D1172340

RAILROADING
IN
EIGHTEEN COUNTRIES

HEADQUARTERS FLAG, MILITARY RAILWAY SERVICE

RAILROADING IN EIGHTEEN COUNTRIES

The Story of AMERICAN RAILROAD MEN
Serving in the Military Railway Service
1862 to 1953

BY

CARL R. GRAY, JR.

MAJOR GENERAL, RTD., ARMY OF THE UNITED STATES
DIRECTOR GENERAL, MILITARY RAILWAY SERVICE, 1942-1945

CHARLES SCRIBNER'S SONS NEW YORK 1955

A

LITHOGRAPHED IN THE UNITED STATES OF AMERICA
BY THE MURRAY PRINTING COMPANY, WAKEFIELD, MASS.

Library of Congress Catalog Card Number 55-10490

Contents

Foreword *xiii*

1 Origin and Development of the Military Railway Service, 1861-1919 *1*

2 Reorganization of Military Railway Service, 1919-1942 *17*

3 Military Railway Service Troops and Their Training, 1942 *24*

4 First Assignments Overseas World War II, 1942 *41*

5 Operations in North Africa, 1943-1944 *57*

6 Operations in Sicily and Italy, 1943-1945 *99*

7 Operations in Northern France and Belgium, 1944 *165*

8 Operations in Southern France, 1944 *194*

9 Operations in Europe after Consolidation of American Northern and Southern Forces, 1945 *219*

10 Operations in Iran, 1942-1945 *256*

11 Operations in India, 1943-1945 *269*

12 Operations in the Philippine Islands, New Caledonia, Australia, and Japan, 1942-1945 *284*

13 Operations in Korea, 1945-1953 *299*

14 Summations and Conclusions *316*

References and Authorities Used *323*

List of Illustrations

Headquarters Flag, Military Railway Service. *Frontispiece facing* iii

CHAPTER 1

Brigadier General D. C. McCallum 3

Potomac Creek bridge 6

Rehabilitation as done in 1864 6

Nashville and Chattanooga Railroad bridge, 1864 6

Nashville and Chattanooga Railroad, March, 1864 7

Military Railway Service, Union Army, near Fredericksburg 7

Behind General Pope's Army 7

Brigadier General W. W. Atterbury 11

Repairing light railroads, France, 1918 13
(Courtesy, The National Archives)

Light Railways of the 21st Light Railway Engineers, France, 1917 13
(Courtesy, The National Archives)

Armored train, France, 1917 14
(Courtesy, The National Archives)

American locomotives, finished, France, 1918 15
(Courtesy, The National Archives)

Boxcar, M.R.S., France, 1917 16
(Courtesy, The National Archives)

CHAPTER 2

Brigadier General John J. Kingman 19
(Courtesy, U.S. Army)

Maj. Gen. Charles P. Gross 22
(Courtesy, U.S. Army)

CHAPTER 3

Officers of the Headquarters M.R.S. May 15, 1942 30

Training M.R.S. troops. Inspection, 1942 34

Training of M.R.S. troops. Battalion on hike, 1942 35

727 R.O.B. in training, 1942 36

CHAPTER 4

General Brehon B. Somervell 40
(Courtesy, U.S. Army)

Alaska Railroads 42

Barging locomotives and supplies to Skagway 43
(Photo by J. K. Hansen)

Hurricane Bridge, Alaska Railroad 44

The PX train at Matanuska, Alaska, autumn 1943 47
(Courtesy, Signal Corps U.S. Army)

The PX car at Fairbanks, 58° below zero 51

Rotary snow plow fleet at McKinley, 48° below zero 51

Thirty below, winter 1944-1945 53
(Courtesy, U.S. Army)

Normal operating conditions, winter 1944-1945 54
(Courtesy, U.S. Army)

Blocked by snow, winter 1944-1945 55
(Courtesy, U.S. Army)

CHAPTER 5

General of the Army Dwight D. Eisenhower 56
(Courtesy, Signal Corps U.S. Army)

The railroads of North Africa 58

U.S.A. equipment. Standard 2-8-0 locomotives 59

General Headquarters, Allied Forces Headquarters, North Africa, 1943 63

Director General decorating Staff Sergeant George Falson 64
(Courtesy, Disabled American Veterans)

753 Railway Shop Battalion, Sidi Mabrouk Shops, Algeria 65

Arabs transferring load to meter-gauge cars 66
(Courtesy, Signal Corps U.S. Army)

Parade, Military Railway Service troops, North Africa, 1943 70-71

Military Railway Service Command, North Africa, 1943 73

Meter-Gauge Railroad, Tunisia 74

Sbeitla-Sousse Line, meter-gauge 74

Meter-Gauge bridge north of Kasserine Pass 76

Bomb wreckage, C.F.T. Shop Yards 77

Supply yards, Maison-Carrée, 1943 80

Livestock travels in *wagon-lits*, North Africa, 1943 82

American refrigerator cars, North Africa, 1943 84

Repair Shops, C.F.A., Algiers, 1943 86-7
(Three Views)

Arab desert fighters passing in review 91

Moving meter-gauge locomotive on well car 95

CHAPTER 6

Field Marshal Earl Harold R. L. G. Alexander 98

Gen. George S. Patton 104
(Courtesy, U.S. Army)

Gen. Mark W. Clark 106

Railroads in Italy 108

General Giovanni di Raimondo 110

A type of German demolition, Italy 112
(Courtesy, Military Railway Service)

Typical German demolition, Italy 113

German attempt to wreck both locomotive and turntable, Rome 113

Reconstructed bridge, Teano, Italy 115

Repairs to Viarano bridge, Italy 115

Repaired bridge, Teano, Italy 115

Welding rail 117
(Photo by Krinke)

Soldier Ghandi Dancers, Italy 117

Track demolition, Line 89 117

Scarified track, Italy, Line 89 120
(Photo by Krinke)

Steel ties bent by Germans, Line 80 120

The Scarifier used by Germans in Italy 120

Scarified track, Line 90 121

Typical track destruction, Italy 121

Steel tie track destruction 121

Villa Literno Yard 122
(Courtesy, Military Railway Service)

Result of our bombing on German train, Arezzo Line 122

Crews of Company B. 713 R.O.B. transfer Italian engine and coaches in Naples 123
(Courtesy, Signal Corps U.S. Army)

Direct hit on troop train, Villa Literno 123

Italian laborers repair rails torn up by Germans 124
(Courtesy, Signal Corps U.S. Army)

North end, Itri Yard, Italy 124

Naples Passenger Station 124

Beginning clean-up job, Villa Literno 125

A portion of Naples Yard 125

Roth Waagner bridging being repaired on Cecina River bridge 127

Test train over newly constructed bridge, Grosetto 127
(Courtesy, Signal Corps U.S. Army)

Volturno River bridge, Capua, Italy 128

Completed Volturno River Bridge 129
(Courtesy, Signal Corps U.S. Army)

Volturno River bridge, Capua, Italy 129

Garigliano River bridge. Start from the west bank 130

Garigliano River bridge, temporary pier 130

Garigliano River bridge. Nearly completed 130

Garigliano River bridge. Roth Waagner prefabricated bridging 131

Garigliano River bridge 131

Molten lava from Vesuvius 133
(Photo by Krinke)

Eruption of Mount Vesuvius, March, 1944 133

Headquarters, First M.R.S., Naples, Italy 134

M.R.S. Diesel electric locomotive 137

M.R.S. standard steam wrecking crane, Italy 137

Loading American hospital train, Italy, 1944 139

Wounded soldiers board hospital train 139
(Photo by Krinke)

Dedication of the "Yankee Dipper," Naples, 1944 141

Anti-aircraft fire, March, 1944 145
(Photo by Krinke)

Fifth Army Plaque faces p. 148

His Royal Highness, Umberto, visits M.R.S. Headquarters 149
(Photo by Krinke)

Diesel electric operation, Italy, July, 1944 150
(Courtesy, Signal Corps U.S. Army)

Secretary Stimson and Generals M. W. Clark and C. R. Gray, Jr., inspecting the Scarifier at Rome 152

Rome passenger terminal 152
(Photo by Krinke)

General Gray, Engineer, General di Raimondo, Fireman. First train into Rome 153

Destroyed bridge, south of Leghorn 155

Railroad yards after bombardment at Brenner Pass 155

Destroyed railroad yard, Florence 156

Ostiense Yard, Rome 156
(Photo by Krinke)

Bombs removed from Vivola Tunnel 158

Po River bridge between Bologna and Verona 159

Destroyed bridge, Cecina, Italy 162

Bridge over the Fioria River 162

CHAPTER 7

Brigadier General Clarence L. Burpee 166

Assembled and made-ready locomotives in England 168
(Courtesy, U.S. Army)

General Omar N. Bradley 170
(Courtesy, Signal Corps U.S. Army)

Lt. General John C. H. Lee 171

Major General Frank J. Ross 172
(Courtesy, U.S. Army)

Brigadier General J. A. Appleton 173

Main lines of railroad, Northern France 174

Coast Guard LST converted into car ferry 176
(Courtesy, U.S. Coast Guard)

Unloading American 2-8-0 locomotive at Cherbourg 177
(Courtesy, U.S. Army)

Double track railroad bridge under reconstruction at Argenteuil, 1945 183

Yank engine with a GI crew pulls out of the bombed railroad yards at Laon, France 184
(Courtesy, U.S. Army)

The "Toot Sweet Special" 193

CHAPTER 8

General Jacob L. Devers 195

Major General Thomas B. Larkin 196

Bridge North Valence 197

Repairing bridge south of Langres 197

Bridge repair at Romans 198

Finishing touches on bridge, Romans 198

Rhone River bridge, Lyon 199

French locomotive demolished by demolition, Avignon 199
(Photo by Krinke)

Bridge destruction on Belfort-Bâle Line 199
(Courtesy, Maison de Photos)

Driving north pier, Seurre 202

Starting bridge construction at Seurre 202

River span in place before jacking down on piers 202

Assembling British trestling and launching nose, Seurre 203

Side view of finished trestle, Seurre 203

Launching a British trestling bridge 203

Demolished bridge, Isère River 204

First train on the double track over the Isère River 205

Durance River bridge 206-7
(Photos by Krinke)

First train crossing temporary pile-bent trestle, Avignon 208

Bridge destruction on Belfort-Bâle Line 208
(Courtesy, Maison de Photos)

Setting 75 foot girders on 112 foot pier at Dounoux 210

Colonel Coudraux and Director General, Lyon 213

Christmas party at Lyon for railroad orphans 215

The French Orphans greet Miss Madeleine Carroll 215

Destroyed yard, Dijon 217

Naval gun on railroad cars, France 217
(Photo by Krinke)

CHAPTER 9

Major General Carl R. Gray, Jr. 220

Colonel Arthur E. Stoddard 221

Staff, General Headquarters Military Railway Service, July, 1945 222

Director General and General Managers 224

Miss Madeleine Carroll 227

10,000th car erected by the 756 Railway Shop Battalion, Marseille, France 229

Dedication of locomotive to Pvt. H. J. O'Brien, killed in action 230

First bridge over the Rhine River, Wesel, Germany, 1945 232

First train over Victory Bridge at Duisburg, Germany, 1945 235
(Courtesy, Engineering Dept., 2nd Military Railway Service)

Celebrating completion of Victory Bridge over Rhine River 235
(Courtesy, Engineering Dept., 2nd Military Railway Service)

Victory Bridge at Duisburg 235

German rail-mounted artillery 236

Double turntable, Cologne 239

Bridge near Bietigheim, Germany 242-3

Dr. Julius H. Dorpmüller 246

First pilot placed on condenser engine, Kassel 249

Dedication of first condenser locomotive built by 757 Railway Shop Battalion, Kassel 249

Condenser engine designed and built by Henschel at Kassel 249

V-8 steam locomotive, Henschel & Son, Kassel 250

CHAPTER 10

Brigadier General Paul F. Yount 257
(Courtesy, U.S. Army)

Railroads of Iran 258

Iranian railroad at Km. 572 259
(Courtesy, U.S. Army)

Iranian railroad bridge at Km. 556 260
(Courtesy, U.S. Army)

Roundhouse at Andimeshk, Iran 263
(Courtesy, U.S. Army)

Roundhouse at Qum, Iran 263
(Courtesy, U.S. Army)

CHAPTER 11

Railroads of India 270

Colonel Stanley H. Bray 272

Comparison of Military Railway Service and Indian transportation, 1944 274
(Courtesy, U.S. Army)

Locomotive on the Bengal and Assam Railroad 274
(Courtesy, U.S. Army)

The shops operated at Assam, India 277
(Courtesy, U.S. Army)

Railroad yards and shops at Parbatipur, India 277
(Courtesy, U.S. Army)

Natives coaling engine, India, 1944 279
(Courtesy, U.S. Army)

The interlocking cabin or control tower of the Bengal and Assam Railway 280
(Courtesy, U.S. Army)

61 Transportation Corps Company awaiting meet at Mogaung, Burma 282

CHAPTER 12

Brigadier General Paul W. Johnston 285

Railroad on Luzon, P.I. 287

Jeep switcher, Philippine Islands 289
(Courtesy, Signal Corps U.S. Army)

Railroad formerly used for sugar plantation and refinery at San José, Mindoro Island, P.I. 289
(Courtesy, U.S. Army)

Major General George C. Stewart 291
(Courtesy, U.S. Army)

American 2-8-2 locomotive in the Philippine Islands 293
(Courtesy, U.S. Army)

Railroad engines in the yard at San Fernando Pampanga on Luzon, P.I. 293
(Courtesy, U.S. Army)

Railroads of Japan 294

CHAPTER 13

Korean railroads 298

Demolition of Yongsan Yard 300

Yongsan Station yard 301
2-8-2 locomotive used in Korea 305
Switching, Korean fashion 305
Colonel W. S. Carr 308
South Han River bridge 311
Bridge demolition, Korea 311
Anyang Highway River bridge 313
Han River bridge 313
Waegwan Railroad bridge being repaired 314

CHAPTER 14
"The Red Shadow," Pfc. Myhers 319
Military Railway Service Chorus 320
Memorial Day, National Cemetery, Algiers, 1943 321

Foreword

AT THE END OF 1953, 30,910,000 Americans had participated in the nine wars which Uncle Sam has fought from 1775 to 1954. The first railroad in America was built in 1828. Railroads did not supply armies in the Revolutionary War and the War of 1812, but were used slightly in the Mexican War. They played an important part in the movement of men and equipment of both the Northern and Southern Armies in the War Between the States. The Spanish-American War of 1898 was of such short duration, and the area of its operation so small, that railroads were not required in Cuba, in the Philippines, and in the Boxer Rebellion. However, they came into their own as the main artery of logistical supply in France in 1917.

This is the story of the use of railroads in World War II and the increment of the American Army known as the Military Railway Service. There were more than 351,000 men and women employees of the American railroads who served in all arms in World War II. Of that number, 43,500—or approximately 12 per cent—were assigned to the various units of the Military Railway Service, and thus rendered a superb technical service. These men, from all sections of the Operating Departments of the railroads, were organized into units corresponding to the divisional organization of a railroad. They operated the railroads in the war zone, and, as nearly as could be done, railroaded in the American way.

This, then, is their story of achievement.

RAILROADING
IN
EIGHTEEN COUNTRIES

1

Origin and Development of the Military Railway Service

1861-1919

THE USE OF RAILROADS for supplying armies was experimented with in Continental Europe prior to the War Between the States, but first reached practical importance in the latter conflict. The armies involved, and the territories over which they campaigned, were so large that it became necessary to utilize every possible means of transportation for their supply and movement. This included highways, which at that time were unimproved and practically impassable in winter or wet weather; waterways, as far as then developed, and the railroad system as it existed in 1860. Armies have to be supplied summer and winter, in good and bad weather, so increasing use was made of the railroad system of the country.

Since the railroads were then operated by private corporations, their first use was by contract between the War Department or Army Commanders and the railroads for the movement of certain supplies between bases and the Army dumps. All of these supplies moved in the same equipment and by the same trains in which commercial goods were transported, and were subjected to the same delays owing to lack of control, destruction of rail lines, and other circumstances brought about by tremendously increased use of rail lines and the exigencies of war.

It was soon realized in Washington that railroads in the theater of operations must be under the absolute control of the military authorities. By the act of 31 January 1862, Congress authorized the President, whenever in his judgment the public safety might require it, to take possession of, and place under military control, the country's telegraph lines and railroads. To carry out the authorities thus vested in the President and directed by him to be executed by the Army, the Military Railway Service was formed as an integral part of the Army.

With the firing on Fort Sumter on 12 April 1861, and the subsequent declaration by President Lincoln on 15 April 1861 of a state of rebellion, the President as of that day seized the railroads of the North so that the supplies for the forming armies could be given priority in movement to designated points. It was decided to concentrate large stores of Army supplies at Baltimore, Maryland. The first Secretary of War in President Lincoln's Cabinet, Mr. Simon Cameron, began the rushing of stores from the North and Northwest by rail.

He called upon Messrs. Samuel M. Felton, Sr., President of the Philadelphia, Wilmington and Baltimore Railroad, J. Edgar Thomson, President of the Pennsylvania Railroad, and Thomas A. Scott, Vice-President of the Pennsylvania Railroad and placed them at strategic points in the general triangle of Harrisburg, Philadelphia, and Baltimore as agents generally to supervise the movement of Army supplies by the seized commercial railroads.

Thomas A. Scott became the Assistant Secretary of War in August 1861, and on 11 January 1862 Mr. Edwin M. Stanton succeeded Mr. Cameron as Secretary of War. Scott, by virtue of his private railroad experience and sensing the requirements of rail transportation, caused the appointment of Mr. D. C. McCallum, General Superintendent of the Erie Railroad, as Military Director and Superintendent of Railroads, with the rank of Brigadier General, by the following War Department order, thereby creating the first organized Military Railway Service of the United States Army:

War Department
Washington, D. C., February 11, 1862.

Ordered. That D. C. McCallum be, and he is hereby, appointed Military Director and Superintendent of Railroads in the United States, with authority to enter upon, take possession of, hold and use all Railroads, engines, cars, locomotives, equipments, appendages and appurtenances, that may be required for the transport of troops, arms, ammunition, and military supplies of the United States and to perform all acts

Brigadier General D. C. McCallum, Director, Military Railway Service, 1862-1865.

and things that may be necessary and proper to be done for the safe and speedy transport aforesaid.

By order of the President, Commander-in-Chief of the Army and Navy of the United States.

EDWIN M. STANTON,
Secretary of War.

A great engineer, Mr. Herman Haupt, Chief Engineer of the Pennsylvania Railroad, a young man of unbelievable engineering achievements who had finished ten years previously the construction of the Hoosac Tunnel in Massachusetts, was commissioned in the rank of Colonel (later Brigadier General) to become the Chief of Construction and Rehabilitation of tracks and bridges destroyed by the Southern forces.

Experience dictated the need of absolute command with respect to the operation of trains in support of the Army, so that on 10 November 1862 General McCallum caused the following Special Order, No. 337, to be issued:

War Department
Adjutant General's Office,
Washington, November 10, 1862.

Commanding officers of troops along the United States military road will give all facilities to the officers of the roads and the quartermasters, for unloading cars so as to prevent any delay. On arrival at depots whether in the day or night, the cars will be instantly unloaded, and working parties will always be in readiness for that duty, and sufficient to unload the whole train at once.

Commanding officers will be charged with guarding the track, sidings, wood, water-tanks, etc., within their several commands and will be held responsible for the result.

Any military officer who shall neglect his duty in this respect will be reported by the quartermasters and officers of the railroad, and his name will be stricken from the rolls of the army.

Depots will be established at suitable points, under the direction of the commanding general and properly guarded.

No officer, whatever may be his rank will interfere with the running of the cars as directed by the superintendent of the road.

Any one who so interferes will be dismissed from the service for disobedience of orders.

By order of the Secretary of War:
F. D. Townsend,
Assistant Adjutant General.

General McCallum, in his final report to the Secretary of War, comments on the above order:

Having had a somewhat extensive railroad experience, both before and since the rebellion, I consider this order of the Secretary of War to have been the very foundation of success; without it the whole railroad system, which has proved an important element in conducting military movements, would have been not only a costly, but ludicrous failure. The fact should be understood that the management of railroads is just as much a distinct profession as is that of the art of war, and should be so regarded.

At that early date, therefore, the operation of the military railways was recognized as an independent command and happily was carried forward as will be shown in World War II.

Mr. James A. Seddon was the Secretary of War in Jefferson Davis' Cabinet, and for some unaccountable reason the central government of the Confederacy failed to recognize and ignored constant requests of General Lee and other commanders in setting up and providing adequate rail transportation in the support of the Southern Armies. Secretary Seddon refused allocation of supplies and purchase of material for maintaining adequate rail supply lines.

The officers of the Southern Army, who were charged with the logistical support of their armies, and the officers and owners of the Southern railroads were never permitted the cooperation that was so evident in the North. There were no organization and no rail transportation and construction and reconstruction men in the South such as were headed by Generals McCallum and Haupt in the Northern Armies. It is believed that the failure of the Southern government to use railroads to their maximum capacity in the logistical support of their armies was the greatest factor in its ultimate defeat.

One of the firsts in the special uses of railroads in wartime was the placing of mortars on railroad cars so that they could be moved up to more advanced positions than could be had by roads or across fields. This, too, was carried on in subsequent wars, particularly in World War I with the Naval Batteries of Admiral C. P. Plunkett.

An interesting fact concerning the Military Railway Service in the War Between the States is also taken from the Military Director of Railways' final report and covers some statistics incident to the extent of the operations over a period of the three and one-half years that the war lasted:

Number of engines run over the road for other than local construction purposes	8,983
Number of loaded cars	30,457
Number of empty cars	20,699
TOTAL NUMBER OF CARS	51,156

It will be interesting to see later the tremendous increase in logistical support by the railroads in World War II.

Potomac Creek bridge built in nine days by M.R.S. troops.

Rehabilitation as done in 1864.

Nashville and Chattanooga Railroad bridge, Bridgeport, Tennessee, 1864.

Nashville and Chattanooga Railroad, Nashville, Tennessee, March, 1864.

Military Railway Service, Union Army, maintaining the railroad near Fredericksburg, Virginia.

Behind General Pope's Army.

The operation of the Military Railway Service was carried on in the War Between the States with a maximum strength as follows:

In Virginia	4,542
In North Carolina	3,387
In military division of the Mississippi	17,035
TOTAL NUMBER OF MEN	24,964

The total length of bridges built and rebuilt upon the Virginia railroads, including those rebuilt in 1863, in Maryland and Pennsylvania, was as follows: Trestle or temporary bridges, 33,336 lineal feet; truss or permanent bridges, 1,595 lineal feet; total, 34,931 feet, or 6.6 miles. The total length of track as it was laid upon the same railroads was 177.4 miles. During the war and up to shortly after its close 129 miles of track were taken up.

To maintain the locomotives and all cars in good working order, extensive machines and carshops were built at Nashville and Chattanooga. These shops were supplied with machinery either seized or purchased from Northern manufacturers.

The Military Railway Service ceased its control over any railroads in the United States by Executive Order of 8 August 1865.

In his final report, General McCallum pays tribute to the railroad men in his command:

> In conclusion, permit me to say that the government was peculiarly fortunate in securing services of civilian officers of great nerve, honesty and capability, to whom the whole country owes a debt of gratitude.

The sinking of the *Maine* in Havana Harbor, 15 February 1898, was the start of the Spanish-American War, but about the only land operations were in the vicinity of Santiago, the landing of American forces at Siboney, and the capture of San Juan Hill. Surrender followed shortly thereafter so that no major amount of rail logistical supply was required. Of course there was a rail movement to ports in the United States incident to transportation by vessels to ports in Cuba, and naturally there was use of existing Cuban railroads in the general distribution of supplies to satisfy the Army of Occupation.

Generally connected with the Spanish-American War is the Philippine

Insurrection, 11 April 1899 to 15 July 1903, in which no major rail movement was used.

Uncle Sam then was at peace until 1917. He, however, had a belief that an adequate national defense was necessary. Up to that time the Armed Forces had consisted of a small and well-organized Regular Army, a Navy, and a Marine Corps, and the states had National Guard units which had been called into federal service in previous wars.

On 3 June 1916 there was passed a National Defense Act which provided for the Army of the United States to consist of the Regular Army, the Organized Reserve, and the National Guard when called into federal service. This National Defense Act contemplated and provided for the commissioning of qualified men in the Officers Reserve Corps, and the enlistment of men in the Enlisted Reserve Corps, who had special experience to cover the various branches of the Army. As an illustration: doctors and nurses were commissioned in the Medical Corps, civil and construction engineers in the Corps of Engineers, telephone and telegraph men in the Signal Corps, business administrators in the Adjutant General's Department, etc. Enlisted men were assigned to that branch of the Army where their experience would serve best.

Since the Army Regulations at that time contemplated the construction, reconstruction, and operation of railways by the Corps of Engineers, operating men and railroad engineers were commissioned in the Corps of Engineers.

At about this same time in 1916 Pancho Villa had been causing a great deal of trouble in the border states, and it was decided to send an expeditionary force under General Pershing to capture him. It was anticipated that this force would have to go south of the border some one hundred to one hundred fifty miles.

On 24 June 1916 the Chief of Engineers at that time, Major General William M. Black, called upon Mr. Samuel M. Felton, Jr., for help. He was then President of the Chicago Great Western Railway and was the son of the man whom President Lincoln had called upon in 1861. General Black asked him to help him form a force of railroad men who could build and operate a railroad of no longer than 150 miles in support of General Pershing's expeditionary force.

At Mr. Felton's recommendation there was formed a regiment of six companies, known as the 3rd Reserve Engineers, one company formed from each of six railways headquartered in Chicago. It was mobilized on Navy Pier, Chicago, on 3 February 1917, but was not used, as, for the first time in history, Pershing's logistical line of support was by motor truck.

This unit was not demobilized, however. With the outbreak of World War I, the 3rd Engineers was reorganized to become the Thirteenth Engineers, and served in France. General Orders No. 61, of 14 May, 1917, authorized the formation of eight additional regiments of Military Railway Service units with railroad men drawn from the railroads of the United States. Five of these regiments were to be construction, three to be operating, and one to be a shop regiment.

Ultimately the force consisted of nine regiments, each operating regiment having an organization totaling 57 officers and 1,839 enlisted men, for an aggregate strength of 1,896 per regiment. The regimental headquarters consisted of 7 officers and 41 enlisted men; the first battalion consisted of a battalion headquarters and four companies and had 28 officers and 1,024 enlisted men. Three of those companies were light railway operating and a fourth was a light railway shop. The second battalion consisted of three companies, the first two being light railway maintenance of way and the third light railway construction. This battalion consisted of 22 officers and 774 enlisted men.

The railway regiments were numbered the 11th through the 19th. The Director General of these troops was Brigadier General W. W. Atterbury, who was then Vice-President of the Pennsylvania Railroad, later its President.

While the regiments were ordinarily commanded by a Colonel of the Corps of Engineers of the Regular Army, the Executive Officers (in the grade of Lieutenant Colonels) were practical railroad men. Among them were such well-known railroad men as William B. Parsons, noted transportation engineer and consultant, 11th Regiment; H. H. Adams, President of the Kansas City Terminal, 12th Regiment; N. L. Howard, of the Chicago, Burlington and Quincy and later President of the Chicago Great Western Railway Company, 13th Regiment; Albert T. Perkins, associated with railroad financial circles and President of the Chicago, Milwaukee and Gary

Brigadier General W. W. Atterbury, Director General, Military Railway Service, World War I.

Railway, 14th Regiment; Carleton W. Sturtevant, 15th Regiment; George H. Webb, Chief Engineer of the Michigan Central Railroad, 16th Regiment; Charles G. Dawes, who at the time of his appointment was President of the Central Trust Company and later became Vice-President of the United States and Ambassador to Great Britain, 17th Regiment; J. R. Holman, Chief Engineer of the Oregon-Washington Railroad and Navigation Company, 18th Regiment; and H. H. Maxfield, Superintendent of Motive Power, Pennsylvania Railroad, 19th Regiment.

To show how the entire railroad industry contributed to the manpower of these regiments, the mobilization points and source of supply were geographically as follows:

11th Engineers, organized at Fort Totten, New York
12th Engineers, organized at St. Louis, Missouri
13th Engineers, organized at Chicago, Illinois
14th Engineers, organized at Boston, Massachusetts
15th Engineers, organized at Pittsburgh, Pennsylvania
16th Engineers, organized at Detroit, Michigan
17th Engineers, organized at Atlanta, Georgia
18th Engineers, organized at Seattle, Washington, and San Francisco California
19th Engineers, organized at Philadelphia, Pennsylvania

The first railroad operation by Military Railway Service troops was by the 13th Engineers, who started operation in December 1917. The theater of the American Army in France in World War I was, generally speaking, in the triangle, being the southwest portion of France with boundaries south of a line Le Havre to Paris, and a line Paris to Marseille west of the Rhône Valley, with the ports of Saint-Nazaire, Brest, La Pallice, and Bordeaux being the major ports of debarkation. Naturally, it was the railroads of that area that the Military Railway Service operated during World War I.

There are some interesting statistics, however, which should be included. One is that the Corps of Engineers and the engineer troops under the direction of the Director General of Transportation constructed 937 miles of standard-gauge track mostly for yards, on docks and sidings to serve warehouses and depots. The largest individual project was the Nevers Cut-Off which was a belt line around the city of Nevers, France, on the main line of communications east from Bordeaux and Saint-Nazaire, and was five and one-third miles long. All construction and reconstruction of railways in France were stopped by General Orders No. 54, Headquarters, Service of Supply, issued 14 November 1918, canceling 827 miles of track that had been authorized for construction, including 37 miles of second main-line track on the Paris-Orléans Railway from Le Mans to Tours.

The gross tons hauled on standard-gauge railroads in France during World War I amounted to 3,430,000 tons.

Further use of railroads in combat was the placing of cannons on rail-

Repairing light railroads, Mouilly, France, 1918.

Light Railways of the 21st Light Railway Engineers, Chepply, Meuse, France, 1917.

Armored train in the north of France, 1917.

road cars as the mortars had been placed on cars in the War Between the States. The United States Navy put ashore in France during the period from 18 August 1918, until the signing of the Armistice, five United States Naval Batteries composed of one 14-inch 50-caliber gun carried on a special railway mount attached to ammunition and auxiliary cars. They bombarded German bases and positions behind the lines in France with remarkable efficiency and important results. This use of big-caliber guns in land warfare by the United States Navy was planned for and arranged by Rear Admiral Ralph Earle, U.S.N., Chief of the Bureau of Ordnance, United States Navy. Admiral Earle consulted with Major General John Hedlam, Royal Artillery, and Captain André Tardieu, French Commissioner, in the development of the plans and specifications for the gun carriages and equipment.

Each battery was made up in a train of: 1 locomotive, 1 gun car, 1 construction car, 1 construction car with crane, 1 sand and log car, 1 fuel car, 1 battery kitchen car, 2 ammunition cars, 3 berthing cars, 1 battery headquarters car, 1 battery headquarters kitchen car, and 1 work-

American locomotives finished, ready for work. Built by 19th Regiment, Engineers, Camp Penhoet, St. Nazaire, France, April 7, 1918.

shop car. The locomotives were built by Baldwin and the cars were built by Standard Steel Car Company.

The batteries were an independent command under Lieutenant Commander Garret L. Schuyler, temporarily in command, in France, until the arrival of Rear Admiral C. P. Plunkett, U.S.N.

The gun trains were assembled at the port of Saint-Nazaire and the first train left there on 18 August 1918.

Another development in the use of railroads for logistical supply of armies in World War I was the use of sixty-centimeter narrow-gauge railroads located and extended forward to battle lines from dumps on standard-gauge track. This relieved motor convoys and other means of supplying front-line troops with all classes of supplies. Narrow-gauge railroads were used by the Germans and French, but extended and developed to a great degree by Americans.

A Manager of Light Railways, who operated under the direction of the Chief Engineer, American Expeditionary Force, was responsible for the construction and operation of light railways. The greatest number of

Boxcar, M.R.S., France, 1917.

officers and men engaged in this work was 13,650. The total tonnage handled by them was 860,652 gross tons, and the tons handled one mile by them was 8,106,700, reaching its peak in October 1918, when the haulage was 8,100 tons per day. The equipment used was 104 steam locomotives, 61 gas locomotives, and 1,695 cars 20 feet long. Special shops were constructed for both running repairs and overhaul repairs to this equipment, the main one being at Abainville. Light railways troops constructed a total of 130 miles and rehabilitated 186 miles of narrow-gauge railroad in France.

During World War I there were 51 units aggregating 69,000 men in the Military Railway Service which served overseas. In all, there were 83,000 men organized for the Military Railway Service, of which 1,970 were officers.

This indicates the great part that the standard and light railways played in the supply and logistical support of Pershing's Armies.

The story of railroads and the use of railroad men during World War I would not be complete without a mention of what the United States Government did at home with respect to its railroads. President Wilson on 28 December 1917 seized the private railroads of America by authority of the Act of Congress of 31 January 1862, which empowered the President of the United States to seize railroads "when in his judgment the public safety may require it."

He formed the United States Railroad Administration under the Director Generalship of W. G. McAdoo. This continued until the railroads were turned back to their private owners 1 March 1920.

2

Reorganization of Military Railway Service

1919-1942

EXPERIENCE HAD SHOWN in the operation of the Military Railway Service in France in 1917 and 1918 that the regiment was not the best form of a unit to have, both as to size and internal organization. Many Engineer Reserve Officers, who were practical railroad men, assisted the Chief of Engineers in the formation of an adequate organization of various units for future requirements of the M.R.S.

The basic decision was to put an American railroad in uniform. A division is the lowest organization on an American railroad where the officer in charge has jurisdiction over all departments. The Division Superintendent has full responsibility for the maintenance of track and bridges, locomotives and cars, and the operation of trains. The basic unit, then, for the M.R.S. took the form of a battalion of four companies: "A" Company consisting of three platoons, two of which were trackmen and the third bridge carpenters; "B" Company, which was the Maintenance of Equipment and likewise made up of three platoons; each of the first two was a complete roundhouse force and the third was a rip track force for the repair of cars. The "C" Company was the operating company (the largest of the three) and consisted of train crews.

In civil operation, when the employees have finished their work, they go to their own homes where they are fed. When they require supplies, they go to a store and purchase them. In the M.R.S., in time of war, however, those needs have to be provided for the men, so a fourth company, the Headquarters and Service Company, was formed for that purpose. In it were placed the dispatchers, operators, and line repairmen. Men handling housing, messing, and supply operations likewise formed a platoon in this company.

The first attempt was the formation of a Railway Company of an Engineering Battalion. It was set up under Tables of Organization 564-P on 21 November 1921, and consisted of 9 officers and 270 enlisted men (peacetime strength) for an aggregate of 279. This company had three units, really platoons, but called companies: a Maintenance of Way Company, a Maintenance of Equipment Company, and an Operating Company, each of 3 officers and 90 enlisted men. Each of these units was commanded by a Captain. The one for Maintenance of Way was to be a Division Engineer; the one for Maintenance of Equipment was to be a Division Superintendent of Motive Power, and the one for the Operating unit was to be a Trainmaster. The assisting lieutenants were to be track supervisors, bridge and building foremen, mechanical engineers, yardmasters, and road foremen of engines.

Shortly after, on 15 December 1921, there followed Headquarters and Headquarters and Service Platoon Engineer Battalion Railway, which had a strength of 9 officers and 93 enlisted men. The Commanding Officer was a Major and a Division Superintendent of a railway. The second in command was an Assistant Division Superintendent. There was also a Signal Engineer and Chief Dispatcher, as well as an Adjutant, each in the grade of Captain. The headquarters was divided into a headquarters section, operation and signal section, and had attached medical.

The next change was to blow up the original railway company into a four-company battalion. This was done through Tables of Organization 563-W, Railway Battalion, Corps of Engineers, dated 2 July 1927. For the first time the battalion became equivalent to the organization of a Division Superintendent of a standard American railroad. There was, of course, the Battalion Headquarters, or Superintendent's office, and a Headquarters and Service Company. Then Company "A" was Maintenance of Way, Company "B" Maintenance of Equipment, and Company "C" operating. In all it had 21 officers and 638 enlisted men, there being 3 officers in the Battalion

Brigadier General John J. Kingman, Assistant to the Chief of Engineers.

Headquarters, 3 officers and 94 enlisted men in the Headquarters and Service Company, 4 officers and 176 enlisted men in each of the three lettered companies; the attached Medical Detachment consisted of 3 officers and 16 enlisted men.

Colonel John J. Kingman was appointed assistant to the Chief of Engineers and was promoted to the grade of Brigadier General on 1 January 1938. He previously had been the District Engineer at Milwaukee, Wisconsin. General Kingman was vitally interested in fulfilling the responsibility of the Chief of Engineers with respect to the M.R.S. and all of its component parts.

The next change occurred on 15 July 1938, when the Table of Organization became known as 5-125, and the number of enlisted men was raised in the Railway Battalion to 759 for an aggregate battalion strength of 780 officers and men.

General Kingman secured the transfer of the writer from a Corps Area assignment in command of the 326 Engineers (Combat), 101 Division, to the Arm and Service Assignment in the office of the Chief of Engineers. Under date of 1 February 1939, the writer was assigned to duty as Manager, Military Railway Service, Engineer Headquarters, Railway. In the subsequent period, General Kingman played a substantial part in the proper organization of the M.R.S., for he unquestionably understood and contemplated its requirements in time of war.

The battalion passed through reorganizations between 15 July 1938 and 28 October 1943, but basically only the aggregate strength was changed. The highest number of officers was 24 and the highest number of enlisted men was 847.

As of 28 October 1943 the Table of Organization for the Railway Operating Battalion became known as 55-225. It has undergone five changes of organization in the intervening years to date, and the current Table of Organization is known as T/O&E 55-225, dated 11 January 1954, and consists of three types of Railway Operating Battalions. For utilizing steam power only, it has 30 officers, 2 warrant officers, and 792 enlisted men. For utilizing Diesel electric power only, it is the same, but the third one, contemplating the use of both steam and Diesel electric power, contains 31 officers, 2 warrant officers, and 796 enlisted men.

Since there are so many electric railroads in Europe, it was necessary to form an electric power transmission company for the Railway Operating Battalion as a "D" Company. Prior to 28 October 1943 there was no published table covering this unit, but T/O 55-217 on that date provided 3 officers and 196 enlisted men. The current organization is under T/O 55-217, dated 11 January 1954, and consists of 4 officers and 190 enlisted men.

American railroad organization consists of divisions. Divisions are grouped into districts with a General Superintendent at the head of each. Districts are grouped into regions in which a General Manager has jurisdiction. General Managers report to the next echelon of command, the Vice-President in Charge of Operation. The President of an American railroad, of course, is responsible for all departments, Operating, Traffic, Law, Finance, etc.

The next conception in the M.R.S. was to create an organization equivalent to that had by a General Superintendent. The Railway Grand Division was the result. This began with Table of Organization 569-W dated 16 May 1927, with 10 officers and 27 enlisted men. This headquarters was divided into departments and the General Superintendent had as assistants Maintenance-of-Way Engineers, Maintenance-of-Equipment men, Transportation men, and Stores men.

The existing Table of Organization is known as 55-202, dated 30 August 1953, and is known as Transportation, Railway Group. It has 25 officers, 2 warrant officers, and 72 enlisted men. The greatest number in the headquarters was under Table of Organization 5-602 dated 5 September 1942, when the unit had 26 officers and 75 enlisted men.

The next step was to organize a General Manager's headquarters. Its first organization was evidenced by Table of Organization 5-302, dated 15 July 1938, with 22 officers and 186 enlisted men. The General Manager had the rank of Brigadier General, and his headquarters staff consisted of four full departments: Maintenance of Way and Structures, Maintenance of Equipment, Operation, and Stores.

The General Manager's headquarters was originally called Engineer Headquarters, Railway, and has undergone nine changes since its original form. The present unit is under Table of Organization 55-302 A, dated 24 August 1953, and is named Transportation Railway Command. It has 36 officers, 4 warrant officers, and 94 enlisted men. The organization has been larger, the greatest force having been under Table of Organization 5-302, 1 April 1942, when it consisted of 30 officers, 2 warrant officers, and 227 enlisted men.

The supreme command of the M.R.S. is vested in an officer in the grade of Major General, called the Director General. His command is known as General Headquarters, Military Railway Service, and was originally organized by Organization Order No. 110 on 16 February 1945. It consisted of 27 officers, 1 warrant officer, and 73 enlisted men. The present organization, called General Headquarters, Transportation Military Railway Service, is under Table of Organization and Equipment 55-210 A, dated 26 Septem-

Maj. Gen. Charles P. Gross, Chief of Transportation for the Army, World War II.

ber 1953, and consists of 60 officers, 7 warrant officers, and 139 enlisted men. The heads of departments in General Headquarters, Military Railway Service, called Directors, are equivalent to Vice-Presidents in American railroad organization.

For overhauling and major repairs there was formed a Railway Shop Battalion, the first organization being under Table of Organization 668-W, dated 23 November 1929, with a Shop Superintendent in the grade of Captain. It consisted of 4 officers and 176 enlisted men. It was actually organized as a company of an engineer battalion. Table of Organization 668, dated 22 September 1932, recognized it for the first time as a battalion organization, and it then consisted of 21 officers and 638 enlisted men. The battalion is organized as a four-company unit, consisting of a Battalion Headquarters and Service Company, Company "A," Erecting and Machine Shop; Company "B," Boiler and Blacksmith Shop; and Company "C," Car Repair. It has undergone some seven changes since the war, and its current organization is evidenced in Table of Organization 55-235 A, dated 6 November 1953. The unit consists of 23 officers, 2 warrant officers, and 635 enlisted men.

With general use of Diesel electric power in war zones, one of those changes was the setting up of Table of Organization and Equipment 55-247, dated 6 November 1953, which is a Diesel Electric Locomotive Repair Company assigned to a Railway Shop Battalion. It consists of 3 officers and 107 enlisted men.

Because of the contemplated general use of Diesel electric power, first in the Iranian Theater, a Diesel Shop Battalion was provided. Its first organization was in accordance with Table of Organization 55-245, dated 18 April 1942, and consisted of 34 officers, 1 warrant officer, and 597 enlisted men. It is a four-company battalion with the companies designated the same as the steam shop battalions.

By virtue of War Department General Order No. 60, dated 5 November 1942, M.R.S. was transferred in total from the Corps of Engineers to the newly created Transportation Corps. Major General Charles P. Gross was Chief of Transportation and continued in that office throughout the war.

The M.R.S. in World War II was expanded by virtue of experience and necessity, and a Table of Organization was provided for some separate smaller organizations under Table of Organization 55-500 dated 17 August 1943. These included Railway Workshops Mobile, Hospital Train Maintenance Sections, Hospital Train Maintenance Crews, and on 25 February 1945, there was added a Station Agency Detachment organization.

Because of the vast amount of material required to maintain track and bridges, and both American locomotives and cars as well as European locomotives and cars, there was organized (and it became a permanent part of the M.R.S.) a Base Depot Company for the securing, storing, and issuing of required stores for the maintenance of track, bridges, locomotives, and cars.

3

Military Railway Service Troops and Their Training

1942

THE AFFILIATION PLAN adopted as the result of the passage of the National Defense Act of 1916 was a plan to get right men in the right places. With the Military Railway Service being simply an American railroad in uniform, individual railroads of America were asked to sponsor, or become affiliated with, the various units of the authorized M.R.S.

The agreement entered into between the railroad and the government was that a railroad would nominate a Superintendent, an Assistant Superintendent, Engineer, Maintenance of Way, and all the other officers in accordance with their technical duties, from among their officers and employees. Those men, when they had passed a physical examination, were commissioned and assigned to the position in that sponsored unit which they were qualified to hold on the railroad.

When a railroad could not furnish all the candidates for every position, individual qualified men from other railroads were commissioned and assigned.

The officers and directors of the Association of American Railroads realized keenly their opportunity in furthering the affiliation sponsorship program as between the carriers of the United States for units of the M.R.S. With the energetic support of the officers and directors of the Association of American Railroads, coupled with the understanding of the problem by the chief executives of the railroads of the United States, the War Department and the Manager soon secured sponsorship for the then-authorized units of the M.R.S.

Prior to 1941 M.R.S. units were numbered in the series 489 to 620, but in that year were renumbered in the 700 series.

When the Japanese struck at Pearl Harbor on 7 December 1941, the organization and sponsorship of units had grown to the following:

UNIT	SPONSOR
Headquarters Military Railway Service	Association of American Railroads
701 Railway Grand Division	New York Central Railroad
702 Railway Grand Division	Union Pacific Railroad
703 Railway Grand Division	Atlantic Coast Line Railroad Company
704 Railway Grand Division	Great Northern Railway
705 Railway Grand Division	Southern Pacific Company
706 Railway Grand Division	Pennsylvania Railroad
707 Railway Grand Division	Southern Railway Company
708 Railway Grand Division	The Baltimore and Ohio Railroad Company
709 Railway Grand Division	Association of American Railroads
710 Railway Grand Division	The Atchison, Topeka and Santa Fe Railway Company
711 Railway Operating Battalion	Training Battalion—No Sponsorship
712 Railway Operating Battalion	The Central Railroad Company of New Jersey
713 Railway Operating Battalion	The Atchison, Topeka and Santa Fe Railway Company
714 Railway Operating Battalion	Chicago, St. Paul, Minneapolis and Omaha Railway
715 Railway Operating Battalion	Illinois Central Railroad
716 Railway Operating Battalion	Southern Pacific Company
717 Railway Operating Battalion	Pennsylvania Railroad
718 Railway Operating Battalion	Cleveland, Cincinnati, Chicago and St. Louis Railway
719 Railway Operating Battalion	Texas and New Orleans Railroad Company
720 Railway Operating Battalion	Chicago and North Western Railway
721 Railway Operating Battalion	New York Central Railroad
722 Railway Operating Battalion	Seaboard Air Line Railroad Company
723 Railway Operating Battalion	Union Pacific Railroad

724 Railway Operating Battalion	Pennsylvania Railroad
725 Railway Operating Battalion	Chicago, Rock Island and Pacific Railroad Company
726 Railway Operating Battalion	Wabash Railroad Company
727 Railway Operating Battalion	Southern Railway Company
728 Railway Operating Battalion	Louisville and Nashville Railroad Company
729 Railway Operating Battalion	The New York, New Haven and Hartford Railroad Company
730 Railway Operating Battalion	Pennsylvania Railroad
731 Railway Operating Battalion	Union Pacific Railroad
732 Railway Operating Battalion	Great Northern Railway
733 Railway Operating Battalion	Central of Georgia Railway Company
734 Railway Operating Battalion	Texas and New Orleans Railroad Company
735 Railway Operating Battalion	Association of American Railroads
736 Railway Operating Battalion	New York Central Railroad
737 Railway Operating Battalion	New York Central Railroad
738 Railway Operating Battalion	Chicago Great Western Railway
739 Railway Operating Battalion	Lehigh Valley Railroad Company
740 Railway Operating Battalion	The Chesapeake and Ohio Railway Company
741 Railway Operating Battalion	Gulf, Mobile and Ohio Railroad
742 Railway Operating Battalion	Pennsylvania Railroad
743 Railway Operating Battalion	Illinois Central Railroad
744 Railway Operating Battalion	Chicago, Milwaukee, St. Paul and Pacific Railroad
745 Railway Operating Battalion	Chicago, Burlington and Quincy Railroad
746 Railway Operating Battalion	Missouri-Kansas-Texas Railroad Company
747 Railway Operating Battalion	The Atchison, Topeka and Santa Fe Railway Company
748 Railway Operating Battalion	The Texas and Pacific Railway Company
749 Railway Operating Battalion	The New York, New Haven and Hartford Railroad Company
750 Railway Operating Battalion	St. Louis-San Francisco Railway Company
751 Railway Operating Battalion	The Denver and Rio Grande Western Railroad Company
752 Railway Operating Battalion	Boston and Maine Railroad
759 Railway Operating Battalion	Missouri Pacific Railroad
753 Railway Shop Battalion	Cleveland, Cincinnati, Chicago and St. Louis Railway
754 Railway Shop Battalion	Southern Pacific Company
755 Railway Shop Battalion	Norfolk and Western Railway

756 Railway Shop Battalion	Pennsylvania Railroad
757 Railway Shop Battalion	Chicago, Milwaukee, St. Paul and Pacific Railroad
758 Railway Shop Battalion	The Atchison, Topeka and Santa Fe Railway Company
763 Railway Shop Battalion	The Delaware, Lackawanna and Western Railroad Company and Lehigh Valley Railroad Company
764 Railway Shop Battalion	Boston and Maine Railroad Central Vermont Railway, Incorporated Boston and Albany Railroad The Delaware and Hudson Railroad
765 Railway Shop Battalion	Erie Railroad
766 Railway Shop Battalion	Association of American Railroads

In addition it was necessary to form special units for special conditions. The 770 Railway Operating Battalion was formed to operate the leased White Pass and Yukon Route, Alaska. The 61 Transportation Corps Composite Company was formed in India as a Provisional Operating Detachment. The 761 Railway Transportation Company was formed for service in England, North Africa, and Europe; the 790 Railway Operating Company (later expanded into a battalion) was originally activated for service in New Caledonia. The 774 Railway Grand Division was an expanded grand division to replace the Headquarters, First M.R.S. in Italy when it went to southern France.

It is interesting to record here that the ultimate force of the M.R.S. consisted of one General Headquarters, M.R.S.; 3 Headquarters, M.R.S.; 13 Railway Grand Divisions; 39 Railway Operating Battalions; 2 Railway Transportation Companies; 10 Railway Shop Battalions (Steam); 2 Railway Shop Battalions (Diesel); 3 Base Depot Companies; 8 Railway Workshops Mobile; 10 Hospital Train Maintenance Crews. Then in order to render protection against pilferage in ports, yards, and on trains, there was assigned as an integral part of the M.R.S. 8 Military Police Battalions and 2 Military Police Companies.

When the affiliation plan was first inaugurated, it was intended to have the written agreement between a sponsor and the War Department in general terms only, non-legal in nature, and in no sense was it to be a binding contract. With the decision reached immediately following Pearl Harbor with the carriers permitting the training of the units back on their own railroad, a complication arose which necessitated working out a definite understanding as between the carrier, the government, and the railroad labor organizations, which was done to the satisfaction of all. Those working this out were Mr. John J. Pelley, President of the Association of American Railroads; Mr. C. H. Buford, Operating Vice-President of the Association of American Railroads; Mr. George M. Harrison, President of the Railway Labor Executives Association; Colonel Lewis T. Ross, Chief, Railway Branch, Office of the Chief of Engineers; as well as the Manager, M.R.S.

The affiliation plan has been made into a very definite program, as is indicated by the plan released under date of 28 April 1947.

On 7 December 1941 the M.R.S. was pretty well organized on an inactive duty basis and a majority of the officers for each unit had been selected, commissioned, and assigned. Key non-commissioned personnel had been enlisted in the Organized Reserve. War Department policies up to that time provided for age-in-grade for the officers. For original appointment, officers were to be between the ages of twenty-one and sixty years, except that lieutenants and captains must not be over forty-five years of age, majors and lieutenant colonels fifty-five, and colonels sixty. Before all of the units were organized a modification of the age-in-grade was made because in many instances competent experienced Trainmasters, Roadmasters, Road Foremen of Equipment, and Round House Foremen, while physically fit, were in excess of the minimum age provided for the grade by regulations.

The Manager created the Railway Grand Division consisting of a Railway Grand Division Headquarters, two or more Operating Battalions, and a Railway Shop Battalion, on paper, as it were, but in accordance with the expected call to active duty of those units. These Railway Grand Divisions and their component parts had been formulated mostly on a geographical basis. As those units were called into active service and began their training period, they were an integral part of the basic M.R.S. organization and functioned accordingly.

Before Christmas of 1941 it had been decided to call into active duty the Headquarters, M.R.S., and one R.G.D. The R.G.D. chosen was the 703 whose headquarters were affiliated with the Atlantic Coast Line Railroad

Company. It consisted of that headquarters, the 727 R.O.B. (Southern Railway System), the 713 R.O.B. (Santa Fe), and the 753 R.S.B. (Big Four). They were immediately designated as the M.R.S. troops to accompany the forces in the invasion of North Africa.

Previously, on 1 May 1941, the 711 R.O.B. had been activated and placed first at Fort Belvoir, the Corps of Engineers Training Center. It was planned to rotate officers and enlisted men through this battalion for a short tour of duty as a practical training program. At the same time it was also to do all of the railroad work, including the switching and spotting of cars throughout the reservation. So, when the Japanese struck they were actually on duty performing that training function as well as rendering an intra-camp rail transportation service.

On 15 March 1942, the 727 R.O.B. was called into active duty, the first unit to be called after the declaration of war. The next activated was the 713 R.O.B. and the 753 R.S.B. on 15 April 1942; then Headquarters, M.R.S., on 15 May 1942, and the 730 R.O.B. (Pennsylvania Railroad) the same date. Headquarters, 703 R.G.D., was activated 1 August 1942.

It was decided that the Headquarters of the M.R.S. and the Manager thereof would be charged with the training and conditioning of the units. Headquarters were established at Fort Snelling, Minnesota, with the office of the headquarters in the Commerce Building at St. Paul, Minnesota.

Technical training of the headquarters took on the form of directing operation of the M.R.S. units then on active duty. One of the most valuable products of that training was the compilation and publication under Colonel B. H. Crosland, Assistant Manager, Engineering, of ten books, which were reports on railroads in foreign countries. The information published was compiled from various books, reports, and periodicals, and covered the countries of Tunis, Algiers, and Morocco; Iraq and Iran, Egypt and Libya; Belgium, Netherlands and northern France; Portugal, Spain, and southern France; Italy, Greece, Bulgaria, and Yugoslavia; Norway, Sweden, and Denmark; Germany; England and the continent of Australia.

Each volume likewise contained an accurate large-scale railroad map prepared on a simplified Lambert projection formula. These books were furnished M.R.S. units in training. When a unit was ordered into one of the countries for which there was a report, it was of inestimable value to

Officers of the Headquarters M.R.S. May 15, 1942.
First Row: Lt. Col. Decker, Lt. Col. McFadden, Col. Knight, Lt. Col. Noyes, Col. Gray, Col. Ryan, Col. Crosland, Lt. Col. Dougherty, Lt. Col. Barrett.
Second Row: Capt. Spector, Maj. Sherer, Maj. Thomas, Maj. Scatterday, Maj. Cheshire, Maj. Wilson, Capt. Sima, Capt. Richards.
Third Row: Lt. Fransen, Lt. Lund, Lt. Hayes, Capt. Garrick, Capt. Scheuble, Lt. Hargreaves, Lt. Sharood, Capt. Kopp.

that organization to have a prior general knowledge of the railroad in that area.

Since agreement was made between the Manager, the War Department, and the sponsoring railroads to give technical training to these units back on the railroad of their sponsorship, the Southern Railroad accepted the 727 R.O.B. for training on the line of their railroad between Meridian, Mississippi, and New Orleans, Louisiana. The unit was encamped at Camp Shelby, Hattiesburg, Mississippi.

The 713 R.O.B. trained on the Santa Fe Railway in the vicinity of Clovis, New Mexico, and was encamped there in a camp built especially for them, called Camp William G. Reid.

The 753 R.S.B. took over an idle but tooled shop of the New York Central at Bucyrus, Ohio. These first units were composed of officers and men of long railroad experience and they soon became an efficient team.

The 753 R.S.B. at Bucyrus took over the maintenance and rehabilitation of rolling stock of the United States Government, thus securing an ideal training as well as repairing motive power and cars utilized by the Corps of Engineers and other branches of the government in their various establishments. It is a pleasure for the Manager to comment on the unprecedented cooperation and assistance rendered in the training of the units of the M.R.S. by the officials and other personnel of the railroads on which these units trained. Unfortunately, space does not permit the naming of these gentlemen. In the training program the Manager worked through the General Superintendent, and the General Superintendent worked with the Division Superintendents and the Railway Shop Superintendents.

In the original planning the writer was to be the Supreme Commander of the M.R.S. in the field. A Vice-President of the Pennsylvania Railroad, Colonel C. D. Young, was to be Chief, Railway Branch, Office of the Chief of Engineers, heading the M.R.S. Branch. Unfortunately, Colonel Young did not get to serve throughout the war. The development of the M.R.S. section in the Chief's office was headed by Colonel (later Brigadier General) Lewis T. Ross, with a group of railroad men as his staff who had been commissioned and called into service for the purpose of assisting the Chief in the development of the M.R.S.

The Manager was fully consulted and his approval secured as to the units next to be called under the plan of mobilization. He had full authority to effect transfers and distribution of men and material. This authority continued throughout the war.

With the establishment of a large training camp, called Camp Claiborne, south of Alexandria, Louisiana, and Camp Polk on the Kansas City Southern Railway Company, approximately 50 miles distant, it was decided to build a railroad connecting the two camps and to use that railroad as a training ground for railway operating battalions. At first it was thought that purchase could be made of an existing lumber railroad, known as the Red River and Gulf Railroad, but that did not work out.

A line was surveyed, which included much of the right of way of an old logging road, long since abandoned, known as the Hillyer-Deutches-Edwards Logging Road. With an eye on expense, as well as creation of conditions anticipated in a theater of operations, the specifications of the railroad were planned to have it not exceed 1.5 per cent in grade and a maximum curvature of 4°. It was necessary in five instances, however, to use 6° curves, and in order to speed construction after the start of the war, the railroad grade was raised to 2 per cent.

The line, as finally built, was 47.66 miles long. It was built by the 711 R.O.B. with the assistance on some of the bridge structures by the 91 and 93 Engineer Battalions. The railroad had twenty-five bridges; all but three were on the old logging right of way.

Big Cut Bridge, which carried the Claiborne and Polk across the Red River and Gulf Railroad, was started late in October. The trestle bents were erected during November, and on 9 December, the steel girder forming the central span was placed in position. The 130-foot frame and steel structure rested on concrete footings, had six single bents with four posts each, and two double bents with five posts apiece. It was approximately 30 feet above the Red River and Gulf rails at the center.

Spring Creek Bridge, a 785-foot pile trestle, was started on 27 January 1942. After the right of way was cleared by the 98 Engineers, the 711 Bridge and Building Platoon, using a 78-ton steam pile driver, completed the essential structure of the bridge in 17 days.

The longest bridge on the railroad was a 2,200-foot bridge across the Calcasieu River. The long and difficult haul of material to the site of the bridge and the frequent floods which filled the bottoms it spanned made construction a most arduous task. By utilizing solid portions of existing piling from an old bridge on the Hillyer-Deutches-Edwards line, it was possible to erect trestle bents for the support of the stringers and track. The first train passed over this bridge on 19 May 1942.

The railroad was made complete as to facilities with the construction of a yard at both Camps Claiborne and Polk, and trains were run on a turn-around basis; therefore, engine-house facilities were provided only at Camp Claiborne. The yard there had six tracks with a capacity of over 150 cars; a three-stall engine house, two rip tracks, and a wye for turning engines. The yard office was in a new building. The telephone and telegraph line over which the dispatching was accomplished was erected by the 26 Signal Construction Battalion. The line was completed in March 1942.

Rolling stock provided was seven 79-ton ten-wheelers and two new 85-ton consolidation type locomotives (all oil burners), two coaches and two combination cars, 16 boxcars, 50 flatcars, 25 gondolas, 12 tank cars, and four refrigerator cars. Six cars were converted into cabooses by the mechanical forces of the 711th. These cabooses had bay windows instead of the time-honored cupolas.

Of course, carloads of government material arriving on the Missouri Pacific at Alexandria and on the Kansas City Southern at Camp Polk were interchanged with the Claiborne and Polk Military Railway. For outbound movement, cars were furnished by those two carriers depending upon the routing off the C. & P.

The railroad was completed and the "golden spike" was driven by the Manager, M.R.S., at Mile 27 near Lacamp, Louisiana. Present at the ceremony as guests of the Commanding Officer of the 711 R.O.B., Major George M. Welch, and Lieutenant Gardner E. Dyke (both from the C. St. P. M. & O. Railway) were such dignitaries as Lieutenant General W. E. Kreuger, Third Army; Major General Richard Donovan, Eighth Corps Area; Major General A. C. Gillan, Armored Divisions; Brigadier General David McCoach, Jr., representing Major General Eugene Reybold, Chief of Engineers; Brigadier General J. W. N. Schulz, Engineer Organization Center, Camp Claiborne; Brigadier General Matthew B. Ridgway, Eighty-second Airborne Division, Camp Claiborne; Colonel Otto Wagner, Camp Polk

Training M.R.S. troops. Inspection, 1942.

commander; Colonel H. M. Pendleton, Camp Claiborne commander; Governor Jones of Louisiana; William Deramus, Sr., President of the Kansas City Southern Railway; and Johnson Couch, Assistant Vice-President, Kansas City Southern Railway. Officers from M.R.S. headquarters at St. Paul who attended along with the Manager were Colonel W. G. Knight, Colonel B. H. Crosland, Lieutenant Colonel C. F. Dougherty, Lieutenant Colonel E. F. McFadden, and Lieutenant J. T. Hayes.

Regular service was established and the first Time Card was issued Sunday, 20 September, 1942, effective at 0001 hours. It provided for two first-class trains in each direction daily with a running time of two hours and thirty minutes. There was also a second-class or local freight train daily, except Sunday, in each direction. Training was provided for telegraph operators at six stations set up along the line.

This railroad was probably the first of its kind in the world. It attracted considerable attention both in railroad and journalistic circles. Two articles were written about this railroad and the training of battalions on it which are outstanding. One appeared in the *Saturday Evening Post* and was entitled: "The Worst Railroad on Earth" telling the story of "Old Crime and

Training of M.R.S. troops. Battalion on hike, 1942.

727 R.O.B. in training, 1942.

Punishment," the affectionately adopted name of the C. & P. Railway. Another very interesting article appeared in the Boston *Globe* by John Barry on 13 April 1944.

When the 730 R.O.B. was called into active service on 15 May 1942 it was trained on the lines of the Pennsylvania Railroad in the vicinity of Fort Wayne, Indiana. It was headquartered in a camp called Thomas A. Scott, named after the Assistant Secretary of War in President Lincoln's Cabinet, who had created the M.R.S. in 1862.

The immediate call for M.R.S. troops in Iran caused the activation of the 702 R.G.D. on 15 October 1942. From an organizational standpoint this unit consisted of the 702 R.G.D. headquarters (Union Pacific Railroad), the

711 R.O.B. (no sponsorship), the 730 R.O.B. (Pennsylvania Railroad), and the 754 R.S.B. (Southern Pacific Company).

As the M.R.S. became more experienced in the activation and training program, the officers were called into duty some month or six weeks prior to the activation of their unit and given a refresher course, first at Fort Leonard Wood, Missouri, later at Fort Slocum, New York. Ultimately most of the unit's officers and some of the enlisted men were given a basic military training at New Orleans Unit Training Center—later named Camp Plauche. When the number of those units called into active service were in excess of the capacity for training at Camp Plauche, the overflow was taken care of at Fort Sam Houston, Texas. During the latter days of the war, when the training was largely completed, the basic training of railway troops was transferred to Fort Francis E. Warren, Wyoming. Technical training continued on the commercial railroads.

The date of activation of the various units of the M.R.S. is as follows:

Unit	Date of activation
Headquarters, Military Railway Service	15 May 1942
701 Railway Grand Division	11 January 1943
702 Railway Grand Division	15 October 1942
703 Railway Grand Division	1 August 1942
704 Railway Grand Division	30 November 1942
705 Railway Grand Division	19 May 1943
706 Railway Grand Division	6 October 1943
707 Railway Grand Division	10 June 1943
708 Railway Grand Division	6 April 1943
709 Railway Grand Division	15 March 1944
710 Railway Grand Division	14 December 1943
711 Railway Operating Battalion	1 May 1941
712 Railway Operating Battalion	25 October 1942
713 Railway Operating Battalion	15 April 1942
714 Railway Operating Battalion	31 October 1942
715 Railway Operating Battalion	31 October 1942
716 Railway Operating Battalion	21 December 1943
717 Railway Operating Battalion	1 December 1943
718 Railway Operating Battalion	14 December 1943
719 Railway Operating Battalion	1 September 1943
720 Railway Operating Battalion	26 August 1943

721 Railway Operating Battalion	14 April 1943
722 Railway Operating Battalion	14 December 1943
723 Railway Operating Battalion	28 December 1943
724 Railway Operating Battalion	28 December 1943
725 Railway Operating Battalion	17 February 1943
726 Railway Operating Battalion	26 June 1943
727 Railway Operating Battalion	15 March 1942
728 Railway Operating Battalion	11 January 1943
729 Railway Operating Battalion	11 January 1943
730 Railway Operating Battalion	15 May 1942
731 Railway Operating Battalion	Was not activated
732 Railway Operating Battalion	12 January 1944
733 Railway Operating Battalion	23 November 1943
734 Railway Operating Battalion	23 February 1944
735 Railway Operating Battalion	10 February 1944
736 Railway Operating Battalion	Was not activated
737 Railway Operating Battalion	30 September 1944
738 Railway Operating Battalion	Was not activated
739 Railway Operating Battalion	Was not activated
740 Railway Operating Battalion	14 December 1943
741 Railway Operating Battalion	12 January 1944
742 Railway Operating Battalion	Was not activated
743 Railway Operating Battalion	12 January 1944
744 Railway Operating Battalion	21 December 1943
745 Railway Operating Battalion	19 May 1943
746 Railway Operating Battalion	4 May 1944
747 Railway Operating Battalion	Was not activated
748 Railway Operating Battalion	12 May 1943
749 Railway Operating Battalion	23 February 1944
750 Railway Operating Battalion	21 March 1944
751 Railway Operating Battalion	Was not activated
752 Railway Operating Battalion	4 May 1944
759 Railway Operating Battalion	1 September 1942
770 Railway Operating Battalion	9 August 1942
790 Railway Operating Battalion	8 July 1943
791 Railway Operating Battalion	21 June 1943

761 Railway Transportation Company	22 July 1942
753 Railway Shop Battalion	15 April 1942
754 Railway Shop Battalion	15 October 1942
755 Railway Shop Battalion	30 November 1943
756 Railway Shop Battalion	11 January 1943
757 Railway Shop Battalion	10 June 1943
758 Railway Shop Battalion	6 April 1943
760 Railway Shop Battalion	15 June 1942
762 Railway Shop Battalion	15 October 1942
763 Railway Shop Battalion	27 July 1943
764 Railway Shop Battalion	25 October 1943
765 Railway Shop Battalion	1 May 1944
766 Railway Shop Battalion	17 July 1944

The Manager and his headquarters were responsible for the training of these units until that headquarters was ordered overseas, the first unit of which departed from St. Paul on 27 January 1943. The direction and training activities were then set up by the Army Service Forces at the Port of Embarkation, New Orleans, Louisiana, under Colonel C. E. Hise, formerly Commanding Officer of the 714 R.O.B. Colonel Hise was appointed Director of Railway Training, Army Service Forces.

General Brehon B. Somervell, Commanding Army Service Forces.

4

First Assignments Overseas World War II

1942

THE CONSTRUCTION and transportation problem in Alaska had become very complex by August 1942. General B. B. Somervell, commanding Army Service Forces, flew to Alaska to acquaint himself with the requirements. On 22 August he was returning and from his plane radioed the Manager, M.R.S., St. Paul, as follows: "Proceed by first Air Priority to White Horse, Yukon Territory, and after consultation with General Hoge take over by lease the White Pass and Yukon Route, retaining it as a Class I carrier and retaining the civilian personnel augmenting with military material, equipment, and personnel sufficient to handle the military traffic." The General was accompanied by Major General Eugene Reybold, Chief of Engineers, and Mr. George A. Benedict, Master Mechanic of the White Pass and Yukon Route.

The General later that day changed his original order and directed the Manager to join him and the party proceeded to Washington on 23 August. Subsequently, the Manager took Mr. Benedict in General Somervell's plane on 28 August, arriving at Pueblo, Colorado, on 29 August. Then, in company with Mr. Sagstetter of the Denver and Rio Grande Western Railroad Company, they went to Alamosa and Salida, Colorado, to inspect the only serviceable narrow-gauge engines known to be in existence in the United States, which were of the same gauge (three feet) as the White Pass and Yukon Route. After inspection, Mr. Benedict indicated that the engines would be satisfactory for use on the White Pass and Yukon Route, so arrangements were made for the purchase of these engines by the government and transportation to Seattle by rail, then by barge to Skagway, Alaska. A total of seven locomotives were thus added to the rolling stock of the railroad.

The White Pass and Yukon Route covers a distance of 110.7 miles from Skagway, Alaska, to White Horse, Yukon Territory. The railroad was completed in the year 1900 and was built as a direct result of the Klondike Gold Rush. Skagway is a port which is free from ice the year around. White Horse, in addition to being the northern terminus of the railroad, was a supply point on the Alcan Highway, which was then being constructed. Large quantities of pipe and other supplies were being shipped to Skagway by boat and then via railroad to White Horse where they were used in the construction of an oil pipeline in that area. Also, much material was being transported to White Horse for the big air base located near there.

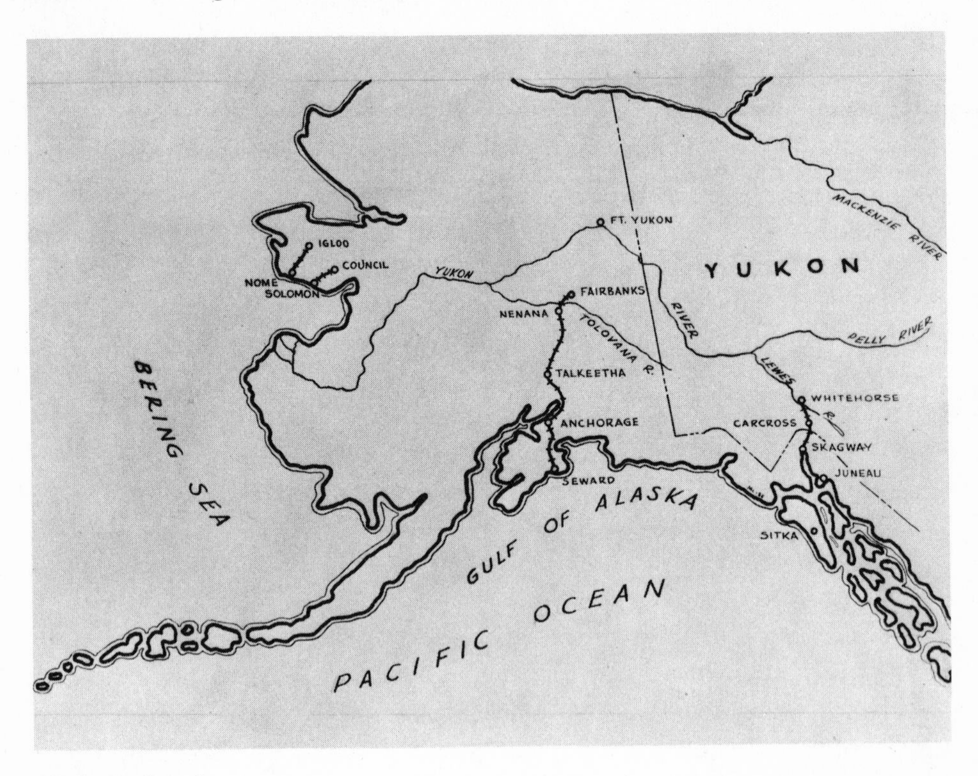

Alaska Railroads.

Barging narrow-gauge locomotives and supplies to Skagway.

In August 1942 it became apparent that the White Pass and Yukon did not have sufficient manpower, locomotives, or cars to move the heavy construction materials required at White Horse. This, of course, resulted in General Somervell's inspection trip and his decision to lease the White Pass and Yukon Route for operation by the M.R.S.

In preparing the lease it was necessary to know the corporate identities of the White Pass and Yukon Route. It was composed of three corporations: The Pacific and Arctic Railway and Navigation Company, which was a West Virginia, United States of America corporation, and owned that portion of the line from Skagway to the international boundary between Alaska and British Columbia, 19 miles; the British Columbia Yukon Railway Company, a Canadian corporation, owning that portion of the railroad between the international boundary and the boundary between British Columbia and Yukon Territory, 34.6 miles; the British Yukon Railway Company, a Canadian corporation, which owned that portion of the line in Yukon Territory terminating at White Horse, and which was 57.1 miles in length. The capital stock of the three named companies was owned by the White Pass and Yukon Route, Ltd., a British corporation with offices in London. The management was then, and is now, headed by an American, Mr. C. J. Rogers, President and General Manager of the railway.

The Manager, M.R.S., then took up to a conclusion the drawing of the necessary contract of lease, the operating procedure, and the M.R.S. force that would be used. An additional trip to White Horse was necessary. On that trip, before he left White Horse, the Manager issued a letter of intent to Mr. Rogers regarding the taking over of the White Pass and Yukon Route by the Government of the United States. Since this was agreeable to the various

Hurricane Bridge, Alaska Railroad, 300 ft. high.

parties concerned, the railroad was actually taken over as of 12:01 A.M., 1 October 1942.

One of the legal difficulties in connection with drawing up the lease was the fact that under Canadian law no foreign corporation could do business within Canada. It was therefore necessary for the Manager, M.R.S., to go to Ottawa on three occasions, where he finally secured an Order of Counsel, which "legalized an illegal action."

From the preliminary contract a formal contract was drawn and the representatives of the holding corporation in London, Sir George Hamilton and Mr. A. H. Martens, respectively Chairman of the Board and the senior partner of Close Brothers, bankers, trustees of the mortgage, flew to America and signed the contract on behalf of the owners. The lease was for the duration of the war and six months thereafter. This was accomplished 22 October 1942, 21 days after the railroad was taken over.

The Manager was very desirous of eliminating the difficulties which occurred in World War I by the taking over of the American Railroads by the United States Railroad Administration and the subsequent claims which came from the carriers. These claims were bitterly contested and long drawn out in their settlement in regard to retirements, additions, betterments, etc., during the government control. So it was agreed to incorporate within the contract for lease a paragraph specifically covering this complex question. That covenant, Article No. 4 of the lease, is quoted here in its entirety:

Article 4. Improvements.—It is contemplated that the Government for the purpose of expeditious and efficient operation of the leased facilities may provide additions and betterments to the property in the form of improvements to the roadway, tracks and structures, to the rolling stock, and to the shop facilities for the maintenance of equipment, and to other property or facilities included within the lease. It is understood and agreed that the Contractor will reimburse the Government currently for additions and betterments to existing facilities or property which are properly chargeable to capital account, and made by the Government in connection with normal maintenance, and that insofar as are concerned additions or movable and mobile equipment, such as cars, locomotives, machines, etc. made by the Government, the Contractor shall be given the option to purchase such equipment or any part thereof within ninety (90) days after termination of the lease at the then fair value, and if such option is not exercised, then at the expiration of said ninety (90) days' period the Government shall have the right to remove all and sundry such equipment at its own expense. In the event that the Government, during the term of this lease shall retire any of the existing property, the Government will reimburse the Contractor currently therefor in an amount equal to the book cost less depreciation accrued on such property as of the date of such retirement under the terms of this lease, but there shall be no right to reimbursement in connection with fixed property which shall be retired and replaced with other property of equal or greater value. Current Interstate Commerce Commission, United States of America, classifications of accounts shall govern with respect to charges hereunder.

In the event it is desired to change the railroad from narrow gauge to standard gauge track a new contract will be negotiated at that time.

In addition to the immediate purchase of the locomotives from the Denver and Rio Grande Western Railway, our government was able to divert some 36-inch gauge steel boxcars destined for South America. They were sent to the White Pass and Yukon Route for use there.

Major John E. Ausland, Acting Chief Construction Engineer, Headquarters, M.R.S., was selected to head a detachment of 402 officers and men, designated as Railway Detachment 9646-A, to proceed to Skagway to operate the W. P. & Y. Major Ausland was chosen because he had had long civilian experience in the location, construction, and operation of transportation facilities in foreign lands, as well as extensive service in World War I.

The group was made up of men from the 713 and 727 R.O.B. The unit departed from Clovis, New Mexico, on 16 September and assumed operations of the railroad as of 12:01 A.M., 1 October 1942. Civilian employees continued in service with M.R.S. personnel supervising. The entire operation remained under the command of Major Ausland, who maintained a close liaison with the staff of the Commanding General, Northwest Service Command.

By authority of the War Department, the Manager, M.R.S., exercised jurisdiction on all matters of technical operation. On 16 November 1942 the name of the unit was changed to the 770 Railway Operating Detachment.

By December 1942 it became evident that because of the tremendous amount of tonnage required in connection with the construction and supplying of airports and the Alcan Highway there was not sufficient force in the M.R.S. in Alaska nor equipment to satisfy the Army's demands. The original force was supplemented by an additional 38 railway men who departed from Fort Snelling on 28 February 1943.

Finally, a new organization was perfected in accordance with the actual requirements gained by the experience of the operation. These were beyond the Table of Organization of a railway operating battalion. Assembly was started at Camp Claiborne of specialists to augment the forces then operating the W.P.&Y.

The result of all the plans and deliberations of experienced staff officers who studied not only the situation at hand but the future requirements caused the formation of a modified railway operating battalion which was called the 770 R.O.B. It had 19 officers, 2 warrant officers, and 708 enlisted men.

A very experienced Colorado and Southern Railway Company narrow-gauge operating Superintendent, Lieutenant Colonel W. P. Wilson, was

The PX train at Matanuska, Alaska, autumn 1943.

chosen to command and Major Ausland was transferred back to Headquarters, M.R.S., and ultimately saw service in North Africa, Sicily, and Italy. Major H. C. Baughn was the Assistant Superintendent of the 770 R.O.B. Other officers and men of northern United States railroad experience with an understanding of operating in snow conditions played no small part in the success of the venture.

The operation of this railroad was hectic, to say the least. Below-zero temperatures, snow, blizzards, drifts, and every factor of winter in all its wrath was visited upon this carrier to disrupt its operations. The area of difficulty in operation during extreme winter conditions was from Milepost 7 northward, but with greater emphasis in the vicinity of Mileposts 15 to 17 inclusive.

Colonel Wilson and the men of the 770 R.O.B. had their worst experience in the period from 5 to 15 February 1943, when the railroad was blocked by snow and blizzards raging throughout the entire time at thirty-degrees-below-zero temperatures.

Colonel Wilson was on the north end, and on 5 February he was stopped at Carcross because of the severity of the storm and high snowdrifts over the railroad. Likewise, a rotary was trying to work north from Skagway, and it was blocked at Milepost 16.5. Conditions got worse, more snow drifted, winds blew, temperatures stayed 30° below zero, but notwithstanding all of those unbelievable weather difficulties these men kept trying to break through with their rotaries. Instead, they were snowbound, coal supplies gave out, they burned ties, and finally secured the assistance of one of the general contractors in that area and got a D-4 tractor to bring rations and coal to the stalled crews.

The weather started to moderate on 11 February and the thermometer went up to 6° below zero and the wind ceased blowing. With superhuman effort they broke through and opened the line on 13 February. Traffic was resumed on 15 February with bad snow conditions, but without the blockades of the preceding two weeks.

Colonel Wilson left the 770 R.O.B. by rotation in July 1943, activated the 745 R.O.B., and took it to Assam, India. Then he was called to Italy and made the Deputy Director, M.R.S., when the Director General moved his headquarters and operations from Italy to southern France. Colonel Wilson was succeeded in the 770 R.O.B. by Major (later Lieutenant Colonel) H. C. Baughn.

The following winter found the White Pass and Yukon again completely blocked. This time it was from 27 January to 14 February 1944. Here again the men of this battalion, with Colonel Baughn himself in the field constantly, had almost identically the same climatic conditions they had experienced the winter before. This time traffic was stopped due to a two weeks' period of heavy snowslides and drifts combined with a serious ice condition on the tracks between Glacier and the snowshed at Milepost 20.9. The line was opened and traffic resumed at 0435 hours on 14 February 1944.

With the transfer of Headquarters, M.R.S., to the North African Theater of Operations at the end of January 1943, the technical supervision exercised by the M.R.S. headquarters over the W. P. & Y. passed to the Commanding General, Northwest Service Command, per letter from the Chief of Transportation, dated 24 February 1943.

The ultimate locomotives and rolling stock in use on the White Pass and Yukon Route were:

	W.P.&Y.	U.S.A.
Locomotives	10	26
Passenger Cars	24	2
Freight Cars	83	258
Work Equipment Cars	22	4

In the work equipment there were two W.P.&Y. rotary snowplows and one U.S.A.

The White Pass and Yukon, as a commercial railroad, for the period 1938 through 1941 had averaged 25,000 tons handled per year. For the first nine months of 1942 it handled 67,496 tons. From 1 October through 31 December 1942, under the operation of the M.R.S., 25,756 tons were handled, and for the calendar year 1943, it handled 281,962 tons; 133,524 tons in the year 1944; and for the year 1945, 38,531 tons.

Up to the time of the discontinuance of the lease on 30 April 1946, 10,570 tons were handled. For the balance of 1946, 25,604 tons were handled. At the end of seven years, since the turn-back of the railroad to private industry, it averaged approximately 64,000 tons hauled per annum.

The leasing of the White Pass and Yukon Route by the United States Government and the operation of it by the 770 R.O.B. of the M.R.S. was a war necessity that proved most satisfactory to both parties to the lease.

A board of officers, headed by Colonel Dawes G. Brisbine, negotiated a termination of the lease in August 1944. Those negotiating, of course, followed the provisions of Article 4 of the lease and by virtue of its clearness and the cooperative attitude of the owners of the property, long-drawn-out controversies such as were experienced at the end of the United States Railroad Administration in 1920 were eliminated.

By virtue of the strategic offense and defense characteristics of Alaska, it early became quite an active area. There was even contemplated, and a preliminary survey made for, a railroad to connect the western terminus of the Canadian National Railways with the Alaska Railroad at Fairbanks. The M.R.S. headquarters was called upon to indicate what personnel and rolling stock would be required, and other operating facilities to handle a maximum of 200,000 net tons of freight per month. This planning and activity were carried out in the summer and fall of 1942. That railroad was never built, but the Alcan Highway was.

The capacity of the Alaska Railroad to handle government freight was more than sorely tried. The Alaska Railroad was built by the United States Government pursuant to two acts of Congress; the first passed in August 1912 authorized the President to appoint a commission to examine into certain problems relating to transportation in Alaska. The second act, passed 1 March 1914, authorized and directed the President to designate and cause to be built a railroad line to connect one or more of the open harbors on the south coast of Alaska with the navigable waters, coal fields, and agricultural lands of the interior.

Pursuant to the act of 1912, President Taft appointed the Alaska Railroad Commission, consisting of Major Jay J. Morrow, Chairman; Alfred H. Brooks, Geologist in charge of Division of Alaska Mineral Resources, Geological Survey, Vice-Chairman; Civil Engineer Leonard M. Cox, United States Navy; and Colin M. Ingersoll, consulting railroad engineer, of New York City. The Commission proceeded to Alaska, and later submitted a comprehensive report, which was transmitted by President Taft to Congress in February 1913.

The PX car at Fairbanks,
58° below zero.

ary snow plow fleet at McKinley,
48° below zero.

By the provisions of the act of 1914 a new commission was created by President Wilson, which was known as the Alaskan Engineering Commission. Its members were Mr. William C. Edes of the Southern Pacific Railroad, Chairman; Lieutenant Frederick Mears of the United States Army; and Mr. Thomas Riggs, Jr., of the Alaska Boundary Survey Commission. They organized, equipped, and sent into the field a number of railroad location surveying parties. The members of the commission then proceeded to Alaska and made a close examination and survey of the recommended routes. This work was carried on during the summer and fall of 1914.

President Wilson, upon receiving the report from this commission, issued an order on 10 April 1915 announcing his selection of a route commencing at Seward on Resurrection Bay and extending northward a distance of 412 miles, more or less, to a point on Tanana River. Later, the line was extended to Fairbanks.

Construction was begun in 1915 and completed on 15 July 1923, when President Harding drove the "golden spike" signifying the completion of the railroad.

Later, a 12.34 mile cutoff to a new port terminal at Whittier was constructed, which reduced the distance from tidewater to the interior of Alaska by 52 miles over Seward. This construction was begun in 1941 and, under the direction of the Corps of Engineers, was completed in 1943. The cutoff included two tunnels, one 13,090 feet long and the other 4,911 feet long. In 1943 the Alaska Railroad was approximately 470 miles long and had a maximum curvature of 15° and a gradient of 2 per cent.

The Alaska Railroad, although government owned, operated as a private carrier. At the time the railroad became of strategic importance in the part Alaska might play in World War II, Mr. Otto F. Ohlson was the highest ranking officer, the General Manager. Because of the tremendously increased activities, the manpower situation on the Alaska Railroad by midsummer of 1942 became desperate. Railroad employees were leaving for more lucrative positions with the contractors and other activities in the territory.

Coupled with this, the heavy demand put upon it and a most severe winter season in 1942-1943, the railroad was confronted with the problems of undermaintained track and equipment, and even of insufficient train-operating forces. Since this railroad was of prime importance in the tactical

Thirty below, winter 1944-1945.

situation of the North Pacific Theater of Operations and since the Army was being constantly called upon for help, a survey of complete requirements by the M.R.S. was ordered at the request of the Commanding General of the Alaska Defense Command.

The situation was not like what was to be expected and planned for in an active theater of operations; however, in February 1943 a decision was made to send M.R.S. troops to augment the civilian employees and maintain and operate the Alaska Railroad. The 714 R.O.B. (C. St. P. M. & O.) at that time in training on the C. & P. Military Railway, was selected.

It was intended that a railway operating battalion would operate a maximum of 150 miles, but the Alaska Railroad was more than three times that; therefore, the battalion was augmented by three additional platoons for "A" Company, each 87 men. The 714 R.O.B., as it took over the Alaska Railroad, had a total strength of 23 officers, 2 warrant officers, and 1,108 enlisted men, for an aggregate of 1,133 officers and men.

The Division Superintendent of the battalion as it arrived in Alaska was Lieutenant Colonel Herbert S. Huron. By reason of rotation of personnel, he was succeeded by Lieutenant Colonel W. Hastedt. The original commanding officer was Lieutenant Colonel C. E. Hise, but he had been relieved to become the Director of Railway Training of the entire M.R.S. training program.

The battalion departed from Camp Claiborne on 14 March 1943, and moved onto the railroad 3 April 1943. Headquarters were established in the

Normal operating conditions, winter 1944-1945.

Alaska Railroad General Office along with the civilian General Manager. Perfect coordination existed as between those two headquarters.

Bad track condition was the paramount difficulty at the time the battalion arrived. To handle this, five grand maintenance sections were set up with a minimum of 66 miles and a maximum of 106 miles. A lieutenant with experience in track maintenance commanded each one of these sections.

A great amount of construction was necessary to augment the facilities of the Alaska Railroad to provide quarters for the men. One of the most troublesome conditions was the distribution of the supplies and messing of the men. A portable PX and supply car remedied the first, but the messing situation with adequately trained cooks for so many small messes troubled to the end of service. Another thing that was troublesome was the fact that the battalion left Camp Claiborne without its basic railroad equipment which had been established by Supply Circular OT-29. Therefore, when the battalion got to Alaska, it required a great amount of miscellaneous equipment from the various branches of the Army. Additional special equipment was required and arctic clothing as well because of the frigid conditions of the weather and the snow conditions affecting the movement of trains and maintenance of track and bridges.

The 714 R.O.B. was on the property for more than 25 months augmenting the civilian personnel of the Alaska Railway in all departments. During that little more than two-year period they effected the following en-

Blocked by snow, winter 1944-1945.

viable record: renewed 240,387 crossties; renewed 75,000 F.B.M. switch ties; installed approximately 63,000 cubic yards of ballast; rebuilt or repaired 50 bridges consisting of 318 spans.

In 1941 the total amount of tonnage handled was 474,884, of which 12.2 per cent was company freight. In 1942 this increased to 519,452 tons handled, with approximately the same percentage being company freight. In 1943 the figure went to 699,246, with a slightly higher ratio handled being company freight. The maximum tonnage handled was in 1944, when 764,775 tons were handled. Thereafter, the figures gradually dropped; however, for the years 1941 to 1946 inclusive there was handled a total 3,632,077 tons of freight of which 19.1 per cent was company freight.

Further, as a comparison, the average number of cars moved per month on the Alaska Railroad during 1942 was 3,150 cars per month; during 1943 the average was 5,080 cars per month. The peak was reached during the month of October 1943, when 6,600 cars were handled.

The 714 R.O.B. was relieved of responsibility in the operation of the Alaska Railroad 7 May 1945, and departed for the United States on 10 May 1945. Numerous leaves were granted, but the battalion was assigned to Camp Claiborne, Louisiana, and took over the operation of the C. & P. Military Railway. The 714 R.O.B. was taken into the Regular Army and on the closing of Camp Claiborne was ordered to Fort Eustis, Virginia; it arrived there 6 January 1946. It is still in service, acting as a training battalion for M.R.S. troops of the Army.

General of the Army Dwight D. Eisenhower, Supreme Commander.

5

Operations in North Africa
1943-1944

AMERICAN AND BRITISH STRATEGY in World War II surprised the enemy, for instead of the invasion of Europe, the first landings were made under the Allied Forces command on 8 November 1942, simultaneously by the Americans north of Casablanca, Morocco, and by the British at Oran and Algiers, Algeria. The occupation of French North Africa by Allied troops was determined in July 1942, when the American and British Governments agreed to launch a Mediterranean operation in the fall of 1942. The invasion, designated in the planning as TORCH, was to coincide with a British advance westward from Egypt.

General Mark Clark carried out one of the most adventurous and dangerous personal undertakings of the whole war when, with the assistance of Mr. Robert Murphy, American consul at Algiers, he went ashore in North Africa from a submarine with a party on 22 October 1942. There he met with General Mast of the French Army and Mr. Murphy at a secret rendezvous at the home of a M. Tessier, approximately 60 miles west of Algiers. Proper data were exchanged and collaboration with the French was fabricated. In later negotiations carried on by the Americans through General Clark and Admiral Darlan of France, a written understanding was agreed upon.

Paragraph XVI of this agreement reads as follows:

In North Africa areas deemed by the Commanding General, United States Army, to be of importance or useful to the purpose set forth in the preamble hereof, from time to time, may be declared by him to be military areas under his control whereupon the maintenance of order and administrative and public services in such areas shall come under the direct control of such Commanding General. The French authorities will be promptly notified in the event such a step becomes necessary.

This agreement had a very definite effect upon the authority and operations of the M.R.S. in the North African Theater of War.

Under the French law of 1875 the operation of railroads in a theater of war comes under the Director of Military Transports. To that end, it was necessary to operate the French railroads in North Africa through Colonel E. Quenard, who was the Director of Military Transports for the French in North Africa.

Allied Force Headquarters (AFHQ) entered into negotiations with the French Government and ultimately worked out a financial arrrangement with respect to the use of their government-owned railroads as lines of communications for the Allied Armies. The French Government furnished the physical railroad and as much of its rolling stock and motive power as were usable.

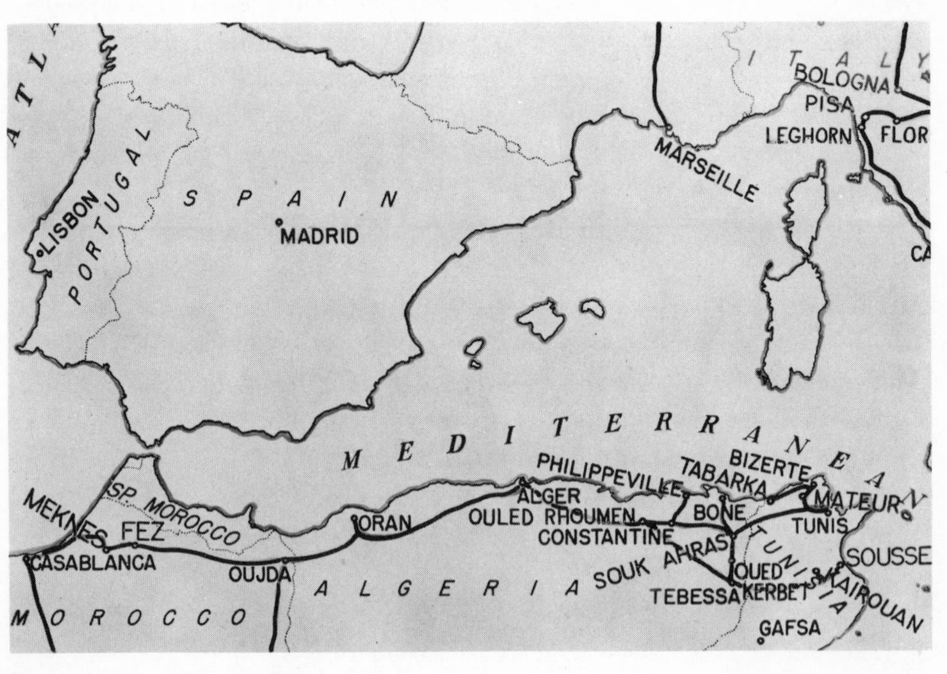

The railroads of North Africa.

U.S.A. equipment. Standard 2-8-0 locomotives, coal or oil.

The Americans and British added materially to the number of locomotives and cars in service, as well as stores, machines, and almost everything to make the railroads available to handle the unprecedented tonnage that required moving.

The contract in North Africa as compensation paid was that the Allied countries paid for the transportation of material and personnel with rates as listed in the North African regular military tariffs. These tariffs had been in effect before the war, and they were applied to the Allied military traffic as they had been applied to the military traffic that was handled before the war. These tariffs were strange to the Americans, for they were based on the capacity of cars. Cars having a capacity of up to 20 tons were charged a certain tariff; a different rate for cars having a capacity up to 40 tons carried was charged, and a still different tariff for cars having a capacity of over 40 tons. Each of these tariffs was based on francs per kilometer transported.

For the transportation of personnel, the North African first and third class rates were used for individual moves, but for the transportation of units there were three rates to apply: one for 16 to 31 men in a 20-ton boxcar, another rate for 40 men in a special coach, and a third rate for 60 men in a special coach.

Then a rental charge for cars furnished by the Americans at $1.00 per day, and a charge for motive power of $.01 per pound of tractive effort per locomotive per day were levied against the French railroads. The net established was paid monthly to the French.

It is interesting to balance those transportation charges of the North African campaign. Under the direction of Captain Stanley R. Beggs, Statistical Officer, a group of 12 enlisted men from Headquarters, M.R.S., checked and verified all freight and passenger bills rendered by the railroads of North Africa against the United States Army, beginning with the original landings. A similar group from the British Transportation Office, composed of Major L. C. Pannel (in charge), a Captain Smith, and 15 enlisted men engaged in the same work for the British.

When Headquarters, M.R.S., moved on to Italy, a detachment of men was left in North Africa in charge of First Lieutenant J. A. Vopatek, Assistant Adjutant, M.R.S., Fiscal Section, North Africa, to complete the checking and auditing of transportation charges levied against the armies of the United States and Great Britain.

Auditing continued until September 1944, and when all warrants had been checked, involving 1,384,277,664 francs, or $27,685,595.68, a total of $1,396,210.76 or 5.04 per cent had been recovered. Breakdown of the total overcharge is as follows:

Overcharge to British Army	$552,501.22
Overcharge to French Army	144,909.62
Overcharge to United States Army	698,799.92

Main items of overcharge were due to duplication of warrants, excessive distance and personnel charges, excessive car capacity weights and charges for the holding of cars waiting for arrival of convoys. The amount chargeable to the French Army was made up mainly of transportation charges on supplies for civilian use, and it was ruled by the French Government that those costs were payable.

Several of the key enlisted personnel who engaged in this work were Technician Fourth Grade George D. Anderson, Technician Fourth Grade George C. Weatherill, Technician Fourth Grade George O. Nygaard, and Technician Fifth Grade Raymond F. Miloston.

The strategical plan was to occupy Tunisia before the Germans and Italians could concentrate in strength there. As Sir Winston Churchill put it: "North Africa is no halting place—it isn't a seat, but a springboard." With the northern coast in Allied hands, the way would be opened to attack the most vulnerable front of the Axis, the "soft underbelly" of southern Europe. Tunisia at the nearest point is only 90 miles from Sicily and 150 miles from the mainland of Italy.

Transportation planning for the North African campaign was begun in London in August 1942 under the British War Office and the First Army Command. Information available on transportation facilities in Algeria and Tunisia was very full and accurate. The railroads of North Africa consisted of a total of 5,082 miles: The Chemins de Fer du Maroc, 867 miles; Chemins de Fer Algériens, 2,741 miles; and the Chemins de Fer de Tunisie, 1,001 miles—all government owned. The Sfax-Gafsa Railroad, 276 miles, and the Tangier Fez, 197 miles, were the only privately owned and operated railroads in North Africa.

The planning in London contemplated that the Americans would look after all transportation matters in Morocco and Algeria west of Orléansville, and the British would be responsible east of there.

In the original planning for the North African Campaign from the American side, the railway plan contemplated that the principal concern was in furnishing supplies from the anticipated ports of debarkation; namely, Casablanca, Oran, and Algiers. It was assumed that 500,000 tons of supplies a month would have to be distributed from unloadings at the three ports. It was further assumed that the greatest resistance would be at the ports in Tunisia.

Because the distance from Casablanca to Tunis was 1,400 miles, and since the railway operating battalions contemplated operating a maximum of only 240 miles, the railways from Casablanca to the border of Tunisia would have to be handled mostly by civilian personnel, supervised by the M.R.S. The over-all final estimate included the necessity for use of one Headquarters, M.R.S., four Headquarters, R.G.D., 19 R.O.B., and four R.S.B., without civilian operation. It was further figured that if the 500,000 tons per month were to be handled it would require 34 trains per day, 190 locomotives, and 2,600 cars to handle the traffic.

A minimum force required to operate the network in Tunisia, if and when the Allied forces got there, would require the use of 40 standard-gauge locomotives, 670 cars, 80 narrow-gauge locomotives, and 1,400 narrow-gauge cars, with an additional force of one Headquarters, R.G.D., six R.O.B., and two R.S.B.

The British Transportation Service was, like the American M.R.S., recruited largely from the railroad men of Great Britain, but was a division of the Engineering troops of the British Army. Through their War Office and through the offices of the Headquarters, British Transportation Service, which were to be a part of the North African Campaign, they planned forces and allocations of those forces during the period of the spring and summer of 1942 in cooperation with the American rail transportation officers then in England.

Preliminary planning for English railway requirements included one Railway Operating Group, two Railway Operating Companies, one Railway Workshop Company, and two Railway Mobile Workshops. Cars and locomotives, in addition to those already in service on the railways in North Africa, were to be provided by the United States.

With the landings in November 1942 the Axis reacted to the Allied invasion by rushing troops to Tunisia by air and sea, and captured the local airfields and ports without opposition. American, British, and French troops drove eastward, and at the end of November and in early December launched their attack against the Axis bridgeheads.

The Allied advance, however, was stopped short of Tunis. Air superiority, for the moment, lay with the Axis. Lack of means to overcome the increased resistance, in addition to weather conditions which interfered with transport and flying, forced the postponement until 1943 of a renewed advance over the difficult terrain of northern Tunisia.

AFHQ were set up in Algiers 1 January 1943, with General Dwight D. Eisenhower as Commander in Chief. Headquarters were basically American and British.

Transportation reverted from First Army (British) to AFHQ command, staff direction being received from the Chief Administrative Officer, AFHQ, Sir Humphrey Gale. There was on the staff a Director of MOV and Tn (British), Brigadier A. T. Philipe, and his opposite on the American side,

General Headquarters, Allied Forces Headquarters, North Africa, 1943.

Front Row: Brig. K. W. D. Strong, OBE; Brig. Gen. C. L. Adcock, Mr. R. D. Murphy, Brig. Gen. B. M. Sawbridge, Maj. Gen. E. M. Cowell, CB, CBE, DSO, TD; Commodore R. M. Dick, RN, CBE, DSC; Maj. Gen. W. B. Smith, Gen. D. D. Eisenhower, Lt. Gen. Sir H. M. Gale, KBE, CB, CVO; Maj. Gen. L. W. Rooks, AVM H. E. P. Wigglesworth, GB, CBE, DSC; Rear Adm. S. S. Lewis, USN; Maj. Gen. L. B. Nichols, CBE; Brig. Gen. T. J. Davis, Maj. Gen. R. G. Lewis, CBE; Brig. Gen. F. A. Blesse.

Middle Row: Brig. Gen. W. C. Crane, Brig. H. M. Hinds, CBE; Col. T. E. Roderick, Brig. G. S. Thompson, MBE; Brig. Gen. G. C. Stewart, Brig. H. S. Pineer, OBE, MC; Brig. Gen. H. Hewett, Brig. W. R. Baddington, CBE; Brig. V. J. E. Westropp, CBE; Brig. E. J. B. Buchanan, DSC; Brig. Gen. C. R. Gray, Jr., Brig. W. E. C. Pickthall, CBE; Brig. Gen. J. C. Holmes, Brig. Gen. T. H. Ramsey, Brig. I. P. Brickman, CBE; Brig. Gen. R. A. McClure, Col. T. J. Tully.

Last Row: Col. The Lord Russell of Liverpool, CBE, MC; Col. G. H. Vogel, Brig. E. S. O. Dunlop, Col. F. D. Sharp, Col. D. J. Crawford, Col. J. W. Ramsey, Col. Dan Gilmor, Col. F. A. Hibbard, Col. C. S. Shadle, Brig. A. H. Fernyhough, MC; Col. L. A. Higgins, Brig. A. C. Baillie, MC; Brig. Gen. H. S. Clarkson, Col. L. H. Sims.

Colonel (later Brigadier General) George C. Stewart, as Chief of Transportation. The Director of British Transportation covering their M.R.S. troops was Brigadier Rex F. O'Dowd Gage, who had set up his headquarters in Algiers.

As indicated previously, the 703 R.G.D. had been designated and was an integral part of the North African invasion. Twelve officers and men of this unit, including Colonel Clarence L. Burpee, Commander, and Master Sergeant Richard J. Flannagan were with the original landing parties on the beaches north of Casablanca at Fedala. Because Casablanca was to be a main port of entry and the origin of rail movement of American supplies, Colonel Burpee went there at once; and thus began the operations of the M.R.S. in the North African Theater.

When our forces landed at Fedala, there was a gentleman standing on the beach waving a white piece of paper. Divine Providence was with him and with us, for he was not shot. When American officers looked at the piece of paper he had in his hand, they found it to be an honorable discharge paper of Sergeant George C. Falson, from the 18th Infantry of the First Division in

Director General decorating Staff Sergeant George Falson, December 2, 1945.

753 Railway Shop Battalion, Sidi Mabrouk Shops of C.F.A. at Constantine, Algeria, August 17, 1943.

World War I. After his discharge from World War I, George had married and lived in France for a while and then moved to Morocco where he had been living for some time. His mother was from the island of Malta and his father was a Frenchman; however, George was a naturalized American when he entered the forces of our Army in World War I.

He was of inestimable value, for he was well acquainted with rail operations in Morocco, and among the first helpful jobs which he was able to do for the M.R.S. was that of securing a few tractors from French concerns for

Arabs transferring load from standard-gauge cars to the meter-gauge cars at Ouled Rhamoun.

switching service at Casablanca. He was even able to acquaint our forces with the whereabouts of the German officers in mufti and their hiding places.

The Assault Commander told Colonel Burpee to take care of George, so Colonel Burpee took him to Casablanca with him. When the Allied Act was passed, which permitted the enrollment in our armies of our Allies, he was enlisted in the M.R.S. and continued to serve in the 703 R.G.D., and later with Headquarters, Second M.R.S., throughout the North African campaign, Italy, and ultimately France, Belgium, and Germany. He spoke fluently the languages of each of those countries, and, in addition, Arabic. It is doubtful whether any other one man helped the cause of liberty and justice any more than did Sergeant George Falson.

The first troops of the American M.R.S. to arrive were those of the 761 R.T.C., commanded by Captain Claude S. Crouser, who came down from England and landed at Oran on 11 November 1942. They immediately took over the terminal operations at the very heavy tonnage port of Oran, switching and dispatching trains from that port in support of the Allied Forces.

The next contingent was the 727 R.O.B. (Southern Railway System), commanded by Lieutenant Colonel Fred W. Okie, which landed at Mers El-Kebir on 26 December 1942 at 10:15 A.M. In the same convoy, and landing the same day, was the 753 R.S.B. (Big Four), less Company "C," commanded by Lieutenant Colonel J. J. Daugherty. This unit was bivouacked at Sidi-bel-Abbès and began what operations it could with respect to maintenance and repairs to locomotives and cars in that area.

The 713 R.O.B. (Santa Fe), commanded by Lieutenant Colonel Charles D. Notgrass, landed at Casablanca on 20 February 1943.

After some delay due to indecision as to where it could best be used, the 727 R.O.B. was moved forward onto the meter-gauge railroad running between Ouled Rhamoun through Tébessa and on to the Sfax-Gafsa road in southeastern Tunisia. Headquarters were established at Tébessa and it took over the operations of the railroad in support of the II Corps.

The 753 R.S.B. was moved from Sidi-bel-Abbès to the very modern shops of the Chemins de Fer Algériens at Sidi Mabrouk, a suburb of Constantine. There it took over operation of the shop with continuation of C.F.A. personnel. Notwithstanding the delay of securing repair parts, they averaged four classified repairs to French locomotives per month in addition to all of the other assembly and roundhouse work that they did. From time to time they sent detachments of experienced men to Tébessa, Oran, and other terminals to assist in major and minor repairs to locomotives and cars.

The 713 R.O.B. on arrival at Casablanca was moved forward and took over the operations of the Chemins de Fer Algériens (C.F.A.) between Algiers and Constantine, with headquarters halfway, at Sétif.

British transportation forces allocated to the North African Theater were: Headquarters, First Railway Operating Group, commanded by Lieutenant Colonel J. E. Bell; 154 Railway Operating Company, commanded by Major C. A. Ireland; 189 Railway Operating Company, commanded by Major D. C. L. Reynolds; 163 Railway Workshop Company, commanded by Major J. Sinclair; No. 2 Railway Mobile Workshop, commanded by Lieutenant W. E. Burke; No. 5 Railway Mobile Workshop, commanded by Lieutenant C. E. J. Cole; 155 Stores Company, commanded by Major W. J. Lake; First Railway Construction and Maintenance Group, commanded by Lieutenant Colonel V. R. Illingworth, with its component parts being the

No. 3 Railway Telegraph Company, commanded by Major Treasure; 29th Railway Survey Company, commanded by Major Glendenning; 150 Railway Construction Company, commanded by Major Barnwell; 160 Railway Construction Company, commanded by Major Miller; 161 Railway Construction Company, commanded by Major Crawford; No. 1 Railway Bridging Section, commanded by Captain Simpson; No. 2 Railway Bridging Section, commanded by Captain Moncrieff; 187 Mechanical Equipment Company, commanded by Major England, and the No. 42 Line Maintenance Section, No. 76 Tele-Op Section, and the 45 and 46 Mechanical Equipment Sections.

Their disembarkation point was Algiers. The operating troops arrived on 13 November and by the 16th they had commenced learning duties in and around Algiers.

At the conclusion of the Casablanca Conference on 24 January 1943, General B. B. Somervell went to AFHQ at Algiers and, in his characteristic fashion, wanted to know what they needed and what he could do to help. On being advised that rail transportation was one of the outstanding difficulties and what they needed was more railroad direction, he radioed the Chief of Transportation, Major General C. P. Gross, in Washington, to send Headquarters, First M.R.S., to North Africa, and directed that the Manager and 25 officers and men of his choice should be flown there immediately.

This information came by phone to the Manager at his headquarters in St. Paul in the late afternoon of 26 January 1943. Being advised that 25 could not be handled in one plane, he was told that 12 men could be moved on the first plane and the balance one week later. General Gross requested advice as to who they would be and when they would be ready to move, which information was telephoned him before midnight of 27 January 1943.

At that time, the Manager advised him that the first party would consist of the Manager and 11 other officers and men; viz., from Headquarters, M.R.S.: Lieutenant Colonel Benjamin H. Decker, Major Carl C. Scheuble, Captain James T. Hayes, Technical Sergeant Julius Fuith, Technical Sergeant Sidney W. Truax, and Technician Fourth Grade Terry E. Drake; from Headquarters, 701 R.G.D.: Lieutenant Colonel Robert J. Crane, Captain Allan A. Bush, and Captain Stephen J. Keating; from Headquarters, 704 R.G.D.: Captain Justin G. Toomey and First Lieutenant Harry J. Surles; and they were to arrive by train in Washington, D.C., the morning of 29

January. The second party would consist of: from Headquarters, M.R.S., Colonel B. H. Crosland, Major Cecil A. White, Captain Frederick T. Richards, Captain Thomas R. Patterson, Master Sergeant Virgil M. Johnson, Staff Sergeant Alfred L. Capra, and Technician Fourth Grade Bernard Andreoli; from Headquarters, 701 R.G.D.: Major Albert G. Hentz, Captain Lyle Bristow, and Captain Arthur G. Teets; from Headquarters 704 R.G.D., Major John M. Budd, Major Oscar R. Diamond, Captain James H. Heron, and Captain Thomas A. Jerrow. They would arrive in Washington one week later.

On arrival in Washington, the Manager reported to General Gross. Letter orders were issued by the War Department, dated 30 January 1943, relieving the Manager from assignment to Headquarters, M.R.S., St. Paul, and assigning him to: "Allied Force Headquarters, Algiers, Algeria. He will proceed . . . to Algiers, reporting upon arrival to the Commanding General, Allied Force Headquarters, for duty as General Manager, Military Railway Service."

Prior to leaving Washington, of course, it was necessary to secure yellow fever, cholera, typhus, and tetanus shots. A special plane was set up and left Washington at 10:20 A.M., 3 February. After all-night stops at Miami, Florida, Georgetown, British Guiana, and Natal, Brazil, the party flew the South Atlantic route and landed at "Yum Dum" Bathurst, Gambia, at 8:28 A.M., 6 February; they left there the next morning and arrived at Marrakech, Morocco. After overnight stops there and at Casablanca, they arrived at Algiers at 5:34 P.M., 9 February 1943.

On the morning of 10 February the General Manager reported to AFHQ and was assigned in accordance with General Orders No. 19, dated 14 February 1943, as "Director General of Military Railways." The order further directed that he would report direct to the Chief Administrative Officer of that Headquarters, Lieutenant General Sir Humphrey Gale, and for certain functions mentioned below, to the Deputy Theater Commander, North African Theater of Operations, United States Army (NATOUSA), Major General E. B. Hughes.

The order further stated that:

> 2. a. He will be responsible for the technical development and operation for military purposes of all railways in the North African Theater.

Parade, Military Railway Service

b. In order that railway operation may be in accordance with the Commander-in-Chief's plans he will make recommendations to the Chief Administrative Officer as to the extent to which such development and operation shall be carried out through the medium of the French railway service or by U.S. or British military personnel.

3. All U.S. and British Military railway personnel and matériel will be at his disposal. Such British technical railway officers as he requires in his organization will be provided under orders of the Chief Administrative Officer.

4. He will dispose railway troops at such points as he considers necessary, and will apply to G-4, AFHQ, for authority and executive orders when he desires to move complete railway units in order that the necessary movement orders may be issued and other administrative arrangement may be made.

5. a. He will be responsible to the Deputy Theater Commander for the development and operation of railway facilities within the U.S. Communications Zone and within depots and installations controlled by the C.G., SOS.

b. For railway development within British installations, he will be responsible to the Chief Administrative Officer.

6. He will be responsible to the Deputy Theater Commander for the well being and discipline of the United States Military Railway troops.

By Command of General EISENHOWER:

W. B. Smith
Major General, GSC, Chief of Staff

OFFICIAL:

T. J. Davis
Brigadier General, AGD
Adjutant General.

troops, North Africa, 1943.

Subsequent changes in the orders were made by AFHQ General Orders No. 38 of 7 June 1943. This order extended the responsibility of the Director General amending Paragraph 6 of General Orders No. 19 as follows:

He will be responsible to the Deputy Theater Commander for the well-being, discipline and training of the United States Military Railway troops.

On arrival in North Africa, the Director General established his headquarters at the General Office Building of the C.F.A. at Algiers, Algeria. Immediate liaison was established with Brigadier Rex F. O'Dowd Gage and Colonel E. Quenard; with M. Ardoin, Director of the Chemins de Fer du Maroc (C.F.M.), who had his headquarters at Rabat; with M. Ducluzeau, Director of the C.F.A., headquarters at Algiers; with M. Barbout, Director of the Chemins de Fer de Tunisie (C.F.T.), headquarters at Constantine at that time, having been pushed back from Tunis by the occupation of that area by the enemy.

The integrated Allied staff of the Director General in North Africa consisted of the Headquarters, M.R.S. (United States). In it were two Assistant Director Generals; viz., the Director of Transportation (British), Brigadier Gage, and the Director of Military Transports (French), Colonel E. Quenard.

The American organization and the ultimate Allied organization consisted of five departments each headed by an Assistant General Manager with adequate staff organization. The Director of Transportation (British) had eight sections in his staff, headed by Assistant Directors. In the coordination of the headquarters, the Assistant General Manager, Transportation,

Colonel C. F. Dougherty, had as his opposite the Assistant Director of Transportation, Tn-3, of the British staff, Lieutenant Colonel L. B. Marson; the Assistant General Manager, Engineering, Colonel B. H. Crosland, had as his opposite the Assistant Director, Tn-2, Lieutenant Colonel J. Ratter; the Adjutant of the American headquarters, Major S. R. Truesdell, had as his opposite the Assistant Director, Tn-1, Lieutenant Colonel J. F. M. Leese. The Americans had an Assistant General Manager, Mechanical, Colonel F. R. Hosack, without counterpart in the British staff. The British headquarters contained four sections of ports and docks for which the Director General, M.R.S., had no responsibility and therefore no staff, this being handled in the American plan by the Theater Chief of Transportation. Colonel Quenard's French headquarters did not have the same sections as the Americans and British.

To coordinate rehabilitation and operation of trains in the forward areas, the British had set up an advanced section for railway construction, railway planning, and railway liaison, under Colonel E. L. Parkes. Under that organization they had the First Railway Construction Group under Lieutenant Colonel V. R. Illingworth in which they had all of their construction and maintenance organization. Operating was done by the First Railway Operating Group under Lieutenant Colonel J. E. Bell.

The American plan, of course, was to place a Headquarters, Railway Grand Division, and its organization covering not only the Railway Operating Battalions and Shop Battalions assigned, but it had an American section for railroad reconstruction, railroad planning, and railroad liaison under Lieutenant Colonel R. J. Crane, later Lieutenant Colonel C. S. Sanderson. This was in the 703 R.G.D., Colonel C. L. Burpee commanding.

As finally organized, the Director General carried out the coordination and utilization of these various troops directly through the American railway grand division and through the British advanced section, while Colonel Burpee and Colonel Parkes coordinated their respective activities in the field.

From a physical standpoint, the North African railroads were not in bad condition. Their gauge was all metric, 1.43 meters being standard. Then they had a 1.00 meter and a 1.55 meter-gauge. A great deal of the railroad in Tunisia was meter-gauge, but the main line from Souk-Ahras through to Bizerte and Tunis was standard.

Military Railway Service Command, North Africa, 1943. *Left to Right:* Brig. Rex F. O'Dowd Gage; Brig. Gen. Carl R. Gray, Jr.; Col. E. Quenard.

Because the heaviest fighting in North Africa was in Tunisia, there was considerable bridge demolition by both sides there. A complete reconnaissance by the Engineering Section of the M.R.S. headquarters under Colonel B. H. Crosland developed the fact that, from an enemy standpoint, the demolitions were not carried on with usual German standards. Many of the larger and more important bridges were not destroyed and some of the smaller bridges were destroyed with much more explosives than were required for their destruction. It looked like a "hit-and-miss" job.

With the combination of the "A" Companies of the Railway Operating Battalions in the theater, Army Engineering troops, and British Railway Construction troops, quick and definite repairs were made to these railroads. This resulted in a much quicker redistribution of material and men than was anticipated.

Meter-Gauge Railroad, Hadjeb el Aioun, Tunisia.

Sbeitla-Sousse Line, meter-gauge, near Hadjeb el Aioun.

There were 32 major bridge reconstruction and rehabilitation jobs. As an illustration of the type and manner of rehabilitation there was a bridge eight and one-half miles east of Hadjeb-El Aioun on the Sbeitla-Sousse line. It was of masonry arch design, three spans, 40 feet to the center of the piers and 41 feet from the top of the rail to the bed of the stream.

Demolition had been carried out by the enemy and consisted of destruction of the center and east arches, and excessive damage to the west arch, which was badly shattered and cracked by the explosion. Repairs were accomplished by the use of British standard steel military railway bridging. Work was carried on by the bridging section of the 713 R.O.B., the 727 R.O.B., two bridging sections of the 167 Railway Bridging Company (British), assisted by the 57 French Military Railway Service Company. Repair was accomplished in ten days.

After arrival in the theater, while complete responsibility and direction for the operation of the North African railroads were the Director General's, it was felt that he should create a committee to coordinate the civilian use of the North African railroads with him. A committee was appointed with M. Ardoin, Director of the C.F.M., as Chairman, and consisting of the directors of the C.F.A. and C.F.T. as members. This arrangement and method of procedure proved to be extremely satisfactory.

It was thought that the M.R.S. was complete. Upon getting into an active theater of war, however, it was discovered that a very important office had been forgotten. Consequently, application was made for an additional officer in the headquarters of the Director General, the General Superintendents, the Superintendents, and the Shop Superintendents for a chaplain's position in each organization. The request was approved and ultimately each organization of the M.R.S. had a chaplain ranging in rank from a Major to a First Lieutenant, according to the headquarters in which he served. Every faith was represented among those chaplains who, of course, came through the Corps of Chaplains, United States Army. The first Chief of Chaplains in the headquarters of the M.R.S. was Major R. F. Alexander. Splendid service was rendered, to the benefit of every man in the organization which these chaplains served. Chaplains are now an integral part of the organization of the M.R.S.

By the first of February, generally speaking, the American II Corps of four divisions; viz., the 1st Armored Division and the 1st, 9th, and 34th Infantry Divisions, were concentrated in the Kasserine Pass area with headquarters at Tébessa and a front thinly occupied extending from Gafsa to Fondouk.

The British First Army had moved into a position in northern Tunisia on a line beginning at La Calle with a battle front extending southeasterly from the Mediterranean to a point south of Bou Arada. A small force of the French Army in the Allied Command was in between the right flank of the British First Army at Bou Arada and extended to connect with the left flank of the American II Corps at Kairouan. This line, generally speaking, was north and south of a point near Tabarka, through Souk Arbe, Sbeitla,

Meter-Gauge bridge north of Kasserine Pass.

Bomb wreckage, C.F.T. Shop Yards. Transfer pit between boiler shops and erecting shop, Tunis, May, 1943.

Fondouk, Maknassy, and just east of Gafsa. The British Eighth Army, under Field Marshal Lord Montgomery, was advancing westward from Egypt across Libya, driving Rommel before it.

Supporting this Allied battle line was the 703 R.G.D., consisting of the Headquarters, 703 R.G.D., the 713 and 727 R.O.B., and the 753 R.S.B. The jurisdiction of the 703 R.G.D. was the total mileage of the C.F.A. under the supervision of the General Superintendent extending from Beni Mancour through to Souk Ahras, from Philippeville to Kroubs, from Ouled Rhamoun to Tébessa and from Oued Keberit to Tébessa. Headquarters of the 703 R.G.D. were established at Constantine.

Units of the British Transportation Service under Brigadier Gage were disposed as follows: Headquarters, First Railway Operating Group at Algiers; 154 Railway Operating Company operated the line Bone to La Calle; 189 Railway Operating Company operated the meter-gauge line Ouled Rhamoun to Tébessa until relieved by the 727 R.O.B.; 163 Railway Workshop Company operated in shops at Algiers; No. 2 Railway Workshop Mobile was at Guelma; No. 5 Railway Workshop Mobile was at Ghardimaeu.

French railroad operation consisted of moving trains in opposite directions by "blocking" as between stations through the action of stationmasters, each of whom called ahead to the next station and got a positive block from that station. When these blocks were long, delays were fearful, so blocking distances were shortened by increasing the number of intermediate block stations. This had the effect of increasing the number of trains moved by shortening the delays incident to train meets. On the line between Algiers and Constantine, five such additional block stations were installed. In addition, a timetable was issued providing for eleven east- and west-bound military train schedules each twenty-four hours.

At first, owing to a shortage of locomotives, it was not possible to utilize all these schedules. An average of five military trains daily, however, were operated for Allied use in each direction in addition to French military and civil traffic and coal trains. At the end of February, the average number of trains worked east of Algiers was six daily.

The Kasserine Pass break-through occurred in February 1943. The ground lost was recovered by the American forces on 21 to 22 February, when the enemy was driven back out of the pass.

The 727 R.O.B. had been on the meter-gauge railroad, learning it, since 21 January 1943. On 8 February it took over full operation from Ouled Rhamoun through Tébessa into southeastern Tunisia on the Sfax-Gafsa Railroad with headquarters at Tébessa. The German offensive against the American II Corps, which resulted in the Kasserine Pass break-through, provided one of the most dangerous and one of the most thrilling demonstrations of American soldier-railroaders' bravery and ingenuity, and justifies special mention.

Colonel Frederick B. Butler, Corps of Engineers, a liaison officer of the II Corps, had established a headquarters at Gafsa with a small detachment. The 727 R.O.B. had moved into that area a small group of approximately

15 men from Company "A," under Lieutenant Edwin B. Connerat. It was rumored, but unfortunately discredited in higher headquarters, that a German offensive was to be made.

Major Roy P. Moss, the Assistant Superintendent, had been in Gafsa on 3 February and really started the program of moving trains and supplies out of that point because of the rumored pending German advance. There were six dead engines in the sheds at Sened, and a live engine was moved over from Gafsa by Engineer J. O. Ling and Fireman J. L. Stump to remove all equipment. A train left Sened with four dead engines and as many carloads of supplies as the engine could haul, bound for Gafsa.

At 1:30 P.M. on 14 February, Colonel Butler reached Lieutenant Colonel Fred W. Okie by telephone at his headquarters in Tébessa and asked him to come to Gafsa. Colonel Okie, sensing what it might be about, took five train crews of five men each, Lieutenant Franklin S. Howie, Company "C," and Lieutenant J. R. Sterling of Headquarters and Service Company. They traveled in ¾ and 2½ ton trucks and reached Gafsa about 4 P.M. that date where they were advised that the stores and railroad equipment had to be gotten out of Gafsa with the troops by midnight, as the Germans were moving to attack.

Due to quick reorganization of combat troops incident to the now-recognized assault, the M.R.S. found itself and its operations ahead of our lines and between them and the enemy.

From 8 P.M. the 14th to 3 A.M. the 15th, the yards at Gafsa were cleared and the trains started toward Tébessa with all equipment loaded to car capacity. The fifth and last train out of Gafsa left at 3 A.M. on the 15th. Four of these trains were stalled behind a bridge at Sidi Bou Baker, which had just been partly destroyed by American forces. Five piers and five spans of the total of 40 thirty-foot spans were out. Only one train had gotten across the bridge before our own destruction.

After the trains were started out of Gafsa, the Colonel and Lieutenants Howie and Connerat left by truck for Metlaoui and Henchir Saoutir to move gasoline by train to a rendezvous for midnight that night arranged for with the Quartermaster of the II Corps. Because of delays, by 1 A.M. of the 16th it was agreed to postpone the rendezvous twenty-four hours. The train was moved into hiding in a tunnel. Later that day further train movements had to be abandoned, locomotives hid in phosphate mines and stripped. Colonel Okie and his men left Metlaoui bound for Tébessa just as a "Jerry" tank came in from the east.

Another very disconcerting situation at this critical time was that as the trucks reached Redeyef en route to Tébessa, they were fired on point-blank by a French-Singhalese detachment with 37-mm. shells; however, they fortunately were able to identify themselves and no one was hit. Colonel Okie led his men on up through a desert wadi because the highways had

Supply yards, Maison-Carrée, 1943. *Left to Right:* Col. E. F. McFadden, Capt. George E. Hargreaves, Capt. R. E. Godley.

been taken over by the German forces, and arrived at Tébessa about 3 A.M. of the 17th.

In the meantime, Lieutenant Sterling went to Thelepte to move out equipment and trains from there on the late afternoon of the 16th. After fulfilling his mission, he was picked up by Captain Beard and returned to Tébessa by car.

The Director General had been in touch with Colonel Okie by phone on the 13th and made an engagement to meet him at the end of the standard-gauge track at Oued Keberit at 8 A.M. on the morning of the 18th. The Director General arrived at Constantine late the night of the 16th and on the morning of the 17th was advised concerning the break-through at Kasserine Pass and the activities of the 727 R.O.B. and its men in getting trains out of southern Tunisia or hiding them so that the Germans could not use them, including the information that Colonel Okie and his men were missing in action for three days and unaccounted for, presumably killed or captured.

These reports came to the Headquarters, 703 R.G.D., from the Headquarters, 727 R.O.B. The Director General and Colonel Burpee took these reports to the War Room of the Task Force at Constantine and found that they had received from the Headquarters, 727 R.O.B., more definite information as to exactly what had happened in southern Tunisia than was known in the War Room itself.

The Director General finished his inspection in and around Constantine and moved that night to Oued Keberit. What a great sigh of relief was his, on pulling into Oued Keberit, to find Colonel Okie standing there as per schedule!

The spring offensive started shortly after the middle of March when the British Eighth Army had reached a point just south of Sousse. The British First Army was just east of Natour, Djedeida, and Pont du Fahs.

As more American M.R. S. troops arrived, the British railway operating troops were gradually concentrated behind their First Army, and at the end of March were responsible only for the main line east of Souk Ahras as well as the Bone-La Calle line and Algiers Base Area.

The final phase began 1 May 1943, when the battle line was shortened from the south by having the British Eighth Army on a line between Bou Arada and Enfidaville.

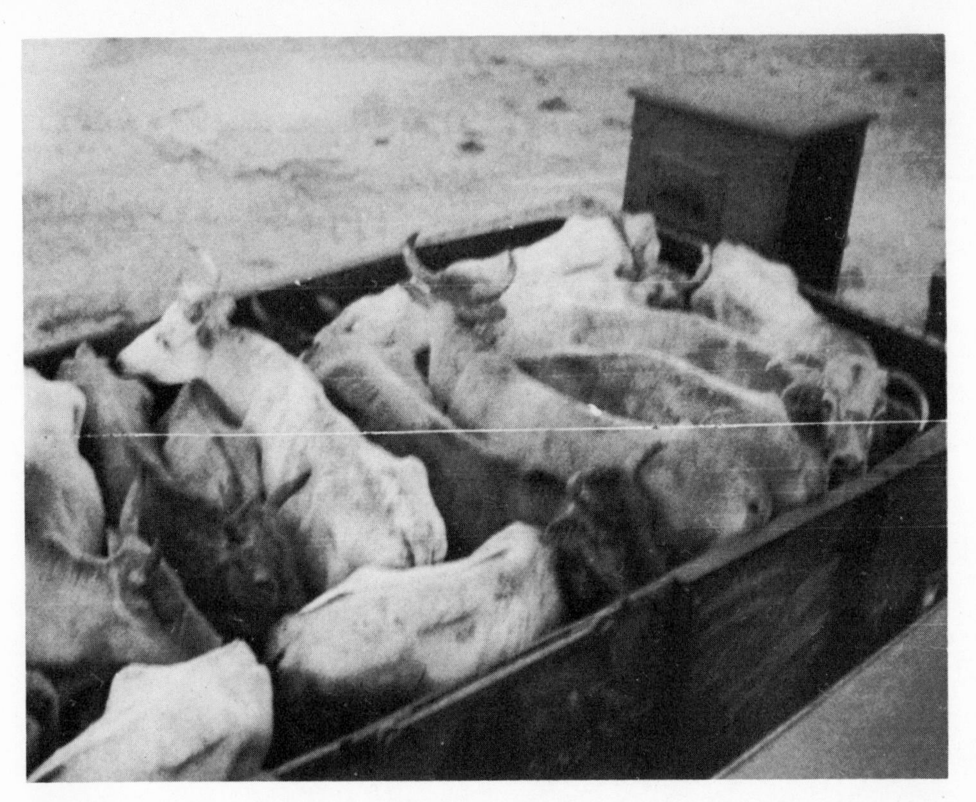

Livestock travels in *wagon-lits*, North Africa, 1943.

The United States II Corps, however, had been transferred onto the left flank and occupied a front from the Mediterranean down to Tebourba. Then came the British First Army and the French units, all moving in a northeasterly direction between the British First Army and the British Eighth Army from a point near Pont du Fahs. This offensive was successful. Bizerte and Tunis were occupied on 7 May, Protoille on 8 May, and hostilities ceased 12 May 1943, near Kelibia. The problem of the M.R.S. now was to supply these armies in the field and to build up supplies for the bases in and near the port of Oran and east.

There were tremendous stores of railroad equipment being received daily from the United States. These not only included American locomotives and cars, but parts for their maintenance and repair. Rail, frogs, ties, spikes, bolts and nuts, angle bars as well as bridge material arrived almost daily.

Inasmuch as the utilization of all these stores was wholly within the Director General's jurisdiction, it was felt that railroad stores separate from the base sections should be provided for their assembly. The first provisional base depot company, M.R.S., was established at Oran where most of the supplies were being received.

All railroad material, both American and British, and Lend Lease for the C.F.M., C.F.A., and C.F.T. were handled and issued through this depot. The Commanding Officer of this first depot was Captain Herbert R. Phillips, and those supply depots established later were all commanded by experienced stores men off American railroads. They operated under the direction of Colonel E. F. McFadden, Assistant General Manager, Stores, Headquarters, M.R.S.

To insure regularity of movement, express schedules were set up between Casablanca and Constantine. The first schedule was established 3 May 1943, and provided the following:

Read Down	EASTBOUND							WESTBOUND		Read Up
Sun. Wed.	Mon. Thur.	Tues. Fri.	Mon. Thur.	Thur. Only	STATION	Mon. Only	Tues. Fri	Mon. Thur.	Tues. Fri.	Tues. Fri.
Lv 0800				Lv 0705	Casablanca	Ar 2010				Ar 1757
Lv 0937				Lv 0836	Rabat	Lv 1836				Ar 1604
Ar 1611 Lv 1708					Fez					Lv 1010 Ar 0915
Ar 1009	Lv 1204			Lv 1915	Oujda	Ar 0812			Ar 1509	Lv 1700
				Ar 2349	St. Barbe de Tletat	Ar 0305				
	Ar 1847	Lv 0831		Ar 0051 Lv 2320	Oran	Lv 0220 Ar 0349		Ar 1833	Lv 0654	
				Lv 0010	St. Barbe de Tletat	Ar 0250				
		Ar 1730	Lv 0718	Ar 0700	Algiers	Lv 1956	Ar 1803	Lv 0808		
			Ar 1818		Constantine		Lv 0732			

Note: Days shown indicate days of departure from first station of schedule.

The transport *Santa Elena* arrived at the Port of Oran on 11 May. On the transport were the additional M.R.S. troops under requisition for the

North African Theater, including the balance of Headquarters, M.R.S., the Headquarters, 701 R.G.D. (New York Central), commanded by Colonel J. E. Guilfoyle; Headquarters, 704 R.G.D. (Great Northern), commanded by Colonel A. W. Campbell; 715 R.O.B. (Illinois Central), commanded by Lieutenant Colonel T. P. Crymes; 719 R.O.B. (Texas and New Orleans), commanded by Lieutenant Colonel Robert F. Williams; and the 759 R.O.B. (Missouri Pacific), commanded by Lieutenant Colonel E. M. Price. These troops were first billeted in the vicinity of Oran pending movement to their designated territories.

While armed resistance officially ended in North Africa at 2015 hours on 12 May 1943, the war was not over for the M.R.S. in North Africa. Use of all M.R.S. troops then in the theater was in the augmentation of the main line of communication to the previous battle fronts and the troops still there.

American refrigerator cars, North Africa, 1943.

They also handled the redeployment and redistribution of those troops and supplies, as they were regrouped and placed for the invasion of Sicily by General Patton's Seventh Army and the British Eighth Army; and the invasion of Italy by General Clark's Fifth Army and the British Eighth Army in the fall of 1943. M.R.S. also moved a tremendous number of prisoners of war and captured equipment to concentration camps in rear areas.

On 12 May the Director General and the balance of his headquarters and the headquarters of the 704 R.G.D. left Oran by train and were pulled by United States Engine 1776. On the train was the first of the assembled "crummies"—quite a novelty to the French "cheminos." There was a wreck at Orléansville involving three C.F.A. trains, but the troop train arrived at Algiers about noon. Headquarters, M.R.S., supplemented the force already established at the Chemins de Fer Algériens General Office building in Algiers.

Stealing of military supplies from trains and cars in yards and from depots caused Major General E. B. Hughes, the Deputy Theater Commander, to call the Director General and Brigadier General J. V. Dillon, Provost Marshal, to his office and say that the stealing had to stop. The Director General indicated that on an American railroad the management was responsible for the security of the lading, but that the M.R.S. was not set up that way.

He further stated that if manpower was given him, he would accept the responsibility. Men were given him and the first battalion of Military Police that was placed under his command was the 794 Military Police Battalion, commanded by Lieutenant Colonel F. H. Owen, who reported for duty 14 August 1943. Other units followed, including the 178 Military Police Company commanded by Captain G. F. Linthwaite, the 181 Military Police Company commanded by First Lieutenant W. T. Hoblitzell, the 185 Military Police Company commanded by First Lieutenant W. A. Schulze; the 186 Military Police Company commanded by Captain M. F. Kernkamp, the 187 Military Police Company commanded by Captain E. J. Leer, and the 193 Military Police Company commanded by Captain W. Sugarman.

The policies as agreed upon by the Director General and Provost Mar-

Repair Shops, C.F.A., Algiers, 1943. *Left to right:* Staff Sgt. Chas. H. Wall, Staff Sgt. Wm. A. Royal, T/5 Wm. D. Ross.

Repair Shops, C.F.A., Algiers, 1943. *Left to right:* PFC Raymond D. Vernier, T/5 Johnnie M. Katterjohn, T/5 Arthur T. Brandon, PFC John J. Ridzik, T/5 Leo (NMI) Rothstein, 2nd Lt. John B. Mattingly, T/5 Albert T. Dold, T/5 Jerry A. Jezek.

Repair Shops, C.F.A., Algiers, 1943. *Left to right:* PFC Clarence F. Dick, PFC Norman H. Price, T/5 Ralph H. Webb, T/5 Noel E. Lahners, Tec. Sgt. Wm. E. DePoister. Other men in picture are C.F.A. employees.

shal were that yards and ports should be guarded, and at least four guards placed on each freight train.

On the basis of four guards to the train, and an operating battalion being capable of running as many trains as 50 train crews could run, a company of Military Police of 250 men was assigned to each operating battalion. They were billeted with the "C" Company and were called "First in-First out" as were the train crews.

Stealing from trains and yards was stopped. By virtue of the success of this strategy, Military Police were assigned thereafter in accordance with a company of 250 for each railway operating battalion.

A Security Section was set up in the headquarters of the Director General, and Lieutenant Colonel Owen became the Assistant General Manager, Security.

It would seem proper at this time to give the geographical location of the various units of the Military Railway Service, both American and British, at the end of May, and list the territories over which they continued jurisdiction until the exodus to Sicily and Italy.

The 703 R.G.D., with headquarters at Constantine, was assigned the territory of the C.F.A. extending from Beni Mancour, Algeria, through to Souk Ahras; Philippeville to Kroubs; Ouled Rhamoun to Tébessa; and from Oued Keberit to Tébessa, Algeria. Its component parts were: 713 R.O.B. with headquarters at Sousse, which was assigned the line Sousse to Tébessa; the 715 R.O.B. with headquarters at Souk Ahras, which was operating the line between Kroubs and Duvivier and Bone to Oued Keberit; the 727 R.O.B., with headquarters at Tébessa, which continued the operation of the narrow-gauge line between Ouled Rhamoun and Tébessa; the 753 R.S.B., which was still operating the shops of the C.F.A. at Sidi Mabrouk, Algeria.

The 701 R.G.D. headquarters (without troops) was assigned to have jurisdiction over and the direction of the railways of the C.F.M. west of the east yard limit board at Oujda.

The 704 R.G.D., with headquarters at Maison-Carrée, Algeria (about six miles from the city of Algiers), was assigned supervision from the East Yard Limit Board at Oujda, Morocco, east along the lines of the C.F.A. through Constantine to Philippeville, Algeria. Its component parts were: 719 R.O.B., which had jurisdiction from the West Yard Limit Board at Sétif, east over the lines of the C.F.A. through Constantine to Philippeville, Algeria; the 759 R.O.B., with jurisdiction from the West Yard Limit Board at Orléansville to Algiers, thence east over the lines of the C.F.A. to the West Yard Limit Board at Sétif, including the line from Beni Mancour to Bougie; 761 R.T.C. which was placed in the 704 R.G.D. and continued terminal yard operations at Oran.

From the British transportation side, the following assignments held: No. 1 Railway Operating Group was headquartered at Souk Ahras; No. 154 Railway Operating Company continued operation of the meter-gauge line from Bone to La Calle; No. 189 Railway Operating Company had half its men operating in the Algiers area and the other half behind the British First Army in its advance; No. 163 Railway Workshop Company was working in the railway shops at Algiers; No. 2 Railway Mobile Workshop was at Guelma, where it assisted the C.F.A. in the shops there; No. 5 Railway Mobile Workshop was at Ghardimaeu repairing locomotives abandoned by Tunisian railway men.

As stated above, the 753 R.S.B. was operating the shops of the C.F.A.

at Sidi Mabrouk. In October 1943 this unit, under the command of Lieutenant Colonel J. J. Daugherty, Shop Superintendent, was directed to prepare a "caravan" for the field use of the Commander in Chief of the Allied Force Headquarters, General Eisenhower.

The British field headquarters of their army groups, armies and divisions, had mobile headquarters in which each of the officers had a "caravan," which was a combination office and sleeping accommodation on a truck. Headquarters thus could be moved and set up very quickly with these caravans at a predetermined location and arrangement.

The caravan for General Eisenhower was built on a G.M.C. cab over engine type 2½-ton truck. The body was fabricated from an abandoned civilian bus body. The interior was arranged with two rooms and a bath, one room being sleeping quarters and the other an office. A half-ton jeep trailer was converted for use in carrying an electric generator. In order to eliminate the possibility of disturbing noises in the caravan from the generator, a reel of 225 feet of wire on a trailer was constructed, thereby permitting the reel trailer and generator to be separated from the caravan. Two telephones were installed by the Signal Corps.

General De Gaulle made an inspection and visit to North Africa in December 1943. Quite a ceremony of reception was given him when he visited Constantine. Company "C" of the 753 R.S.B. had completed the assignment of erection of cars at Oran and was with the battalion. They were signally honored by being chosen to represent the American Army as a unit of the parade given in General De Gaulle's honor.

Other units in the parade were British, French, and Moslem chieftains who, with their colorful tribal dress and magnificently groomed mounts, added much to this spectacular demonstration, but the American soldier car men made the big hit of the parade with their soldierly appearance and alignment.

Immediately after the capture of Tunis, contact was made with the director, M. Barbout, and other principal officers of the C.F.T. In a very short time satisfactory arrangements were made for reopening rail traffic. The first train entered Tunis on 13 May. It was greeted on arrival by a large joyous crowd. The first train ran into Bizerte on 20 May 1943.

With the cessation of hostilities a series of conferences began with the officers of the C.F.A., C.F.T., British, and American M.R.S., in connection with capacity and ability of the local authorities to handle tonnage requirements of the armies as well as the need of American assistance, both as to manpower and equipment. At the same time, a very definite field inspection and a number of conferences were held by Colonel Crosland and the various engineer officers of the headquarters, grand divisions, engineering section of the British, including Colonel E. L. Parkes, and with Colonel Quenard with reference to the rehabilitation of bridges and track on the recently recovered C.F.T. mileage.

There were not enough engineer troops of either the British or American railway forces to rehabilitate bridges on the captured rail lines. On 21 May the "A" Companies of the 715, 719, and 759 R.O.B., commanded by Captains John R. Wartchow, James N. Fuller, and H. H. White, respectively, were detached from their normal maintenance work in their areas and were assigned to bridge rehabilitation in the area of Sousse, Enfidaville, and the Gabes-Graiba sections.

Train operation in North Africa was exceptionally difficult because the lines were up and down hill and the French engines were equipped with poor steam brakes. The normal operation was to place brake cars through the train. These brake cars had little cupolas at one end of them in which an Arab "brakeman" rode. He was supposed to set and release brakes on whistle signals from the locomotive. Many times he fell asleep and did not respond to signals.

American engineers, of course, were not accustomed to that type of operation and had to learn it the hard way. Some amusing and even tragic incidents of operation resulted. For instance, Engineer George Franks and Fireman Ed Hess of the 713 R.O.B. on a U. S. Army 1,700-class engine were called to handle a train from Constantine to Philippeville. The locomotive stalled on a hill, backed up, and took slack and started again, broke in two, and the crew finally realized that the brake car had likewise broken in two due to faulty brakes setting only on the rear pair of wheels, which the Arab had not released in time.

Another illustration happened on a train operated by the 713 R.O.B., as told by Sergeant William B. Jones of that organization. This occurred between Kasserine and Sbeitla. In this instance, the lead engine stalled on

Arab desert fighters passing in review.

a hill. There was a helper engine on the hind end. The lead engine backed up, took slack, and started up the hill again, and stalled the second time, but the rear engine kept on coming and piled up several cars in the middle of the train. This was due to non-observance of whistle signals.

The G-4 Section of the general staff is responsible, among many other things, for the supply of the Army. The various units of the service put in their tonnage requirement figures, which were coordinated, and at a priority movement meeting in the office of the Chief of Transportation the various units of service bid for the movement of their freight.

The Director General, M.R.S., set up the capacity of the railroads. MOV and Tn (British), together with the Chief of Transportation, accepted weekly from each service their requirements for tonnage movement. After the estimates were in, MOV and Tn made allocations to the various services and advised the Director General, who in turn advised each of the units what their tonnage would be and from whence it would come.

In other words, the Chief of Transportation and the various services acted, as it were, as the Traffic Department of a railroad, securing business, and the M.R.S. was to be prepared to handle the "business" gotten for them.

It is interesting to record that there was handled in North Africa under such an arrangement for the month ending 12 December 1942, over 1,326 miles of track, 9,069,713 tons hauled one mile. For the period of a month, ending the middle of March, then over 1,748 miles of track, there was hauled 19,150,699 tons one mile. For the month ending mid-June over 1,958 miles of railroad, 32,562,743 tons were hauled one mile.

The latter figure was during the period approximately when the maximum tonnage was moved, for hostilities had ended on 12 May and redistribution was being made and stores assembled in preparation for the invasion of Sicily and Italy.

It is pleasing to report that the above record of tonnage hauled was military freight only, and did not include troop movements, prisoners of war by passenger train, hospital trains and empty car trains.

The M.R.S. got set up and was capable of handling, beginning about the first of June 1943, an average of 90,000 tons of military freight a week. The average priority movement schedule for the M.R.S. was to handle 60,000 tons per week.

For the week ending 28 July, 1,114 trains handling 26,857 loads, 528,788 gross tons were run, or an average of 159 trains a day handling 3,836 loads containing 75,541 tons. For the week ending 4 August, 1,222 trains, 26,126 loaded cars, 434,035 gross tons were handled, which averaged 175 trains, 3,746 loads containing 62,005 tons per day. Included in that and causing a considerable difference in the tonnage and trains was the fact that for the week ending 28 July there was handled a total of 130 trains exclusively for troops, hospital trains, and prisoner-of-war trains, and for the week ending 4 August there were handled 127 such trains.

The highest tonnage handled was for the week ending 18 August, when 66,000 net tons were handled. At no time did the M.R.S. fail to handle in excess of the P.O.M. tonnage bid in.

The original estimate for the number of freight cars that would be needed in the North African Campaign was 5,000; the number of standard-gauge 2-8-0 locomotives was 250; the number of meter-gauge 2-8-2 locomotives was 175. In the handling of this equipment from America to North Africa the freight cars and the meter-gauge locomotives came knocked down in crates; the standard 2-8-0 locomotives were received assembled.

The Port of Oran was designated as the place to handle this equipment. Company "C" of the 753 R.S.B., commanded by Major F. J. Kossuth, was set up there to assemble freight cars.

Because of the long distance from Oran to Ouled Rhamoun, the meter-gauge 2-8-2 locomotives in crates were moved on flat cars to the 753 R.S.B. at Sidi Mabrouk, assembled there, then placed on specially designed well flatcars and moved to Ouled Rhamoun where they went onto the meter-gauge track.

The same was true of the meter-gauge freight equipment which was transported knocked down to Sidi Mabrouk, erected there, and placed in service at Ouled Rhamoun.

By the first of March 1943 a complete estimate of the power and car situation was re-evaluated and the requisition for locomotives and cars was materially reduced—freight cars from 5,000 to 1,500; the 2-8-0 standard-gauge locomotives from 250 to 105; and the meter-gauge 2-8-2 locomotives from 175 to 60.

As of 24 July there were 1,000 freight cars (U.S.A.) in service in North Africa. There had been 149 2-8-0 locomotives received, 135 assembled and 126 in service, with nine stored in white lead. In addition, there had been erected 60-meter gauge freight cars and 25-meter gauge 2-8-2 locomotives. By October there had been erected seven more 2-8-2 locomotives, making a total of 32 placed in service.

All of the French locomotives had a very shrill and penetrating, high-pitched steam whistle. The Director General asked if those "sopranos" couldn't be made "bassos." This was done by the shop forces at Sidi Mabrouk; consequently the American locomotives were "bassos," much to the amusement and surprise of the French and natives of North Africa.

The War Department in late September 1943 hit upon a very clever program for raising the morale among war workers when it decided to bring home to those so employed the story of how the goods they manufactured were being used. One of the first units of the Army to be asked to report was the M.R.S. Quoted below is the report sent home from North Africa concerning locomotive No. 1864. Its number has a significance in historical annals.

"No. 1864 is a 2-8-0 consolidated type engine built by the Baldwin Locomotive Works to government specifications which were given to the nation's three foremost locomotive manufacturers in order to speed production and to assure power units whose parts would be interchangeable, no matter who built them.

"She was completed in December 1942, one month after the invasion of North Africa, and was earmarked immediately for service on the Dark Continent. She arrived at Oran early in May of 1943 and was immediately set up by the M.R.S. provisional erecting detachment assigned to that port to put into service the considerable amount of railroad machinery then arriving.

"There was not a great deal of work to do on 1864, because she came overseas nearly entirely assembled, as deck load on a freighter. So the job of getting her ready for the rails went fast, and on 11 May she got her hydrostatic test and was pronounced fit for the road.

"Unlike some of the locomotives that disembarked at Oran, she did not linger there to do prosaic short-haul or yard duty, but was sent forward immediately to help replace the overworked French power upon which the American soldier-railroaders had been forced to depend at the outset. She worked for some time in the Algiers area, there receiving her 'baptism of fire.' She came unwounded through a number of German air raids, some of which were quite evidently aimed at her and her sisters, for the enemy well knew the importance of the railroads in the Allied plan of supply. At present she is somewhere in North Africa. Her exact whereabouts is a military secret, but she is working on what is well known among railroaders as one of the toughest pieces of road anywhere in the world.

"Recently, in addition to her normal duties, she underwent a nerve-racking experience. Somebody tried to steal her. She was sitting peacefully in the yards, her back to an open turntable pit, her head turned toward the open road. She had steam up. Her crew, in this well-guarded establishment, were nearby, picking up a cup of coffee and a sandwich before starting their run.

Moving Meter-Gauge locomotive on well car.

A man dressed in regulation GI coveralls climbed aboard and opened the throttle. The Johnson bar was in reverse. The brakes, fortunately, were set, so nothing happened. Technician Fourth Grade Oswald B. Dusina, a Southern Pacific employee from Oakland, California, came along about this time and saw the would-be thief busily pulling levers. He called Private First Class Anthony P. Dwyer of St. Louis, Missouri, formerly with the Missouri Pacific, and Technician Fifth Grade Keith McCafferty of Steubenville, Ohio, who once worked for the Pennsylvania Railroad. The three of them pulled their quarry out of the cab and turned him over to the military police. No saboteur, he turned out to be nothing more than a merchant seaman who, spurred on by a bottle or two of the potent North Africa red wine, wanted to see the countryside and figured 1864 would be just the vehicle for him.

"Getting back to 1864's present run, it is a single track and steep. Two per cent grade is not unusual, and sometimes it is worse. Winding through barren mountains, the U.S.A. locomotive meets curves for mile after mile and looks down into deep canyons at every bend. There are a great many tunnels, and one of them is particularly dreaded. So steep is the grade outward bound that it takes from fifteen to twenty minutes to get through. Coming back, 1864 runs through it in five. The climb through this bore is best described by the engineer, Technician Fourth Grade Paul Marin, Madisonville, Texas, in civilian life a fireman on the Southern Pacific: 'There is absolutely no ventilation in this tunnel. We hit the mouth climbing, take a big breath, and hang on. Within a minute it is next to impossible to breathe. The noise is deafening. It is blazing hot; we get right down on the deck and lie there. Sometimes she starts slipping and then I have to get up and ease her out of it. When I do that, I get new respect for my fireman, because most of the time he has to stand up there and feed her.' The fireman is Technician Fifth Grade Hugh Bartholomew, New York City, formerly of the Long Island Railroad.

"Other facts and figures about 1864: she does nearly 400 miles before she gets in again. She gets no repairs on the road—only a little oil and a wrench where needed. She is operated and maintained entirely by Americans. The man to whom she looks for maintenance is Lieutenant Julius R. Gott, of Osawatomie, Kansas. He does the same thing here that he did in civilian life. He is a general roundhouse foreman. He worked for the Missouri Pacific back home. For fuel, she burns briquettes—not the little ones, but big things that must be broken up in the cab before they can be fed into the fire. For company in the yards she finds herself next to French, Belgian, British, and German locomotives. She—and her crews—thinks she is better than any of them."

In closing this episode of the M.R.S. in North Africa, it is believed fitting that the commendation of the Commander in Chief in that theater should be quoted. In *Crusade in Europe*, General Eisenhower said:

"At the same time our Military Railway Service engineers were working miracles in improving the decrepit French line leading to the front. When we went into North Africa the railway could daily deliver a maximum of 900 tons of supplies. By introducing Yankee energy and modern American methods of operation the Military Railway Service increased the daily tonnage to 3,000 and this before they received a single extra engine or boxcar from the United States."

Field Marshal Earl Harold R.L.G. Alexander, Commanding Mediterranean Theater of Operations.

6

Operations in Sicily and Italy

1943-1945

EVEN BEFORE THE END of hostilities in Tunisia, top-level planning covered the invasion of Sicily and then Italy. The assault plan covered the British Eighth Army under Field Marshal Lord Montgomery, landing in the vicinity just south of Syracuse at Pachino. The American Seventh Army, under Lieutenant General George S. Patton, Jr., landed on the south center of the island at Licata. One of the greatest armadas in history made up this force, as there were over 2,500 ships carrying troops and supplies and hundreds of escorting warships from six allied navies which included Greek, Polish, and Dutch.

The attack started with a group of paratroopers dropping at 10 P.M. on the night of 9 July 1943. They were quickly followed by the first landing of ground troops, which occurred at 3 A.M. in the morning, 10 July.

The British Eighth Army, after landing at Pachino, started northward along the coast until a very stubborn line of resistance was met just south of Mount Etna. The American Seventh Army, after landing at Licata, started in a northwesterly direction through Caltanissetta, on to Marsala, and went on to capture Palermo on 25 July, and then started eastward. In the meantime, the Germans and Italians had been forced into the northeast quarter of the island behind a line of which Mount Etna was the anchor.

Sicily has approximately 1,500 miles of standard- and narrow-gauge railroad, all steam operated. Starting at Palermo and extending eastward to Messina, the railroad then runs southward to Ragusa, thence westward through Licata and Agrigento and, completely encircling the island, connects again at Palermo. There are one or two standard-gauge railroads inland; for instance, the one between Licata and Fiumetorto. It likewise has an east and west line connecting it with the west coast line at Catania.

There was a modern and extensive railroad car ferry operating across the Strait of Messina from Messina to Reggio di Calabria. All trains operated through and across the ferry, making a very efficient operation from Italy to any part of Sicily.

American planning provided for the utilization of the 727 R.O.B. and special officers from the 703 R.G.D. British Transportation Service contemplated the First Railway Operating Group, two Railway Operating Companies, one Railway Workshop Company; in addition, for railroad rehabilitation, plans included one Headquarters, Railway Construction Group, two Railway Construction Companies, one Bridge Section, one Section Railway Survey Company, and one Separate Mechanical Equipment Company.

The first British railhead was opened on 22 July at Scordia and then they pushed it on to Bicocca, Motta, and finally to Catania, a total of 106 miles. By early August they were operating seven trains daily of 1,500 tons each. By 1 September they had placed in service and were using 90 locomotives and approximately 900 freight cars which they had captured.

The advance party of the 727 R.O.B., consisting of Colonel F. W. Okie, Major C. O. Butler, Captain J. M. Boles, Lieutenants M. L. Horton, F. S. Howie, J. M. Norris, and J. R. Sterling and 61 enlisted men, arrived at Licata on 12 and 15 July 1943. The first train ran out of Licata the day of their arrival, 12 July, to make a reconnaissance and checkup of the railroad between Licata and Campobello, some fifteen miles to the north. Headquarters and Service Company and Company "A" arrived on 21 July and Companies "B" and "C" within that next week. The entire battalion was in Sicily by the end of July.

The first operations of the 727 R.O.B. were in support of the Third Division, which had started north from Licata. On the first day of operation, which was 12 July, 400 tons were moved inland from Licata; on the second day, 600 tons; and on the third day 800 tons of freight. The 727 R.O.B. had to do more than operate the railroads, as they had done in Tunisia, for they had to establish Rail Transportation Offices and had to detach officers and men for that purpose. They did R.T.O. work in five ports, dumps, and at railheads.

For all practical purposes, there was an unlimited supply of cars and locomotives in good condition in Sicily. Storeroom stock and even critical materials were more than adequate with a few exceptions. For Captain H. N. Wittekind, the supply officer, it was a storekeeper's paradise.

One of the earliest and most difficult problems was water supply—supplying locomotives with water and washing out boilers in roundhouses. At one time a locomotive on the shoreline was supplied with water pumped through a hose from a warship into the tank of the locomotive. Ultimately, however, their water section and the engineers collaborating provided adequate water facilities.

Another great difficulty was in the communications and dispatching system. What telegraph and telephone lines there had been along the railroads were destroyed or sabotaged in one way or another and everybody wanted a line—the Air Forces and the Ground Forces. Repair and replacement of lines along the railroad were made difficult by the fact that there was not a road parallel to the tracks from which to work. It became necessary to use radio in the dispatching and handling of trains on the ever-increasing operated mileage. Three dispatching headquarters were established: one each at Licata, Palermo, and Caltanissetta.

Because of no direct through-dispatching wires, it became necessary in several instances to go back to the station-by-station block-system operation, which was the type of operating method found originally in North Africa.

The narrow-gauge railroad from Licata to Margonia was opened and a few supply trains operated. After 20 July there was no further need for the line and operation was stopped. While other sections of the narrow-gauge lines could have been opened, there was no military need for them.

The advance of the Seventh Army through most of the island and the withdrawal of the Germans and Italians made it possible for the 727 R.O.B. to open and operate most of the rail mileage of Sicily. On 12 August the Director General received a report from Colonel Okie that the railroad had been opened from Palermo to San Stefano on the north and Licata to Enna in the south. It was further stated that the main effort was being exerted along the north coast handling all tonnage offered.

By 1 September the tonnage and troops movement averaged better than 3,000 tons daily. Colonel Okie had moved his headquarters from Licata to Palermo on 28 July 1943.

On 24 July, at about 4:30 A.M., three runaway cars loaded with gasoline, ammunition, and other supplies crashed into several loaded cars in the railroad yards at Licata, starting a fire and burning up about 25 carloads of supplies. Majors Moss and Butler, with several other officers and enlisted men, in spite of danger of injury from bursting gasoline drums and flying shrapnel, managed to clear the yards of other loaded cars of supplies, thereby keeping the loss of damage down to a very small area. The incident was caused by sabotage.

The Palermo yards were bombed by the enemy on 1 August and again on 4 August, with a resulting serious effect, as the leads to the yards were almost completely obstructed. Tracks were cleared and rehabilitated promptly, however, by the "A" Company of the 727 R.O.B., assisted by civilian laborers.

On 2 August a serious fire (sabotage again) broke out in the Centrale Yard Freight House, Palermo, in which was stored a large supply of combustible oil and Italian ammunition. Trains adjacent to the freight house, which were being loaded with military supplies, were in serious danger. Due to the personal efforts of Colonel Okie and Sergeants N. L. Stone and C. Swan and two other enlisted men, a serious disaster was averted. Only a few cars of Italian supplies stored in the vicinity were lost, but a yard interlocking plant was set on fire by exploding drums of tar.

The Director General, accompanied by a few members of his staff, inspected the operations in Sicily when that party flew to Palermo on 28 August. It was a great source of satisfaction to see what the battalion had accomplished under most difficult circumstances, but the most pleasing was the complete understanding between all members of the battalion, officers and men alike, and the technical staff of the Seventh Army headquarters, particularly with the G-4 of the Seventh Army, Colonel W. J. Muller.

In Sicily also was captured the first depot containing the famous German-designed Roth Waagner prefabricated bridging, which was to be used so extensively and advantageously later in Italy where even larger stocks of this bridging were captured.

One of the "firsts" that M.R.S. engineering reconstruction officers secured was the use of the prefabricated American Bailey type of bridging developed by the Corps of Engineers for road bridges. The M.R.S. men used this for railroad bridges both horizontally for spans and vertically as piers. To our best belief, Bailey bridging was first used for railroad bridging about seventeen miles east of Cefalu, Sicily, between 4 and 8 August 1943. A through-type, triple-truss, double-story bridge was built there approximately 120 feet in length. It was decked to take motor traffic as well as railway traffic. This bridge was built by Company "C," 20th Engineers, Seventh Army.

On 30 August the 727 R.O.B. opened the line from Catania to Geribini in the British Sector because great stores were being moved into and out of the great airport at Geribini.

By 1 September, the battalion was suffering, as were all the troops in Sicily, from malaria. About 5 per cent of all troops were afflicted. The 727 R.O.B. Medical Detachment, under Captain J. G. Peeler, M.C., established its own hospital. With the very efficient medical detachment under him, he rendered great service to those affected.

On 19 July the Allied Forces based on Sicily undertook a very careful spot bombardment of Rome. Greatest care was taken in bombing only transportation facilities, and by intent and design not a single historical or religious shrine was touched with the exception of the Basilica of San Lorenzo. It was slightly damaged, but that circumstance was unavoidable, as the structure was located at the very edge of the San Lorenzo railway yards. Growing unrest and virtual revolution in Italy by that time caused the announcement on the Rome radio at 2300 hours on 25 July that Premier Mussolini had resigned and departed from Rome.

The 727 R.O.B. took over and operated a total of 1,373 miles of Sicilian railroads, captured and used 300 locomotives and 3,500 freight cars of all classes, all of them in first-class shape and many of them brand-new cars of German ownership.

From the date of the landing in Sicily on 10 July to 30 August, approximately 170,000 net tons of military freight were moved, or an average of 3,400 net tons per day, with a maximum of 4,000 net tons in any one day. A great point to note is that in all the operations of the M.R.S. in Sicily, the

Gen. George S. Patton, Commanding 7th U.S. Army.

Sicilians were very cooperative, many of them working more than thirty hours at a stretch, often without food.

The 727 R.O.B. was nominated for service in Italy as a part of the original 703 R.G.D. of which it had been a member in North Africa, together with the 713 R.O.B. and the 753 R.S.B. "A" Company was sent to Italy 13 October 1943. Headquarters and Headquarters Company and "B" and "C" Companies left Sicily for Naples, Italy, 8 November.

The Seventh Army under General Patton waged a fast and furious war in Sicily and captured a great amount of country rapidly. Notwithstanding the rapid advances of the elements of that army, the M.R.S. never failed from the beginning until the end to carry all tonnage offered from each port to the desired destination—a thoroughly remarkable feat. It is believed that no better way to indicate the achievement can be found than to quote General Patton, Commanding General of the Seventh Army, in his commendation of the 727 R.O.B.:

During the initial operations of the Seventh Army in the Gela-Licata-Porto Empedocle Area, an Advance Party of the 727 Railway Operating Battalion landed at Licata on 12 July. This advance detachment made a reconnissance of the railroad yards, organized native rail workers, located equipment, had steam up, and made a reconnaissance of the rail lines within four hours after landing. Within twenty-four hours after landing, supplies were being moved by rail to the 3rd Division on 13 July 1943. On 15 July, the second increment of the Advance Party landed at Licata. They immediately made reconnaissance of rail lines, communications and equipment, placed key men in strategic rail junctions, established RTO's at railheads and port clearances, and effectively organized the Italian rail system in spite of many handicaps of demolition and enemy destruction. This accomplishment relieved the truck transportation for use at more critical points in advanced area. The main body of the Battalion arrived on the 23d of July and the necessary plans had been so well formulated by the Advance Party that the entire Battalion was moved into action in numerous rail operations extending over the entire western part of Sicily. The opening of the rail lines and organization of the Italian railroad personnel were made so rapidly that rail service was immediately available in the port of Palermo when it opened on the 28th of July, and service maintained from that port in spite of bombing attacks and sabotage. This Battalion worked day and night to accomplish its mission and was a strong influence in the movement of supplies to the front lines during the Sicilian Campaign. The initiative and the perseverance of the officers and enlisted men of the 727 Railway Operating Battalion, working on a strange railroad with strange equipment, without regard to personal safety, are a credit to the Military Railway Service and traditions of service as a whole.

According to plan, the invasion of the mainland of Italy occurred on 3 September, when two divisions of the British Eighth Army ferried across the Strait of Messina to Reggio di Calabria and entered Italy at the "toe" and started, without too much opposition, up the "instep" toward the "heel" to the cities of Brindisi and Bari.

At 6:30 P.M. on 8 September General Eisenhower announced the unconditional surrender of Italy. The Armistice had been signed 3 September, the same day that the British had landed at Reggio di Calabria.

At 4 A.M. on 9 September the United States Fifth Army, under Lieutenant General Mark W. Clark, landed in strength in the vicinity of Naples at Salerno and south. There was terrific resistance to the landing. The Germans had anticipated the main landing to the north of Naples near the mouth of the Tiber River, but took no chances and had a great number of troops in

Gen. Mark W. Clark, Commanding 5th U.S. Army.

the vicinity of Naples and Salerno, which moved immediately in an attempt to drive the Fifth Army from the beachheads. Through a series of gallant actions, the Fifth Army maintained its position, advanced steadily northward, and captured Naples on 1 October.

In the meantime, the British Eighth Army had advanced through the Liri Valley, had captured the Foggia airfields, and by 1 October the battle line stretched from the west coast of Italy, just north of Naples, to a position north of Foggia on the Adriatic Sea.

First planning of the M.R.S. in connection with the operation and ultimate forces and necessary supplies to support it began with the conferences in London and the over-all plan of strategy to be used in the European Theater of War. Final planning took place with Colonel Tate, G-4 of the Fifth Army, on 21 August.

Colonel B. H. Crosland, Assistant General Manager, Engineering Headquarters, M.R.S., and Colonel John Ratter, Assistant Director, Tn-2 (British), made the M.R.S. Engineering estimates and plans for the campaign. They arbitrarily phased the campaign, Phase I being south of the Apennine Mountains and Phase II north thereof. They estimated the probable destruction of bridges in the two phases and requisitioned bridge material in accordance with their plans. By 1 October 1944 a checkup between those two officers showed, to their amazement, that their estimates had been within 3 per cent of being correct.

The 703 R.G.D., under Colonel Burpee, was nominated to head the first M.R.S. troops to support the Fifth Army and its operations. Subsequently all of the M.R.S. troops in North Africa were moved to Italy: the 701 and 704 R.G.D. Headquarters, the 713, 715, 719, and 759 R.O.B., the 761 R.T.C., the 753 R.S.B., and the 760 R.S.B. Diesel which came direct from Egypt to Naples.

British transportation service was to use the forces from Sicily, North Africa, and the Middle East in their support of the British Eighth Army.

Italy's railroads are state owned and operated. Generally speaking, the Italian State Railroads (I.S.R.) consisted of a main line from Reggio di Calabria, a single-track electrified railroad, running up the "toe" and "shin" through Naples and Rome, Line 89, then to Genoa and Milan and on into southeastern France. Running north out of Naples to Caserta are two double-track electric railroads forming a loop connecting with Line 89 at Caserta. The eastward side of the loop, continuing through Caserta to Rome, is Line 90. There is also an electric line from Caserta through Benevento to Foggia, Line 91. A single-track and steam-operated rail line runs from Reggio di Calabria around the "instep" to Taranto and then on into Bari with a branch out to Brindisi, then extends with a double-track railroad from Bari to Foggia, then a single-track railroad up the "calf" to Ancona, where it double-tracks into Bologna, and then on into Venice and eastward.

From Rome there is a double-track electric railroad through Florence, Verona, and north to the Brenner Pass. Another double-track electric railroad runs northwest from Bologna toward Milan and north connecting up at Piacenza with an east-and-west line through Alessandria and Turin, and on into France. East and west there are many cross single-track railroads;

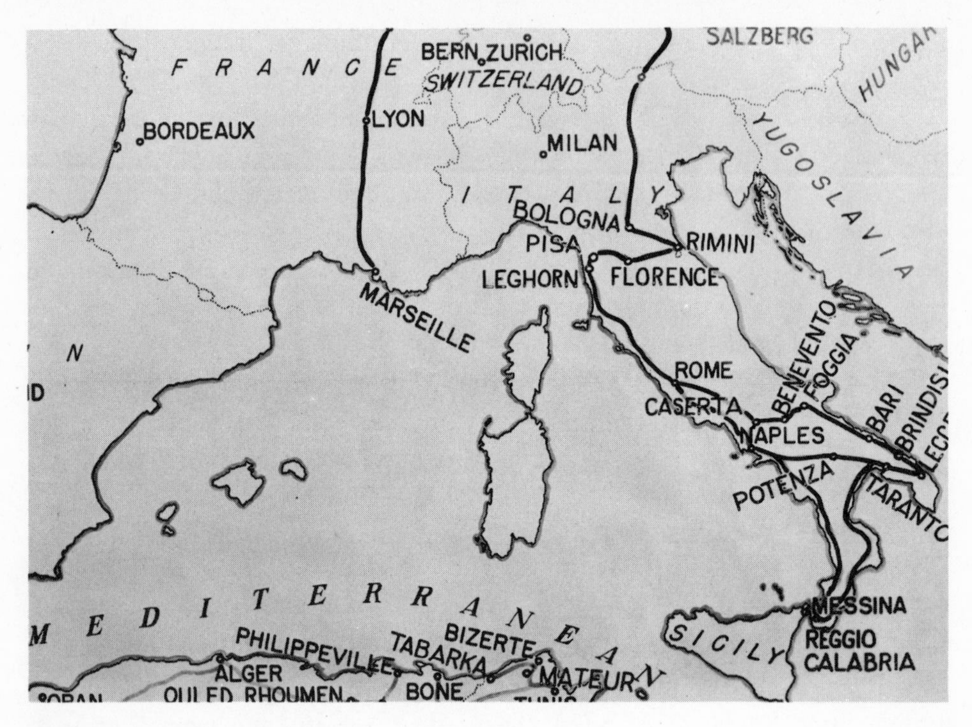

Railroads in Italy.

the most useful at the beginning of the invasion was one from Naples through Potenza and Taranto to Brindisi and Bari.

Colonel Burpee was in the original forces landing at Salerno as he had been in the landings in North Africa north of Casablanca. Lieutenant Colonel C. S. Sanderson was placed in charge of the advanced echelon of the Headquarters, 703 R.G.D., and moved from Constantine to Oran with eleven officers, one warrant officer, and eighteen enlisted men on 9 September. Lieutenant Colonel L. E. Covin, acting General Superintendent of the 703 R.G.D., moved with the balance of the headquarters to Oran on 27 September. The advance echelon, Headquarters, 703 R.G.D., landed at Naples on 4 October and established headquarters temporarily in a building on one of the piers. The balance of the headquarters arrived in Naples on 10 October when Colonel Burpee again took command of the unit. Headquarters were established at 35 Prince Umberto Square where office space, quarters, and messing facilities could be provided. That headquarters immediately took over the direction of the rehabilitation of tracks in the yards at Naples, on the docks, and the main line from Naples to Aversa.

The British Transportation Service, following the invasion of the British Eighth Army at Reggio di Calabria, had worked up the "instep" and began operations of the Italian railroads in the vicinity of Brindisi, Bari, and on to Foggia.

The first rail movement in the American sector after General Clark's landing was from south of Naples into Naples. This line was rehabilitated by Company "A" of the 345 Engineer General Service Regiment, commanded by Colonel John D. Matheson, who will be remembered as the first of the Regular Army officers who trained with the General Manager, M.R.S., in 1939 in anticipation of being the Adjutant or Executive Officer of a railway unit. He really was the Executive Officer of the 711 R.O.B. in 1941 and 1942 when that battalion built and operated the Claiborne and Polk Military Railway. The first train into Naples over this line was named and publicized as the "Mark Clark Special."

After the Port of Naples was cleared, virtually all of the supplies for the American Army were received and unloaded at Naples; thereby, Naples became the hub of M.R.S. activities in the Italian Campaign.

On 27 September the Director General received a radiogram from the British Eighth Army headquarters that Major General Giovanni di Raimondo, Director General of Military Railways, I.S.R., had reported to that headquarters for service and they requested information as to what should be done with him.

The reply was to send him to the Director General at Algiers. In company with Lieutenant Colonel Wynn Davis of the British Transportation Service, he arrived in Algiers on 28 September. General di Raimondo did not speak English, but through an interpreter it was learned and recognized that he was a highly capable officer, thoroughly imbued with railroad capacity, and had a very keen desire to be helpful in the operation of the railroads in the logistical support of the Allied armies in Italy.

After consultation with the members of the staff of the Headquarters, M.R.S., and Sir Humphrey Gale, the Chief Administrative Officer of AFHQ, the Director General flew to Italy, accompanied by General di Raimondo and Colonel Davis, with verbal orders from AFHQ to take over the operation

General Giovanni di Raimondo, Director Military Railways, Italy.

of the Italian State Railways. Verbal orders were later confirmed by General Orders No. 60, AFHQ, dated 22 October 1943.

Landing at Taranto, the Director General immediately had a consultation with Signor Fransi, Director of the Italian State Railways in that "Compartimento." Then, after consultation with Lieutenant General Sir Brian H. Robertson of the British Second District, the representative of the Chief Administrative Officer, AFHQ, in Italy, the Director General proceeded to inspect facilities in Brindisi, Bari, and Foggia, then went on by car to Naples for consultation with Colonel Tate and Colonel Burpee.

Through the verbal authority had by the Director General, at Naples he issued Field Memoranda Nos. 1 and 2, under date of 7 October 1943, which read as follows:

ALLIED FORCE HEADQUARTERS
MILITARY RAILWAY SERVICE
TRANSPORTATION CORPS
OFFICE OF DIRECTOR GENERAL

APO 782
7 October 1943

Field Memorandum No. 1

1. The provisions of GO 19, AFHQ are extended to cover all the railways of Italy.
2. The undersigned assumes command of all British Tn and U.S.A. Military Railway Service troops in Italy with headquarters at Naples.
3. Colonel C. L. Burpee, Commanding Officer, 703 Railway Grand Division, is announced as Deputy of Director General and will exercise the authority of the Director General during his absence.
4. The primary mission of the Military Railway Service is to give rail supply support to the Allied Armies in the field.

and:

ALLIED FORCE HEADQUARTERS
MILITARY RAILWAY SERVICE
TRANSPORTATION CORPS
OFFICE OF THE DIRECTOR GENERAL

A.P.O. 782
7 October 1943

Field Memorandum No. 2

1. Under the provisions of Field Memorandum No. 1, the Railways of Italy in the hands of the Allies are divided for reconstruction and operating purposes into two districts.
2. The First District will be composed of the lines of the Bari and Reggio-Calabria Compartimenti. Commanding Officer will be Colonel Pottle, D.D. Tn (Br), with headquarters at Bari.
3. The Second District will be composed of the lines of the Naples Compartimento and the terminals and port of Naples. The Commanding Officer will be Colonel C. L. Burpee with headquarters at Naples.
4. There is hereby established a division of the office of the Director General

A type of German demolition, Italy.

> known as the Reconstruction Division under the command of Colonel E. L. Parkes, D.D. Tn (Br). This division is charged with the responsibility of repairing the tracks and facilities of the 1st and 2nd Districts and all the construction and maintenance troops and their equipment are placed at his disposal.

These two field memoranda definitely set up responsible agencies for the rehabilitation and operation of the Italian State Railways looking toward the complete logistical support of the Fifth and Eighth Armies.

The first over-all ground command in the Italian Campaign was Headquarters, Fifteenth Army Group, commanded by Field Marshall Sir Harold R. L. G. Alexander. Lieutenant General Jacob L. Devers was the Commanding General of NATOUSA and second in command in the Fifteenth Army Group headquarters. In the support of the Fifteenth Army Group operations in Italy, the Director General had three forces under his command: the American M.R.S. troops under his direct command, the British forces under Brigadier R. F. O'D. Gage, and the Italian railway forces under Major

Typical German demolition, Italy.

German attempt to wreck both locomotive and turntable, Rome.

General Giovanni di Raimondo, just as he had had a joint command in North Africa with British forces under Brigadier Gage and the French railway forces under Colonel Quenard of the French Army.

The general program included the American M.R.S. being assigned to the west coast ports and west coast lines, including the cross line from Salerno through Potenza to Taranto. The British units of the M.R.S. were assigned to the east coast ports and lines and the Calabrian ports and operations. This division of American and British M.R.S. units was continued nearly throughout the Italian Campaign.

There were three phases of rail operation in Italy: Phase I, operation exclusively by Military Personnel and methods; Phase II, operation by civilian personnel, supplemented and supervised by M.R.S.; Phase III, operation by civilian organization under general direction of the military.

Immediately behind the battle lines on both coasts Phase I operation was followed; and on the west coast, due to extensive demolition and damage, and disorganization of civilian personnel, Phase I operation was inaugurated in and out of the Port of Naples.

In Calabria and on the east coast it was possible in the main to operate under Phase II except in immediate battle areas, and the progress made by the small number of M.R.S. troops in service was made possible by the ever-increased Phase II and Phase III form of operation in the support of the armies.

One of the first tasks confronting the management of the M.R.S. was to make available locomotives and equipment. Another was the necessity for determining what additional locomotives and equipment of various types and what operating personnel would be required as the armies advanced. This was particularly difficult, as there was no reliable information available as to what would be the extent of demolitions in advance of the armies, and how much rolling stock of the I.S.R. would be available.

An inventory was made of all serviceable locomotives and equipment to be moved in from Africa and the United States, as well as Diesel locomotives from the Near East. As a result of this early planning and prompt transfer of locomotives and equipment, together with the efficiency of mechanical M.R.S. units, sufficient power and equipment to supply the armies and maintain port clearance were provided at all times.

Reconstructed bridge, Teano, Italy.

Repairs to Viarano bridge, Italy.

Repaired bridge, Teano, Italy.

Due to the fact that there were M.R.S. troops in North Africa, Sicily, and Italy, and in order to carry out his responsibilities, the Director General requested authority to issue travel orders for all officers and men of his command, including permanent changes of station, anywhere in the theater. This request was concurred in by the Commander in Chief in accordance with his letter of 20 October 1943.

The Italian Railway men followed the orders and the action of General di Raimondo, their Director General, in affording complete and intelligent assistance in the rehabilitation and operation of their railroads. There existed in the Italian Army an organization of construction engineers, known as the "Raggrupamento Ferrovieri," commanded by Colonel Umberto Dutto. It consisted of the First Railway Battalion, commanded by Major Salvatore Rapino, in which were the 2d Railway Company, commanded by Captain Mario Fidecadori, the 7th Railway Company, commanded by Captain Paolo Scarnecchia, and the 20th Railway Company, commanded by Captain Antonino Celone; the 13th Railway Battalion, commanded by Major Francesco Botta, in which were the 8th Railway Company, commanded by Captain Arduino Martinetti; the 21st Railway Company, commanded by Captain Tommaso Carpi; the 31st Railway Company, commanded by First Lieutenant Filippo Topa; and the 3d Railway Battalion (forming), commanded by Major Alberico Maiatico.

These troops, with the "A" Companies of the 715, 719, and 759 R.O.B., all of which arrived at Naples 17 November 1943, and assisted by civilian laborers, totaling about 10,000 men, began the rehabilitation and reconstruction of the railroad yards and dock tracks at Naples. It is doubtful if any Roadmaster ever had an extra gang of 10,000 men before or since. Very fast and excellent work was done by these men.

Another interesting action on the part of the Italians was that after they had surrendered unconditionally to the Allies on 3 September 1943, they declared war on Germany on 12 October.

As the railroads became rehabilitated in the vicinity of Naples and south thereof and parts of them were being turned back to the Italian State Railways, it became necessary to issue orders to the I.S.R. officials that they could not run trains without the authority of Headquarters, M.R.S.

As indicated before, there are two main-line railroads running north

Welding rail.

Soldier Ghandi Dancers, Italy.

Track demolition, Line 89, north of Naples.

from Naples forming a circle that closes at Caserta, twenty-five miles from Naples. About halfway, or ten miles north of Naples on the western side of the circle, is Aversa, a junction with a double-track line running from Aversa to Villa Literno on the coast line. Inside the circular nature of the track through Aversa is a large yard of some ten or fifteen tracks, each capable of accommodating 75 to 100 cars. At the time of the enemy withdrawal from that area each of the tracks of that yard was full of cars.

With characteristic thoroughness, the Germans in their retreat had destroyed that yard by blowing out the center of every other rail, placing a time bomb in the journals of the cars, and then covering the entire mass with gasoline and setting it all afire.

Colonel Burpee and the Director General inspected this; at first sight, it didn't seem possible that the yards could be cleared and rebuilt through for a matter of weeks.

The German soldier, however, was disciplined to do as he was told to do, but nothing more. He was told to destroy the yard tracks. That is what he did. But behind the station was a house track on which was standing ten flat-cars loaded with brand-new rail and fastenings. The house track was not a part of the yard; therefore, it had not been destroyed by the Germans. Bull-dozers shoved clear some 25 feet of the debris and M.R.S. men walked a distance of not over 100 feet, got the new rail and ties, and had a fine track through in a matter of hours.

The Germans used two forms of track demolition. They placed a time bomb about the size of a K-ration box in the center of every other rail. When the sixty-second time fuse exploded the bomb, it blew out approximately sixteen inches in the center of the rail. Our method of rehabilitation was to cut off and square the broken edges of the blown section with an acetylene torch, and then pull down the remaining rail. When the gap was of sufficient size, work crews reached over to the other track of a double-track system and took out the undamaged every-other rail and filled in the gap. In that way, work of rehabilitation proceeded unbelievably quickly in the restitution of one track of a double-track system.

The other form of track demolition was the use of the "Scarifier," which in reality was nothing more than a big plow on an axle with wide wooden wheels which ran along outside the rails on the ballast shoulder. The Germans would hook four engines to that Scarifier and go down the track cutting every tie so that when they were finished the rails were separated, every tie was broken, and the track had to be completely retied. If the ties were iron, as some were, the iron was bent and impossible to straighten and so had to be replaced with wooden ties; concrete ties were broken like the wooden ones and also had to be replaced.

Detailed and lengthy have been the accounts given of the paralyzing destruction wreaked by our bombers on the rail transportation facilities, but possibly not so well publicized has been the additional destruction of individual units of rolling stock by the demolition squads of the enemy. Individual locomotives were immobilized in a very methodical and thoroughly efficient way. The enemy employed a set formula in this and the procedure was followed wherever the equipment might have been located.

In the case of a steam locomotive, a charge was usually placed under the rail directly below the driving wheels of the engine. The resulting explosion blasted a section of the rail so that the locomotive could not be moved and at the same time cracked the driving-wheel tire and sometimes the wheel itself. This precluded moving the locomotive to the shops until extensive repairs had been made to the track and locomotive at the site.

In addition to this, it was a regular feature to place a charge in the firebox and smokebox of the locomotive, and the tank portion of the tender, and usually a charge was placed in one of the cylinders. The right cylinder was invariably blown, thereby eliminating the cannibalizing of other locomotives to repair a few.

Along the electrified rail lines they not only destroyed the catenary, poles, and substations, but they destroyed the electric locomotives themselves. The usual procedure was to place a charge in each of the traction motors, another charge in the cab, destroying the control panel and instruments, and in addition the usual charge under the rail, directly below the wheels.

Ordinary freight and passenger cars were treated in much the same way as the motive power, with several new twists to render almost complete destruction. In addition to the usual charge under the wheels, splitting both rail and wheel, it was quite customary to place a charge in the journal box or next to the spring. The resulting explosion rendered useless the complete truck.

Scarified track, Italy, Line 89 between Aversa and Rome.

Steel ties bent by Germans, Formia, Italy, Line 80.

The Scarifier used by Germans to demolish track in Italy.

Scarified track, Line 90, Naples-Rome, Italy, 1944.

Typical track destruction, Italy.

Steel Tie track destruction.

Villa Literno Yard.

Result of our bombing on German train, Arezzo Line.

Tank cars, or any liquid-carrying container cars, were given special additional attention in the form of a charge directly under the underside of the tank itself, blowing a large jagged hole up into the tank.

In Italy there is a type of gasoline motor or Diesel motor-powered rail car in service, used on short-distance and high-speed runs. These cars are somewhat longer than the conventional passenger coach with motors and control panels at either end to eliminate turning at terminals. These cars, too, were not spared; the usual procedure was the placing of the now-familiar charge under the rail and wheel, then a charge under each of the motors, and then a final burning of the interior of the car.

The 713 R.O.B. came ashore on the mainland of Italy at Naples on 7 October. Actual battle lines were very close, as the enemy was only fifteen miles away and Naples had been occupied by Allied troops for only four days. It was about impossible to find a building that had not been damaged.

Crews of Company B. 713 R.O.B., starting to transfer Italian engine and coaches in Naples, Italy, Railroad Yard.

Direct hit on troop train, Villa Literno.

After bivouacking in a warehouse the first two days, and it seemed ready to crumble at any minute, the troops moved into another building near the station and yards because it looked better.

For two days they labored at cleaning things up. Then an American major, an expert on such things, rushed up to declare the place was loaded with time bombs, ready to go off at any moment. It was speedily evacuated. For days after their arrival buildings skyrocketed without warning as clock-work detonators set by the Germans did their work. At night the city was a ghost town. Shots and explosions were continuous overtones. Day and night the rumble of artillery from the front could be heard, and flashes lit the sky. The railroads were in bad shape. There was hardly a track that had not been blown apart every hundred yards or so, either by our own bombing before the occupation or by the thorough demolition tactics of the enemy. Cars were blown about the yards. In some cases there were long strings of rolling stock

Italian laborers under supervision of M.R.S. repair rails torn up by retreating Germans.

North end, Itri Yard, Italy.

Naples Passenger Station.

Beginning clean-up job, Villa Literno.

A portion of Naples Yard.

on the sidings, burned to a crisp, the frames standing like charred skeletons. Blowing a railroad into a state of total uselessness, however, is a tough job. The 713th set about to prove it.

Perhaps the most amazing exploit in the rehabilitation of the road was performed by an operating platoon that had nothing to operate and decided to become a track gang. That platoon became known as "Sergeant Tomer's Reclamation Department." Sergeant Fred A. Tomer was a conductor. Giving himself some new titles, he became all at once track gang foreman, wreck foreman, and rip track foreman. He chose Private Alexander Parker, who had had some track-gang experience, for his right-hand man.

Sergeant Tomer and his "gang" set to work early one morning. At dusk that night the gang of engineers, firemen, and brakemen, wielding picks and shovels, had opened a good-sized piece of track and put eight serviceable cars on it; they had filled in huge bomb craters, had cleared away demolished rolling stock that sewed in serviceable equipment, and had gotten a switch engine running.

The next day the gang reclaimed 12 cars and put some more track back in operation. They filled more craters and fixed more switches. On the third day they found a German wrecker crane that wasn't badly damaged. Tomer's gang didn't even bother to call the battalion's expert mechanics. They repaired the crane and then built 75 yards of track to get it to where it could be used. From then on in, it was easier. It made no difference whether the repairable cars were crosswise or sidewise or upside down. They merely hooked the big chain around a car, set the German gears to grinding, and put the car back on good rail.

The names of the train crew of the 713 R.O.B. who took the first train up to the front were Sergeant Woodrow Boice, conductor; Technician Fourth Grade William J. McMeans and Technician Fourth Grade Lyman R. Mills, engineers; Technician Fifth Grade Alfred C. Ricketts and Technician Fifth Grade Paul H. Dahlin, firemen; and Private First Class Harvey D. Bradley and Private First Class Victor F. Schaefer, brakemen.

Officers shared the risks of that first trip with their men. Aboard were Lieutenant Colonel Ernest E. Foulks, Captains R. D. McGee and J. W. Scott, and First Lieutenant L. G. Shields.

This first train ran northward with Army supplies on 10 October and by 23 October there were nine locomotives in service and as many German and Italian cars as were necessary. At the start trains averaged 350 net tons, but by 16 October the 713th was handling regularly an average 700 net tons of freight per train. By 29 October the unit was operating military freight trains from the port to dump area in the vicinity of Aversa. By the first week in November it operated into Caserta, handling an average of 4,700 net tons per day. By 11 November port clearance capacity of 4,800 net tons per day and railhead capacity of 6,000 net tons per day to railheads were established, mounting gradually to reach a maximum of 15,000 tons port clearance in December.

The question of stores and supplies fortunately was taken care of promptly. The Germans had to leave a considerable amount of stores in and around Naples, but possibly the most useful captured by the Americans was some 25,000 tons of German Roth Waagner prefabricated truss bridging found in reconnaissance by Sergeant C. E. Quist at Gricignano, Italy, on the line between Aversa and Caserta.

This prefabricated bridging went together like a Meccano toy and great use of it was made in the drive north through Italy. Other captured German stores, as well as Italian stores at Bagnoli, came to the M.R.S. on 19 November.

The "A" Company, 727 R.O.B., arrived at Naples from Palermo on 15 October and the balance of the battalion, "believe it or not," moved by truck from Palermo, Sicily, to Salerno, Italy, a distance of 500 miles, ferrying the entire convoy across to the mainland. The 160 trucks they used in moving had been through the campaign of Sicily and had been repaired by the motor section of the Headquarters Company, the mechanics of "B" Company, and even the engineers and firemen of "C" Company. It left Palermo 8 November 1943, and arrived at Salerno four days later. It re-

Roth Waagner bridging being repaired on Cecina River bridge by 727 R.O.B.

Test train over newly constructed bridge, Grosetto, Italy.

Volturno River bridge,
Capua, Italy.

lieved the 192 Operating Company (British) and was assigned by Colonel Burpee the operating and maintenance of the Italian Railways between San Giovanni Barra and Potenza; Battipaglia and Agropoli, and between Avellino and Nocera Inferiore via Codola, and the assignment included all yards except the Potenza Yard. In the first five days of operation out of Salerno, they averaged 700 gross tons of freight daily. The Director General, however, was not relieved of responsibility in the operation of the Sicilian railroads until they were returned to civilian operation effective 18 March 1944, per letter orders from AFHQ.

On arrival in Italy, "A" Company, 727 R.O.B., was teamed up by Colonel B. H. Crosland, Assistant General Manager, Engineering, with the "A" Company of the 713 R.O.B. and Italian Engineer Construction troops to carry on track and bridge rehabilitation on Line 90 north of Caserta.

On 28 October the "B & B" Platoon of the 713 R.O.B. and the "A" Company of the 727 R.O.B. moved to Capua and began reconstruction of the bridge over the Volturno River. The original structure was 532 feet of through plate girders completely destroyed except for three masonry piers. The new structure was fabricated with 531.6 feet of Roth Waagner steel

Completed Volturno River bridge, 525 feet long, completed in 24 days, by bridge platoons of "A" Companies of 713 and 727 R.O.B.

Volturno River bridge, Capua, Italy.

bridging and 21 feet 2 x 5 Bay British Steel Trestling. All steel was loaded on trucks at Aversa and hauled to Capua. The bridge was ready for trains in twenty-two days. In the repair of the bridge the "A" Company, 727 R.O.B., had expended 22,375 man-hours of labor; the "A" Company of the 713 R.O.B., 1,294; and Italian Railway Troops had expended 13,734 man-hours.

Because of the numerous mountain streams there were many bridges on the I.S.R., and the American bombers in their attacks and the Germans in their retreat destroyed virtually every one of the major ones. It is impossible to explain the rehabilitation of so many of them, but one of the unique and quick jobs was the work performed by the bridge platoons of the "A" Companies of the 713, 715, 719, and 727 R.O.B. on the destroyed double-track, single-span bridge over the Garigliano River on Line 89 between Naples and Rome.

Garigliano River bridge, Minturno, Italy. Start from the west bank.

Garigliano River bridge. Temporary pier is floated out into river to support the span during construction.

Garigliano River bridge. Nearly completed.

Captured German Roth Waagner bridging was used and construction started with the erection from the south bank. Because there were no piers, it was necessary to erect as much bridge backward as forward to keep it from tipping into the stream. This use of material and time was out of the question, so units of Roth Waagner bridging were formed into temporary

Garigliano River bridge. Roth Waagner prefabricated bridging assembled with nuts and bolts.

Garigliano River bridge.

piers approximately 70 feet in length, hung on pontoons taken to the proper place in the stream and set; the bridge was then built to them, making it unnecessary to have counterbalance on the back end. The bridge was thus erected by steps to the piers and then on to the north abutment, a distance of 240 feet. After the completion of the bridge the temporary piers were removed and the single-track, single-span bridge was in operation in eleven days from the time work started until the first train passed over it. The track was 47 feet above the surface of the river, and the stream was 22 feet deep.

The capture of the Roth Waagner bridging material from the Germans was a Godsend. Augmented by strong American prefabricated Bailey type bridging, it was possible for the "A" Company bridge men to perform near miracles in crossing gaps occasioned by the demolition of masonry arch bridges which were so prevalent in southern Italy.

A great tragedy occurred on 3 March 1944. The Corps of Engineers had found standing timber of sufficient size south of Potenza in the "instep" and had put a forestry battalion there to cut bridge timbers which were very vital in the rehabilitation of bridges in the wake of the Army. M.R.S. scheduled train service to handle this bridge timber and was operating empty trains regularly out of Battipaglia through Torrenza and south from Metaponto through Sibari and Spezzano into the "toe," to be loaded and returned in special trains.

Italian civilian employees were operating these trains. The loaded trains were double-headed, and in order to balance power, the empty trains were also double-headed. There were many heavy ascending grades between Battipaglia and Potenza eastbound and there were many tunnels. Delays were incurred frequently and, while instructions were definite and every effort was made to insure that no unauthorized person was transported in these empty trains, in the darkness of the night at station stops refugees would climb aboard without the knowledge of train crews. On one such train, when it had pulled into a tunnel (two miles in length) east of Potenza, the drivers on both engines started slipping and the train stalled inside the tunnel. The tunnel filled with gases from the two engines and before the situation could be corrected and the train pulled into the clear, 426 refugees and trainmen were asphyxiated.

This was the only accident of this nature suffered in the operations in Italy. The use of Diesel electric power had much to do with overcoming the hazards of asphyxiation in tunnels and accidents of a similar nature.

The railroad men of the world have had to overcome many serious obstructions which have blocked their main lines and interfered with the normal flow of traffic, but there are very few who experience the unusual occurrence of having their railroad blocked with 27 inches of ashes from an active volcano.

On 13 March 1944 Mount Vesuvius erupted. The inner cone, which rose to some 300 feet above the other crater, partially collapsed and fell into the throat of the volcano. The eruption continued through the 23d day

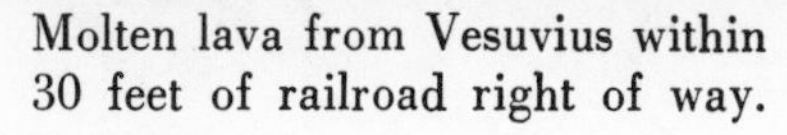

Molten lava from Vesuvius within 30 feet of railroad right of way.

Eruption of Mount Vesuvius, March, 1944.

of March. By the 24th the residents of the stricken towns in the immediate vicinity of the volcano were allowed to return to their homes. Water had been turned on and shops were beginning to reopen.

During the succeeding days the activity of the volcano continued with decreasing intensity and on the 28th finally died out. Danger from the lava had ceased but a very definite and equally grave situation had been created by the enormous volume of ash and volcanic dust which had been deposited over the countryside. Molten lava actually flowed to within 30 feet of the track of the I.S.R. The M.R.S. was out of operation for twenty-four hours commencing at 1600 hours 22 March as a result of the ashes and cinders on tracks and in switches. As far away as the yards at Nocera Inferiore approximately eight inches of ashes fell. By 1400 hours on 23 March all lines had been cleared and traffic resumed.

AFHQ, having decided that Headquarters, M.R.S., and its force should move to the now active Italian campaign, the Director General issued General Orders No. 26, dated 22 October 1943, which closed M.R.S. headquarters in North Africa and opened them in Naples.

This order likewise established territorial directives as follows: Brigadier Rex F. O'Dowd Gage, DTn (British), was named Deputy to Director General with headquarters at Algiers, Algeria; Colonel E. L. Parkes, DDTn

Headquarters, First M.R.S., No. 2, Piazza Nicola Amore, Naples, Italy.

(British), Deputy to Director General, with headquarters at Naples, Italy; Colonel Burpee, Commanding Officer of the 703 R.G.D., was assigned as Director, Military Railway of Italy, with headquarters at Naples; and Colonel A. W. Campbell as Director, Military Railway of North Africa, with headquarters at Algiers, Algeria.

On 24 October the advance party of the Headquarters, M.R.S., consisting of Colonel Crosland, Lieutenant Colonel Dennis, Major Hartzog, and Captain Murphy, departed by air for Italy. The balance of the headquarters, consisting of 10 officers and 113 enlisted men, arrived at Naples, Italy, on 17 November.

Upon establishment of Headquarters, M.R.S., there was immediately formalized and extended the understanding had between the 703 R.G.D. and the Movement Control Section of AFHQ. From the middle of November, a representative of Headquarters, M.R.S. (Lieutenant Colonel E. F. Barnes), attended the daily AFHQ Staff Conferences covering and providing for volume and priority of tonnage and troop movement.

A transportation subcommission was also formed by the Allied Control Commission in conjunction with AFHQ for the regulation of civilian traffic and tonnage. The Headquarters, M.R.S., worked very closely with all of these controlling bodies.

A movements section was made up corresponding to Superintendent of Transportation and car service organization, but due to the necessity for close supervision and coordination also functioning as a super Chief Dispatcher's setup. In charge of this movements section was Major J. M. McLellan, assisted by Captain R. W. Hartzel and First Lieutenant F. D. Lucas and some very competent enlisted personnel. All movements were cleared through this section and the nature of the work necessitated virtually twenty-four-hour duty. The performance and functioning of this movements section were most efficient notwithstanding the early difficulties due to lack of poor communications, etc.

In conjunction with movements section, numerous graphic and running records were maintained covering M.R.S. operation. In addition to the normal movement of military traffic there was a very considerable "special movements" such as troops, prisoners of war, hospital trains, etc., all of which were lined up, coordinated, and followed through by the movements section.

It is interesting to analyze the officers and men of Headquarters, M.R.S., and discover the number of railroads and experiences involved:

Representing 34 American railroads, the officers and enlisted men of M.R.S. Headquarters injected into their army jobs a wealth of civilian experience garnered from every corner of the nation—from the Bangor and Aroostook in Maine to the Southern Pacific in California; and from the Great Northern through the heart of the great Northwest to the Atlantic Coast Line in the Southeast.

Out of 35 regularly assigned officers in M.R.S. Headquarters, 34 of them were railroad men in civilian life. Of the 165 enlisted men, 91 (or 55 per cent) were railroaders. There were enlisted men in Headquarters from 29 different lines, and officers from 21. Topping all other roads by a wide margin was the Union Pacific, which contributed 19 enlisted men and 1 officer. The 33 other companies are represented as follows:

A. C. L. Railroad Company, 2 officers, 1 enlisted man
B. & A. Railroad Company, 1 officer and 3 enlisted men
B. & M. Railroad, 1 enlisted man
C. & N. W. Railway, 1 officer, 3 enlisted men
C. B. & Q. Railroad, 3 enlisted men

C. G. W. Railway, 1 officer, 1 enlisted man
C. M. St. P. & P. Railroad, 2 officers, 4 enlisted men
C. P. Railway, 1 enlisted man
C. R. I. & P. Railroad Company, 1 officer, 2 enlisted men
C. St. P. M. & O. Railway, 5 officers, 5 enlisted men
D. & R. G. W. Railroad Company, 2 officers, 5 enlisted men
D. & S. L. Railroad, 1 enlisted man
D. L. & W. Railroad Company, 1 enlisted man
G. N. Railway, 2 officers, 7 enlisted men
I. C. Railroad, 1 officer, 1 enlisted man
K. C. S. Railway Company, 2 enlisted men
L. V. Railroad Company, 1 enlisted man
M. & St. L. Railway Company, 1 officer, 5 enlisted men
M. P. Railroad, 4 officers, 2 enlisted men
M. St. P. & S. S. M. Railroad Company, 7 enlisted men
N. & W. Railway, 1 officer
N. P. Railway, 1 officer, 7 enlisted men
N. Y. C. System, 1 officer, 2 enlisted men
N. Y. C. & St. L. Railroad Company, 1 enlisted man
N. Y., N. H. & H. Railroad Company, 1 officer
N. Y. O. & W. Railway, 1 enlisted man
Pennsylvania Railroad, 1 officer, 2 enlisted men
P. M. Railroad, 1 enlisted man
The Pullman Company, 1 officer, 1 enlisted man
R. F. & P. Railroad Company, 1 officer
St. L.-S. F. Railway Company, 1 officer
S. P. Company, 1 officer, 1 enlisted man
W. M. Railway, 1 officer

Arriving along with the Headquarters, M.R.S., on 17 November, were elements of the 794 Military Police Battalion. Others followed during the month of December. One of the most tragic accidents which befell any of the units of the M.R.S. occurred on 2 January 1944, at 1:45 A.M., when the *Largs Bay*, a British transport, carrying personnel of Company "B" of the 794 Military Police Battalion, struck a mine in the Bay of Naples. Of the 149 "B" Company men aboard, 14 were killed and 62 injured.

In the spring of 1942 two Railway Shop Battalions Diesel were authorized and organized with the American Locomotive Company, Baldwin Locomotive Company, and the Electro-Motive Corporation as sponsors. One of

M.R.S. Diesel electric locomotive.

M.R.S. standard steam wrecking crane, Italy.

them, the 760 R.S.B. Diesel, under command of Lieutenant Colonel A. R. Walker, was activated at Camp Claiborne, Louisiana, on 15 June 1942, underwent training, and sailed from Charleston, South Carolina, to the Middle East on 7 October, arriving at Suez Harbor 12 November 1942.

There had been 140 Diesel-electric engines ordered for use on the railroads in the Middle East, and this R.S.B. was sent there to maintain these locomotives. It was a rather difficult assignment as these locomotives were used in Egypt, Libya, Palestine, and Syria, which necessitated the utilization of the battalion in widely separated detachments.

By the end of October 1943 it was believed that there were sufficient other units to maintain these locomotives. Consequently, arrangements were made to move the 760 R.S.B. Diesel from the Middle East to Italy. Lieutenant Colonel Walker arrived 17 November 1943, and the balance of the unit arrived in separate detachments between then and 17 July 1944. One unit arrived at Naples on 9 January 1944 with 49 Diesels which had been transferred from the Middle East to Italy. Headquarters and operations were set up in the Diesel electric locomotive repair shops at Campi Flegrei just north of Naples.

As a result of Allied bombing and German demolition, an appalling amount of repair work had to be performed before the shops or any of their equipment could be placed in operation. Shop facilities had been most extensive and modern. It was discouraging and disheartening when viewing the almost wholly inoperative condition of the locomotive and carshops, roundhouses, and enginehouse terminals and service points. But, seemingly hopeless or not, military necessity demanded immediate attention and operation with the least delay. From this chaos, surprisingly soon there emerged at first a semblance of some restoration and repair, quickly followed by production in the form of repairs, light and heavy, to cars and locomotives. Eventually lathes, boring mills, presses, forges, furnaces, and cranes were in operating condition again.

Another serious problem was the matter of civilian personnel normally employed in these shops. The passing of a full-scale war through their immediate vicinity and the resultant destruction of life, homes, property, and transportation, had a demoralizing and deterrent effect on the civilian population. Temporary lack of proper nutrition, inconvenience, and privation resulting from destruction of the utilities, all resulted in the appalling low productive standards of this personnel. In many instances these men lived quite some distance from the shop with no way of getting to and from work, except walking. It was necessary to provide transportation to and from work. During the temporary shortage of food, it was necessary to provide their midshift meal. In many instances, their lack of necessary clothing had to be supplied. Investigation disclosed that many skilled machinists and

Loading American hospital train, Italy, 1944.

Wounded soldiers board hospital train in forward area.

mechanics had been deported to Germany for forced labor, thereby creating an even greater shortage of skilled craftsmen than normally is prevalent during wartime.

Possibly one of the most satisfying accomplishments of the mechanical department and the shops was the construction of hospital trains for the United States Army. Passenger coaches were deemed the most fit to become a part of a hospital train, but due to the urgency of the demand for hospital trains it was necessary to use only those in first-class condition. Promptly upon these coaches being located, they were brought into the car repair shops which had been used exclusively for the repair of passenger equipment during peacetime. It was necessary to strip the coaches almost entirely of their interior furnishing and install fixtures and apparatus necessary for the care and transportation of the wounded.

The first hospital train was delivered for use by the Medical Corps on 21 November 1943, and made its first trip carrying 354 wounded back from the front the following day, the 22d. A second hospital train was delivered on 11 February 1944, and additional hospital trains went into service on 14 May 1944.

As a general rule these hospital trains consisted of several cars for litter or stretcher patients, several more for "ambulatory" or less seriously wounded, a pharmacy car, several kitchen and dining cars, and several quarters cars for the medical personnel attached to the train.

The American Red Cross Clubmobile Division under Tom Beatty of Ellsworth, Kansas, was responsible for the M.R.S. providing something most unusual. They had been running trucks up to the rear of the front line with coffee and doughnuts for the combat troops, but because trucks couldn't get along railroad right of way, M.R.S. troops in Italy were being deprived of this generous and worth-while action of the Red Cross people.

When this was brought to the attention of Mr. Beatty, he wanted to do something at once to provide this assistance for M.R.S. men, so Company "C" of the 753 R.S.B. constructed, under the supervision of Captain Frank J. Kossuth and Lieutenant T. E. Wilder, Jr., a coffee and doughnut car from an Italian coach. The car was equipped with quarters for six persons, storage room for supplies, icebox, screened windows, a 150-gallon overhead water tank, a 5-k.w. electric generator for light and power, kitchen fans, and doughnut machines brought over from the United States.

A contest was conducted for a suitable name for the car. Company "C" men who had built the car participated in the contest. The final choice was a most appropriate one, "Yankee Dipper," which was painted on the side of the car.

Miss Mary Jepp from Carmel, California, was the hostess in charge. Usually she had an additional Red Cross lady with her and one or two Italian helpers. While she worked from fourteen to sixteen hours a day happily and gladly, one of the things that a great many switchmen, trainmen, and trackmen will remember is that many times after she had retired these men would come along, strike the side of the car next to Mary's quarters, and immediately the cheery voice would call out: "Just a minute until I get decent and I'll serve you," and that she did.

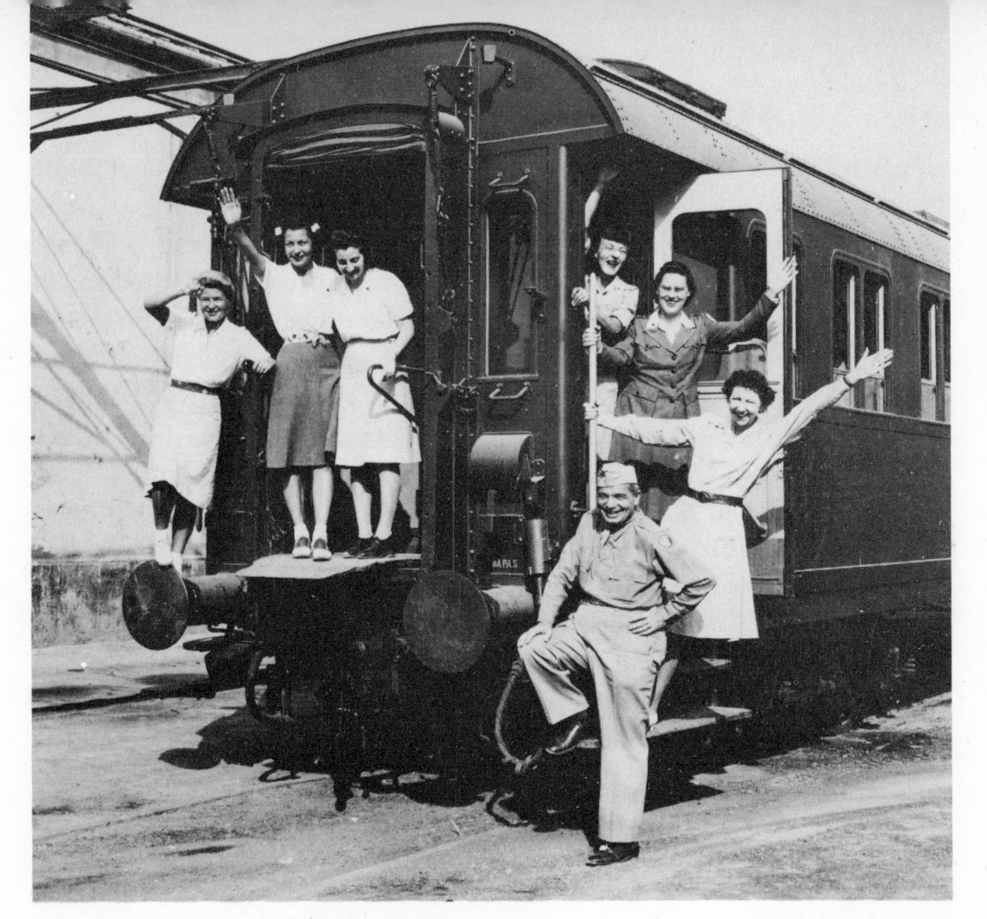

Dedication of the "Yankee Dipper," Naples, 1944.

The Yankee Dipper was indeed a welcome sight to the M.R.S. men when it arrived, and it operated extensively and continuously throughout the entire campaign in Italy.

General Eisenhower left the command in the Mediterranean to become General of the Army and to assume duties as Allied Commander in Europe. He was succeeded in the Mediterranean Theater by General Sir Henry Maitland Wilson, who assumed command of AFHQ 8 January 1944. General Eisenhower went to London to direct preparations for the invasion across the Channel.

Lieutenant General Jacob L. Devers became Deputy Commander, AFHQ, and succeeded General Eisenhower as Commanding General of the North African Theater (NATOUSA). He remained at that post until 22 October 1944, when his headquarters became Headquarters, Sixth Army

Group in France. He was succeeded by Lieutenant General Joseph T. McNarney as Commanding General, NATOUSA.

The North African Theater was redesignated Mediterranean Theater of Operations, United States Army (MTOUSA), 1 November 1944, continuing under General McNarney. About the same time General Sir Henry Maitland Wilson went to Washington as a member of the Allied joint Chiefs of Staff to be succeeded as Commander in Chief of AFHQ by Field Marshal Sir Harold R. L. G. Alexander. Lieutenant General Mark W. Clark (later General) succeeded to the command of the Fifteenth Army Group; Lieutenant General Lucian K. Truscott took command of the Fifth United States Army, and Lieutenant General Sir Oliver W. H. Leese succeeded in command of the British Eighth Army; Field Marshal Sir Bernard L. Montgomery, who had commanded the British Eighth Army, accompanied General Eisenhower to England to command all ground forces.

While all of these changes were taking place and even before many of them were more than in the rumor stage, General C. P. Gross, Chief of Transportation, War Department, Washington, visited the theater to view operations and observe firsthand how things were being done and what he and his office could do to assist.

One of the problems which had to be solved was the establishment of a second Headquarters, M.R.S., to command the M.R.S. troops in the cross-Channel operations.

Because of experience gained by his being the first M.R.S. officer ashore in North Africa, his excellent direction in North Africa, Sicily, and Italy, as well as his all-around railroad capacity, the Director General recommended as the General Manager for the Headquarters, Second M.R.S., Colonel C. L. Burpee, General Superintendent of the 703 R.G.D. This was acceptable, and Colonel Burpee left Italy for New Orleans to organize and command the Headquarters, Second M.R.S. He was succeeded in command of the 703 R.G.D. by Lieutenant Colonel (later Colonel) L. E. Covin of the 703 R.G.D., who commanded it for the balance of the war.

On 17 November 1943 Colonel Chester K. Harding left the M.R.S. and was succeeded by Colonel James K. Tully. Colonel Harding was Executive Officer of Headquarters, M.R.S., and was appointed Allied Military Governor of the Island of Sardinia.

Colonel Tully was a classmate of Generals Clark, Collins, and Ridgway in that rather famous class of 1917. He had resigned from the Army after World War I and had been with The Pullman Company continuously from that time. He made an ideal Executive Officer in Headquarters, M.R.S., because of his familiarity with Army regulations and procedures, his personal friendship with the highest ranking officers in the theater, and his some twenty years' experience in the Operating Department of The Pullman Company.

Because Major S. R. Truesdell, Adjutant, Headquarters, M.R.S., was returned to the United States to command the 706 R.G.D. being formed there, Major Stanley R. Beggs, who had done such a remarkable job in connection with the handling of the fiscal account of the M.R.S. in North Africa, was appointed Adjutant, Headquarters, M.R.S., 17 January 1944. He held this position until he became Adjutant of General Headquarters, M.R.S., when it was formed in France.

Even with the sponsorship by various railroads of additional units of the M.R.S. training in America, there were not enough experienced officers to go around. As a result, the Director General was asked to nominate officers for transfer back to the United States for promotion and assignment to higher positions in the units then being formed. The following named men were nominated and left on 10 January 1944, for reassignment and promotions: Captains R. D. McGee, E. F. Oviatt, C. Patterson, J. H. Ritter, and R. A. Sharood; First Lieutenants W. E. Cobble, S. S. Gillespie, L. B. Griffin, L. W. Howard, F. S. Howie, H. E. Linningston, J. H. Morris, C. J. Strieff, W. J. Winfree, and V. O. Zimmerman; Second Lieutenants J. B. Deakyne, J. R. Graham, M. D. Kelly, and R. J. Laurent.

To take their places, the Director General was given authority to promote experienced and efficient non-commissioned officers. On 12 January the following non-commissioned officers were commissioned Second Lieutenants in the M.R.S.: A. W. Arnall, D. C. Beach, R. H. Bryant, G. M. deLambert, R. J. Flannagan, R. D. Frye, H. W. Johnson, H. E. Latham, H. R. Lawrence, W. Luscaleet, R. B. Mann, L. C. McCarty, C. H. McConnell, L. R. Mills, T. C. Netherton, C. E. Quist, J. W. Shannon, T. E. Troxler and L. E. Ward. A total of 44 M.R.S. enlisted men eventually received direct commissions in the field.

Changes in command also affected the British Transportation Service in Italy. The Deputy Director General, M.R.S., Brigadier R. F. O'D. Gage, Director of Transportation, was relieved in order that he might command the British Transportation troops of the 21st Army Group in the invasion across the Channel. He was ordered out and departed on 23 February 1944, and was temporarily succeeded by Colonel E. L. Parkes until the arrival of Brigadier R. D. Waghorn, who reported on 23 March 1944.

The 715 R.O.B. under Lieutenant Colonel T. P. Crymes was relieved in North Africa and arrived at Naples on 8 January 1944. Its first assignment with headquarters at Benevento, Italy, was the territory between Caserta and Foggia, including the operation of the Caserta Yard.

One of the greatest helps in connection with fuel and lack of steam motive power in good serviceable condition was the rapid rehabilitation of electric lines. On 16 January the first rehabilitation was completed between Salerno and Cava. By 16 March the electric line, Benevento to Foggia, was in working order also.

As of 22 January 1944, the battle line was at Formia, Italy, on the west coast, and ran directly across Italy to a point just south of Pescara on the east coast. The railhead facilities had definitely caught up with both the Fifth and Eighth Armies, and pending the next big forward move of these two armies, the rail lines were generally in reasonably good condition to give maximum service to both.

The 2682 Base Depot Company (Provisional), commanded by Captain Herbert R. Phillips, arrived at Naples on 20 February 1944, and was assigned to the 703 R.G.D. at Naples. Later, on 21 May 1944, it became the 788 Base Depot Company.

The Headquarters, 701 R.G.D., commanded by Colonel J. E. Guilfoyle, was relieved in North Africa and arrived at Naples on 29 February 1944. Headquarters were immediately established in the Hotel Cavour, located at Piazza Garibaldi, Naples, Italy. Limits of its jurisdiction were the Naples Terminal, and Naples to Sant' Eufemia, Lamezia, Paola to Castiglione to Cosenza and Battipaglia to Potenza. The 719 R.O.B. (less Company "A"), 727 R.O.B. (less Company "A"), and 759 R.O.B. (Company "A" only) were assigned to that grand division as well as the 2682 Base Depot Company.

Anti-aircraft fire, Naples, March, 1944.

The 719 R.O.B., commanded by Lieutenant Colonel R. F. Williams, was relieved in North Africa and arrived in Italy on 6 March 1944. It was given jurisdiction of operations between San Giovanni Barra and (but not including) Potenza; Nocera Inferiore and Avellino; Nocera Inferiore and (but not including) Cancello; Sicignano and Lagonegro; Battipaglia via Sant' Eufemia Marina and Reggio di Calabria and (but not including) Metaponto.

The 753 R.S.B., commanded by Lieutenant Colonel John J. Daugherty, was relieved in North Africa and arrived at Naples on 7 March 1944. It continued as an integral part of the 703 R.G.D. It took up assignment for the repair of locomotives and cars and the erection of American cars in the Pattison and Bufola shops of the I.S.R. at Naples.

With the introduction of American steam motive power in Italy, an interesting situation resulted at Naples, where there were two adjacent roundhouses with a large back shop in the immediate vicinity.

Both Italian and American power was being used. Experience showed that the American M.R.S. personnel were more familiar with the maintenance and repair of their own American power, and such was the case with the Italians as concerned the Italian power. Therefore, in the interest of efficiency and productiveness, it was decided that the Americans would take over one of the roundhouses exclusively for the running repairs of American power. The Italians would take over, under American supervision, the other roundhouse for the running repairs of Italian power. This arrangement worked out extremely well, eliminating the usual complications arising from the difference in languages when mixed personnel work on the same job; different shop practices and methods; and a myriad other minor, yet plaguing, differences.

The adjacent back shops, occupied by the 753 R.S.B., had been almost entirely stripped of heavy machinery by the Germans and the building itself suffered material damage because of bombing activity. Within forty days after moving in, the M.R.S. was making heavy or classified repairs to Italian locomotives. This is more remarkable when taking into consideration the repair and rebuilding necessary to the buildings themselves and installing and preparing for operation the various light and heavy back-shop machinery. To rather complicate and hinder even this progress there were several bombing raids by the enemy. The shop on one of these occasions received two direct hits.

The small amount of available coal in Italy was not good. In the interest of economy and efficiency a program was inaugurated to convert all United States steam locomotives and a certain type of Italian locomotive from coal burning to oil burning. Simplicity of design and installation and operation were the prime requisites in this conversion.

While the conversion of all United States power was performed by American M.R.S. personnel, on some of the Italian locomotives so converted the work was done entirely by I.S.R. shopmen, under direct and close supervision of competent American mechanical officers. This gave satisfactory production. They maintained and at times even exceeded the set schedule. The type of Italian locomotive selected was a 2-8-0 "Class 735" consolidation type of locomotive, American built, which had been sent over and used in Italy during World War I. These locomotives had been in almost continuous service since that time and, in service, proved to be the most efficient steam power found on the Italian railroads.

An unusual incident occurred during this conversion from coal to oil burning. A boiler-maker in the 715 R.O.B. was just finishing a job of converting a locomotive. His gaze happened to fall on the engine number—2737. "That's funny," he thought, "that number seems awfully familiar. Wonder where I could have seen it before?"

Then his memory caught up. He had seen a picture of that same locomotive in a story in the magazine, *Railway Age*. It was the 70,000th locomotive constructed by the Baldwin Locomotive Company in Philadelphia.

This fact was called to the attention of Lieutenant Colonel T. P. Crymes, Commanding Officer of the 715 R.O.B., who thought the Baldwin President, Mr. Ralph Kelly, might be interested in knowing where his 70,000th locomotive was and what it was doing. He wrote to Mr. Kelly:

"I thought it of interest to you to know that this engine now performs a highly important service for the Army. It is one of the large pool of similar locomotives being used in Italy in a mission of transporting troops, matériel, and supplies from ports of debarkation to final destination. American steam locomotives have proven the most dependable and satisfactory of all types of power in use. Up to the present time they have been manned exclusively by American railway soldiers, who take real pride in the operation.

"Due to the difficulty in securing coal we are converting all U.S.A. engines to oil. This is done by American shop forces located in several terminal points. Conversion has been completed on a large number of locomotives and has proven entirely satisfactory. Your 70,000th was just converted. It might also be of interest to know that only seventy-two hours elapse from the time the engine enters the shop as a coal burner and it is again in service as an oil burner."

In line with the policy of AFHQ and the capacity of the Italians to do it, the Director General turned back as fast as possible rails south of Bari and Naples to I.S.R. operation under M.R.S. direction. On 29 March the British were ordered to turn back the Bari Compartimento to Signor Fransi, the former director of that sector of the I.S.R. On 7 July the Reggio di Calabria Line was turned back to the Italians.

General Mark W. Clark was at all times complimentary concerning the great service rendered by the M.R.S. in supplying his Army. In a surprise ceremony on the night of 14 April 1944 he caused Brigadier General Laurence B. Keiser, his Deputy Chief of Staff, to make presentation of the Fifth Army Plaque to the Allied Forces M.R.S. for excellence in discipline, performance, and merit for the years 1943 and 1944, with the following citation:

"ALLIED FORCE MILITARY RAILWAY SERVICE is awarded the Fifth Army Plaque and Clasp for meritorious service 1943-1944. During the early days of the Fifth Army's Campaign in Italy, this organization reconstructed inoperative railroads which were able to carry substantial tonnages. In subsequent stages of the Italian Campaign they have enabled freight and hospital trains to come within close proximity of the front lines. The services performed by the Allied Force Military Railway Service have contributed materially to the military operation of the Fifth Army." It is understood that this presentation was the only one made by General Clark to a unit not an assigned part of the Fifth Army.

There were constant air raids by the Germans over the elements of the American Fifth Army and the British Eighth Army, with particular emphasis laid to bombing the great port of Naples. While well protected with anti-aircraft batteries, numerous bombs fell on vital points causing damage to railroad facilities and stores. On 24 April, in one of these raids, nine men of the 753 R.S.B. were injured.

One of the most distinguished visitors to familiarize himself with the operations of the M.R.S. in Italy was His Royal Highness Umberto, Prince of Piedmont, Lieutenant General of the Realm. He evidenced such an interest in the operations of the railroads that he was invited to come to headquarters and see what "made the wheels go round." He picked 13 May 1944 as the day and remained more than four hours visiting and talking with every officer and enlisted man of the Headquarters, M.R.S. He was profoundly interested in the Engineering Department and its map reproduction plant with which it did so much. Afterward he bestowed the Order of the Crown of Italy on many of the officers of Headquarters.

Possibly one of the most difficult decisions that General Clark had to make was in connection with Cassino. On the top of this mountain was a monastery. The height of the mountain was very advantageous for the Ger-

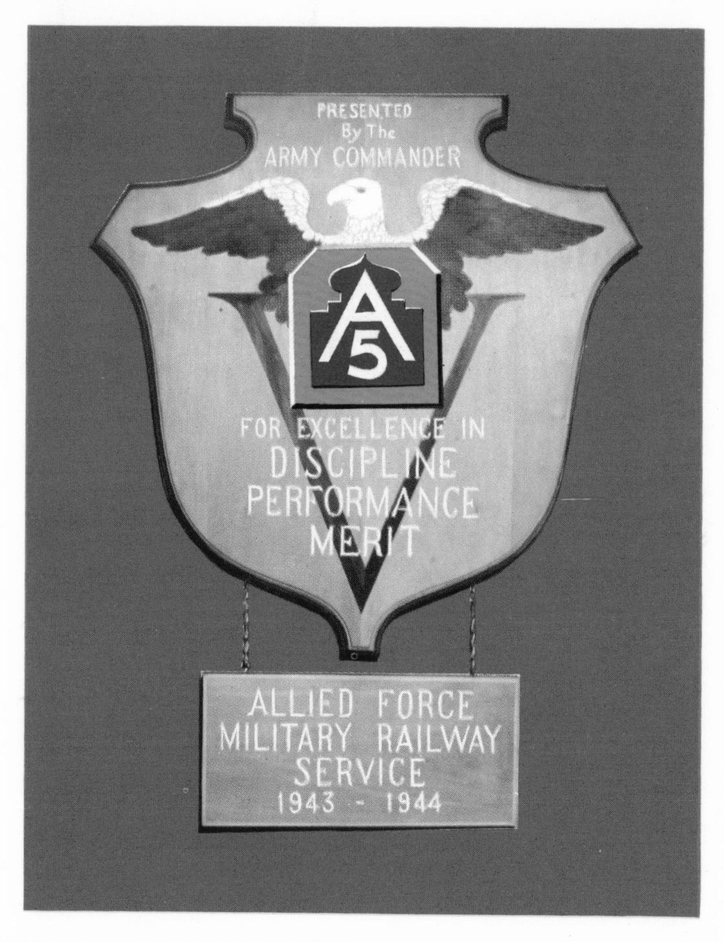

FIFTH ARMY PLAQUE PRESENTED BY GENERAL CLARK, 1944

His Royal Highness, Umberto, visits M.R.S. Headquarters and listens to Colonel B. H. Crosland's plans for rehabilitation.

mans to observe and direct fire and even carry on fire on the advancing Fifth Army. They totally disregarded the spiritual significance of the location.

The Americans were loath to bombard the monastery or any other religious or ancient historical landmark, but finally Cassino was captured and fell on 18 May 1944.

The Fifth Army captured and entered Rome on 4 June 1944. The battle line as of 6 June 1944 extended in a rather curved fashion from a point on the west coast of Italy just north of Rome in a northeasterly direction, and then over a southeasterly course to a point just south of Pescara.

The 761 Transportation Company, commanded by Captain Lloyd E. Hatley, was relieved from switching operations in Oran, Algiers, and arrived in Naples on 22 June. It was immediately placed in charge of switching in the yards and on the docks of Naples.

Diesel electric operation, Italy, July, 1944.

With the capture of Rome and new lines available for rehabilitation and use, the 701 R.G.D. had its jurisdiction extended northward from Caserta on Line 90 to end of track. The Germans had used a scarifier on this double-track railroad with tragic effect, as well as blowing most of the bridges, including the Volturno River Bridge. The position of the battle line up to approximately the end of May had placed all of Line 90 up to Isoletta in our hands and work of rehabilitation had gone on rapidly.

When the Director General went to Rome on 13 June there was only the bridge over the Liri River at Isoletta unfinished on Line 90. This bridge was 140 feet long and 60 feet above the stream. The work of rehabilitation was done by the 161 Railway Construction Company (British). Work was begun on 9 June and the first train was a train of coal for Rome which passed over at 0812 on 2 July 1944.

During his trip to Rome on 13 June, the Director General indicated to General H. H. Johnson, commanding in Rome, that according to the best estimate, Line 90 from Caserta to Rome, with only one large bridge still to be repaired, could be rehabilitated and trains run so that the first train appropriately could be run into Rome on the Fourth of July. The Director General proposed to do that, and the first train was to consist of 40 carloads of coal. The people of Rome had not seen coal in months and it was intended to deliver the coal to Major General E. E. Hume of the Allied Military Government. The piazza in front of the Victor Emmanuel World War I Memorial was an ideal place to hold a regular old-time American Fourth of July celebration, and in addition celebrate the arrival of the first train into Rome.

General Johnson agreed to do that, and without telling anyone what their plans were, preparations for the event went on secretly.

On 26 June the Director General got a call from General J. L. Devers from his headquarters at Caserta, indicating that he would like to see the Director General as soon as possible. When he reached there, the Director General was greeted with one of the most interesting questions propounded to him during the war: "Can you handle the Secretary of War from Naples to Rome—all rail?" The Director General asked when, and was told 4 July. The reply was made instantly: "Yes, sir!" The Director General then advised General Devers of the plans that he and General Johnson had made and said that the only change in the plans would be that the Secretary of War would deliver the coal to the people of Rome.

It is satisfying to record that, with consultation of staff, a schedule for a three-car Diesel electric train which the Director General had prepared for his inspection trips, with cars 9, 99, and 999, was set up to leave Garibaldi Station at Naples at 0835 on 4 July 1944 and arrive at the Rome terminal at 1600 hours, with a forty-five minute stop at Cassino in order that the Secretary might be taken in a jeep to the top of the mountain and back.

The plan was carried out. The trainload of coal actually proceeded to the outer yards of Rome at about 10 A.M., 2 July, as the bridge at Isoletta was finished at 0811 that morning. The Director General then left from Rome at 0004 on 3 July, reached Garibaldi at Naples at 0650 hours, and completed final arrangements for the trip of the Secretary of War the next day.

The trip on 4 July was made without incident. The Secretary of War was able to see to the best advantage the terrible destruction wrought by the

Secretary Stimson and Generals M. W. Clark, and C. R. Gray, Jr., inspecting the Scarifier on arrival at Rome, July 4, 1944.

Rome passenger terminal.

General Gray, Engineer, General di Raimondo, Fireman. First train into Rome, July 4, 1944.

retreating Germans and the effect of our air and artillery fire. The train reached the interlocking plant at the entrance to the Rome Terminal at 1555 hours, pulled up alongside the already parked 40 carloads of coal, and at 1557, with the Director General as engineer and General di Raimondo as fireman on the Diesel of the coal train, they pulled down parallel tracks simultaneously and stopped shy of the bumping posts at 1559/50, ten seconds ahead of time.

On the tracks at the station there was mounted on a flatcar one of the scarifiers which was used in the plowing and breaking of ties in the destruction of the railroads by the Germans, of which the Secretary had seen many miles in his trip that day. Escorted by Generals Clark, Johnson, and the Director General, the Secretary inspected the scarifier and the then-uncompleted and undamaged massive Rome Main Railroad Terminal.

At 2359 on 8 July 1944 the 704 R.G.D., commanded by Colonel A. W. Campbell, closed its headquarters and moved to Italy with temporary headquarters at Naples and general jurisdiction over the 715 R.O.B. and the line from Naples north to Rome as far as it was then opened. The last elements of this railway grand division arrived in Italy on 9 July 1944. Rome had been captured on 3 June 1944, and on 16 July 1944 the 704 R.G.D. moved with its headquarters to Rome and took over jurisdiction of the Rome Terminal, Line 50, from the North Yard Limit Board at Rome to the end of track and Line 263 from Civitavecchia Marino to Civitavecchia. Its component parts were the 727 R.O.B. with the "A" Companies of the 713, 715, 719, and 759 R.O.B. attached.

The 759 R.O.B., commanded by Lieutenant Colonel E. M. Price, was relieved from duty in North Africa and arrived in Naples on 15 July 1944. It was placed in the 703 R.G.D. and had jurisdiction over the operation of the Tiburtina and Rome Terminal Yards.

With the arrival of the 759 R.O.B., all M.R.S. units that were in North Africa and Sicily in previous campaigns had arrived in Italy. On 17 July 1944 General Orders No. 38, issued by Headquarters, M.R.S., became effective and placed all the units as follows:

The 701 R.G.D., with headquarters at Naples, had the 715 R.O.B. (Rome), 719 R.O.B. (Naples), 761 R.T.C. (Naples), and the 788 Base Depot Company (Naples) as its component parts. It had under its jurisdiction the Naples Terminal, Line 89, from Naples to Rome, Line 90 from Naples to Rome, Line 91 from Aversa to Cervaro, Line 94 from Naples to Potenza, Line 283 from Cancello to Codola, Line 284 from Codola to Nocera, Line 287 from Campi Flegrei to Villa Literno, Line 290 from Sparanise to Minturno, and Line 265 from Nettuno through Campo Leone to Ciampino.

The 703 R.G.D., with headquarters at Rome, had the 713 R.O.B. (Rome) and the 759 R.O.B. (Rome) as its component parts. It had jurisdiction over Line 65 north from Rome to the end of track.

The 704 R.G.D., with headquarters at Rome, supervised the 727 R.O.B., also with headquarters at Rome. It had under its jurisdiction the Rome Terminal, Line 50, north from Rome to the end of track, and Line 263 Civitavecchia Marino to Civitavecchia.

The 753 R.S.B. (Naples) and the 760 R.S.B.D. (Bagnoli), as well as the 794 Military Police Battalion (Rome), were under the direct jurisdiction of Headquarters, M.R.S.

While there were still divisions, corps, and operation in North Africa,

Destroyed bridge, south of Leghorn on coast route.

Railroad yards after U.S. air bombardment at Brenner Pass.

Destroyed railroad yard, Florence, Italy.

Ostiense Yard, Rome.

the need of all possible troops of the M.R.S., equipment, and stores from North Africa in Italy was imperative. In keeping with the general policy of AFHQ to move its own headquarters to Italy, by General Orders No. 18, dated 8 July 1944, the Director General was relieved of all responsibility for railroad operation in North Africa.

British Transportation units now in Italy consisted of a Director of Transportation and his headquarters, one Railway Operating Group Headquarters, two Railway Operating Companies, and one Railway Workshop Company, two Railway Construction and Maintenance Group Headquarters, one of which came from North Africa and the other from the Middle East, five Railway Construction Companies, one Mechanical Equipment Company, one Railway Survey Company, and two Railway Bridging Sections. In November 1943 the Railway Construction Group of South African Engineer Corps arrived in Italy. It was composed of a group headquarters and three companies. A South African Tunnelling Group, consisting of a Headquarters and two Tunnelling Companies, arrived in March and was assigned to the South African Construction Group. In September 1944 an Indian Railway Construction and Maintenance Group Headquarters arrived. Three Railway Construction Companies followed. There were two British Railway Telegraph Companies, and a third South African Railway Telegraph Company.

These British troops rehabilitated and operated the railroads in the heel and up the east coast of Italy in support of the British Eighth Army.

The next phase of the Italian Campaign can be called the northern sweep of the Fifteenth Army Group, the American Fifth Army on the left flank and the British Eighth Army on the right flank. This was from the capture of Rome on 3 June until the fall of Pisa to the Americans on 2 September, while the British and their Allies broke through the Gothic Line the same day in the vicinity of Pesaro and tore a gap in the line 20 miles wide. The Gothic Line, generally speaking, was 150 miles in length, reaching from the west coast of Italy just north of Leghorn and Pisa to the north of Pesaro and the Foglia River on the east coast of Italy. It protected the cities of Milan, Turin, Bologna, La Spezia, Genoa, and Pola, and was as near impregnable as German ingenuity could devise and construct.

North of Rome there are in reality only three north-and-south lines of railroad. Line 50 along the west coast, a continuance of Line 89, runs north

Bombs removed from Vivola Tunnel placed for demolition, Italy.

through Leghorn, Pisa, and then northwest to Genoa. Line 65 runs due north and south from Rome to Florence and Bologna and as Line 69 runs on north through Verona to the Brenner Pass. Line 86 runs along the east shore of Italy along the Adriatic Sea from Foggia and Ancona and then runs northwesterly to Bologna. There is another important line between Orte and Ancona, Line 87, which has a connection at Terni with the line between Rome and Pescara. Then there is a connection across from Chiusi to Montepescali on Line 50, with a north-and-south line connecting with the Pisa-Florence line.

So, north of Rome, the three main lines of railroad are Lines 50, 65, and 86, but there were several secondary lines also that were used for the rail support of the Fifteenth Army Group. One line, No. 65, was found to have extremely heavy bridge damage, particularly in the fifteen-mile portion between Arezzo and Montevarchi; in this stretch there were 25 destroyed bridges. With one exception all were brick or masonry arches. There were three major viaducts which were completely destroyed to the ground level and included one 525 feet long and 75 feet high built on a curve; one

800 feet long and 105 feet high and on a ten-degree curve. Another was 480 feet long and 70 feet high. In that short distance there were also seven tunnels all of which were blown at the portals.

With the shift northward the port of Civitavecchia was opened and became the port through which the food supply for Rome and the territory north thereof was received. This saved the port of Naples and the rail haul from Naples to Rome of this tremendous tonnage.

By the spring of 1944 virtually everything south of Rome had reverted to Phase II and III form of operations by the Italians. It was fortunate that this condition existed, for the M.R.S. in Italy was called upon to furnish troops and rail logistical support to NATOUSA's planned invasion of southern France at Marseille, which invasion was made 15 August 1944. It was

Po River bridge between Bologna and Verona, Italy, built by A Company, 715 and 719 R.O.B. and the 175 British BNCN, 1565 feet long, work completed in 43 days.

necessary to rearrange the M.R.S. units in Italy in order to provide troops for the southern France invasion.

In the planning with General J. L. Devers and his headquarters, the Director General indicated that it was necessary to retain a Headquarters, R.G.D., two R.O.B., and two R.S.B. in Italy. The planning then included the 701 R.G.D. to consist of the 715 and 719 R.O.B. For the first time the 753 R.S.B. was taken from the 703 R.G.D. supervision and placed under the 701 R.G.D., as well as the 760 R.S.B.D. These were the permanent troops to remain in Italy. The Headquarters, 703 R.G.D. and the 704 R.G.D., the 713, 727, and 759 R.O.B., and the 761 R.T.C. were nominated to support the invasion of southern France. Headquarters, M.R.S., was likewise to go on to France.

It became necessary to form a supervising headquarters; consequently, Colonel A. W. Campbell, Commanding Officer of the 704 R.G.D., was named Director, Military Railways-Italy, and Lieutenant Colonel John M. Budd was appointed Commanding Officer of the 704 R.G.D. Colonel Campbell remained in this capacity until the arrival of the 774 R.G.D. from the United States. This unit took over the supervisory control of the M.R.S. It contained more officers and men than were in a R.G.D. because of its increased responsibilities. This railway grand division was under the command of Lieutenant Colonel (later Colonel) William P. Wilson, and Colonel Campbell then returned to take command of the 704 R.G.D., as it moved to France.

The Director of British Transportation was a Brigadier, while the General Superintendent of the 774 R.G.D. was a Colonel; therefore, Brigadier R. D. Waghorn, who had succeeded Brigadier Gage, became the Director, M.R.S.-Italy, and Colonel Wilson was appointed Deputy to Director, M.R.S.-Italy. The British then assumed direction of both the British Transportation Service supporting the Eighth Army and the American M.R.S. supporting the Fifth Army, both in the Fifteenth Army Group.

Because of the quantity of stores, particularly Roth Waagner bridging that had been captured in Italy, and other railroad stores that had been transferred from North Africa to Italy, it was possible to move large quantities of railroad stores to Marseille shortly after the successful capture of that port.

The spring offensive of 1945, which resulted in final victory, began 16

April, and by 27 April the Germans had been driven north of Verona to Milan. On 3 May the remaining German and Fascist forces in Italy unconditionally surrendered and the war in Italy was over.

The railroad situation north of Bologna is not unlike that north of Rome. Line 50 extends northwesterly to Genoa along the Mediterranean coast. Line 59 extends on northward from Bologna through Verona as Line 53 and on to the Brenner Pass, and Line 86 from Ancona comes into Bologna and extends northwesterly through Piacenza to Milan and eastward to Turin.

Much of the terrain was such that even trucks could not be used because of the mountainous grades. Mules in pack trains and even our own soldiers had to carry supplies from the railheads to the troops. At this time Headquarters, 701 R.G.D., with its two units, the 715 and 719 R.O.B., was operating in Phase 1 operations over Lines 50 and 59 north of Rome.

During this same period the British Transportation Service, which had its railhead at Ancona for a long period, continued to develop Line 86 from Ancona to Bologna as the battle progressed, and in mid-November of 1944 took over the operation of the line from Orte to Arezzo.

The Po River was crossed at Revere, Italy, on Line 69 during this final drive. A bridge of M.R.S. design such as had been the first bridge across the Rhine River at Wesel was built in forty-eight days, and completed on 8 July 1945. The troops that built this bridge were the Engineering Section of Headquarters, M.R.S.-Italy, Engineering Section of the 701 R.G.D., 1st Battalion, 175 Engineers General Service Unit, "A" Companies of the 715 and 719 R.O.B., detachments of the 3483 and 3491 Quartermaster Truck Company, and the 9 and 23 Companies of Italian Railway Engineers.

The United States Army troops put in 123,439 man-hours of labor, the Italians 22,128, and the equipment hours were 23,259. The bridge was 1,527 feet in 29 spans, consisting of eight 40-foot sectional girders, four 75 and 80 U.C.R.B., seven 41-, and six 45-meter beam spans. There were 526 tons of steel in the superstructure.

The opening of this bridge made possible the connection of Brenner with all major points south, and in the first thirty days following completion a total of 525 trains passed over this bridge. The total included 382 trains carrying 248,603 gross tons of military freight, 19 refugee trains with over 26,000 refugees, 95 troop trains, and 29 prisoner-of-war trains.

Destroyed bridge, Cecina, Italy.

Bridge over the Fioria River north of Montalto di Castro, Italy.

During the campaign in Italy, 49 Diesel electric locomotives were transferred from the Middle East, 49 steam and Diesel locomotives from North Africa and Sicily. There was received up to the end of the war 114 locomotives and 225 cars from the United States. If it had not been for the prompt arrival of this American equipment it would have been impossible to have supplied either the American Fifth Army or the British Eighth Army in their campaigns in Italy. Tremendous stores were received in Italy and mostly through the Port of Naples from an American standpoint. As lines were rehabilitated and placed in service, the tonnage handled in support of the Fifth Army increased tremendously.

Tonnage moved out of the Port of Naples for the month of January 1944 was 137,108 tons. The peak of the tonnage moved was in April 1944, when 209,522 tons were moved northward from Naples. From January to and including September 1944 there was moved out of the Port of Naples 1,229,105 tons, an average of 136,567 tons per month. This was accomplished in 84,089 carloads.

There was an average of some 250 military trains operated daily, averaging some 10 million gross ton miles per day in addition to the civilian passenger and freight train service, and not including operations in the Calabria section which Phase III operation made effective in May 1944. With the improvement in port facilities, additional power and equipment, and notwithstanding lengthening of the lines of communication, M.R.S. was able to offer the armies 15,000 net tons port clearance per day from the west coast ports, 10,000 net tons port clearance per day from east coast ports, 8,000 net tons road haul to the Army on the east, and 7,500 net tons road haul to the armies on the west coast from Naples to Rome and north. In addition they were able to offer some 4,000 net tons per day cross-country movement, there being some 3,000 miles of main track in operation under M.R.S. supervision during the peak.

Within the 10 months' period November 1943 to September 1944 there were allocations made through the movements section for some 650,000 Allied troops, quite a number of which moved the entire length of the railroad from "toe and heel" points to Rome and north. During this same period in excess of 60,000 sick and wounded were handled in 10 hospital trains, approximately 75,000 refugees were evacuated from various forward sectors to points in southern Italy and Sicily, and some 30,000 prisoners of war were moved. There was also heavy movement of pack horses and mules, some 18,000 to supplement the supply transport problem of the Army in the very difficult mountainous terrain.

Throughout the campaign M.R.S. was called upon on various occasions, particularly preceding and in preparation for the Allied drives beginning 11 May 1944, to move within a short time divisions or major units from the east to the west coast and to the front, including tanks, tank destroyers, gun carriers, and other armored force vehicles. During the ten months' period, some 5,000 tanks of the Sherman and Churchill classes and in excess of 2,000 guns, half tracks, tank destroyers, ducks, and other mechanized implements of war were transported by rail. These movements necessitated special types of equipment which were arranged for by Headquarters, M.R.S.

With the surrender of the Germans and Fascists in Italy, World War II was not over. Immediately began a reassignment, realignment, replacement, and withdrawal of troops and supplies anticipating their use in the still active war with Japan in the Pacific. The atom bomb was dropped and Japan surrendered. World War II officially ended. There was need however, for assistance in Italy and help in the rehabilitation and reconstruction of the crippled railroads.

The 774 R.G.D. was not discontinued until 30 June 1946 by General Orders No. 33, Headquarters, MTOUSA. The 6603 Railway Supervisory Group was formed from the personnel thereof effective 1 July 1946. General Orders No. 56, Headquarters MTOUSA, redesignated the 6603 Railway Supervisory Group as the 7107 Railway Supervisory Group on 12 October 1946, and it was inactivated and went home on 4 November 1947.

The Headquarters, 701 R.G.D., was relieved and left for home on 25 September 1945. Its component parts, the 715 R.O.B., left 7 August 1945, the 719 R.O.B. left 19 August 1945, the 753 R.S.B. was sent to the Philippine Islands, the 760 R.S.B.D. was inactivated in the Mediterranean Theater 5 October 1945, and personnel returned to the United States individually.

7

Operations in Northern France and Belgium

1944

THE PLANNING and the build-up of troops and supplies in England, called BOLERO by code name, was set up in 1941 shortly after the declaration of war by Germany and Italy against the United States. The invasion of France was known as Operation OVERLORD.

The General Manager had activated his headquarters in St. Paul on 15 May 1942, and soon was asked for nominations of experienced railroad officers to be sent to England. He nominated, and there was ordered from his headquarters at once, Colonel Norman A. Ryan, Lieutenant Colonel Edward T. Barrett, and Major Herbert L. Thomas. In addition he was ordered to form an especially organized transportation company to be used in switching cars in American depots and to assist in operating railroads serving American stores depots in England.

The 761 Transportation Company, under the command of Captain Chris H. Anderson, was activated and mobilized at Camp Shelby, Mississippi, on 28 July 1942. Men were drawn from the M.R.S. units then in training; viz., the 713, 727 and 730 R.O.B. This Transportation Company arrived in Scotland on 5 September 1942, certified to handling under English Railroad Rules, and began the operation of the Melbourne Military Railway, as well as providing switching service in several depots then being established by the American forces.

Brigadier General Clarence L. Burpee, General Manager, Headquarters, Second Military Railway Service.

In the original planning of OVERLORD, the M.R.S. troop assignment contemplated a headquarters, M.R.S., five headquarters, R.G.D., twenty-one R.O.B., and seven R.S.B.

The first troops to arrive in England after the 761 R.T.C. were those of the 729 R.O.B. (The New York, New Haven and Hartford Railroad Company) commanded by Lieutenant Colonel W. S. Carr, who arrived there on 15 July 1943. The build-up continued until by D-Day the following additional M.R.S. troops were in England:

Headquarters, Second M.R.S., commanded by Brigadier General C. L. Burpee, arrived 27 February 1944.

Headquarters, 707 R.G.D. (Southern Railway Company), Lieutenant Colonel W. W. Greiner, arrived 22 December 1943.

Headquarters, 708 R.G.D. (The Baltimore and Ohio Railroad Company), Major Ralph D. Jensen, arrived 30 September 1943.

712 R.O.B. (Reading Company and The Central Railroad Company of New Jersey), Lieutenant Colonel F. R. Doud, arrived 16 April 1944.

717 R.O.B. (Pennsylvania Railroad) arrived 23 May 1944. (Not used as a battalion.)
720 R.O.B. (Chicago and North Western Railway), Lieutenant Colonel C. J. Freeman, arrived 29 January 1944.
728 R.O.B. (Louisville and Nashville Railroad Company), Lieutenant Colonel C. D. Love, arrived 29 December 1943.
755 R.S.B. (Norfolk and Western Railway), Lieutenant Colonel M. G. Stevens, arrived 12 December 1943.
756 R.S.B. (Pennsylvania Railroad), Lieutenant Colonel H. U. Bates, arrived 4 September 1943.
757 R.S.B. (Chicago, Milwaukee, St. Paul and Pacific Railroad), Lieutenant Colonel J. W. Moe, arrived 15 May 1944.
763 R.S.B. (The Delaware, Lackawanna and Western Railroad Company), Lieutenant Colonel James Purcell, arrived 15 May 1944.

As American M.R.S. units arrived in England, they were immediately put to work in preparation for D-Day and subsequent service on the Continent. The technical men received further training at technical schools; and during their training they assumed these responsibilities:

1. Supervision of American troop movements by rail over the United Kingdom railroads.
2. Supervision of rail switching services of all ports of embarkation and debarkation.
3. Actual operation of rail switching and civilian interchange service at all United States Army General and Sub-Supply Depots.
4. Actual operation of rail switching service at some sub-ports of debarkation and embarkation.
5. Supervision of the construction of storage yards for Transportation Corps railroad equipment awaiting movement to the Continent.
6. Actual construction of prefabricated boxcars, flatcars, and gondolas, which had been shipped to the United Kingdom for erection.
7. Maintenance of Transportation Corps Equipment, cars and locomotives in actual operation in the United Kingdom.
8. Supervision of the shipment of all United States troops and military supplies by rail to the ports of embarkation for movement to the Continent.
9. Assistance in the central control of rail movements from the Office

of the Chief of Transportation of the European Theater of Operations.

10. Shop work necessary on the steam and Diesel locomotives shipped from the United States to the United Kingdom to get them ready for operation on the Continent.

Generally speaking, the shop battalions, while in England, erected cars that had been received knocked down and stored there. They likewise assem-

Assembled and made-ready locomotives in England before being transported to France, March, 1944.

bled and placed in running condition the standard 2-8-0 consolidated locomotives as well as 0-8-0 switch locomotives (Diesel) and the 350, 650, and 1,000 horsepower Diesel locomotives, which had also been shipped there.

Great storage yards, the largest of which was at Hainault, were built and both locomotives and cars were stored in them preparatory to movement to ports of debarkation in southern England. This large storage yard at Hainault had been built as a new depot for the subway, and the British turned it over for the use of freight-car construction by the M.R.S.

A sub-depot was established at Morton-on-Lug to take care of overflow tonnage at such times as Hainault was choked. There were several other base depots scattered throughout England, and all depots were operated under the Chief of Transportation.

The main theme, of course, was preparation for invasion and movement to the Continent. To show the degree of preparedness: American steam locomotives had water placed in the boilers. Wood and paper were placed in the fireboxes ready for the match upon arrival on the Continent, and enough water was placed in the tenders to keep them moving.

All of the work in England, of course, necessitated the closest liaison between the American military transportation authorities, the British military transportation authorities, and civilian railroad management. This was accomplished through a British liaison officer placed at each of the depots so that proper timing and scheduling were perfected and carried out. The cooperation of the English was magnificent.

The Supreme Command for the forces covering the invasion of France was known as Supreme Headquarters, Allied Expeditionary Force, which, of course, was immediately called SHAEF. General Eisenhower, in command of this headquarters, continued the organizational plan that he had utilized in the Mediterranean, and so the Naval, Air, and Ground Chiefs occupied a double command status, being on his staff as well as being responsible for the execution of his part of the operations.

A difference, however, was that the M.R.S. did not report to SHAEF headquarters. The British Transport Service was under the Chief of British Transportation, Brigadier Rex F. O'Dowd Gage, who had been with the M.R.S. in North Africa and Italy. It supported the Twenty-first Army Group, which was Field Marshal Montgomery's command in the invasion on the

General Omar N. Bradley, Commanding Twelfth Army Group, France.

left flank. It consisted of the British Second Army under General Dempsey and the Canadian First Army under General Crerar. Brigadier General C. L. Burpee commanded the Headquarters, Second M.R.S., which was to supply the Twelfth Army Group under General Omar N. Bradley. At the time of the invasion it consisted of the First United States Army under General Hodge and the Third United States Army under General Patton.

SHAEF had a simply worded directive, but an unbelievably difficult one. General Eisenhower, in his book, *Crusade in Europe*, quotes its significant paragraph as: "You will enter the continent of Europe and, in conjunction with the other Allied Nations, undertake operations aimed at the heart of Germany and the destruction of her Armed Forces."

After long and greatly detailed planning conferences, changes, and alterations, the plan was finally complete. Men and equipment were ready, the ships were assembled, and D-Day was fixed as the morning of 6 June 1944. The places chosen as the landings for the Americans were known as

Lt. General John C. H. Lee, Commanding European Theater of Operations.

Omaha and Utah Beaches on the Bay of the Seine, east of the Cherbourg Peninsula, almost directly south of Portsmouth, England, the main point of debarkation. The British were to land on the three beaches immediately east of the Americans' left flank.

The line of communications to support the force was under the command of Lieutenant General John C. H. Lee and his command was known as ETOUSA. The M.R.S. came into the line of communications command through the Chief of Transportation, ETOUSA, Major General F. T. Ross. Brigadier General Burpee, General Manager, Second M.R.S., as had the General Manager, First M.R.S., in North Africa and Italy, exercised the command to carry out the operations of the M.R.S.

The policy of General Eisenhower as to who would do what in connection with the operation of railroads in the campaign was published as Administrative Memorandum No. 24, dated 18 July 1944, and was a continuation of his original NATOUSA program of three-phase operation. This

Major General Frank J. Ross,
Chief of Transportation,
ETOUSA.

was further clarified and accentuated by his Administrative Memorandum No. 28, dated 27 August 1944, in which he set up an Inter-Allied Railway Commission. The members of that commission were Brigadier General J. A. Appleton of the Pennsylvania Railroad (American), Brigadier W. T. Kelly (British), and General Bergess (French).

This is the quotation from Administrative Memorandum No. 28 which sets up this commission:

Constitution: An Inter-Allied Railway Commission will be set up forthwith with the United States, British and French representation. It will sit initially under the Chairmanship of the Director General of Military Railways, Supreme Headquarters, Allied Expeditionary Force, and at a later stage under a French representative.

Duties and Responsibilities: a. The Inter-Allied Railway Commission will be responsible for advising this headquarters and the French Provisional Government on all questions of policy affecting the railways of France. b. The Commission will be responsible for recommending dates for the progressive changes in the stages referred to in Adm. Memo 24, and designating the area to which these stages will apply.

Brigadier General J. A. Appleton, Chairman Inter-Allied Railway Commission.

The Commission will be responsible for the re-establishment of Commissions Regionales de Chemin de Fer and Sous-Commissions, with United States and British military representation as necessary, Commissaires Militaires and Commissaires Techniques. These Sous-Commissions will conform as far as possible to the old Arrondissements d'Exploitation.

Operation of the Railways. The British and United States authorities will be responsible for the operation of the railways during stages 1 and 2 as laid down in Adm. Memo 24, except insofar as this responsibility is delegated to the French authority. In stage 3, operation of the railways will be a French responsibility.

Centralized control of traffic, and, to a large extent, the distribution of supply depots were handled by the Inter-Allied Railway Commission under SHAEF. The operation and maintenance of railroads, however, were never consolidated in the European Theater as they had been in North Africa and Italy. Operations under SHAEF were divided, with the British Transportation Service reporting to the Commander in Chief of the British Twenty-first Army Group, and all M.R.S. in the American zones was operated first by the

Second M.R.S. supporting the Twelfth Army Group, and later the First M.R.S. supporting the Sixth Army Group in southern France in that invasion. After the two American Army Groups joined in eastern France, General Headquarters, M.R.S., was formed, and consolidated and coordinated all of the American railroad operations through the European Theater command.

Along the boundary between the Twenty-first Army Group and the Second M.R.S. great volunteer coordination and consolidation occurred. Possibly the most illustrative of this resulted from a conference held in Paris as between the Director General and Major General C. S. Napier, Chief, British MOV and Tn Branch, G-4 Division, SHAEF, when General Napier indicated the lack of a bridge within the British lines over the Rhine and desired to secure the Wesel Bridge. That, of course, was impossible, but an understanding was worked out as between the British and American M.R.S. by which the British operated, from their lines from the north and west bank of the Rhine, then across the Rhine River at Wesel, and then back to their

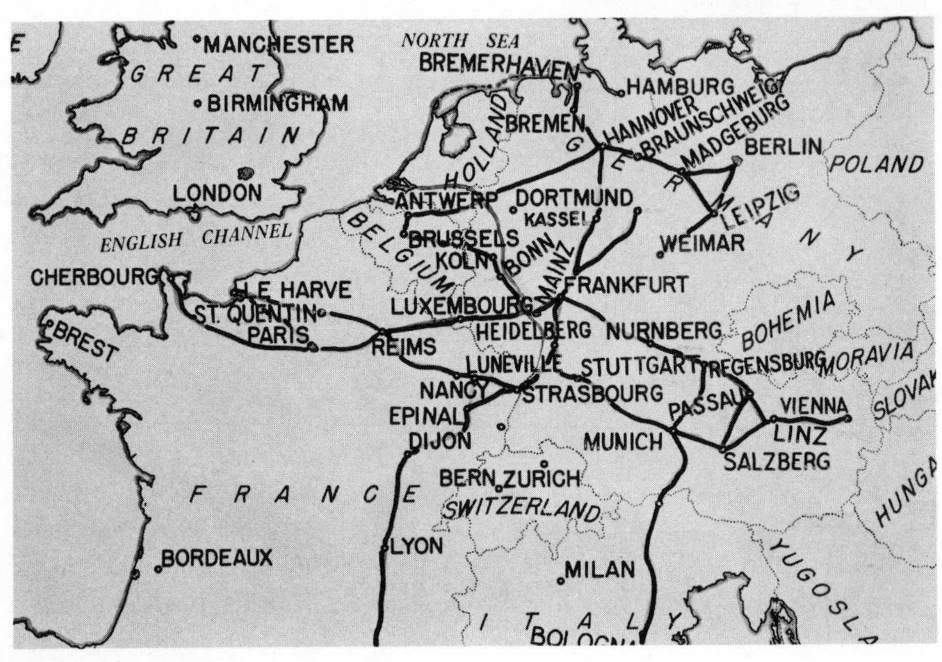

Main lines of railroad, Northern France.

own lines north on the east bank of the Rhine, three military freight trains each day in each direction.

This the Americans were able to work in notwithstanding the fact that American operations required an average of eighteen trains per day and, with the acceptance of six British trains, gave the British, in reality, 33 per cent of the train capacity of the bridge.

To provide for the unloading of troops and supplies and evacuation of wounded, there were also planned two types of protected anchorages familiarly known as "Gooseberry" and "Mulberry." These temporary dock facilities were provided with all the modern apparatus necessary for quick unloading of cargo. One "Mulberry" each was provided for the British Twenty-first Army Group and the American Twelfth Army Group, and five "Gooseberries" were divided between the two forces.

The contribution of the M.R.S. to this unusual type of port construction and operation was the plan and design of Colonel S. H. Bingham. LST 2 and LCT 4 ships were reconstructed and adapted for use as car ferries for the transportation of loaded railway cars, as well as engines, across the Channel. The high tide of 28 feet in the Channel made an essential part of this operation the design and construction of "breathing bridges" at the amphibious landing ramps at Cherbourg and Dieppe to enable running these cars directly off the landing craft and onto the railway tracks at shore installations regardless of the height of the tide.

By D-Day plus 25, four "breathing bridges" had been put down on the Normandy beach. Thirteen days later the converted LST's and LCT's started carrying locomotives and cars across the Channel, each ship carrying 22 cars. By mid-October 1,300 locomotives and 20,000 loaded cars had thus been delivered to the shores of France.

For the purposes of this narrative, the campaign in Europe may be considered to have four phases. The first phase was from the landing on Omaha and Utah Beaches on 6 June 1944, the capture of Saint-Lô, and the beginning of the drive eastward on or about 25 July 1944. The second phase begins about the 1st of October with a battle line off the Channel north of Antwerp and swinging eastward to include Aachen, then south to include Luxembourg, Metz, Dijon, and southeasterly to the Swiss border, a line facing the Siegfried Line of resistance of the Germans.

Coast Guard LST converted into car ferry handling loaded cars from England to France.

As of 1 March 1945 the battle swung over south of Holland to a line just west of the Rhine River, then through Strasbourg and Mulhouse to the Swiss border. At the time of the surrender, 8 May 1945, the battle line began at the southern boundary of Denmark and the North Sea, northwest of Hamburg and down the Elbe River, and found the Third United States Army driving on Pilsen, Linz, and Dresden, the First United States Army driving on Berlin, the Ninth United States Army driving through Dassel toward Berlin; the Seventh United States Army, with the First French Army on its right, was driving southeast and south through Austria toward the Italian border; the British Second Army was driving on Hamburg, and the Canadian First Army on Amsterdam.

Meanwhile, in Italy, the American Fifth Army was driving on Innsbruck and the British Eighth Army toward Trieste. The Fifteenth United States Army, which became operative in France 24 December 1944, was really in

Unloading American 2-8-0 locomotive at Cherbourg, France, August, 1944.

reserve, but had taken over the occupational area behind the First United States Army.

The operations and achievements of the M.R.S. in connection with this campaign will be phased in accordance with these time and place locations of the Allied Forces.

The M.R.S. followed the campaign troops in the invasion of western France very promptly. In the period from D-Day to the capture of Paris there had arrived from England and were in operation Headquarters, Second M.R.S., commanded by Brigadier General C. L. Burpee, which arrived on 8 July 1944, and three headquarters, R.G.D., viz.:

707 R.G.D. (Southern Railway Company), commanded by Lieutenant Colonel W. W. Greiner, arrived 25 July 1944;

706 R.G.D. (Pennsylvania Railroad), commanded by Colonel L. G. Jamison, arrived 16 August 1944;

708 R.G.D. (The Baltimore and Ohio Railroad Company), commanded by Colonel W. S. Carr, arrived 16 August 1944;

five R.O.B., and the sequence in which they arrived were:

729 R.O.B. (The New York, New Haven and Hartford Railroad Company), commanded by Lieutenant Colonel W. C. Smith, arrived 2 July 1944;
720 R.O.B. (Chicago and North Western Railway), commanded by Lieutenant Colonel C. J. Freeman, arrived 15 July 1944;
740 R.O.B. (The Chesapeake and Ohio Railroad Company), commanded by Lieutenant Colonel S. H. Pulliam, arrived 13 August 1944;
712 R.O.B. (Reading Company and The Central Railroad Company of New Jersey), commanded by Lieutenant Colonel F. R. Doud, arrived 14 August 1944;
718 R.O.B. (Cleveland, Cincinnati, Chicago and St Louis Railway), commanded by Lieutenant Colonel R. A. Wright, arrived 16 August 1944;

three R.S.B. arrived also:

757 R.S.B. (Chicago, Milwaukee, St. Paul and Pacific Railroad), commanded by Lieutenant Colonel J. W. Moe, arrived 18 July 1944;
755 R.S.B. (Norfolk and Western Railway), commanded by Lieutenant Colonel M. G. Stevens, arrived 16 August 1944;
764 R.S.B. (Boston and Maine Railroad, Central Vermont Railway, Inc., Boston and Albany Railroad, The Delaware and Hudson Railroad), commanded by Lieutenant Colonel Emil Ringberg, arrived 20 August 1944.

The military operations covered the drive toward Saint-Lô and around to the northwest side of the peninsula toward Cherbourg by the American forces, and a drive by the British forces directly south from the beachheads toward Caen. As of 25 July the battle line extended easterly from a point on the Cherbourg Peninsula just west of Saint-Lô to Caen and then north to the Channel.

The break-through at Saint-Lô occurred on the 25th day of July; then there was a steady movement of the armies, so that by D-Day plus 120, or approximately the 1st of October, the action had been extended along the beach northerly as the Twenty-first Army Group drove forward and captured Antwerp. The battle line then extended from north of Antwerp directly east to the Rhine River, and then south, but east of Aachen, Metz, and Dijon. Carentan had been captured on 12 June, Cherbourg on 26 June, Caen on

9 July, Saint-Lô on 18 July, Paris on 25 August, Antwerp on 4 September, Brest on 17 September, and Aachen on 21 October 1944.

As of 1 September 1944, General Eisenhower, commanding SHAEF, had in the field an Army of 37 Divisions comprised of 20 United States Divisions, 12 British, 3 Canadian, 1 French, and 1 Polish.

To follow the advance of the armies, the line of communication in general was covered by the French National Railways, with a line from Brest through Rennes to Le Mans, and Châteaudun; and south from Cherbourg through Saint-Lô, Vire, Mayenne, and on to Le Mans; and from Le Mans to Chartres and Paris through Versailles; from Vire through Argentan, Surdon, Dreux, and into Paris; and also between Surdon and Le Mans. A line was also operated south from Paris to Orléans. There were lines from Pontabault through Fougères to Mayenne and from Granville to Vire.

The task assigned to the M.R.S. in northern France was to move 20,000 tons of supplies daily from the beaches and ports to depots and railheads behind the advancing armies over these lines of railroad.

When Headquarters, Second M.R.S., arrived, it established headquarters at Cherbourg, and had direct jurisdiction over M.R.S. troops until the arrival of the Headquarters, 707 R.G.D., which also set up headquarters at Cherbourg and had jurisdiction over the lines in the Cherbourg Port area to Vire.

On arrival of the Headquarters, 708 R.G.D., it first set up headquarters at Pontabault, and then moved to Rennes and had jurisdiction over the lines from Brest to Le Mans, from Pontabault via Fougères to Mayenne, and from Granville via Vire and Flers and Mayenne to the line between Brest and Le Mans.

The 706 R.G.D., as tracks were opened, took control of the line from Vire through Surdon, Dreux, and Paris, from Surdon to Le Mans, and from Le Mans to Paris. Its headquarters were at Le Mans.

The 757 R.S.B. on landing was set up in the shop facilities at Cherbourg; the 764 R.S.B. moved into Le Mans and took over the back-shop facilities there about 1 September; the 755 R.S.B. on landing went to Rennes, France, and stayed there until it moved to Namur, Belgium, early in 1945.

The 729 R.O.B., the first unit of M.R.S. to land on the Continent, immediately set up operations at Cherbourg and operated the lines from Cherbourg south through Sottevast, Valognes, Montebourg, and Carentan to Lison.

The 720 R.O.B. when it arrived established headquarters at Lison on 23 July and started immediately the rehabilitation of tracks and operated about 62 miles of railroad east through Bayeux, Caen, Mézidon, and Lisieux. These battalions became units of the 707 R.G.D. when it arrived.

After landing, the 740 R.O.B. went by truck to Mayenne, arriving there on 14 and 15 August 1944. When it arrived at Mayenne, it was without supplies or equipment, insufficient time having been allowed in the United Kingdom to accumulate them. It found trains waiting to be run east, only one track open, all buildings severely damaged by bombing, no communication lines to the east, and the one to the west inoperative; very little water in the tank and the pump broken; only fifteen tons of coal on hand with the nearest supply 65 kilometers away; no roundhouse facilities available, and no flagging equipment.

Orders were issued for the movement of 31 trains of ammunition, rations, and gasoline that General Patton said were required to enable him to take Paris in twenty days. These trains were moved from the beachheads in the vicinity of Cherbourg down through Saint-Lô, Flers, Mayenne, and Le Mans, and in all the 720 and 740 R.O.B. handled those 31 trains in six days.

From this beginning at Mayenne, trains were operated to the east on manual block systems; then linemen opened a circuit to the east, and assisted in the repair of the line west to Fougères; track laborers, with a motley and inadequate collection of tools, restored three yard tracks at Mayenne and started on the removal of slow orders between that point and La Chappelle; an old reciprocating steam pump that had not been used for years was repaired and used for pumping water to the tank from the river; a small open-air engine terminal was established; a supply of very poor coal was sent in, and an additional water point was provided at Ernée as the pump at Mayenne continually gave trouble.

Le Mans, one of the largest rail terminals in France, was found to have been given a severe bombing and was almost completely destroyed. As of the 22 August only one main line into the terminal and two yard tracks had been restored. Orders were given to begin the rehabilitation of the yard. This was a stupendous task. The terminal was a twisted mass of wrecked locomotives, cars, rails, ties, buildings, etc. The work was planned and proceeded under the supervision of the 706 R.G.D. As soon as the 712 R.O.B. and 740 R.O.B. arrived at Le Mans, the "A" Company men of those units were assigned to this reconstruction work.

When the Maintenance of Equipment Company of the 740 R.O.B. moved into the engine terminal at Le Mans on 20 August they found it deserted. One roundhouse had been completely destroyed, the other badly damaged, and the machine shop about two thirds wrecked. Bomb craters, collapsed walls and beams, wrecked locomotives and machinery proved a great obstacle in setting up shop. Inspection revealed that one track could be used with a little repair work. When a search failed to locate tools, blacksmiths were assigned the task of making wrenches, hammers, screw drivers, punches, chisels, etc., so that the other crafts could go to work. Oil, however, was no problem; the Germans had left a large quantity. The mechanism of the turntable had been damaged and had to be manually operated, requiring the services of eight to ten men each time an engine left the roundhouse. Despite these handicaps, engines were serviced and light repairs made and there was no delay of movement due to lack of power. When the 764 R.S.B. moved into Le Mans, it took over the back shop about 1 September. Jurisdiction of the entire terminal was assigned to the 712 R.O.B. on 30 August. "B" Company men of the 712 R.O.B. continued to work in the shops until the battalion was assigned to another sector on 15 September.

Journal brass was a problem until a Frenchman informed the car force that some American brass had been stored in an old warehouse uptown. On investigation, it was found that this brass had been sent over in 1918 for use on World War I equipment. It was collected and immediately put to use.

Naturally every expedient was used to get bad-order equipment running, and a help that came from Technician Fourth Grade Frank Palmisano of the 757 R.S.B. was his erection of a large-scale portable blowtorch made entirely from scrap metal which was very effective in helping to straighten bent sills on cars while the cars were still on the track.

For the first few days of operation between Mayenne and Le Mans the very crudest of operating conditions prevailed. On the completion of the communication circuit, dispatchers and operators were placed. At night, absolute blocking was in force, with both permissive and absolute blocking, depending on conditions, prevailing during the daytime. Trains were operated and switching performed at night by signaling. Crews were on the road as long as ninety-six hours, catching cat naps in cabs and cabooses. The Germans who had been by-passed at Mayenne by the combat forces cut the wires night after night, and sniped at passing trains and at yard and engine-house men.

M.R.S. stores naturally were in the supply-picture incident to supporting the invasion at Omaha Beach. The first stock of M.R.S. supplies was established in an apple orchard some eight or ten miles from Omaha Beach. As the lines advanced eastward, the next real M.R.S. store was established at Paris in a S.N.C.F. stores location with modern storage facilities, cranes, and stores-handling equipment.

A depot was next established at Liége, Belgium, which was headed by the very experienced storekeeper, Captain R. M. Heflin from the B. & O. Railroad. Immediately upon taking Antwerp, supplies from the United States began to move into Liége, and by January 1945, 75 per cent of the rail supplies on the Continent were at Liége. The progress of the Battle of the Bulge brought consternation with respect to M.R.S. stores, and loading of the stores for removal started shortly after the battle began. At its close, approximately 50 per cent of all stores were loaded and ready for movement to a place of safety.

In Germany nearly all rail supplies were obtainable from the Germans, who, up to that time, had a fair stock remaining. There was established a mutual-aid committee of French, British, and Americans which met each month, alternating between zones; thus each benefited by the aid of the other.

The Purchasing and Stores Department of the German railroad was reorganized and headed by a very competent man, Herr Mittman. A depot at Karlsruhe, Germany, for heavy transportation stores, was established and another was established at Bremerhaven for stationery and light supplies.

The 706 R.G.D. pushed the rehabilitation of the line into Paris with all they had and could get. On 29 August 1944 an inspection of the capacity of this line was made by an inspection Diesel autorail car. Thus Lieutenant D. C. Hastings, Assistant Engineer of Track of the 706 R.G.D. on this car, was the first American to enter Paris by rail. The rehabilitation progressed rapidly and the next rail entry into Paris was made by General

Superintendent Colonel L. G. Jamison, accompanied by Lieutenant Colonel George W. Covert, Superintendent of Equipment, 706 R.G.D., on a Diesel engine, No. 8125, coupled with two cars which made the final inspection before service was authorized. They arrived at Paris at 1710 hours on 30 August and were met on arrival by M. LeNesueray, President General of the French Railways.

It was most proper that the first supply train to move on this route was a sixteen-car medical supply train which was moved forward and spotted at the Batignolles Team Yard in Paris at 0600 hours on 1 September 1944. That supply train was operated into Paris by the 712 R.O.B. with Conductor Sergeant Lee Zelmer and Engineer Technician Fourth Grade S. Wilson.

By the end of August the Second M.R.S. was operating a total of 1,006 miles of track over which only 211 miles were double tracked. They had run 251 passenger trains carrying 29,450 people and had run 991 freight trains delivering to the front 136,169 net tons of military freight.

The situation had become so enlarged, with the activities shifting to the east as the armies progressed, that General Burpee opened his headquarters, Second M.R.S., at Paris on 9 September 1944 at Saint-Lazare Station.

Double track railroad bridge under reconstruction across the Seine River at Argenteuil, France, 1945.

Allied progress materializes as a Yank engine with a GI crew pulls out of the bombed railroad yards at Laon, France, damaged by American planes during German occupation. October, 1944.

During September the railhead serving the Twelfth Army Group had been extended beyond Paris to Laon.

The 718 R.O.B. also landed on famous Utah Beach, and after a march of some three or four miles boarded trucks and were taken to Folligny, France, where headquarters were set up in an apple orchard adjacent to the ruined railroad yards. It began immediately the rehabilitation and operation of the railroad from Folligny to Mayenne and to Rennes, and was also given the responsibility of maintaining the single track from Pontabault to

Mayenne and from Pontorson to Fougères, the double track from Folligny to Dol, and supervision of French maintenance of the double track from Dol to Rennes.

As the battle front pushed eastward, the following additional units arrived in France, and were assigned to the Second M.R.S.:

722 R.O.B. (Seaboard Air Line Railroad Company), commanded by Lieutenant Colonel C. A. McRee, arrived 26 August 1944.

723 R.O.B. (Union Pacific Railroad), commanded by Lieutenant Colonel Doyle Gresham, arrived 26 August 1944.

716 R.O.B. (Southern Pacific Company), commanded by Lieutenant Colonel W. C. Morris, arrived 27 August 1944.

724 R.O.B. (Pennsylvania Railroad), commanded by Lieutenant Colonel J. D. Shea, arrived 27 August 1944.

710 R.G.D. (The Atchison, Topeka and Santa Fe Railway Company), commanded by Colonel O. D. Crill, arrived 28 August 1944.

744 R.O.B. (Chicago, St. Paul, Milwaukee and Pacific Railroad), commanded by Lieutenant Colonel W. J. Hotchkiss, arrived 28 August 1944.

728 R.O.B. (Louisville and Nashville Railroad Company), commanded by Lieutenant Colonel C. D. Love, arrived 31 August 1944.

733 R.O.B. (Central of Georgia Railway Company), commanded by Lieutenant Colonel W. P. Schopper, arrived 29 September 1944.

732 R.O.B. (Great Northern Railway), commanded by Lieutenant Colonel T. J. Brennan, arrived 1 October 1944.

735 R.O.B. (M.R.S.), commanded by Lieutenant Colonel H. C. Baughn, arrived 1 October 1944.

741 R.O.B. (Gulf, Mobile and Ohio Railroad), commanded by Lieutenant Colonel L. E. Thornton, arrived 1 October 1944.

743 R.O.B. (Illinois Central Railroad), commanded by Lieutenant Colonel F. G. Cook, arrived 1 October 1944.

709 R.G.D. (Association of American Railroads), commanded by Colonel F. E. Cheshire, arrived 8 October 1944.

717 (R.O.B., Detachment "A" (Pennsylvania Railroad), commanded by Captain George P. Hayes, arrived 8 October 1944.

750 R.O.B. (St. Louis-San Francisco Railway Company), commanded by Lieutenant Colonel J. J. Stockard, arrived 6 November 1944. This comprised the advance detachment of this unit only. The balance of the unit arrived at Marseille in First M.R.S. and were joined by the advanced detachment for assignment actually in First M.R.S.

763 R.S.B. (The Delaware, Lackawanna and Western Railroad Company and Lehigh

Valley Railroad Company), commanded by Lieutenant Colonel James Purcell, arrived 13 November 1944.

734 R.O.B. (Texas and New Orleans Railroad Company), commanded by Lieutenant Colonel R. E. Johnson, arrived 17 December 1944.

746 R.O.B. (Missouri-Kansas-Texas Railroad Company), commanded by Lieutenant Colonel W. C. Pruitt, arrived 25 January 1945. This battalion had an extra "D" Company for Diesel operation and maintenance; therefore, the total strength of the battalion consisted of 1200 officers and men.

752 R.O.B. (Boston and Maine Railroad), commanded by Lieutenant Colonel R. E. Triggs, arrived 25 January 1945.

765 R.S.B. (Erie Railroad), commanded by Lieutenant Colonel L. H. Lewis, arrived 13 February 1945.

During the month of September the M.R.S. in Northern France consisted of Headquarters, Second M.R.S., four R.G.D., twelve R.O.B. and three R.S.B., comprising a total of 472 officers and 9,993 enlisted men.

They were operating the railroads south of Antwerp and east of Cherbourg and Brest to Laon, France, and into Belgium and Luxembourg, a total of 4,788 miles of main-line track of which 2,776 miles were double-tracked lines. During the month of September they handled 355,020 net tons of military freight. The LST and LCT car ferries brought over loaded 11,288 freight cars of all types and 702 locomotives.

The 724 R.O.B., after operating west of Paris on its arrival in France, had its territory changed to that east of Paris with headquarters at Soissons and then went farther east with headquarters at Compiègne, where a magnificent job was done cleaning up the yard tracks and terminals and logistically supporting the First and Third Armies.

As of 1 October assignments made by Headquarters, Second M.R.S., covered the railroad lines indicated previously and the assignment of M.R.S. troops and additional lines were as follows:

The 706 R.G.D., with headquarters at Toul, France, was assigned the mission of operating and maintaining military railways from the east connecting switch Valenton Yard at Paris to Nancy via Sommesous and Commercy and to railheads off this line except within Belgium and Luxembourg; from east switch Pantin Yard, Paris, to Belgium and Luxembourg border via Meaux, Reims, Verdun, Conflans, and to army railheads in France and

Germany off this line. Its units were the 712 R.O.B. at Coulommiers; the 718 R.O.B. at Sézanne, and the 733 R.O.B. at Toul.

The 707 R.G.D., with headquarters at Cherbourg, France, was assigned the mission of operating and maintaining military railways from Cherbourg to north switch at Vire via Lison, Sottevast to Folligny, Carteret to Carentan; Saint-Lô to Coutances; Granville to west switch at Vire; Lison to west switch at Lisieux via Caen. Its component units were the 728 R.O.B. at Cherbourg; the 729 R.O.B. at Cherbourg; the 720 R.O.B. at Lison; 735 R.O.B. at Coutances; and the 757 R.S.B. at Cherbourg.

The 708 R.G.D. established headquarters at Liége, Belgium, having been assigned the mission of operating and maintaining military railways from Erquelinnes and Quiévrain on the French-Belgium border to Liége via Charleroi, Gembloux, and Landen; Gembloux to Namur to Liége; Athus to Namur and Liége including branch lines; Liége to railheads of armies in Belgium, Holland, Luxembourg, and Germany. Its component units were the 740 R.O.B. at Liége, the 741 R.O.B. at Liége, and the 755 R.S.B. at Namur.

The 709 R.G.D., with headquarters at Compiègne, France, was assigned the mission of operating and maintaining military railways from Versailles-Matelots Yard to the Belgian border via Creil, Tergnier, Busigny, Cambrai, Denain, and Valenciennes, from Le Havre to Creil; from east connecting switch, Batignolles Yard, Paris, to the Belgian border via Soissons and Laon, and from Laon to north switch, Reims. Its component units were the 722 R.O.B. at Valenciennes, the 724 R.O.B. at Compiègne, and the 743 R.O.B. at Beauvais.

The 710 R.G.D. was assigned headquarters in Paris, with the mission of operating and maintaining military railways from west and north switch Vire to last connecting switch east of Valenton Yard, Paris; Argentan to south switch, Mézidon; Valenton Yard to last connecting switch north and east of Batignolles Yard, Paris. Its component units were the 716 R.O.B. at Versailles, the 723 R.O.B., Dreux, the 732 R.O.B. at Argentan, the 744 R.O.B., Vire, and the 764 R.S.B. at Paris.

The terrain of Belgium is irregular, and while superb engineering was used in the location of the railroads, there were very heavy grades and curves. As an illustration, one of the most difficult grade lines was in the territory of the 722 R.O.B. between Mons and Namur. Ruling grades of 1.3 per cent eastbound between Mons and Charleroi required helper service on all trains of more than 700 tons. Grade of 2.5 per cent between Charleroi and Gembloux required from two to three pusher engines to assist each eastbound train out of Charleroi Yard and grade of 1.7 per cent between Gembloux and Namur required helper service on most trains.

Notwithstanding the damaged track, the gradient, and the fact that a war was being fought in its very lap, the M.R.S. handled the freight. Every unit made records, an example of which is that set by the 744 R.O.B. in October when they handled over their division 71,724 train miles consisting of hospital, freight, troops, and prisoner-of-war trains. Following this, during November that unit handled from Cherbourg to Paris 298,304 net tons of military freight.

The great Port of Antwerp, second largest in the world, was opened on 28 November 1944. It was in the territory assigned to the 709 R.G.D., and the 743 R.O.B. switched the port while the 729 R.O.B. handled the trains out of the port. They were ready when the first ship docked at the port. Empty cars were on the docks ready to load. Unfortunately, forward depots had not been completely established, and before they were, congestion of sea-borne traffic to the Port of Antwerp sadly interfered with scheduled train operation. This was finally remedied by mid-February 1945 and thereafter traffic flowed freely by rail from the port of entry. The M.R.S. handled promptly all traffic offered.

December was a momentous month as to action and counteraction in the general area northeast and east of Paris for the Twelfth Army Group, which was rail logistically supplied by the Second M.R.S. The most noteworthy action was the Battle of the Bulge, when Von Rundstedt counterattacked the Third Army. In the thick of this action were the troops of the 706 R.G.D., the 708 R.G.D., and the 709 R.G.D. Among those operating battalions directly involved in this action were the 718, 722, and 732 R.O.B. One of their exploits is contained in an official communication which is a commendation by Brigadier General Walter J. Muller, Assistant Chief of Staff, G-4, Third Army, in which he stated: "Particularly I would like to mention the work of the 732 R.O.B., which operated magnificently prior and subsequent to the Bastogne Bulge—these troops have developed a flexibility which enables them to meet the ever-changing situations in a most efficient manner. Their ready understanding and prompt action have insured the uninterrupted flow of supplies to the army and has contributed immeasurably to the success of the Third United States Army.

"At the time referred to, the 732 was operating railheads literally up to the front line. On occasions the artillery ammunition was delivered by rail right to the guns without the necessity of trucking on up from railheads. At the nearest point to Bastogne being operated, the troops and trains of the 732 were frequently under bombing and strafing attacks from the enemy, but they kept the trains moving with the vital supplies under the most trying conditions."

During the period of the Battle of the Bulge the 718 R.O.B. accomplished a rather remarkable feat in that they moved within forty-eight hours four divisions, including supply, of the Third Army laterally across the front and into the south flank of the Bulge. At the same time, one division of the Seventh Army was moved into the line. The forty-eight hours was from the withdrawal of the first division to commitment combat of the last division. A double-track railroad was operated in one direction (both tracks) for sixteen hours, then reversed for eight hours. Trains were operated in blocks of six trains at a time on each track, holding to ten minutes' minimum headway.

All of the operations in the area were severely handicapped by a heavy snowfall and without the proper snow equipment; much of the clearing of railroads had to be done in the good old-fashioned way, by shoveling.

Throughout the entire period M.R.S. units were under constant fire both as to trains en route and the yards in which they switched them. Typical of the danger was the experience of Sergeant Edward E. Loneker and Technician Fifth Grade Leonard R. Angel of "C" Company of the 712 R.O.B. On 23 December 1944 incendiary bullets fired by snipers set a car of five-gallon cans of gasoline afire. The car was in the middle of a train of 40 cars loaded with gasoline. With complete disregard for their own safety, they cut the train one car on either side of the blazing car and pulled the front and rear portions of the train away from the then three blazing cars. With gasoline cans exploding over the area, they returned and pulled a trainload of ammunition imminently in danger of exploding from an adjacent track to a place of safety.

Enemy planes strafed a number of trains. Two of the trains carried Captain Von O. Zimmerman and First Lieutenant Harvey H. Sparks of the 735 R.O.B. At Ramillies Yard an ammunition train was set on fire and "C" Company men acted with dispatch in moving other trains out of danger. At Gembloux, under enemy strafing, a train was moved out of the yards.

Even with the danger, the bombarding, the strafing, and the fires, the business of the M.R.S. was to move trains, and in order to move trains it is necessary to have cars and engines in order, so complete running repairs for both locomotives and cars were set up in many instances in demolished roundhouses. As an illustration of the capacity to repair equipment, the two roundhouse platoons of the 735 R.O.B. set up classified repair work at Landen, Belgium, and by the end of the month of December the men were turning out a heavy repaired locomotive each twenty-four hours.

The phenomenal tonnage movement of the M.R.S. supporting the Twelfth Army Group for the month of December totaled 1,308,937 tons, which meant the operation of 3,136 trains. By the end of the year there had been received from the United Kingdom and placed in service 1,523 locomotives and 19,383 freight cars of all types.

Some unusual mistakes occur always, and what appeared to be a very serious affair was easily solved by Master Sergeant Robert E. Lane, Chief Stock Record Clerk of the 709 R.G.D. Six 0-6-0 locomotives assigned to the 709 R.G.D. were in transit when that headquarters were advised about them, but upon arrival it was discovered that they were without main rods, eccentric rods, and eccentrics. The 709 R.G.D. asked at what port these engines had been unloaded and, upon being told, Master Sergeant Lane took a 6 x 6 truck and went to the port. After a great deal of checking that could almost be classified as sleuthing he tracked the parts down and had them loaded on his truck. The rods and eccentrics were delivered to the R.O.B., who had the engines waiting for the parts. Upon receipt, the engines were placed in active service within six days.

By the first of the year the total force of the Second M.R.S. troops in northern France and Belgium was 17,500, made up of 750 officers and 16,750 enlisted men.

With the coming of the New Year, Allied strategy was to drive the Germans out of the Siegfried Defenses and face them across the Rhine River for the final push in the spring, which was to bring victory. The responsibility of the M.R.S. was to move supplies and ammunition closer to the front for that spring offensive.

Take, for instance, the 744 R.O.B. in whose territory supply and storage dumps grew by leaps and bounds. Almost every type of equipment was handled and stored. Medical, ordnance, air corps, engineer, and signal supplies poured in from the ports and had to be held until needed. There were also large food, POL, and clothing depots established in its area. These activities, aside from the regular operation, called for much planning, created problems in man power, and brought new wrinkles into the foreheads of the car distribution men. By March, the total had grown to 42 depots.

The M.R.S. naturally operated over bad track. Its worst wreck, however, was caused by sabotage. A trainload of ammunition ran away down a four-mile 3 per cent grade and piled into a train of rations. Sergeant Joseph Cushman of Company "C," of the 718 R.O.B., engineer of the ration train, died in his attempt to back up his train when warned of the approach of the runaway train in order to cushion the impact. The ammunition on the runaway train, exploded by the impact, devastated the countryside.

Another accident occurred on 16 February at Châtelineau-Châtelet in 744 R.O.B. territory. Fortunately, there were no lives lost. There was considerable damage done, however, to tracks and adjacent property, loss of 14 cars of package POL, an 0-6-0 engine, and approximately 75 per cent destruction of a Diesel locomotive. A runaway train manned by Technician Fourth Grade Benjamin Tate and Private Clarence Chandler ran unchecked downhill into the yard at Châtelineau-Châtelet where it crashed into a yard engine. Engineer Tate stayed in the cab of his engine, using the steam jam and also set up the hand brake, but the momentum of the train was too great to be stopped. Private Chandler did what he could, jumping from car to car applying hand brakes. When they saw the crash was going to occur, they both jumped and escaped serious injury, but Jerry cans of gasoline spilled out and started a fire.

Lieutenant Gongaware witnessed the accident and with quick thinking uncoupled an engine from a passenger train standing in the yard and used it to pull 20 cars of precious supplies to safety. During all this time exploding Jerry cans were flying through the air like hailstones.

A very bad fire occurred 1 February 1945 when fire broke out in a group of about 100 cars in the railroad yards at Soissons, France. The fire caused numerous explosions and intense heat from burning phosphorus. Captain George T. Maguire and Captain C. G. Price, Jr., of the 709 R.G.D., took immediate action. Utterly disregarding their own safety under such dangerous circumstances, they succeeded in clearing the tracks around the burning cars with a net result of only four cars destroyed.

One of the most threatening fires that occurred in units of the M.R.S. happened on 26 May at Giessen, Germany, while gasoline was being transferred by the Quartermaster Corps from tank cars to Jerry cans by means of dispensers. One of the dispensers ignited gas that had been spilled on the ground and this in turn fired many cans on the loading platform which had been filled previously. City Security Guard and all available men were called to the scene of the fire to assist in removing the loaded gas cans from the vicinity of the fire; all fire companies in the city were called out to help as well as all available personnel of the 746 R.O.B. Under the direction of Lieutenant Raymond F. Delaney, Company "B," necessary cuts were made in the train and numerous tank cars and carloads of gasoline were removed to safety. Due to the prompt and heroic efforts of the railroad men, probable loss of the entire station, loading sheds, and platforms was averted.

A fire broke out in the yards at Domgermain, France, in the territory of the 733 R.O.B. Great bravery was shown by members of the battalion when in utter disregard for their lives they switched and isolated the burning cars. Lieutenant Colonel W. P. Schopper, Commanding Officer of the unit, and First Lieutenant Thomas C. Moran each received the Soldier's Medal for their bravery in this action.

One of the innovations which was worked out in conjunction with the Quartermaster Corps was the establishment of a train to handle meat from a freezing plant that had been rehabilitated not too far from the Port of Cherbourg. The meat was handled from ship to port, taken to the plant, and refrigerated as necessary and then, on a regularly scheduled train, was taken virtually to the front lines. This train was called the "Meatball Express."

Due to the very heavy congestion on the roads as well as adverse weather conditions, uniformity of delivery of fresh meats by truck to the front-line troops had been impossible, but with the establishment of the "Meatball Express" front-line troops secured fresh beef, pork, and chicken with the regularity desired by the Quartermaster Corps.

The "Toot Sweet Special," Cherbourg to end of rail, Second M.R.S., 1945.

Recognizing the need of special daily movement, the "Toot Sweet Special," an L.C.L. and carload freight train, was established between Cherbourg and forward areas. It made its initial run on 22 January 1945.

Throughout the spring offensive of the Allied Forces retreating Germans in their haste had to leave railroad equipment which was immediately captured and placed in service by the Allies. As an illustration, by the end of February, along the lines operated by the 708 R.G.D., there were 82 locomotives, 4,718 boxcars, 2,403 flatcars, 3,022 gondolas, 128 refrigerator cars, and 192 tank cars that had been captured and put into service.

Later in June the Equipment Department of the Second M.R.S. reported that up until that time a total of 29,646 cars had been catalogued as captured equipment taken over in Germany. Moreover, by the end of June a total of 2,905 German engines were listed as equipment captured in Germany.

The operations of Headquarters, Second M.R.S., and its troops in northern France and Germany will be continued as a part of the history of General Headquarters, M.R.S., established 12 February 1945.

8

Operations in Southern France

1944

THE INVASION OF SOUTHERN FRANCE, made by NATOUSA, occurred in the vicinity of Marseille near St. Raphael and St. Tropez on 15 August 1944. Marseille fell on 28 August. The invading forces drove up the Rhône River Valley until they met the troops of the Third United States Army under the Twelfth Army Group just west of Dijon on 11 September 1944.

The invading force was the Sixth Army Group under the command of General J. L. Devers, and consisted of the Seventh United States Army under Lieutenant General A. M. Patch, Jr., and the First French Army under General of the Army Jean de Lattre de Tassigny. The Seventh United States Army was comprised of three corps of twelve divisions, while the First French Army was composed of two corps of seven divisions.

This invasion was supported logistically by a command known as SOLOC (Southern Line of Communications), with Major General T. B. Larkin as Commanding General and Brigadier General Morris W. Gilland as Chief of Staff. It reported to the Commanding General, NATOUSA. On 17 November 1944 NATOUSA became MTOUSA (Mediterranean Theater of Operations, United States Army).

After the joining of the American armies on 11 September, a meeting was held at Dijon on 11 October, which laid the groundwork for the transfer of the logistical support of the Sixth Army Group in southern France from MTOUSA to ETOUSA. On 12 February 1945, SOLOC was dissolved and absorbed by COMZONE, ETOUSA (Communications Zone, European The-

General Jacob L. Devers, Commanding Sixth Army Group.

ater of Operations, United States Army), with Lieutenant General J. C. H. Lee commanding, and Major General Larkin became the Chief of Staff.

It is interesting to note that the drive of the Twelfth Army Group from Cherbourg to Paris, and then southeasterly, and the drive of the Sixth Army Group up the Rhône Valley, cut off, as it were, the entire southwest corner of France south and west of those lines. There were no American troops in that zone and the ports of Brest, Bordeaux, and St. Nazaire were but little used. In World War I almost the entire American operation was in that southwest corner of France and those ports were almost solely used.

According to the plans for rail support in the invasion of southern France, M.R.S. troops from the Mediterranean Theater were to come from Italy. The Headquarters, 703 R.G.D., arrived in France on 29 August. Its two operating battalions, the 713 R.O.B. and 727 R.O.B. (less Company "A"), arrived on 29 and 30 August and all established headquarters at Marseille.

Major General Thomas B. Larkin, Commanding SOLOC.

By General Order No. 52, Headquarters, First M.R.S., dated 11 September 1944, the headquarters was closed in Rome and established at Lyon, France, effective 15 September 1944. The advanced echelon arrived there on 14 September and set up headquarters in the Hotel Bristol-Savoy. The balance of headquarters arrived at Lyon 1 October.

Company "A" of the 727 R.O.B. and the 759 R.O.B., a portion of the 788 Base Depot Company and the advance echelon of the 794 Military Police Battalion, all under the command of Lieutenant Colonel Frederick H. Owen for the movement, left Naples, Italy, 12 September, and landed at Marseille, 14 September. The 794 Military Police Battalion was shortly augmented by the second battalion of the 65 Infantry Regiment. These were Puerto Rican troops.

The 703 R.G.D. was first assigned all lines in southern France under the control of the Director General, M.R.S. As of 1 October its component parts were the 713 R.O.B. and a detachment of the 788 Base Depot Company,

Bridge North Valence, France.

Repairing bridge south of Langres, France.

Bridge repair at Romans, France.

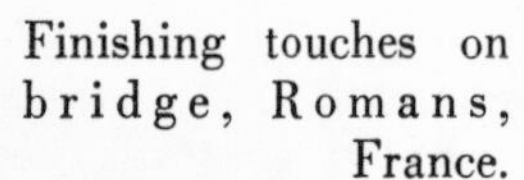

Finishing touches on bridge, Romans, France.

all headquartered at Marseille. Actual lines of operation were: Marseille Terminal, Marseille-Valence, San Raphael-Toulon, Marseille-La Barque, Aix-en-Provence to Grenoble, Valence-Moirans, Port-de-Bouc-Avignon via Miramas and Cheval Blanc-Pertuis.

At that time, Headquarters, First M.R.S., at Lyon, had the 727 R.O.B., then established at Lyon, and the 759 R.O.B., which had arrived from Italy

Rhone River bridge, Lyon, France.

Bridge destruction on SNCF, Belfort-Bâle Line.

French locomotive demolished by demolition, Avignon.

22 October and set up headquarters at Dijon. These units were responsible for the operation of the Lyon Terminal, Valence to Lyon, Lyon to Dijon, lyon-Chagny-Grenoble, Grenoble-Bougr, Bourg-Railhead, and Dijon-Railhead. All reported direct to First M.R.S.

Other elements of the First M.R.S. as they arrived and were assigned to service were: 750 R.O.B. (St. Louis-San Francisco Railway Company), commanded by Lieutenant Colonel J. J. Stockard, arrived at Marseille, 6 November 1944, and was assigned the main line east of Dijon. The 756 R.S.B. (Pennsylvania Railroad), Lieutenant Colonel H. U. Bates, commanding, which had been erecting knocked-down cars and locomotives in England, arrived 18 November 1944. They and their shop were established on Pier "R" at Marseille. The first week's capacity of the erecting shop was better than 30 cars per day and climbed steadily to a maximum of 100. It erected forty 9,900 gallon tank cars within 30 hours. By the 1st of August 1945 it had erected 17,584 miscellaneous types of freight cars.

The 704 R.G.D. arrived from Italy 20 December 1944; 761 R.T.C. arrived from Italy the same date and was placed at Sarrebourg operating in advance of and reporting to the 750 R.O.B. The 766 R.S.B. (M.R.S.), commanded by Lieutenant Colonel E. K. Hobbs, arrived 6 April 1945, and likewise was established at Marseille.

Lieutenant Colonel Benjamin H. Decker, Executive Deputy of First M.R.S., arrived in southern France on 16 August. He arranged for rail service which started with the placement of cars for loading at Fréjus on 23 August. The first train, manned by French "cheminots," left Fréjus at 0015 hours on the 24th and arrived St. Maximin at 1700 hours with 275 net tons. The second day two trains were run, one for Draguignan and the other for St. Maximin. Thus, the first rail service was established in southern France "D" plus eight days.

The railroads first utilized were the lines from St. Raphael through Gardanne and then northward up the Durance River Valley through Sisteron and on up along the west slope of the Alps over extremely heavy grades through to Grenoble and Montmelion, thence west to Lyon and northwest to Bourg.

Movement of freight was steady from the Port of Marseille area to depots and from depots to the rear of the Sixth Army Group troops. At all times the capacity of the M.R.S. was greater than tonnage offered. For the month of October, Headquarters, First M.R.S., operated in the Rhône Valley behind the Sixth Army Group a total of 1,897 trains hauling 640,561 net tons of freight.

With the completion of the Livron Bridge at Lyon at 1800 hours on 20 September, the double-track line on the east bank of the Rhône was open from Marseille to Lyon. This permitted scheduled trains in that territory, the first one of which left Marseille at 0300 hours on 25 September.

The situation was further improved when on 27 September the Auxonne Bridge and the Rhône River Bridge at Lyon were completed, giving access to the double-track line on the west bank of the Rhône River from Marseille to Lyon. The line was then opened also from Lyon to Dijon and Vesoul.

The first scheduled train left Lyon via Dijon for Besançon at 2330 hours on 28 September. The opening of these lines virtually closed down military operations on the difficult Grenoble line from the south.

The 703 R.G.D., which had jurisdiction over the Port of Marseille and over the lines in southern France north to Dijon, operated over the two double-track railroads from Marseille north, one pair on each side of the river. For the month of November 1944, over these lines it handled 415,404 net tons in 798 trains with 32,951 cars.

This vast tonnage handled up the Rhône Valley by the 703 R.G.D. continued at the same volume, for in March that unit handled 413,996 net tons in 716 trains with 29,280 cars.

General Devers, commanding the Sixth Army Group, commended the M.R.S. for its logistical support in a letter addressed to the Director General, which is quoted:

> I want to send my congratulations to you and your splendid achievement in opening and maintaining the railroad system in southern France since the invasion of our forces. Knowing this fine work could not have been possible without the unceasing effort of those in your organization, let me through you congratulate the men in those units of the Military Railway Service who have contributed so much to this work.
>
> Supplies carried by your trains are now reaching the forward areas. There could be no finer compliment to pay them than to say that you have the thanks and appreciation of each individual soldier receiving those supplies.

Driving north pier, Seurre, France.

Starting bridge construction at Seurre, France. Foreground shows ¼ yard Lorraine crane placing piles.

River span in place before jacking down on piers.

Assembling British trestling and launching nose. Seurre, France.

Side view of finished trestle, Seurre, France.

Launching a British trestling bridge with launching nose.

Demolished bridge, Isère River, Romans, France.

First train on the double track over the Isère River near Tain, France.

It is of vital interest that the railways be kept in the best operational condition, that they improve continuously, and that they be extended as fast as the situation will permit. I know I can count on you and the men of the Military Railway Service to achieve the same results in the future that you have so admirably achieved in the past.

The M.R.S. fulfilled the General's desires and requests. Let's see what they had to do to accomplish it:

Between Marseille and Dijon they had to build 42 bridges with a total of 4,450 lineal feet and had to repair nine bridges of 1,000 lineal feet. The most serious was the first undertaken over the Rhône River at Avignon. There it was necessary to build a 1,877-foot pile trestle with two openings—one 131 feet and one 141 feet. Roth Waagner spans were placed near the center of the bridge to permit continued navigation on the Rhône River. Of the total length, 1,479 feet consisted of timber bent open deck trestle bents on 15-foot centers. The bridge was built by the 713 and 727 R.O.B., assisted by the 1051 Engineer General Service Regiment.

The second really serious bridge was at Orgon over the Durance River. The Germans had blown this five-span through truss bridge in two places, causing the dropping at one end of the 284 and 113 foot section of the truss.

Durance River bridge between Orgon and Cheval Blanc, France.

First train crossing temporary pilebent trestle, Avignon, France.

Bridge destruction on S.N.C.F. Belfort-Bâle Line.

The sections were jacked back to their original elevation through the construction of two cantilever trusses which were used to jack the four ends together. Four 18-foot trestle piers were erected temporarily to support the trusses until final erection was completed, after which the trestles were removed. The two spans were welded together. Work was done by the 713 R.O.B. and the 94 Engineer General Service Regiment under the supervision of the 703 R.G.D.

Possibly the most unique adaptation of available material for major repairs was accomplished by the "A" Company of the 759 R.O.B. when they replaced a blown 112-foot-high masonry arch pier on a bridge at Xertigny between Besançon and Dinozé, France. The repair of the bridge was handled by first building the 112-foot pier by the use of standard U.C.R.B. bridge material and then launching two 75-foot deck spans from the two masonry abutment piers which were still intact on either end, and joining the spans on the newly constructed pier. This work was started 15 January 1945 and completed 28 February 1945.

The greatest assistance and cooperation were extended by the Seventh Army Engineer, Brigadier General Garrison H. Davidson, and the loan of general service regiments of his command to assist Colonel Crosland in his rehabilitation of bridges. During the period from 15 August 1944 to the spring of 1945 the M.R.S. was given the use of the 343 and 344 Engineer General Service Regiments and the 40, 540, and 1175 Engineer Combat Groups.

All of the planning, design, and supervision of construction fell on the Engineering Department of Headquarters, First M.R.S., the grand division headquarters, and the "A" Companies of the operating battalions. The 94 Engineer General Service Regiment, which had been assigned to the M.R.S. in Italy, was brought to southern France and continued through the war as an integral part of the M.R.S. It assisted materially the "A" Companies and the borrowed General Service Regiments in the completion of these bridge repairs and rebuildings.

Repairing the battered communication lines along the right of way also required its share of cooperation and ingenuity. French railway and U.S. Signal Corps men worked side by side with signal groups of the M.R.S. to put back into service the telephone and telegraph facilities so systematically

Company A, 759 Railway Operating Battalion, setting 75 foot girders on 112 foot pier at Dounoux, France, 1944.

destroyed by the retreating Germans. Meanwhile short-wave radio played a vital part in keeping the trains moving. Set up readily at points along the line, these portable radio outfits, originally from the 794 Military Police Battalion, moved in quickly wherever regular ground communications were out of commission. By the first of the year, 800 miles of telegraph and telephone line had been repaired and 50 miles of new telegraph and telephone lines had been constructed.

By the first of the year, 1945, First M.R.S. had 4,000 miles of track in operation. The greatest length of direct line was 563 miles between Marseille and Strasbourg. Also 800 miles of track had been repaired, four tunnels had been repaired (the longest one 4,400 feet), ten water stations had been built, nine repaired. It had a maximum of 3,500 troops on construction projects at any one time, with an average of 2,000 troops employed.

From a transportation standpoint it was a question of locomotives and cars. Colonel B. H. Decker, in his original survey, indicated that only about 10 per cent of the locomotives which existed in southern France before the war were still available; rolling stock was down from about 440,000 to around 200,000 cars, even including the German cars that fell into Allied hands. To supplement this supply it was decided to bring in, as quickly as possible, a number of standard oil-burning locomotives and Diesel electric road switchers, along with some 1,000 special-type cars from North Africa. These included 10,000-gallon tank cars, 56-ton war flatcars to carry tanks and other heavy equipment, refrigerator cars, etc. The first Diesel electric engines were received 25 October, soon to be followed by six American 2-8-0 steam locomotives. The ultimate power requirements were estimated to be another 147 2-8-0 locomotives, steam.

By the first of the year, 1945, on the Sud Est Region of the S.N.C.F., there were in serviceable condition 812 French locomotives and approximately 15,000 French freight cars. There had been brought in from North Africa 249 American cars consisting of 101 86-ton war flats, 74 9,900-gallon tank cars, 22 40-ton refrigerator cars converted from boxcars, and 52 high-side 20-ton gondolas. There was received a total of 102 American locomotives and 87 were in service. The balance of 15 were being assembled and repaired. M.R.S. virtually had to completely overhaul each of the American locomotives brought in from North Africa because of neglect of maintenance by the French forces in North Africa after the M.R.S. departed.

One pleasant surprise to the M.R.S. railroaders when they got to France was air brakes. No longer did they have to rely on sleepy Arabs or slow-moving Italian boys to operate hand brakes on the downgrades.

Effective 1 October a system of symbolizing trains was inaugurated which identified the movement of all northbound trains from point of origin to destination. Trains moving over the main double-track line (Rhône River Route) were given the prefix letter "A" and numbered consecutively throughout any given month, followed by a second number indicating the day of forwarding from point of origin. On the eastward (Sisteron-Grenoble) route, the prefix letter "B" was used in the same manner. Local trains were prefixed with the letter "C." This system simplified identification, location, and movement of trains.

General Devers continued the policy established in North Africa and Italy and by letter dated 30 October 1944, which was further strengthened and clarified by his Administrative Memorandum No. 7, 9 December 1944, placed on the Director General the responsibility for rehabilitation and operation of railroads in southern France and established priority of effort for rehabilitation and operation of lines best suited to serve the tactical plans. Those lines were:

Priority 1 (for Seventh Army) Epinal-Blainville-Lunéville-Sarrebourg-Strasbourg
Priority 2 (for First French Army) Vesoul-Lure-Belfort-Mulhouse
Priority 3 (for Seventh Army) Epinal-St. Dié-Strasbourg.

Maintenance of railways, when placed in operation, was entirely a responsibility of the M.R.S. Guarding of bridges and other essential structures was a responsibility of the army concerned.

In both the repair and operation of railroads in southern France, the M.R.S. received cooperation from French railroad officers and employees. The director of the French M.R.S. was Colonel Henri Coudraux who organized and pushed cooperative action between the French railway service and the American M.R.S. This officer was promoted and moved to another assignment 23 March 1945.

In the middle of December 1944 this splendid cooperation which existed with the French railways was further accentuated by the Director General's trip to Paris for consultation with general officers of the S.N.C.F., including M. Goursat, Director General of the S.N.C.F., and M. Lévi, Chief Engineer. M. Lévi and René Mayer, Chairman of the Board of Compagnie Internationale des Wagons-Lits, and since in most cabinets and finally Premier of France, first worked with the Director General when they were refugees in North Africa in 1943.

Original plans called for the continuation of the three-phase operation of railroads in France, subject always to United States control. These phases were: Phase I, operation out of face by American M.R.S.; Phase II, French civilian operation with United States supervision; and Phase III, complete operation by French civilians.

From the very first the desire of the S.N.C.F. to cooperate was so wholehearted that in many instances it was possible to skip the first step altogether.

Colonel Coudraux and Director General, Lyon, France, January, 1945.

Thus Phase II operations began immediately, with the French civilians doing the operating and the GI's just supervising—double crewing on the runs. This supervision naturally varied, depending on the amount of traffic and proximity of trains to the front lines.

By the middle of April 1945 Phase II and III operations were extended then to the Rhine, releasing M.R.S. troops for battle-line operations.

Receiving high priority for movement over the lines operated by the M.R.S. were a number of United States and French hospital trains which carried Allied wounded back from the battle front. United States shopmen rebuilt French passenger cars to make suitable hospital trains. There were six hospital trains in service; one 10-car train shipped from the United States and five 14-car trains converted from French passenger equipment.

A great many reports were rendered to higher headquarters in the European Theater. At one time there were submitted Lend Lease and Reciprocal Aid reports to the Fiscal Director, ETOUSA, covering gasoline, Diesel fuel oil, and coal turned over to the French for civilian train operation. Civilian labor reports were made to SOLOC. The December report showed a total of 61 interpreters, 75 laborers, and 22 prisoners of war utilized by all units of the First M.R.S. during the month of December 1944.

Emergency troop movements necessitated in some instances superhuman accomplishments. In December, battle conditions necessitated moving the 70th Infantry Division from Marseille to Strasbourg, which was first scheduled to move in six trains at the rate of two trains per day (between 22 and 25 December). This was speeded up to have complete movement in 36 hours between 20 and 22 December. Troops were moved on a 36-hour schedule to destination. The efficient and expeditious handling of this movement by Grand Divisions and Operating Battalions brought favorable commendations to the M.R.S. from SOLOC. The movement of three other Infantry Divisions was completed between 14 and 31 December.

Railroad men are family men. The men of the M.R.S. in far-off France in memory and in love of their own children at home staged a series of Christmas parties for the children and citizenship of southern France. This was one of the best public relations efforts ever made because it was so sincere.

One Christmas party, including a properly attired Santa Claus, who

727 Railway Operating Battalion Christmas party at Lyon, France, 1944, for railroad orphans of SNCF.

The French Orphans greet Miss Madeleine Carroll.

arrived in a jeep, was sponsored by the 727 R.O.B. on the afternoon of 24 December at Lyon. The party was for the benefit of the orphans of the former S.N.C.F. employees of the Lyon District.

Members of the 727 R.O.B. and the 794 Military Police Battalion saved up candy and other items, partly from their PX rations, and partly from their packages from home. Mess sergeants managed to keep enough precious sugar, flour, cocoa, milk, etc., to prepare cookies and hot chocolate for the big event. A large hall was decorated especially for the occasion. Originally planned for 600 children, the party swelled to three times that size. The "Rails" confessed they had as much fun as the kids did. Captain H. C. Mauney, with First Sergeants Frank Sykora, Paul J. Hubble, and Floyd L. Huston, coordinated most of the work in connection with decorations, programs, refreshments, etc., while First Lieutenant S. P. Davis made arrangements for the music. A play was put on by members of the S.N.C.F. Actors Guild.

General Azan, Commander of French Headquarters at Avignon, said in a letter of appreciation to Captain James G. Beard of the 727 R.O.B. "A" Company:

. . . you have responded with results . . . that will help fill with joy the hearts of many unfortunate children, who up to now have seen but the cruel side of life, and none of its sweetness. . . . This deed honors you, as it honors all of America. We will not forget your kindness.

A salvageable pair of coveralls painted red, a pair of overshoes, a stocking cap, and a cotton beard made Technician Fifth Grade George Applebaum top man when the 783 Base Depot Company celebrated its first Christmas in France with a number of children from the neighborhood as guests. "Père Noël, Père Noël!" the kiddies shouted as Applebaum made his appearance, distributing toys and candy donated by men of the company. A decorated tree was in the mess hall. Empty evaporated-milk cans were painted in a variety of colors and hung from the branches as ornaments.

On the day before Christmas the 750 R.O.B. staged a party for children of the neighborhood in which that unit was stationed. Plans for the event were arranged by Chaplain Val B. Strader. Invitations, made by Corporal William S. Thompson, were sent to the families of the community for whom the war had brought particularly severe reverses. The mayor of the town was present, accompanied by Sergeant Yves Jaules of the French Army who served as interpreter. A response to the mayor's welcome was given by Major James J. Stockard, Commanding Officer of the 750 R.O.B.

By 1 January battle conditions had changed. Consequently, on 3 January, General Devers changed priority lines to be First Priority: Lure-Belfort; Bruyères-St. Dié-Saales-vicinity of Molsheim; Sarrebourg-Berthelnung-Sarralbe. Second Priority was: Belfort-Mulhouse; connection from St. Dié to St. Marie and vicinity of Sélestat; any other lines considered necessary by Commanding General SOLOC, to provide improvement of service.

Stores operations of the First M.R.S. were established and developed from Marseille, which was the main port of entry of supplies for the support of the Sixth Army Group. General supervision of supply operations in southern France rested with Colonel E. F. McFadden, Assistant General Manager, Headquarters, First M.R.S., and his staff operating through the Stores Department of the R.G.D. to the Headquarters Companies of the operating and shop battalions.

Main stores stock was maintained at Marseille until rearrangements as to stores were made in Germany immediately after the unconditional sur-

Destroyed yard, Dijon, France, 1944.

Naval gun on railroad cars, France.

render. Coal requirements were about 15,500 tons of coal per month. Diesel fuel-oil requirements were 336,000 gallons a month. For the steam oil-burning American locomotives it required a maximum of 90,000 barrels of Navy Special black fuel oil per month.

From a transportation standpoint, the capacity of the lines north from Marseille was 15,500 net tons of military freight daily which was the estimated maximum out of Marseille; 6,000 net tons were to be delivered to Strasbourg, with an additional 5,000 tons a day port clearance to any point south of the Durance River out of Marseille. The highest number of trains moved out of Marseille during any 24-hour period was on 26 October 1944, when there was moved 24 trains with 1,023 loads, 13,394 net tons. The greatest tonnage delivery in any 24-hour period to Seventh Army railheads was 923 cars with 15,045 tons on 14 January 1945. For the First French Army it was 578 cars with 6,358 net tons on 21 December 1944. The maximum of military trains run in any one day was on 23 November 1944, when 233 were run northbound and 166 southbound, a total of 399 trains.

It became necessary during February to augment oil-carrying capacity and so arrangements were completed with the Swiss government for lease of 500 of their rail tank cars for use in France. These cars were received in trainload lots and forwarded to Calais and Châlons-sur-Marne areas to relieve an acute tank-car shortage created by vast tonnages of gasoline being shipped to forward areas. Further request for 500 additional rail tank cars from Switzerland was rejected, but the Swiss government later leased an additional 25 tank cars.

While the winter was reasonably severe, freezing weather caused a number of engine failures and temporary congestion, but the troops worked out of it in fine shape by throwing into service the American power that didn't freeze up because it was tight. Those American engines did splendid service, especially the oil burners. During the severe portion of the winter it was necessary to reduce tonnage by 25 per cent.

There were two contract- and one company-owned locomotive repair shops on the Sud Est at Nevers, Lyon, and Marseille. There were also eight repair shops between Dijon and Marseille. There were approximately 15,000 civilian mechanical employees on the Sud Est at work. There were 49 officers and 1,376 enlisted American mechanical railroad men at work. That number included, of course, the 756 R.S.B. of 23 officers and 634 enlisted men erecting knocked-down American freight cars at Marseille. On the Sud Est there was repair capacity for 66 classified locomotive repairs per month and 500 general freight-car repairs.

Railroading in southern France in January 1945 not only had the difficulties of a devastating war, airplane bombardments, bridge and track demolitions, and enemy snipers, but M.R.S. was also subjected to possibly as heavy a snowfall as France had had for a long time. The general area of the fall was north of Lyon and in the Dijon area through to Nancy and Strasbourg. Snow even fell south at Marseille and in the Riviera district, although it melted about as fast as it fell.

The leaky French engines froze, train schedules were interrupted, while in one or two instances snow blockades stopped the flow of traffic, but at no time was the Sixth Army Group without its necessary supplies. Conditions were such, though, that the men of the 704 R.G.D., sponsored by the Great Northern Railway, and operating in this area, thought they were back in the northwestern portion of the United States along their own railroad during big snowstorms. Snow blockades occurred in the general vicinity of Langres and Andilly, which completely closed traffic down on 28 January. The weather moderated on 31 January and the first trains were moved at 1330 hours on that day.

With the establishment of General Headquarters, M.R.S., and the transfer of the Director General to command it, the history of the First M.R.S. will be continued in the history covering General Headquarters, M.R.S., from 12 February 1945 to the end of the war.

9

Operations in Europe after Consolidation of American Northern and Southern Forces

1945

THE BATTLE LINE as of March 1945 extended from Arnheim near the German-Netherlands border down the west bank of the Rhine River to Switzerland, and included most of the famed Saar Region, but did not include the Ruhr on the east side of the Rhine River. The spring offensive carried the Twenty-first Army Group on the extreme left flank in a drive northeasterly. The Ninth United States Army was on its right flank, the First United States Army on its right flank, and the Third United States Army on its right flank.

The Ninth, First, and Third United States Armies composed the Twelfth Army Group under General Omar N. Bradley. The Sixth Army Group under General J. L. Devers had the line south of Kaiserslautern with the Seventh United States Army on the left flank and the First French Army on the right flank driving almost due east in the vicinity of Colmar and Mulhouse.

On the basis of the continuous battle line of the Sixth and Twelfth Army Groups and the uniform direction, units of the M.R.S. in the logistical support of these armies were reorganized with the formation of a General Headquarters, M.R.S., headquarters in Paris, established 12 February 1945, in accordance with General Orders No. 16, Headquarters, ETOUSA, dated 6 February 1945.

Major General Carl R. Gray, Jr., Director General, Military Railway Service.

By General Order No. 2, G.H.Q., M.R.S., Colonel Arthur E. Stoddard, originally commander of the 702 R.G.D. (Union Pacific) with service in Iran, who had been rotated to France, was appointed by the Director General as his successor as General Manager, Headquarters, First M.R.S.

In accordance with Tables of Organization and Equipment approved by the Commanding General COMZONE, ETOUSA, Organization Order No. 110, dated 16 February 1945, assignments of the following staff officers, G.H.Q., M.R.S., were announced:

Executive Officer—Colonel James K. Tully
Director Transportation—Colonel Alexander W. Campbell
Director Equipment—Colonel Frank R. Hosack
Director Engineering—Lieutenant Colonel Robert J. Crane
Director Supply—Colonel Edward F. McFadden
Director Security—Lieutenant Colonel Frederick H. Owen
Adjutant—Major Stanley R. Beggs
Aide de Camp—Captain James T. Hayes

When Colonel A. W. Campbell was appointed Director of Transportation, Lieutenant Colonel F. W. Okie succeeded him in command of the 703 R.G.D. He, in turn, was succeeded in command of the 727 R.O.B. by Lieutenant Colonel John W. Budd from the 703 R.G.D.

Then the Director General, as of 3 March 1945, by General Orders No. 4, established a boundary between the First and Second M.R.S. as being "a line extending from Paris along the divisional line between the Nord and Est Regions of the S.N.C.F. to Hirson and thence along the Belgian and German boundaries and thence in a northeasterly direction north of the railway lines connecting Merzig, Otz, Kirn, Bingen, Rüdesheim, Wiesbaden, Frankfurt, Hanau, Gelnhausen, Schulchtern, Fulda, Hersfeld, Bebra, Gerstungen, Horschel, Eisenach, Gotha, Erfurt, Weimar, Bad Sulza, Leipzig, Wurzen, and Röderau."

Territory north and west of this defined line, exclusive of locations named above but inclusive of Paris Terminals of East and South East Systems, was under the jurisdiction of the Second M.R.S., which had been transferred to Brussels after the establishment of G.H.Q., M.R.S., in Paris.

Colonel Arthur E. Stoddard, General Manager, Headquarters, First Military Railway Service..

Staff, General Headquarters Military Railway Service, July, 1945.

Territory south of and east of this line inclusive of locations named above and exclusive of Paris Terminals of the East and South East Systems, was under the jurisdiction of the First M.R.S., with headquarters still at Lyon.

By General Order No. 7, the Director General activated, effective 24 March, the Railway Security Department (Provisional) for Headquarters, Second M.R.S., as it had been in Headquarters, First M.R.S., since service in North Africa. The position of Assistant General Manager, Security, was thus created and he reported to the General Manager, Second M.R.S. He was charged with the direction of protection of war materials, supplies, and equipment which were being transported by rail or set out under load awaiting shipment or delivery to consignee. That protection was afforded through the use of assigned or attached military police personnel. Lieutenant Colonel Fred L. Oliphant was announced as the Assistant General Manager, Railway Security, Headquarters, Second M.R.S. When Colonel Owen was appointed to G.H.Q., M.R.S., Lieutenant Colonel Oliver W. Kempster succeeded him as Assistant General Manager, Security, First M.R.S.

A number of Military Police units were assigned and attached and distributed to the two General Managers' commands. These included the 382, 383, 385, 388, 390, 397, 400, and 794 Military Police Battalions and the 182 and 189 Military Police Companies.

One of the first acts of the Director General was to see that proper accounts were kept in order that suitable payments for transportation charges and countercharges might be made in accordance with the ordinance of 20 June 1944 by the Provisional Government of the French Republic which provided that railroad installations, facilities, and personnel would, in the liberated territories of the nation, be under the control of the government's military representatives to the extent necessary to meet the needs of the military forces. It also provided the basis of transportation charges to be made against the Allied Forces which were to be the same as those applying to the French Army as had been in effect in North Africa beginning in 1942. In the main the charges were based on cost of service and were set up at an average cost per ton moved for troops and military equipment and supplies. The S.N.C.F. was the agency to levy the charges against the United States Forces.

Charges for the use of United States cars and locomotives were assessed

Director General and General Managers, First and Second Districts. *Left to right:* Director General; Colonel A. E. Stoddard, General Manager, Headquarters, First M.R.S.; and Brigadier General C. L. Burpee, General Manager Headquarters, Second M.R.S.

according to the American standard charges per day for the use of railroad cars and locomotives, and such charges were included in the final settlement.

The net amount due the S.N.C.F. for rail transportation charges for the period 6 June 1944 to 1 September 1945 was handled in accordance with Lend-Lease agreements.

The S.N.C.F. presented its claims for transportation charges to the Ministry of Public Works and Transports and the French War Office, who in turn were required to obtain approval of the expense through the service for aid to Allied Forces and specifically to United States Theater Service Forces, European Theater, Headquarters. (M.R.S. did not audit or approve the tonnage figures or cost data.)

The final settlement was concluded by the signing of the Blum-Byrnes agreements on 28 May 1946.

Following close upon the Sixth Army Group in its advance eastward, the rehabilitation and repairs to the South East (Sud Est) Region of the S.N.C.F progressed most satisfactorily, and on 22 February 1945 operation of the railroad was extended to Mulhouse. During the month of February

1945, operating behind the Sixth Army Group, and from Dijon to rear dumps, the 704 R.G.D. handled 175,013,186 gross ton miles.

Railroad men go about their transportation jobs without being excited, in a manner far different from a great many other industries. Every man in the M.R.S. knew that his job was to get supplies of all kinds up to the fighting armies. One of the most startled men in the Field Artillery was a battery captain of a battery of 240's supporting the Third United States Army who had the ammunition for his battery delivered right opposite his gun positions by train. This train crew of the 732 R.O.B. seemed to think nothing about it at all. They were only doing their job.

One of the reasons why rehabilitation and reconstruction of bridges and track were carried on so expeditiously was the fact that really every operating man in the battalions knew how to maintain a railroad and therefore how to build one, and knew what tools it took and knew how to use them.

A great many people confuse and use inaccurately the terms "operation" and "transportation." The Operating Man on a railroad has full and complete knowledge of the three important parts of running a railroad, viz., 1, maintenance of track and bridges; 2, maintenance of locomotives and cars; and 3, switching cars and running trains. He may have his specialty but he also has full knowledge of the other two factors in operation. For instance, if he is a train service man, he knows a great deal about maintenance of track and bridges and also about maintenance of locomotives and cars. This experience and capacity were what made the M.R.S. "click" so well. It also made it possible for the battalion officers, regardless of their specialty, to secure the closest cooperation and coordination of the Engineer General Service regiments and battalions who so tremendously assisted in the rehabilitation of the lines.

Difficulty in securing and moving coal for locomotives' use caused the adoption, in the early stages in North Africa and Italy—and this was carried on in Europe also—of making over the American 2-8-0 steam locomotives into oil burners. Europeans were not accustomed to oil-burning locomotives, and so in Phase II and Phase III operations it was necessary to set up schools and teach European enginemen how to handle oil-burning locomotives. It must be said they were apt pupils, with excellent instructors, however, and soon the Europeans understood the great value of oil-burning locomotives.

Division of transportation was assigned on as nearly a uniform basis as possible. Sometimes units carried for a time tremendous burdens out of proportion to some of the other units. As an illustration, during February 1945 the 712 R.O.B., in the very center of the line with headquarters at Verdun and supporting the First United States and Third United States Armies, moved up 649,280 net tons and spotted them and switched 12 active railheads.

For one period, while Headquarters of the 740 R.O.B. were at Liége, the battalion served a total of 31 railheads. Because of the number of railheads, conductors and brakemen were utilized as Yardmasters. Non-commissioned officers were placed in charge at the majority of those places, and, without exception, turned in outstanding performances.

The 765 R.S.B. only hesitated in England and then went on to France, where it was set up as a part of the 706 R.G.D. in the Basse Yutz Shops outside Thionville. It specialized in Diesel locomotives' general repair and because of that a detachment of four officers and 100 enlisted men of "C" Company (the car company) on 23 April 1945 was attached to the 756 R.S.B. at Marseille to assist in the car-erection program there. At the same time a similar detachment of the 766 R.S.B. was also sent to Marseille to aid in the car-erection program.

The 765 R.S.B. continued Diesel locomotive repair at the Basse Yutz Shops until it was relieved 12 June 1945 for redeployment to the Pacific Theater.

During the winter of 1944-1945 the American Red Cross certainly made life easier for the M.R.S. men. It collaborated with them not only for service to them, but particularly to the orphans and widows of French railway employees. In addition to the various Christmas parties given, the 724 R.O.B. supported and assisted by Miss Madeleine Carroll of the American Red Cross, gave a party for 200 younger war victims of S.N.C.F. employees at Creil, France. Truly, the M.R.S. endeared itself to the families of the French "cheminots," and the relationship was outstanding throughout the war.

As of 1 March assignments of the various M.R.S. units were as follows:

G.H.Q., M.R.S., were at Paris, and under it were Headquarters, First M.R.S., with headquarters at Lyon and Headquarters, Second M.R.S., with headquarters at Brussels. Under First M.R.S. were the 703 R.G.D. with

Miss Madeleine Carroll, American Red Cross, Creil, France.

headquarters at Marseille and the 704 R.G.D., with headquarters at Nancy. Under Second M.R.S. were the 706 R.G.D., with headquarters at Luxembourg, 707 R.G.D. at Wesel, 708 R.G.D. at Liége, 709 R.G.D. at Brussels, 710 R.G.D. at Paris.

The 706 R.G.D., per General Orders No. 5, G.H.Q., M.R.S., 5 March 1945, was transferred to Headquarters, First M.R.S., without change in territory, component units, or headquarters.

Detachment "A" of the 717 R.O.B. had been operating on the continent of Europe since its arrival on 8 October 1944. Detachment "B" of this unit arrived on 16 March, and Detachment "C" arrived 26 March. It was then grouped and operated as Detachment "B," 717 R.O.B., under the command of Captain George P. Hayes. This unit was never brought to full strength nor did it have complete organizational equipment, so until the end of the war this unit was assigned to augment other railway operating battalions in the theater.

March saw many "firsts" in the M.R.S. The 718 R.O.B., operating in Luxembourg and north thereof, had the distinction of running its first train into Germany on 30 March, when it ran from Luxembourg City to Bleialf,

Germany. The train was in charge of Major Merle F. Savage and Captain Ralph E. Bean, and consisted of mail, rations, gas, oil, and coal.

The 741 R.O.B., on 15 March 1945, with a Company "C" operating crew consisting of Conductor Sergeant Patrick Brennan, Engineer Technician Fourth Grade Hugh M. King, Fireman Technician Fifth Grade Richard H. Fox, and Brakeman Private First Class Glenn E. Downing, ran its first train into Krefeld, Germany, commonly known as the Rhine River City. On arrival it was requested by a Signal Corps unit to repull into the station. Signal Corps photographers were on hand to take pictures of "the first train and first crew into that section of Germany."

The 732 R.O.B., a component part of the 706 R.G.D., had its headquarters at Thionville. The first M.R.S. operated train on German soil was operated by the 732 R.O.B. on 10 February and consisted of a train loaded with military supplies which was placed at the unloading platform of the Moselle Valley town of Perl, Germany. The crew consisted of First Lieutenant James R. Holmes, Staff Sergeant Estil H. Fields, Sergeant Anthony L. Garino, Sergeant James J. Jackson, Corporal Clyde P. Shepherd, Corporal Lloyd N. Payner, and Private John J. Faulkner.

Because of the rapid advance of the Third Army into southeastern Germany and the extension of M.R.S. operation of the Reichs Eisenbahn, the General Manager, Headquarters, First M.R.S., secured permission from the Director General to change his headquarters from Lyon to Strasbourg, France, and he opened it there 10 April 1945, in the office building of the S.N.C.F. On 12 April the French railroad building received two direct hits by German artillery fire during a two-hour bombardment commencing about 1430 hours. The French Ordnance judged them to be 210-mm. shells. The area surrounding the building was struck by approximately 20 shells. The first shell that hit the building struck the office below the Adjutant's office but the only damage to offices occupied by the M.R.S. was broken windows. The second shell hit Technical Sergeant Jack W. D. Mann, Equipment Department. Sergeant Mann died the same day from the wounds. Memorial services were held for Sergeant Mann the evening of the 13th in the enlisted men's billet; interment was made 14 April at Bensheim, Germany, in the American Military Cemetery.

The 756 R.S.B. had been making unbelievable records in the erection

10,000th car erected by the 756 Railway Shop Battalion, Marseille, France.

of freight cars on the pier at Marseille. Marking the completion of the 10,000th car erected in France by the 756 R.S.B. at Marseille, the Director General officiated at a battalion ceremony on 19 June at its shop there, dedicating the car to Sergeant Mann. Major E. C. Hanley, in the absence of Lieutenant Colonel Bates, Commanding officer for the 756 R.S.B., introduced the speakers. The ceremony opened with an invocation by Chaplain Lieutenant Colonel Fey, followed by a brief address by Colonel Oscar R. Diamond, head of the Equipment Section at First M.R.S. headquarters, who represented Colonel Stoddard.

The Director General in the dedicatory address said:

"Therefore, on behalf of the 26,000 soldier-railroaders in ETOUSA, the million and a half railroaders who are doing such a splendid and tremendous job at home, the hundred thousand French railroad men who have helped us carry these millions of tons of freight to our fighting armies, and the thousands of Belgian and Dutch railroaders who have entered into the spirit of railroad workmanship with us, I hereby dedicate this American erected boxcar, the 10,000th car to come from the production line of the 756th Shop Battalion, to the memory of an enlisted man whose sense of duty and adherence to a principle justifies us in awarding any honor we might bestow."

At the conclusion of this address the Director General stepped to the side of the car and unveiled the commemorative plaque on the door, as Chaplain Alexander arose and made the dedication prayer.

Dedication of locomotive to Pvt. H. J. O'Brien, killed in action.

The 10,000th car, USA 2203651, was completed on 29 May and differed from its predecessors only in the plaques attached to both doors, carrying the inscription:

The 756th Railway Shop Battalion dedicates this, its 10,000th car erected on the European continent, to the memory of Jack William Davis Mann, Jr., and the many other men of the Military Railway Service who have laid down their lives for their country.

The last car erected by the 756 R.S.B. rolled off the assembly line 29 August 1945. It was a non-cupola side-window caboose, No. 900820, and was the 28,801st car completed by that organization since it arrived overseas on 4 September 1943.

In addition to the car-erection activities of the 756 R.S.B., a detachment of the 764 R.S.B. was set up on the docks at Marseille for the purpose of unloading and processing new 2-8-0 American locomotives for ultimate delivery to the French. This detachment was commanded by Lieutenant Blizard assisted by Lieutenants Etheridge, Hickey, Stimson, and Linehan. The general foremen were Master Sergeant Mason and Staff Sergeant Riach. Together they achieved a production of four locomotives per day.

Another very striking sense of loyalty to comrades was demonstrated by the dedication at Liége, Belgium, on 27 February 1945, of a standard

2-8-0 American locomotive No. 2582, to the memory of Private H. J. O'Brien of St. Paul, Minnesota, a member of "A" Company of the 741 R.O.B., then a part of the 708 R.G.D.

This one dedicatory ceremony was symbolic of sixteen others by the placing on the sill under the cab window of the name of the soldier railroader who had been killed in action. Seventeen in the 741 R.O.B. were killed by enemy bombs and shell fire in the central thrust of the Germans in what was known as the "Battle of the Bulge." Ceremonies in other railway-operating battalions cherished the memory of their fallen comrades by similar dedications to members of their outfits killed in action.

While consumption of oil for the mechanized armies was tremendous, the M.R.S. was also a great factor in oil consumption with all its oil-burning locomotives. The 759 R.O.B. in its operations in southern France consumed alone during the month of March 1945 an average of 19,279 gallons per day, and on one day, 13 March, it burned 30,284 gallons of oil.

The French system of engine assignments with movement forward and back to their own enginehouses within their own subdivisions necessitated too much power and left too much terminal delays per locomotive. One of the first corrective measures was inaugurated by the 716 R.O.B. when it set up the system of running engines through these sub-terminals. This immediately decreased delays to trains and to locomotives, reduced the number of enginehouses in service, increased manpower by transfer to where needed, and provided much faster through trains from the back depots to forward dumps.

Operation was indeed difficult because the M.R.S. really kept on the very heels of the advancing army. One illustration of the difficulties and extent of this front-line operation was that experienced by the 712 R.O.B. when the line from Hanau to Würzburg was opened for traffic on 20 April 1945, handling as much as 30 trains, totaling 24,581 gross tons in a twenty-four-hour period, while hampered by complete blackout and enemy strafings at night, yet only one minor train accident occurred during the period.

Army engineers, cooperating with the Second M.R.S., completed the first rail link across the Rhine on 8 April. The link consisted of a 1,752-foot single-track bridge over the Rhine, a 463-foot bridge spanning a near-by canal, approximately two miles of connecting track, 36,246 track feet includ-

First bridge over the Rhine River, Wesel, Germany, 1945.

ing bridge approaches, and rearrangement and provision of yard facilities at Wesel and Büderich, Germany. Starting construction on 29 March at 1800 hours and working night and day, Army Engineer troops had the main bridge ready for traffic ten days, four hours, and forty-five minutes later.

Twenty-five minutes after the bridge was declared open, the M.R.S. operated the first train across this "last barrier" to Berlin and moved the train east for the unloading at Münster, Germany. The bridge was named for and called the Major Robert A. Gouldin.

Unlike civilian projects of this type, the location of military rail bridges is often decided upon on short notice, depending upon the developments in the tactical situation. In thinking over the problem before the actual crossing by combat troops, preference had been given to locating the first rail bridge at Duisburg, Düsseldorf, Cologne, or Wesel, with Wesel as fourth choice. It was fully expected that additional new bridges would have to be built, however. In pushing toward the Rhine the First Army established the first bridgehead by capturing a rail bridge near Remagen, south of Cologne, on 7 March. Immediately steps were taken to exploit the use of this bridge for rail traffic by rehabilitation of rail lines on the west bank giving access to the bridge. Then, on 17 March, the Remagen span collapsed. Planning by Second M.R.S. reverted to the original blueprints. On 22 March the Third Army crossed the Rhine south of Mainz. The Second British Army crossed the river north of Wesel on 24, 25, and 26 March. Then the envelopment around the Ruhr was completed, leaving Duisburg, Düsseldorf, and Cologne still in enemy hands. The rail crossing of the Rhine was decided upon for Wesel.

Decision on the actual location of the bridge was given the Army Engineers at 2200 hours on the night of 26 March. Reconstruction of the old destroyed railroad bridge at Wesel or use of its piers for a new bridge was rejected because of its former excessive height and length (3,500 feet) and the damage it had suffered. A point 1,500 feet upstream from the old railroad bridge was selected, adjacent to the piers and wreckage of a former highway bridge that the Germans themselves had planned to use, and partially completed, as a dual highway and railroad structure. Here, beginnings of completed approach tracks and embankments were available, connections could be made to Wesel Yard, and some protection from floating debris could be provided by the wrecked highway bridge. It was estimated that two weeks could be saved as compared to reconstruction at the old railroad bridge site.

The work was accomplished by the following Engineer, Quartermaster, Transportation Corps, Sea-Bees, and the M.R.S. units: 1056 Engineer P.C. & R. Group, 355 Engineer General Service Regiment, 371 Engineer Construction Battalion, 1st Battalion of the 341 Engineer General Service Regiment, Companies "A" and "B" of the 1317 Engineer General Service Regiment, 1533 Engineer D.T. Company, detachments of the 368 Engineer General Service Regiment, 433 Engineer D. T. Company, 482 Engineer Heavy Equipment Company, 469 Amphibious Truck Company, Sea-Bees, 980 Signal Service Company, 3112 Signal Service Battalion, 3901 and 4260 Quartermaster Truck Companies (Transportation Corps), and from the M.R.S. the Headquarters, Second M.R.S., and the 720 and 729 R.O.B.

During the first thirty days following the completion of the bridge, 273,141 tons were moved eastbound over it, 403,656 tons westbound, and 309,000 displaced persons.

A great territory was opened behind the Ninth United States Army with the completion on 14 April of the bridge over the Rhine at Mainz by the 347 Engineer General Service Regiment. The first train over was a work train operated by the 732 R.O.B. for the 347 Engineers who had constructed the bridge. Lieutenant General George S. Patton, Colonel Hulen, commanding officer of the 347 Engineers, and other officers were on that work train. The train crew consisted of Conductor Sergeant Bill Odum, Engineer Technician Fourth Grade Bill Dunmire, Fireman Private First Class Ralph Upshaw, Brakeman Private George Morton, and Pilot Technician Fourth Grade Anthony Garino.

The first playload to cross consisted of 34 cars of rations powered by two Transportation Corps Diesels and operated by a crew from the 718 R.O.B. Colonel L. G. Jamison, Commanding Officer of the 706 R.G.D., and Lt. Col. R. A. Wright, Commanding Officer of the 718 R.O.B., rode the lead engine. Tonnage commitment agreed upon for the line from the Metz-Thionville area over the bridge at Mainz was equivalent to 10,000 net tons per day.

The railway bridge over the Rhine River at Ludwigshafen, Germany, was completed and open to traffic on 23 April. First movement over the bridge was made by a light Diesel engine on that day. Two trains of the 727 R.O.B. equipment followed the test train.

The bridge over the Rhine at Karlsruhe, Germany, was completed and put into operation 29 April 1945. "Victory Bridge" over the Rhine at Duisburg was completed 12 May 1945. With its opening an alternate route over Wesel was provided and likewise made the handling of coal from the Ruhr coal fields more direct. While it was a single-track bridge, double tracks extended from both abutments and the peak movement was on 26 June, when a total of 32 trains passed over this bridge containing 1,113 loaded cars and 286 empties, with a total of 14,702 net tons. The last bridge over the Rhine River was completed at Strasbourg, France, 7 July, in the territory of the 704 R.G.D.

What bridges on a main line of communications mean when the freight has to go through is shown by the difficulties encountered in the movement of freight by the 729 R.O.B. Until the completion of the Weser Bridge on 25 April 1945 food and POL were unloaded from trains west of the Weser River and trucked east of the river, then reloaded on waiting trains destined for railheads 120 miles east. The first train crossed the Weser Bridge at 1824 hours on 25 April 1945, manned by a 729 R.O.B. engine and train crew.

One of the main problems also encountered in moving units up into Germany was that of always having to maintain communication between the headquarters and field units. Extra precautions had to be taken on all tele-

First train over Victory Bridge at Duisburg, Germany, 1945.

Celebrating completion of Victory Bridge over Rhine River, Duisburg, Germany, 1945. Demolished bridge is in background.

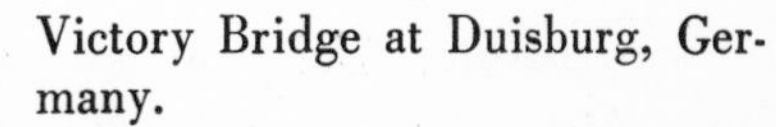

Victory Bridge at Duisburg, Germany.

German rail-mounted artillery.

phone and telegraph communications going into and coming out of Germany. When the units were first established in German territory it was necessary to inaugurate motor courier service between railways units, grand divisions, and the headquarters of both the First and Second M.R.S. in order to maintain daily contacts with the organizations in the field. That the problem was solved was due in no small measure to the Signal Corps network and the S.N.C.F. and the S.N.C.B. telephone networks.

Possibly the greatest volume of business during this period was handled by the 752 R.O.B. During the month of April it was operating in the vicinity of Namur, Belgium, and handled 3,108 trains hauling 1,347,344 net tons using 84,668 train miles, which produced 105 million net tons hauled one mile.

The final assault which led to the unconditional surrender of Germany and the proclamation of VE-Day on 8 May 1945 began with the British twenty-first Army Group on the extreme left flank and covered a period between 8 February and 10 March. The assault and drive of the Twelfth Army Group in the central sector began on 23 February and the Third and Seventh United States Armies began their assaults on the Saar Salient on 13 March.

The military situation at the time of the German surrender was a battle line which in reality was along the Elbe River with a small pocket east of the river still in the hands of the Germans in the vicinity of Magdeburg and Dessau; then beginning near Dresden and Karlsbad in Germany, the Germans held territory south of there into Czechoslovakia and Austria to a point south of Zagreb in Yugoslavia. The Russians in the meantime had pushed forward and occupied that region east of the Elbe from Wismar on the Baltic Sea, had crossed the Oder River, and had occupied Berlin and south including Brünn and Vienna, Austria.

The assignment of the M.R.S. at the time of the unconditional surrender of Germany was as follows:

General Headquarters, M.R.S., office of the Director General, was at Paris. Headquarters, First M.R.S., office of the General Manager, was at Strasbourg, France. Troops of the First M.R.S. were located as follows:

703 Railway Grand Division—Fürth, Germany
- 712 Railway Operating Battalion—Hanau, Germany
- 728 Railway Operating Battalion—Nürnberg, Germany
- 750 Railway Operating Battalion—Würzburg, Germany
- 761 Railway Transportation Company—Augsburg, Germany

704 Railway Grand Division—Nancy, France
- 713 Railway Operating Battalion—Ludwigshafen, Germany
- 727 Railway Operating Battalion—Heilbronn, Germany
- 733 Railway Operating Battalion—Neustadt, Germany

706 Railway Grand Division—Frankfurt, Germany
- 716 Railway Operating Battalion—Metz, France
- 718 Railway Operating Battalion—Metz, France
- 732 Railway Operating Battalion—Saarbrücken, Germany
- 759 Railway Operating Battalion—Hanau, Germany

The 756 Railway Shop Battalion at Marseille, France, the 765 Railway Shop Battalion at Thionville, and the 766 Railway Shop Battalion at Bischheim all reported direct to Headquarters, First M.R.S., and were not a part of any Railway Grand Division.

Headquarters, Second M.R.S., office of the General Manager, was at Brussels, Belgium, with the following units under its command:

707 Railway Grand Division—Wesel, Germany
- 720 Railway Operating Battalion—Wesel, Germany
- 723 Railway Operating Battalion—München-Gladbach, Germany
- 729 Railway Operating Battalion—Hanover, Germany
- 735 Railway Operating Battalion—Hamm, Germany

708 Railway Grand Division—Warburg, Germany
- 722 Railway Operating Battalion—Warburg, Germany

740 Railway Operating Battalion—Bonn, Germany
746 Railway Operating Battalion—Warburg, Germany
757 Railway Shop Battalion—Kassel, Germany
709 Railway Grand Division—Brussels, Belgium
734 Railway Operating Battalion—Maastricht, Holland
741 Railway Operating Battalion—Liége, Belgium
743 Railway Operating Battalion—Antwerp, Belgium
744 Railway Operating Battalion—Charleroi, France
752 Railway Operating Battalion—Namur, Belgium
755 Railway Shop Battalion—Namur, Belgium
763 Railway Shop Battalion—Louvain, Belgium
710 Railway Grand Division—Paris, France
724 Railway Operating Battalion—Compiègne, France
764 Railway Shop Battalion—Paris, France

On 9 May the 704 R.G.D. moved to Esslingen, Germany, and took over the general territory of Karlsruhe, Neustadt, Heilbronn, and Augsburg, and during the month of May the gross ton miles operated by this unit were 106,399,107.

With the surrender and re-establishment of lines, M.R.S. units moved into newly acquired Allied territory. Railroad transportation conditions were spotty. Some of the fine German facilities were not damaged at all, others were completely destroyed, and there were many between those two extremes. A few illustrations will explain.

At Nürnberg and Fürth in the territory of the 728 R.O.B. conditions were very bad. Enormous amounts of damage had been done to the tracks, bridges, roadbeds, terminal facilities, buildings, roundhouses, railway stations, etc. With all available personnel from the battalion and all available German railroad workers, and working on a 24-hour basis, the battalion set about to rehabilitate the facilities and start the operation of trains. By the end of the month of May most of the difficulties had been overcome and thought was given to turning over the operation of the railways to the German civilian personnel.

Also at Nürnberg and Fürth each were located sixty stall roundhouses. Company "B" of the 728 R.O.B. operated these two facilities and during the period from 8 May to 31 May, 92 locomotives were made serviceable at Fürth roundhouse, and according to the records during a twenty-four-

Double turntable, Cologne, Germany.

hour period a total of 133 locomotives were turned at Fürth roundhouse. The roundhouse at Nürnberg was used as a repair point.

At Hamm, Germany, under the 735 R.O.B., the Second Track Platoon under Lieutenant Joseph P. Green started the task of rebuilding the Hamm Passenger Station facilities and the roundhouse. His force for the job included part of "A" Company of the 717 R.O.B. and German labor. All bridge and water work necessary was done by the Bridge and Building Platoon under Lieutenant Nicholas V. Back of the 735 R.O.B. The job was pushed to a finish in thirteen days to meet the opening of the bridge over the Rhine at Duisburg on 12 May 1945.

Demolition of bridges across the Saar River delayed the rehabilitation of many miles of railroad. One of the bridges was rebuilt by the 733 R.O.B. It was an opening 297 feet and 52 feet above the river. A total of 10,880 man-hours were required in its rebuilding; 92½ tons of structural steel, and 330 cubic yards of concrete.

It became obvious shortly that the railroads could soon be turned over to the Germans for operations under M.R.S. supervision. At Kassel, in territory under the 708 R.G.D., Herr Bauer of the Reichs Eisenbahn reassumed operation of the railroad on 10 May 1945 in that sector.

Within a month some 21,000 German railway workers had returned to work and additional lines radiating out of Kassel and Hanover were placed under German railway workers with M.R.S. supervision. The German operation was successful and at no time did they fail to meet the traffic requirements as outlined by the American military authorities.

Rolling stock was operated on a pool basis and "per diem" was recognized. This general operation made it possible to move M.R.S. troops off the Reichs Eisenbahn. The 743 R.O.B. was transferred from the vicinity of Hanover for service in the Port of Antwerp as a result.

The Germans, likewise, at M.R.S. direction, began the repair to and rehabilitation of the catenary on their electrified lines with great success. The M.R.S. had been operating Diesel electric engines in this area, but with the success of the reestablished catenary lines and sub-stations German electric locomotives handled the business and American Diesel electric engines were discontinued on those lines. The first catenary system so restored was on 2 June 1945 on the line between Augsburg and Neu Offingen. Catenaries between Albach and Plechinger also were made ready for electrical service during the first part of June. Lines between Pasing and Ulm sub-station were energized, and the first electric train was operated from Ulm to Unterturckheim on 15 June 1945, and consisted of 50 cars. The electric line between Neuringen and Neu Ulm was put into service 27 June 1945. Leave trains were operated between Bietigheim and Augsburg, a distance of approximately 115 miles, on a four-hour schedule.

The 722 R.O.B. was assigned the line south out of Bremerhaven and Bremen and ran the first train into Bremen on 18 May 1945. This was a coal train in charge of Lieutenant Barnett and a train crew, all of whom, strangely enough, were New York, New Haven and Hartford Company employees prior to entering the Army, although they were serving in a Seaboard Air Line operating battalion.

While the actual fighting stopped with the complete surrender of Germany, it almost seemed that the difficulties of the M.R.S. and its railroad operation increased, at least temporarily, for the freight had to go through —and it did!

Possibly as busy a spot as could be found was that confronting the 729 R.O.B. at Herford, where the Army had a large ration dump. Prior to VE-Day, 1,400,000 United States personnel were fed from this dump. A typical operational month on this Hanover Division was reflected by the May activity report of the Train Movement Section. Trains moved totaled

977, divided almost equally as between eastbound and westbound; train miles covered were 61,529; tonnage handled, 772,391 net tons; number of DP's handled, 153,240; prisoners of war, 88,800.

At the same time the 735 R.O.B. moved a total of 1,222 trains handling 1,588,600 tons. Many of the trains were prisoner of war and displaced persons trains, an important and sizable job in itself, in addition to the regular supplies handled by rail.

There was not a balanced movement, and tremendous peaks occurred in train movement. On 25 May 1945, in the 741 R.O.B., 58 trains were put on the dispatcher's train sheet in seven hours and forty minutes. The average number of military trains moving over its territory were 96 per day. During May 1945, this battalion serviced a total of 3,153 locomotives in the four enginehouses under its jurisdiction; inspectors were working trains in seven yards; 518 cars were given light repairs during their short stay in the yards; they handled approximately 2,905 trains covering 56,507 train miles of military traffic.

During the six-month period January to June 1945, while operating in Belgium, Holland, and Germany, the 734 R.O.B. handled an astounding volume of traffic comparable to any civilian operation back in the United States. That battalion moved 18,179 trains with 341,757 loads, 96,227 empties and an estimated 6,835,140 net tons.

Lieutenant General Lucius Du B. Clay returned to Europe in April 1945 to serve as deputy for the military government of Germany. The policy was that a civil agency of government should eventually take over the control of Germany. His whole organization was separated from the military staff, and in this way were prepared to turn over the military government to the State Department with no necessity for complete reorganization.

General Eisenhower and General Clay sensed the opportunity of helping to make Germany self-supporting more quickly by an immediate restitution of coal mining in the Ruhr. That would provide work and capital for the Germans and permit them to export and import and improve their economy more quickly. This heavy coal traffic, which followed, likewise had important effects upon the operation of the railroads controlled by the M.R.S.

The ending of the war and the discontinuance of the Supreme Command (SHAEF) as well as the zoning of Germany as between the Americans,

Bridge near Bietigheim, Germany.

British, French, and Russians created rail transportation problems for the M.R.S. In the first place, traffic was reversed, and instead of moving from the ports of debarkation to depots and front lines there was much local traffic throughout the area going in every direction, accentuated by a tremendous passenger business occasioned by the return of prisoners of war, displaced persons, and those civilians who had homes somewhere in Europe and who desired to return to them at once.

An amusing incident concerning the handling of refugee trains was that experienced by Sergeant Jim Haag, Conductor and Pilot on a 732 R.O.B westbound refugee train. His German engine was having difficulty pulling a long train, his passengers were pretty unruly, and when the train stalled on a hill, Conductor Sergeant Jim was about ready to give up. But not so his customers. They intended to get to France and a little hill could not stand in their way. The entire train load piled off the cars, and as one man "put their shoulders to the wheel" almost literally, and pushed the train over the hump. Such was railroading in the Falck-Kreuznach division in May.

Not only was transportation of these prisoners of war and refugees a part of the M.R.S. responsibility, but their messes fed them as well. During the month of June 1945 the 724 R.O.B. messes served 7,600 meals to French civilian refugees and German prisoners of war.

This change of direction of traffic also necessitated new main routes of travel; therefore, new priorities incident to rehabilitation. This new program was handled by the M.R.S. with the G-4 sections of SHAEF, Sixth Army Group, Twelfth Army Group, American Military Government, and ETOUSA, and was finally approved by 12 May.

Conquered Germany was occupied by the four powers basically on the basis of the area that their troops occupied on the date of surrender. Berlin, however, almost in the geographical center of the Russian conquest, was divided into quarters: the Russians had the eastern half, the Americans the southwestern quarter, and the northwestern quarter went to the British with a small north and south area on the east side of the British section going to France. In the American Zone was the Tempelhof Airport and the large railroad hump classification yards. There was some difficulty, eventually ironed out, in establishing American railway movement between the west edge of the Russian-occupied section at Stendal and the American area in Berlin. The railroad gauges, however, were the same, and through trains could be run, the difficulty being in the Russians' control of the time and the amount of traffic to be moved.

The first train interchange with the Russians occurred between the 729 R.O.B. and the Russians at Magdeburg, Germany, on 17 May 1945, when 5,000 Russian prisoners of war were turned over to Colonel Roscofsky of the Russian forces.

Magdeburg had taken a terrific pounding from the Allied Air Forces. Before the town fell into the hands of the Ninth United States Army, they ringed the town, hub to hub, with every type of artillery including the giant 240-mm. Long Toms; consequently, the railroad yards looked anything but like one of Germany's largest railroad terminals. German labor, equipment, and materials were utilized to accomplish the rehabilitation of these railroad yards. Communications were partially restored to take care of train movements and the blocking of trains. German train crews were pressed into service but were told to stay away from the trains when the actual train transfer took place with the Russians. Most of this first train originated in the Ruhr Valley, and contained liberated Russian prisoners of war the Germans had taken during the battle for Stalingrad.

Another incident involving establishment of rail communications between the zones of the Allied Armies was one experienced by Captain James R. Thorne of the 722 R.O.B. An American crew on a caboose bounce had been told by their Trainmaster at Bremen to proceed to Northeim, Germany. This they did, but misunderstood their directions and proceeded on to Nordhausen, some twenty miles inside the Russian Zone, where they were detained by the Russians. Captain Thorne proceeded by motorcar and after insufferable delays by sentries at the border and ultimately by officers, including the Russian officer commanding in that area, he pushed his way to headquarters of the commanding Russian officer at Nordhausen. With a combination of diplomacy, direct statements, and unusual perseverance, he succeeded in getting the American crew with their locomotive and car back into the American Zone after a delay of three days. On the trip with Captain Thorne was the battalion Medical Officer, Captain Charles A. Kruse, as well as a driver, Corporal Flody C. Snipes, and an interpreter.

Railroad gauges in western Europe were uniform. This was not true

Dr. Julius H. Dorpmüller, Director, German State Railway.

of the Russian gauges and therefore the gauges of the Polish and German railroads had to be changed in order to handle through traffic from Russia to their western line of occupation, or transfer freight at junction points.

On or about 26 May the Director General was called by General Eisenhower, who said to him: "The war is over. Reorganize the Reichs Eisenbahn on a ministerial level, turn it over to the Germans, and go home."

Dr. Julius H. Dorpmüller had organized, rebuilt, modernized, and managed the German State Railways for years and a superb railroad it was. It was generally known and substantiated by our Intelligence Service that he was in no way a Hitlerite or Nazi. He was just an excellent railroad man who, if Hitler or his agents told him to move 10,000 troops from here to there, did it promptly; or if he was told to move 100,000 tons of freight from here to there, he did that promptly too.

Because he knew the German railroads and because he was not Nazi in any way, shape, or form, the Director General recommended that he be reinstated and called upon to reorganize and manage the German railroads as he had done so successfully in the past. This recommendation was approved. On 10 May 1945 the Director General told Colonel Sidney Bingham of his headquarters: "Go to Berlin and bring me Dr. Dorpmüller." The Colonel departed the same day, but nothing was heard from him until the late evening of 25 May 1945 when a telephone call from the Palace at Versailles from Colonel Bingham was received. He said: "Well, here I am with old man Dorpmüller. What will I do with him?" He was told to keep him incommunicado until eight o'clock the next morning when the Director General would be there. At the specified time he was.

The Director General had met Dr. Dorpmüller in 1936 when the Doctor was visiting the United States in the capacity of the President of the International Power Congress and made a tour after the convention to the West coast of the United States from where he proceeded to Germany.

When the Director General saw Dr. Dorpmüller he did not see the strong, stalwart German individual he had met in 1936. Then he learned why it had taken fifteen days to bring him from Berlin. When Colonel Bingham got to Berlin, Dorpmüller was not at his office. He was found in a small hospital just outside of Flensburg, Denmark, where he had undergone an operation and was convalescing. He still had a rubber tube draining him. Colonel Bingham was told by hospital authorities that he was able to travel, so he got the doctor out of bed, arranged for an elderly German nurse to accompany them, and then brought them to Paris.

It was quite an interesting conference the Director General had with Dr. Dorpmüller. It resulted in the conviction that Dorpmüller was not in any way a Nazi sympathizer or actionary and that he, Dorpmüller, would enjoy the opportunity to direct the rehabilitation and reorganization of the German railroads. He gladly accepted the situation offered him by the Director General. This appointment was approved by General Eisenhower's headquarters, and Dr. Dorpmüller was then sent to Frankfurt to open his headquarters. Unfortunately he had to have an operation for another ailment, and he died in Frankfurt 5 July 1945. Another gentleman, a Herr Bauer, was chosen as his successor. When the Director General and units of the M.R.S. departed from Europe in late October, this man was busily engaged in the rehabilitation of the German railroads.

During Dr. Dorpmüller's tenure of office the M.R.S. staff and the German railroads had a total of somewhere around 30,000 employees in the Kassel-Frankfurt-Nürnberg-Augsburg-Munich-Stuttgart area who were setting up and actually operating many trains with German crews and American conductors as pilots. German civilian maintenance-of-way employees, shop laborers and mechanics, station employees, interlocking tower operators, and train engine men returned to work rapidly. They went right about cleaning up and repairing the railroads. Being accustomed to taking orders they accepted in good faith American direction and control.

In the territory of the 733 R.O.B. in the vicinity of Neustadt, Russian laborers from the displaced persons' camp at Homberg and German civilian labor were used to good advantage in the rehabilitation of the tracks and yards.

The 757 R.S.B. moved from Cherbourg, France, to Kassel, Germany, during the period 2 May to 6 May 1945. Allied bombing had destroyed practically all railroad facilities, yet this shop battalion was able to begin operations at the famous Henschel Plant No. 1 at Kassel.

Heavy machinery from several smaller Henschel plants, located as far away as 120 miles, was brought to the main plant at Kassel and installed to speed the work of locomotive construction. Soon 4,000 Germans were employed in eight railroad manufacturing plants in the Kassel area, all under the jurisdiction of the 757 R.S.B.

One of the most interesting things that the M.R.S. found at the Henschel plants was the condenser-type engine—3,500 gallons of water was all the tank in the tender carried. The tender was a large one and contained condensing machinery, so that all of the steam used by the locomotive went through these condensers and the water went back into the tank and was used over and over again. It could go 700 miles on an original tank of water.

Possibly one of the most interesting facts about its development is the statement made by the German Shop Superintendent that these engines were designed for the purpose of the German invasion of Russia, where water is bad and is hard to get at that.

Lieutenant Colonel John W. Moe, Commanding Officer of the 757 R.S.B., found to his amazement quantities of completely fabricated parts of

'st pilot placed on condenser en-
ıe, Kassel, Germany.

Dedication of first condenser locomotive built by 757 Railway Shop Battalion, Kassel, Germany, 1945.

Condenser engine designed and built by Henschel at Kassel, Germany.

V-8 steam locomotive, Henschel & Son, Kassel, Germany.

a goodly number of these condenser engines and upon reporting this, he was told to commence erecting them.

The first condenser engine so erected was completed during May 1945, and dedicated to the Director General in an appropriate ceremony in the presence of the 757 R.S.B. officers and men as well as the German employees. This engine was erected exactly as planned, but it bore an additional interest, for there was fabricated on it the only pilot of any engine operating in Europe.

Another interesting locomotive that Henschel and Sons manufactured was a streamlined 4-6-2 V-type engine steam locomotive, the V-engines being mounted on both sides of the forward and rear main drivers.

Great difficulty was experienced by the M.R.S. throughout the North African and European Campaigns because of the fact that the Americans designated locomotives by wheels while the Europeans designated them by axles. Thus a 4-6-2 with us was a 2-3-1 with them.

Naturally, with the surrender, military tonnage decreased rapidly. Possibly the handling of 7 June will indicate the size and scope of the M.R.S. operations. This was approximately one month after VE-Day. On that day, just an average day in the M.R.S., there was handled 1,219 military freight trains, hauling 47,614 freight cars loaded with 529,274 net tons, which produced 77,000,000 net tons hauled one mile in twenty-four hours. Breaking that down again, the average shows 22,053 tons handled per hour.

It is also interesting to note the division between the First and Second M.R.S. The First handled 537 trains, 21,832 cars, and 207,174 net tons. Figures for the Second M.R.S. are 682 trains, 25,782 cars, and 322,100 net tons.

Loading reports for 7 June indicate that 1,805 cars were loaded at the main ports and 5,143 at depots and dumps. The highest number of trains run in any one day from the ports was on 29 March, when 123 trains containing 4,176 cars with 57,470 net tons were moved toward the front.

Effective 15 August 1945, the boundary between First and Second M.R.S. General Managers' districts was changed by General Orders No. 39, G.H.Q., M.R.S., 3 August 1945, which stated that: "Effective 15 August 1945, the boundary between First and Second M.R.S. General Managers' Districts is a line beginning at the North Sea thence south along the boundary line between Germany and The Netherlands, thence south along the boundary line between Germany and Belgium, thence south along the boundary line between Germany and Luxembourg, thence south along the boundary line between Germany and France, thence south along the boundary line between France and Switzerland, thence south along the boundary line between France and Italy, ending at the Mediterranean Sea. All United States Military Railway matters and interests west of this defined line are assigned to the General Manager, First M.R.S., with the exception of the Belgium District comprising Belgium and The Netherlands, which territory is assigned to this Headquarters. All United States Military Railway matters and interests east of this defined line are assigned to the General Manager, Second M.R.S."

The same order established a Belgium District and included the territory of Belgium and The Netherlands. This district was under the jurisdiction of the Commanding Officer, 706 R.G.D., who reported directly to the Director General.

Headquarters, Second M.R.S., moved from Brussels where it had been since February 1945 to Frankfurt on 12 August 1945. Brief outlines of units under its command and their moves are as follows:

The 707 R.G.D. was at Haltern-Herne, Germany, with the 720, 723, 729, and 735 R.O.B. in its command. The 707 R.G.D. moved to Fürth, Germany, on 21 July 1945, and had under its command at that time the 716, 735, 746, 750, and 752 R.O.B. and the 762 R.S.B.

The 708 R.G.D. had its headquarters at Warburg and the troops under its command were the 723, 729, 734, 740, and 741 R.O.B. and the 755 R.S.B. As of 1 November 1945, that R.G.D. took over the operation of the line Bremen and Bremerhaven, Bebra, Frankfurt, Mainz, and Mannheim.

The 709 R.G.D., with headquarters at Brussels, had the 722, 744, and 752 R.O.B. under its command. In June 1945 it was moved to Marseille and on 1 August moved to Calais, France, to the staging area there, departed there 16 August 1945, with destination as Manila. VJ-Day intervened, and the destination was changed to Boston, U.S.A. The unit docked there 30 August 1945; personnel were given furloughs and the unit reassembled on 16 October 1945 and moved to Fort Eustis on 26 January 1946, with nine officers and one enlisted man. The unit was disbanded in 1950.

Headquarters, 710 R.G.D., in Paris, directed the operations of the 754 and 757 R.S.B. and under Phase II and III operated the lines west of Paris to the ports of Le Havre, Rouen, and Cherbourg. The unit was moved to Brussels, Belgium, on 5 June 1945, and to Marseille on 30 July 1945.

To handle the rail transportation problems of the Reims Redeployment Area, where the camps were nostalgically named for famous American cities, the Paris Railway Grand Division (Provisional) was formed on 1 June 1945. This provisional unit was composed of officers and enlisted men from both the First and the Second M.R.S. and was charged with a twofold responsibility: first, giving the necessary supervision to rail traffic in and out of the redeployment area, and secondly, the direction of Phase III operations in the Nord, Est, and Ouest (North, East, and West) Regions of the S.N.C.F.

Colonel M. M. Shappell, by that time veteran overseas railroader, was named Commanding Officer of the Paris Railway Grand Division (Provisional) and opened headquarters of the new unit in St. Lazare Station, Paris. Units assigned to this newly formed grand division included the 724 and 733 R.O.B., the 130 Mobile Workshop, and the 117, 119, 120, 140, and 141 Hospital Train Maintenance Detachments.

Approximately at the same time this headquarters opened, the redeployment program began. Cars of material were and had been piling into the vast area too fast for the depots to unload and consequently they could not accept any more. This grew and grew until nearly 12,000 loads were set out short of destination. By 1 July the set-out total had been cut in half. As the first month reached its end, the movement of personnel out of the area began.

M.R.S. units were assigned and moved to render service. This brought about some unusual and interesting history as is evidenced by the record of the 740 R.O.B., which in the course of its service in Europe gave rail service to all Armies on the Continent except the Seventh. Third Army railheads were served west of Paris; First Army in Belgium and Germany; Ninth Army in Holland and the Fifteenth Army in Germany. In addition, railheads of Advance Section, Communications Zone, were served in France, Belgium, Holland, and Germany. Air Corps supplies were delivered in Belgium and Germany; British supplies in Holland and Germany, and French supplies in Germany.

At one time the 712 R.O.B. was actually operating a railroad in four different countries at the same time. This was during the period its headquarters were at Longuyon and Luxembourg City and it operated in France, Germany, Luxembourg, and Belgium.

Several innovations in train operations were established in order to facilitate Army movements. There was a heavy official passenger movement between Paris and Frankfurt and so the "Paris-Frankfurt Express" was established. Its inaugural run was made on 25 August 1945, leaving St.

Lazare Station, Paris, at 4:50 P.M. Its running time was 15 hours and 10 minutes. Colonel Frank R. Hosack, Director of Equipment, General Headquarters, M.R.S., broke a bottle of champagne on the locomotive at a brief ceremony before the train's departure from Paris.

The train consisted of one baggage car, two sleepers, one diner, and three first-class coaches. It was designated for the use of American military personnel traveling between Paris and Frankfurt on official orders. Dining service was under GI supervision. Reconstructed German cars were used in the train, painted olive drab.

With the unconditional surrender of Germany, plans were immediately made incident to the units of the M.R.S. for the following: 1, which units were to remain to provide logistical support to the Army of Occupation; 2, which units were to be redeployed to the Pacific Theater of War; and 3, the units to be returned to the United States for discharge.

In ETOUSA at the time of the surrender there were 1 General Headquarters, M.R.S., 2 Headquarters, M.R.S., 7 Headquarters, R.G.D., 24 R.O.B. and 8 R.S.B., 1 R.T.C., 10 Hospital Train Maintenance Detachments, 5 Railway Workshops Mobile, and 3 Base Depot Companies handling rail supplies exclusively.

Beyond 1 January 1946 it was planned that there would remain in Germany two headquarters, R.G.D., five R.O.B., and one R.S.B.

In connection with the transfer of the M.R.S. units direct to the Pacific Theater of Operations there were to be two Headquarters, R.G.D. (the 709 and 710), one R.O.B. (the 732), and one R.S.B. (the 765).

The general principle of the return of units to the United States in the M.R.S. was to be on the old railway principle of "First In—First Out."

The main line of communication was to start at the Port of Bremerhaven and come down through Bremen, Hanover, Bebra, and Frankfurt. The authority for American operation of the ports of Bremerhaven and Bremen and through territory occupied by the British was established by SHAEF on 3 April 1945. At Frankfurt the main line of communication was to break and one line was to go out through Würzburg, Nürnberg, and Regensburg. The other line extended south and southwest of Frankfurt through Mannheim and Karlsruhe and on southeast through Ulm, Augsburg, and Munich. There was a line connecting up those two lines east of Frankfurt between Nürnberg and

Augsburg. The total mileage to be operated was 1,071 miles, which averaged out very equally to a little over 200 miles of railroad to each of the railway operating battalions.

In the fulfillment of this demobilization plan, many officers and men were to go home on points, and many units were inactivated in France and Germany. The last units of the M.R.S. in Europe were the 734, 735, 741, 746, 750, and 752 R.O.B. and the 766 R.S.B., which were inactivated there 10 February 1946. Headquarters, Second M.R.S., was inactivated 13 February 1946. The last unit, the 716 R.O.B., left for the United States 15 February 1946.

10

Operations in Iran

1942-1945

UNITS OF THE M.R.S. served in the Middle East and Far East beginning in 1942. The first M.R.S. troops to serve in the Middle East were the units of the 702 R.G.D. (Union Pacific Railroad Company), Colonel A. E. Stoddard, commanding, and consisted of the 711 R.O.B. (M.R.S. sponsored), Lieutenant Colonel George M. Welch, the 730 R.O.B. (Pennsylvania Railroad), Lieutenant Colonel J. J. Clutz, the 754 R.S.B., Steam (Southern Pacific), Major Oscar E. Cole, and the 762 R.S.B., Diesel (Alco), Major William C. Rogers, commanding.

Subsequently, Headquarters, Third M.R.S., was formed with Colonel Paul F. Yount as General Manager, and also formed in the theater was the 791 R.O.B. on 1 July 1943, commanded by Lieutenant Colonel Worthington C. Smith, from the Northern Pacific Railway. When Headquarters, Third M.R.S., was formed on 10 April 1944, Headquarters, 702 R.G.D., was inactivated.

It is believed essential to describe the Iranian State Railway (I.S.R.) which the 702 R.G.D. was called upon to operate. In 1927 Reza Shah Pahlevi was the ruler of Iran and he decided that he wanted a railroad. So, with direct cash payments from his subjects, he started the construction of a standard (4′ 8½″)-gauge railroad to extend from Bandar Shahpour on the Persian Gulf to Bandar Shah on the Caspian Sea through his capital at Teheran. When completed, this railroad was 866 miles in length. Subsequently, there were several branch lines built, one of which was from the port of Khor-

Brigadier General Paul F. Yount, General Manager, Headquarters, Third Military Railway Service.

ramshahr to Ahwaz, being built by the British, and covered a distance of 77 miles. There was likewise built a line of 272 miles northwest from Teheran to Mianeh. These lines with the other branch lines in 1942 totaled some 1,448 miles.

The country is exceptionally mountainous and largely desert, and from Bandar Shahpour at sea level the railroad rises to a height of 7,271 feet at Arak on an average 1.5 per cent grade, and descends to Bandar Shah, which is 85 feet below sea level, with a ruling grade of 2.5 per cent. Because of the terrifically high mountain ranges this railroad has 231 tunnels totaling 53 miles in length, and 4,102 bridges, from 16 feet to the longest one, which is 3,512 feet over the Karoune River at Ahwaz. When completed, this railroad cost the people of Iran 2,400,000,000 rials ($145,454,000), but was unique in that it had no debt.

Germany's proposed invasion of Russia created a crisis, as it were, in Iran, and the British and Americans found themselves allies of Russia by reason of their having a common foe, Hitler. The British moved into Iran in force and their Transportation Service took over the operation of the Trans-Iranian Railroad from Bandar Shahpour to Teheran. The Russians moved

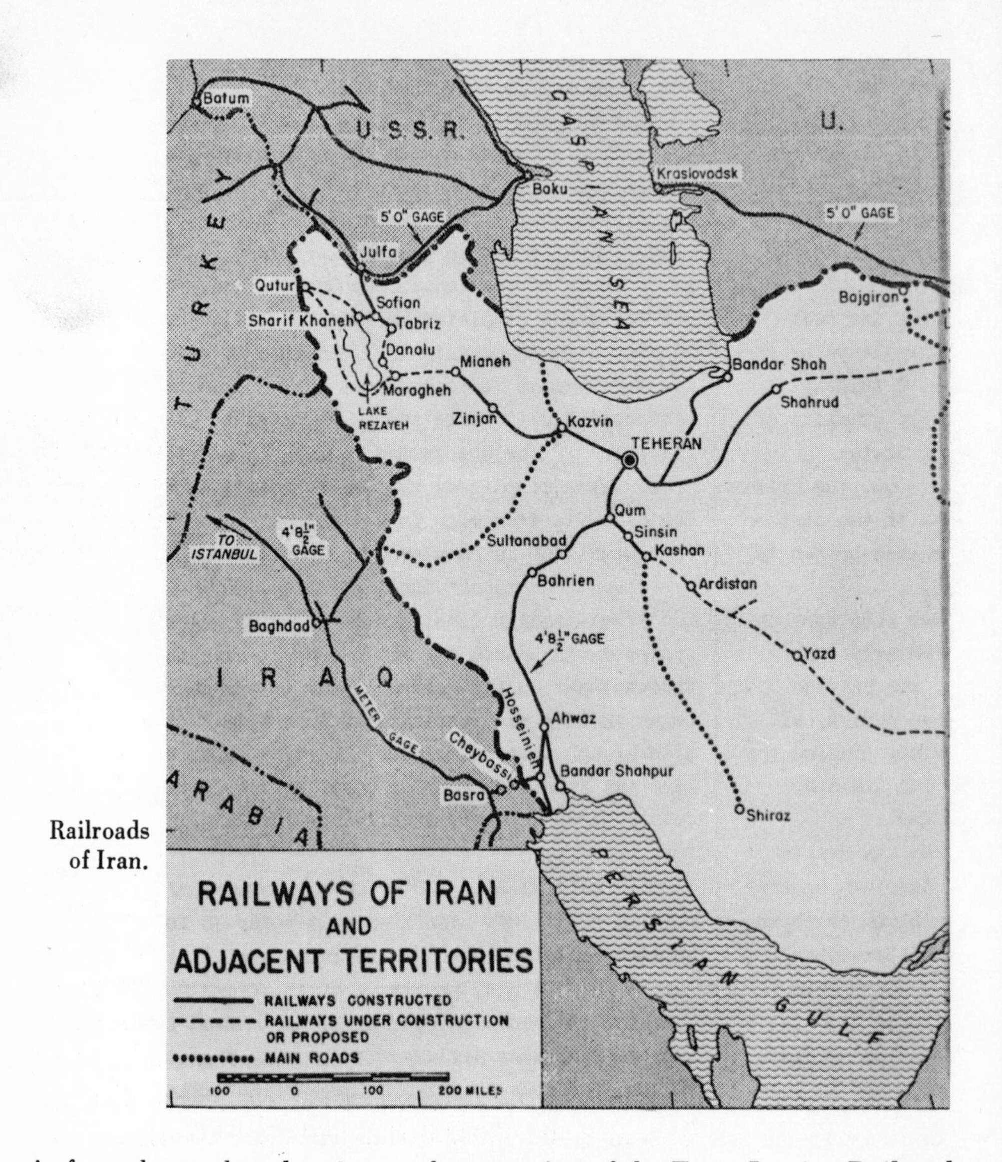

Railroads of Iran.

in from the north and took over the operation of the Trans-Iranian Railroad from Mianeh east and west through Teheran to Bandar Shah. The Russians likewise took over the only other railroad in Iran before 1927, which was of 5′ 0″ gauge, from Tabriz to Julfa (92 miles) and met the 5′ 0″ gauge Caucasian Railways at the Soviet frontier.

The I.S.R. was international in character and built by contract with

Iranian railroad at Km. 572.

companies from the following countries contributing: United States, Germany, Russia, Sweden, Denmark, Poland, Switzerland, France, Australia, Iraq, Italy, Japan, and Czechoslovakia. Such famous names as Mitsui and Mitsubishi of Tokyo, Krupp of Essen, Skoda of Prague, Storch-Nielsen of Copenhagen, les Petit Fils de François de Vandel et Çie, Paris, and Ford, Buick, Chevrolet, and Dodge of Detroit furnished material.

There was formed by the United States originally the United States Military Iranian Mission headed by Brigadier General Raymond W. Wheeler. Through subsequent changes this Iranian authority became the Iran-Iraq Service Command, then the Persian Gulf Service Command, and lastly the Persian Gulf Command, and was then commanded by Major General Donald H. Connolly.

An Allied Conference was held in Cairo in midsummer 1942, which included Prime Minister Winston Churchill from England and W. A. Harriman from the United States. After that conference, Prime Minister Churchill communicated Top Secret with the President of the United States and ac-

Iranian railroad bridge at Km. 556.

cepted the President's proposal that American M.R.S. troops take over the operation of the I.S.R. for the purpose of transporting American war supplies to Russia.

Mr. W. A. Harriman, who was not only American ambassador to Russia, but was also the special liaison representative of the United States in matters pertaining to Lend Lease, inspected the area and concurred heartily in the request that the M.R.S. troops be sent for the purpose of operating the I.S.R. By virtue of his railroad connections, he indicated that because of the tremendous heat and the many lengthy tunnels on the Iranian railroad, Diesel electric power be provided.

Mr. William J. Jeffers, President of the Union Pacific Railroad (and at that time the "Rubber Czar" for the United States Government), and the Manager, M.R.S., attempted to secure the necessary Diesel electric power to satisfy this requirement. It was felt that the 1,000-horsepower combination road switcher was the best type to send and it was found that 57 of these locomotives had just been delivered to American carriers or were in the process of being completed by the manufacturers. They were all secured and shipped as the motive power to be used by the M.R.S. troops in Iran. In addition to that it was recommended that 2,200 freight cars likewise be sent to Bandar Shahpour.

In early September 1942 the Manager, M.R.S., then with headquarters at St. Paul, Minnesota, was asked to nominate a Railway Grand Division for immediate service in Iran. He indicated to the War Department that the 703 R.G.D. was the only one ready. That having been set up and allocated to the invasion of North Africa, the War Department refused to utilize the 703 R.G.D. It became necessary then to create the 702 R.G.D.

The British had been attempting to transport 3,000 tons of military supplies per day, but the requirement set for the Americans was 6,000 tons per day.

In order to permit the officers of the 702 R.G.D. and its units an opportunity to see what they had to do, what they had to do it with, and where each unit was going to be, two echelons were flown in advance over to Iran via Africa. The first was headed by Colonel A. E. Stoddard, and consisted of Lieutenant Colonels John P. Johnson, John J. Clutz, and George M. Welch, and Captain William M. Martin. The first four arrived in Basra on 31 October 1942 and Captain Martin arrived 2 November. The other group left Washington in November and arrived in Basra 8 December, and included Major James H. Gildea, Captain Carl O. Scannell, Captain Philip W. Michaud, First Lieutenant Glenn E. Miller, and First Lieutenant Walter Aye.

The 711 R.O.B. was the first unit of the M.R.S. to arrive. It landed at Khorramshahr on 11 December 1942. In accordance with the previously approved plan of operation it was assigned the territory between Khorramshahr and Ahwaz with divisional headquarters at Ahwaz. Its duty was to spot cars at the docks, make up trains and move them out of the port. Subsequent road assignments along the line of railroad included its taking over the operation of the Iranian State Railway from Bandar Shahpour to Ahwaz on 9 January 1943, from Ahwaz to Andimeshk on 16 January, and from Andimeshk to DoRoud on 18 January.

When Headquarters 702 R.G.D. arrived on 3 February it took over the supervision of the I.S.R. and established headquarters at Teheran on 6 February 1943. Colonel P. F. Yount assumed command of the Headquarters,

702 R.G.D., on 9 February 1943, and Colonel Stoddard assumed other railroad duties.

Other members of the staff then comprised Captain Leslie D. Curtis, Executive Assistant to the General Manager; Colonel Ralph E. Knapp, Assistant General Manager; Lieutenant Colonel Lionel E. Hammond, Engineer of Track and Structures; Major Aubrey M. Bruce, Superintendent of Equipment; Major Raymond H. Wonnenberg, General Storekeeper; Captain Jourdan Rigby, Security and Safety Officer; Captain Henry Dawes, Public Relations and Labor Officer, and Captain Carl E. Steeves, Adjutant.

The 730 R.O.B. arrived 1 February and was established on the north end of the railroad with headquarters at Arak at first and took over the operation of the I.S.R. from DoRoud to Teheran.

The 762 R.S.B. Diesel arrived 10 March 1943 and set up its shop operations on the I.S.R. at Ahwaz. The 754 R.S.B. Steam arrived on 22 March and took over the shop facilities of the I.S.R. at Teheran.

From a practical standpoint the two operating battalions had too much mileage for the business to be handled. So the First Provisional Operating Battalion, later to be known as the 791 R.O.B., was activated in the theater on 1 May 1943. This organization was formed by transfers from other units and many officers were commissioned in the field. The first two to receive such commissions were First Sergeant Francis J. Lewis and Technical Sergeant James S. Hooper, both of the 702 R.G.D., who were commissioned Second Lieutenants.

The newly formed unit took part of the line from the 711 R.O.B. and part of the line from the 730 R.O.B. and thus operated the line between Andimeshk and Arak, a distance of 220 miles.

The assignment of the three units was that the 711 R.O.B., with headquarters still at Ahwaz, had all rail line south of Andimeshk through Ahwaz to the ports of Tanuma, Khorramshahr and Bandar Shahpour. The 791 R.O.B., with headquarters at Arak, operated between Andimeshk and Arak, and the 730 R.O.B., with headquarters then moved to Teheran, operated from Arak to Teheran.

Unlike in other theaters, the M.R.S. units in Iran did not have to rehabilitate the railroads from war ravages and damages before they could start running trains. While improvements and more modern railroading

Roundhouse at Andimeshk, Iran.

Roundhouse at Qum, Iran.

practices were established by the M.R.S., they did not have to rebuild bridges, clear tunnels, and rebuild track damaged by enemy action. It was more like commercial railroading.

Heroism in the line of duty should be, but is not always, recognized. On 13 February 1943 Private Herbert J. Powell of Company "C" of the 711 R.O.B., while riding the tender of an engine backing up, leaped from the tender and knocked an Arab off the track who would otherwise have been killed but for Private Powell's quick thinking and heroism. For this he was awarded the Soldier's medal on 24 April 1943 with appropriate ceremonies.

The M.R.S. had to "Americanize" many practices, particularly in the Accounting Department where a system of American accounts was established covering Material Accounting, Revenue Accounting, and Payroll Accounting. The Stores and Accounting Sections of the M.R.S. remained after the soldier-railroaders went home.

Supplies for the Russians were coming very fast and the tonnage built up very rapidly. In February 1943 the total tons handled were 22,835, and by June had reached 67,729, an increase of approximately 300 per cent.

The 711 R.O.B. showed its capacity early. Its first record was set on 3 March 1943, when it exceeded in tons handled all previous records of freight handled on the railroad by the Iranians or for that matter after the British took control, when it hauled 6,402 gross tons that day. It continued to improve by hauling 7,376 tons on 5 April, and on 21 May, 9,318 gross tons.

Diesels played no small part in these records. The first Diesel-powered train moved on 10 March 1943, from Ahwaz to Andimeshk, and by 16 April Diesel power was uniformly used between Bandar Shahpour and Khorramshahr and Andimeshk.

There was at least one similarity between operating conditions on the Iranian Railroad and those on American railroads from which the men came. That was that Mother Nature causes floods and washouts everywhere. Their first trouble occurred on 21 March 1943, when several thousand feet of track and one bridge were washed out on the Khorramshahr-Ahwaz line. As a result, train movements were suspended from the 22d to the 31st of that month. Service was resumed first with a single train in each direction on alternate days.

The men of the 711 R.O.B. on 29 March had the distinction of handling the Queen Mother of Iran on a special passenger train, Diesel powered, from Ahwaz to Teheran and established between Ahwaz and Andimeshk the fastest time ever made by a passenger train on that railroad. They covered the distance in two hours, thirty-eight minutes. After the return of the railroad to Iranian hands, regular passenger train schedules between these two points were three hours.

On Sunday, 23 May 1943, the M.R.S. men in the vicinity of Teheran had the pleasure of meeting and attending services held by the Military Vicar of the United States Armed Forces, His Excellency, the Most Reverend Francis J. Spellman, Archbishop of New York.

In June 1943 they were honored by a visit from the famed World War I hero Captain Eddie Rickenbacker.

In order to handle the 6,000 tons daily goal of the Persian Gulf Command in the logistical supply to the Russians, it was necessary to build up the rolling stock and engines materially. In August 1941 the I.S.R. had 67 locomotives, 49 passenger cars, and 1,113 miscellaneous freight cars. They had under order, and there were delivered within the next year, 32 Diesel switchers. During British control there was added 200 steam locomotives and 1,696 freight cars to the rolling stock of the I.S.R.

When the Americans took over they brought in 57 1,000-horsepower road switchers as well as 91 2-8-2 steam locomotives and 2,906 miscellaneous freight cars. Thus, the M.R.S. finally carried all the tonnage with 390 locomotives and 5,088 freight cars.

The capacity of the M.R.S. to handle tonnage was constantly reduced by the unfortunate delay in unloading cars at destination in Russian territory and in the failure of the Russians to accept interchange at Teheran. The situation got so desperate that all the cars were on the north end under load so that it became necessary to establish an embargo which lasted from 8 to 13 August 1943, at which time no freight was put aboard cars or moved out of the southern ports. As an illustration of the congestion, it was taking tank cars thirty days to move from Khorramshahr to Bandar Shah and return, which was twice as great a time as M.R.S. calculations contemplated. Had there been action on the north end, the fifteen-day turnaround could easily have been accomplished.

By September, the situation had ironed out sufficiently so that the handling for September totaled 102,261 tons.

In reciting experiences in Iran, one finds the same problem of railroading that the M.R.S. found in North Africa, Italy, and the Continent. That was stealing. As in other theaters, the situation was handled by the creation of a Security Section with special troops guarding stations, yards, and riding trains. In Iran, however, the Security Section likewise had to cover additionally the question of sabotage by German agents.

Extreme heat in the summer and extreme cold in winter, as well as lack of water, made hard railroading. It is recorded that a thermometer in the cab of a second engine of a double-headed steam train in one of its trips to Teheran recorded the unbelievable figure of 145° (Fahrenheit).

Company "A" of the 730 R.O.B. spent most of its time in water supply along the Iranian railroad. In its headquarters camp at Teheran, the 730 R.O.B. provided 500,000 gallons of water per day, all of which had to be treated. Company crews built 4,000 feet of pipe lines in various water-distribution systems to expedite rail facilities at outlying stations.

On 23 October Indian guards accidentally turned over an oil stove in a car in the Ahwaz yards, setting a fire which exploded a carload of ammunition. This caused considerable damage and injuries to M.R.S. personnel. Lieutenant Colonel Mattson, the Superintendent of the 711 R.O.B., was badly injured and hospitalized, as well as nine other 711 R.O.B. men. First Lieutenant Claude W. Hovis of the 711 R.O.B. died of his injuries on 25 October 1943. The severe damage to the yard and equipment was cleaned up and normal operations resumed in 18 hours.

A rather unusual set of circumstances deprived the American troops of displaying "Old Glory" in their encampments, because they were operating in a neutral country. This limitation was lifted when on 9 September 1943 Iran declared war on Germany and American troops could fight under their flag in their successful attempt to protect that portion of the world against Hitler and Mussolini.

Many M.R.S. men had entered the service shortly after their arrival in the United States and were not naturalized citizens of the United States. This was happily corrected in a series of naturalization ceremonies, and the first American railroad men to become naturalized in this fashion in the Persian

Gulf Command were: Private First Class Stanley B. Mars (who at the same time streamlined his name from Marsowicz), Private First Class Herbert Otley, and Private Michael A. Maruscak, all of the 754 R.S.B. Steam.

By the first of the year 1944 the tonnage increased. For January 1944 the M.R.S. handled a total of 146,685 tons. In March the tonnage hauled amounted to 125,726, and for the month of May 1944, 113,583 tons. Tonnage in August 1944 amounted to 164,253 tons, and in November 1944 there were 112,218 tons hauled.

On 11 May 1944 Colonel Frank S. Besson, Jr., succeeded as Director and General Manager of the Third Headquarters, M.R.S., in place of Colonel Yount who departed for other duties in the C.B.I. Rotation of officers out of the theater caused a reorganization of the M.R.S. forces in Iran when in September 1944 Colonel A. E. Stoddard, Lieutenant Colonels M. M. Shappell, J. H. Gildea, C. T. Warren, and W. C. Smith were sent to the European Theater. With the reorganization, Lieutenant Colonel Clutz became General Superintendent, Lieutenant Colonel R. E. Mattson became Superintendent of Transportation, Lieutenant Colonel A. L. Hunt became Assistant General Superintendent, and Major W. T. Rice became Commanding Officer of the 791 R.O.B. Lieutenant Colonel W. C. Rogers became Commanding Officer for the 762 R.S.B. Diesel, Major George Taylor became Commanding Officer of the 730 R.O.B., and Captain Herbert M. Curtiss became Commanding Officer of the 711 R.O.B. On 31 December 1944 there were 158 officers, 6 warrant officers, and 3,809 enlisted men in the Third M.R.S.

During the month of January 1945 the M.R.S. handled 105,706 gross tons, and during the month of May 1945, which saw the end of the war in Europe, the M.R.S. handled 31,330 tons. This reduced tonnage figure reflected the opening of a shorter and new supply route in January from the United States to Russia. This route was through the Bosporus and the Dardanelles, but the operation of the I.S.R. was held in reserve.

How well the M.R.S. accomplished its mission and fulfilled the confidence that the American government officials had when they directed their taking over the Iranian State Railway is evidenced by the final result. From 1 April 1943, when the M.R.S. assumed complete control of the I.S.R., to 1 June 1945, when its mission was completed, it handled 4,144,122 long tons of freight of which 2,749,190 long tons was military freight for the Russians and 1,394,932 long tons was civil Lend-Lease freight for the Iranians. This was an average of 3,524 long tons daily during the 26 months of operation.

The M.R.S. had a passenger business of no small proportions in addition to its great freight volume. During the same 26 months' period on special passenger trains, it handled 16,000 Iranian military passengers, 14,000 Polish war refugees, 40,000 British troops, and 15,000 Russian ex-prisoners of war, while 80,000 British military personnel traveled on regular passenger trains. The New Year season on the Moslem calendar likewise caused a heavy passenger business. During the period from 22 February to 21 April 1944, 21,000 pilgrims were moved on regular and special passenger trains from Teheran or Ahwaz to and from Qum, the Holy City.

It must be said that the Russians recognized the tremendous work done by the M.R.S. in Iran in moving their supplies. At that time they apparently were appreciative, for on Memorial Day, 1945, they, in formal ceremonies, awarded the Order of the Fatherland, First Class, to Lieutenant Colonels Clutz, Bruce, Mattson, and Cole. Lieutenant Colonels Smith and Gildea were awarded the Order of the Fatherland, Second Class. Technician Fifth Grade Harry C. Slick of Company "C," 730 R.O.B., was awarded the Order of the Red Star. Earlier that month four officers and 38 enlisted men received commendation from the Soviet Transport Department in Iran for their assistance in clearing a portion of the I.S.R. under Russian operation that had been damaged in floods.

Because the end of the war saw the diminution of operations, plans were immediately developed for the return of the I.S.R. to its owners and the moving of M.R.S. troops out of Iran. On 1 June the Persian Gulf Command relinquished control and indicated that its mission was fulfilled. The actual turnover by the Military Railway Service was to the British on 25 June 1945. The British lost no time in passing the railroad operation over to the Iranians.

M.R.S. troops were moved out of Iran as follows: the 791 R.O.B. and the 762 R.S.B. Diesel departed in May 1945; the 730 R.O.B. departed in June 1945; the 711 R.O.B. departed in July 1945; Headquarters, Third M.R.S., departed in August 1945. The 754 R.S.B. Steam was inactivated 25 July 1945 in Iran, and its personnel sent home.

11

Operations in India

1943-1945

THE M.R.S. had a second call for service in the Middle East and fulfilled that mission in the operation of a portion of the Bengal and Assam Railroad in northeastern India. As in Iran, it is believed that the background of this railroad should be indicated, as well as the justification for the use of M.R.S. troops in that area.

The Bengal and Assam Railway in Assam, India, is state-owned with the exception of the railroad line between Tinsukia and Ledo, which was a privately owned and operated railroad. As had been found in North Africa, the Bengal and Assam had various gauges; from the port of Calcutta, the railroad runs almost due north to Siliguri, a distance of about 300 miles, and has a gauge of 5′ 6″. North from there, to the resort town of Darjeeling, the gauge is 2′; then beginning at Khatihar and running eastward to Parbatipur the railroad extends across the Brahmaputra River to Tinsukia, Ledo, and Sakkhoa Ghat. This is meter gauge. This portion of the B.&A. was constructed almost parallel to the Brahmaputra River, first on one side, then on the other, but at no place is that river bridged by the railroad. Trains are ferried across instead.

There is a loop south of this line of railroad which extends southeast from Parbatipur to Akhaura, and then northeasterly to connect up with the main line at Lumding. There is likewise a branch line extending southeasterly from Akhaura through the towns of Laksam, Cittagong, and Dohazari. All of this portion of the railroad is also meter gauge.

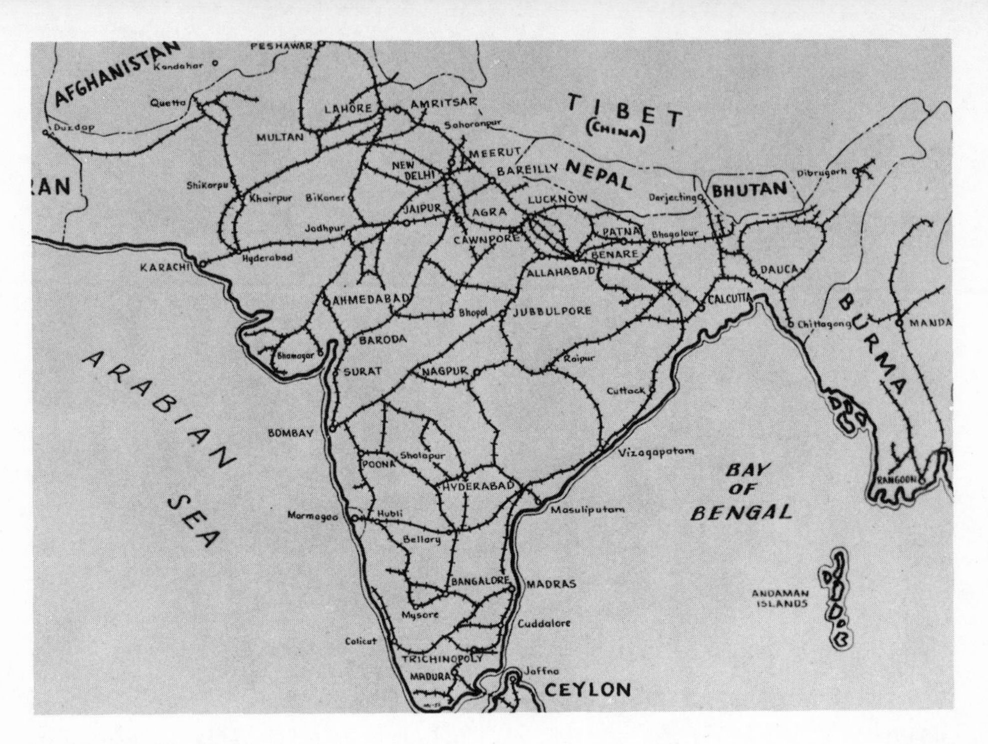

Railroads of India.

In all, the Bengal and Assam has 3,478 miles of railroad. The route of military goods from Calcutta to Ledo was 738 miles. The operation by the M.R.S. covered only that portion of the road from Khatihar east to Ledo on the direct and northern route, a distance of 658 miles. With branch lines, it operated a total of 804 miles of the Bengal and Assam Railway.

The Supreme Commander in Chief of the Southeast Asia Command in 1942 was Lord Louis Mountbatten. Lieutenant General J. W. Stilwell, who commanded the United States Army Forces in the China-Burma-India Theater (USAFCBI), was his deputy. The American High Command in this theater of operations was changed on 24 October 1944 to the United States Forces in the India Burma Theater (USFIB) under Lieutenant General D. I. Sultan, and then Lieutenant General W. A. Wheeler, Major General T. A. Terry, and finally Major General V. Evans.

Previously, M.R.S. troops had been used only in operating railroads in the logistical support of the Allied Forces fighting Germany. The situation was changed by the Japanese tying up with Hitler and in their attempt to conquer China. In the India-Burma Theater, the M.R.S. was to haul supplies the greater part of the distance to the Chinese troops who were attempting to repulse the invasion of the Japanese. Thus, as in Iran, where M.R.S. troops handled supplies to the Russians, in India and Burma the M.R.S. mainly was delivering supplies to the Chinese.

It was impossible to have a railroad constructed and in service from Ledo to the Chinese dumps, so the railroads hauled to Ledo and then supplies were flown by air lift to China or hauled by trucks over the Ledo and Burma Roads. These were relocated and ultimately called the Stilwell Road.

The British had had transportation service troops in India and likewise had formed Indian transportation troops. It was recognized that the Assam line of communications was essential for military purposes and had to be improved, so early in 1942 British and Indian Transportation Service troops were placed along this line in order to bring it up to the required standards for handling the ever-increasing tonnage that it would be necessary to move over this route.

In December 1942 Brigadier General J. A. Appleton, General Manager, New York Zone of the Pennsylvania Railroad, in company with General Harrison and Colonel Thomas Farrell, was directed to go to Europe and Asia to make an inspection of the United States Service Forces installations. General Appleton's particular part of that mission covered the adequacy of railroad equipment and troops in the various countries the commission visited.

The situation in the Pacific became critical. The high command in India requisitioned M.R.S. troops for operation of a portion of the meter gauge of the B.&A. By November 1943 the decision had been made. An augmented Railway Grand Division was designated for India. The grand division chosen was the 705 R.G.D. headquarters, sponsored by the Southern Pacific Railway and commanded by Colonel Stanley H. Bray, General Superintendent. Five R.O.B. were assigned to that grand division, and they were:

721 R.O.B. (New York Central), Lieutenant Colonel Karl F. Emmanuel.

725 R.O.B. (Chicago, Rock Island and Pacific Railroad Company), Lieutenant Colonel George Branch.

726 R.O.B. (Wabash Railroad Company), Lieutenant Colonel Harvey Pilcher.

Colonel Stanley H. Bray, General Superintendent, 705 Railway Grand Division.

745 R.O.B. (Chicago, Burlington and Quincy Railroad), Lieutenant Colonel W. P. Wilson.

748 R.O.B. (the Texas and Pacific Railway Company), Lieutenant Colonel Alva C. Ogg.

758 R.S.B. (The Atchison, Topeka and Santa Fe Railway Company), Lieutenant Colonel Clarence V. Conlisk.

General Appleton again went to India in company with Sir Robert Inglis, General Manager of the London and North Eastern Railway, in November 1943, and they made and reported to the Viceroy of India a complete survey of the transportation picture. Just as General Appleton departed from Washington to go on this assignment, he received additional orders from General Somervell, who was then in India, placing him in command of the M.R.S. troops there.

M.R.S. was to support the building of the Ledo Road and the airfield under construction for the air lift over the Himalaya Mountains. It was also needed to supply the British Army and General Stilwell's forces in Burma who were battling the Japanese in their attempt to move through northern Burma after the fall of Singapore on 15 February 1942. The British Transportation Service had been directing the operation of the Bengal and Assam Railway since the outbreak of the war. The British Railway troops in the theater on the railroad at that time consisted of one Railway Operating Company and two Railway Construction Companies.

The Indian and Burmese Rail Transportation Units in India and Burma had been formed and recruited and trained by the English, much as the M.R.S. troops of the United States had been. They took experienced men off the railroads, formed them into units, and trained them along a line of railroad. In all, the British had organized the following units:

9 Indian Railway Construction and Maintenance Group Headquarters
4 Indian Railway Survey Companies
22 Indian Railway Construction Companies
20 Indian Railway Maintenance Companies
4 Indian Railway Bridging Companies
10 Indian Railway Operating Group Headquarters
34 Indian Railway Operating Companies
5 Indian Railway Yard Operating Companies
2 Indian Railway Workshops Group Headquarters
9 Indian Railway Workshops Companies
2 Indian Railway Control Groups
1 Indian Railway Telegraph Maintenance Section.

Colonel Bray of the 705 R.G.D. and certain of his staff formed an advanced echelon and arrived in New Delhi, India, shortly after 1 December 1943. They immediately set up the plan of operations, the portions of the railroad that each unit would operate and their headquarters, and started the preparation of quarters for these units.

The American command, by virtue of the experience gained in North Africa and Italy, made sure that in the M.R.S. taking over the responsibility for the logistical supply of the British and American armies and in support of the Chinese no interference would be had from any source. In other words, the M.R.S. of the United States Army was to have full and complete control over the operation of the lines taken over.

The form of operation ultimately in use was such as the M.R.S. troops had had in North Africa and Italy—Phase II and III operations. With Phase

Comparison of Military Railway Service and Indian transportation, 1944.

Locomotive in India on the Bengal and Assam Railroad.

II operation, certain units of the M.R.S. and their manpower were superimposed upon the military and civil operations; in Phase III the M.R.S. units supervised and directed the operations of the Indian civilian employees.

The main body of M.R.S. troops started to arrive at Bombay 11 January 1944. Operation of the Bengal and Assam Railway by M.R.S. began officially 1 March 1944. The previously agreed assignment of these M.R.S. units was that the 705 R.G.D. headquarters would be located at Gauhati. The 721 R.O.B. headquarters were established at Parbatipur; they were to run the railroad from Khatihar, some 80 miles west of Parbatipur, where the B.&A. joined the Oudh and Tirhut Railway, eastward through Parbatipur to Lalmanirhat, a total distance of 120 miles. They were also assigned the transshipment of freight at Parbatipur from the broad-gauge railway coming north from Calcutta to the narrow-gauge line operated by the 721 R.O.B. This battalion immediately installed floodlighting at Parbatipur over the transfer tracks and platforms so that operations could go on twenty-four hours a day.

The 725 R.O.B. headquarters were established at Lalmanirhat, and operated from there to Amingaon, on the bank of the Brahmaputra River, a total of 175 miles.

The 726 R.O.B. established its headquarters at Pandu, on the other side of the Brahmaputra River, and operated 160 miles from Pandu to Lumding. The 726 R.O.B. was also assigned the ferry operations at Pandu in bringing the trains across the river, which, as mentioned above, was not bridged.

This battalion started its operation auspiciously with a near catastrophe. Vacuum-braked cars were placed on the head end and hand-braked cars on the rear end of the trains. On the first day of operation, out of Pandu, on an ascending grade, Engineer Emmet P. Doughty realized that nine cars had broken off and were running away downgrade backward. Operating under the positive block, when his train didn't show up within a reasonable time at the next station, Kamakhya, the agent there communicated with the agent back at Pandu who sent a light engine with First Sergeant William J. Cearfoss and Private First Class James Piazzy to find out what had happened ahead. Proceeding eastward, they soon saw the runaway cars fast approaching them. Reversing their engine, they gathered speed and a light collision occurred as they coupled up with the runaway cars and brought them to a stop. Cearfoss and Piazzy were congratulating themselves on having stopped the runaway string when a second string of 18 cars, which had also broken away, crashed into them, scattering cars and equipment all over the right of way. Fortunately no one was hurt.

The 745 R.O.B. established headquarters at Lumding and operated 108 miles to Mariana, including branch lines.

The 748 R.O.B. established headquarters at Mariana and operated over 100 miles to the cities of Tinsukia, Ledo, and Dibrugarh.

There was also activated in the theater on 22 May 1944 the 61st Transportation Corps Composite Company by drawing personnel from the operating and shop battalions. This unit was the first M.R.S. unit to leave India, departing from Calcutta for New York on 30 August 1945.

The 758 R.S.B. set up in the shop facilities of the Bengal and Assam Railway at Dibrugarh. It immediately made itself felt. The output of locomotives from those shops before its arrival was three a month. This was immediately raised to nine, an increase of 200 per cent, and subsequently the unit did better. By the installation of electric lights it could, and for much of the time did, run twenty-four hours a day. Pneumatic riveters took the place of hand hammers; the manufacture of locomotive and car springs was increased from 20 to 110 a week; in the foundry, output of castings was raised from 40 to 90 tons a month.

This shop battalion, working in the Indian-manned civil shops, as well as the "B" Company men of each of the operating battalions at their roundhouses and rip-track facilities, ran up against something brand new to them as they and the Indians worked together. The caste system in India is profound and the mechanic is known as a "mystery." The actual Indian laborer is called a "khalassis," and he waits on his "mystery," handing him tools and material as he requires them.

At the time the M.R.S. assumed responsibility, the B. & A. Railway had 713 locomotives, 401 being meter gauge, 154 of them United States Lend-Lease engines. By March 1945 there were 442 meter-gauge 2-8-2 locomotives of which 262 were of War Department issue. The Army ordered an additional 10,000 cars which were double the capacity of the Indian cars, thereby tripling the rolling-stock capacity of the railroad.

The normal European positive block system of train dispatching and

The shops operated by the 758 Railway Shop Battalion at Assam, India.

Railroad yards and shops at Parbatipur, India.

movement was in effect on the B. & A. when the Americans assumed control of the railroad. Telegraph, telephone, and signal communications were in very meager use. The M.R.S. troops continued the positive block from station to station because there weren't enough Americans to act as operators at each station 24 hours a day and it was realized that natives could not be educated to handle train orders. Modern communication systems of teletype and telephones were installed by the headquarters of the M.R.S. installations to Army headquarters at New Delhi and Calcutta.

The B. & A. Railway was laid on wooden ties with 60-pound rail. The ballast was hand-crushed rock and of six to twelve inches in depth. The weight of the power and the speed of trains in the civilian operation were not too great for this weight of rail, but with the heavier power and the longer trains and higher speeds attained by the M.R.S., a difficulty of "running track" arose and caused kinks and derailments, and for a time trains had to be slowed down until rail anchors could be secured and installed.

The question of tonnage rating was interestingly developed. The old class of B. & A. cars, all iron, were four-wheeled and were given a count of one; there were other cars of six wheels which were given a count of one and one-half; and the American equipment supplied with two four-wheeled trucks was given a count of two. The tonnage of the locomotive was then set on a car-count basis. The various classes of equipment with their ratings were used to limit tonnage of trains.

Civilian labor, both male and female, was available and utilized supplementing maintenance forces. One of the most outstanding accomplishments from the standpoint of American ingenuity and experience is evidenced by the action taken by the M.R.S. management in connection with the elimination of the difficulties on account of constant washouts of the bridge over the Beki River, which the Bengal and Assam crosses. In the United States many problems of a like nature had been solved by diversion. Lieutenant Colonel George Branch, Commanding Officer of the 725 R.O.B., made an aerial survey and found that there was another river, the Bhulkdoba, which came within half a mile of the Beki about four miles above the bridge. Ground surveys indicated that the overflow from the Beki River could be thrown into the other river if a channel could be dug between the two rivers at their narrowest separation. All the dirt-moving equipment of the "A" companies of the five operating battalions was thrown into digging that channel, which solved the problem of the washout of that very important bridge. For the first time in nearly thirty years the railroad was kept in service during the monsoon period.

Constant high water caused other difficulties, too. There were any number of places where the water frequently overflowed the track and these spots had a concrete foundation for the track. Markers alongside the track indicated the depth of the water over the rail, and when it wasn't—and most of the time it wasn't—in excess of the clearance of the locomotives, trains could be and were operated over the track through the water without severe delay. These concrete-spotted sections were known as "Irish" bridges.

Tonnage handled was averaging 15,000 to 20,000 long tons a month. The requirements were a minimum of 25,000 long tons; the desired figure was 30,000 tons.

As in other theaters, there was an established board under British Control in India, called "Movement Control." This board consisted of representatives from the United States and British Armies, Civil Government, and the M.R.S. The board met in Calcutta daily and set up what would move and how, after the M.R.S. representative had given them the tonnage capacity that could be hauled by rail. If there was any tonnage that the railroad

Natives coaling engine, India, 1944.

The interlocking cabin or control tower of the Bengal and Assam Railway, India, operated by the M.R.S. Pvt. Aubrey D. Gillem is showing the Indian helper which lever to pull. March, 1944.

couldn't handle, this traffic control board directed its movement by barge, truck, or pipe line.

There were improvements made by the M.R.S. on the B. & A. The most outstanding was the construction of more than 150 miles of double track between Lumding and Manipur during 1944.

An operating improvement which brought great results was that with the current of traffic, trains of 100 cars were run double-headed eastbound. Westbound trains of 50 cars (the length of the passing tracks) took siding at all meets which permitted the flow of traffic eastward to be doubled by the larger trains. Of course, this method of operation meant double-crewing eastbound trains.

Double-heading, double-crewing trains increased the volume tremendously; however, for speedier operation, it was necessary to lengthen the passing tracks. Sixty-seven passing tracks were lengthened east of the Brahmaputra River crossing to handle 100 cars each, and west of the river crossing 26 were lengthened to 150 cars.

One of the most interesting operating procedures was found by the M.R.S. in India. When Diesel or steam power was not available, cars were switched with elephants. One of the most remembered elephants was "Moonbeam" which the 748 R.O.B. used in the vicinity of Bogpani.

Elephants also caused trouble. Sometimes they had to be moved on trains in especially designed elephant cars. On one occasion, notwithstanding the fact that the engineer had just taken water, the injectors broke, indicating a lack of water in the tank. On investigation, it was found that an elephant in an elephant car, the first car in the train, was sucking the water out of the tank and giving himself a continuous shower bath.

The nature of the country and the advance of the Japanese contributed to some real war conditions along the railroad. In the spring of 1944 the railroad became an armed battle line. At one time the Japanese penetrated to within four and one-half miles of the yards at Mariana. British and American troops were rushed to the danger spot by rail, consuming only twenty-four hours as against the previous best record for that distance of forty-eight hours. This quick movement by train saved the day. The Japanese were driven back, but constantly there were wandering bands of Jap snipers who were trying to destroy the railroad, the trains, and their cargo. It became necessary during this period to run rail motorcars with mounted machine guns ahead of the trains to watch for damage to track and structures and to draw and reply to any attacking Japanese fire.

There were not enough facilities in support of car handling on either side of the car ferry at Pandu over the Brahmaputra River. Many of the tracks in the yards on both sides of the ferry were lengthened up to 100 cars which speeded up the ferry tremendously. Also added were two ferry terminal landings. Steam tugs spotted barges and went about their business instead of standing there while cars were being moved on and off the ferry. Prior to the operations by the M.R.S., the maximum car ferry capacity was 200 cars in each direction daily, but soon the Americans were ferrying 800 cars a day in each direction.

Contrary to European practices, it was necessary that locomotives be equipped with headlights in the India-Burma Theater. There were too many sacred cows, wild elephants, and pedestrians using the right of way as a thoroughfare, so all engines furnished by the United States for the India-Burma Theater were equipped with extra-bright headlights.

As in other theaters, pilferage was a deadly foe in the operation of the Bengal and Assam, but had some interesting differences. One of the things that caused considerable trouble was the stealing of headlight globes from

61 Transportation Corps Company awaiting meet at Mogaung, Burma.

the locomotives. These items brought a large price on the black market, as did the rubber hose connections on the vacuum brakes. Headlight globe stealing was stopped by placing a heavy wire netting over the headlights. Another favorite way to steal was by throwing items of freight off onto boats in the Brahmaputra River when the cars were being ferried across. All this was eventually stopped by the assignment of Military Police to guard both yards and trains.

Some conception of the job done by the M.R.S. on the B. & A. can be conveyed by the fact that from the time it began operation in February 1944 until the departure of the last unit in September 1945, it handled a total of

6,217,143 tons. The maximum month was May 1945, when 506,616 tons of miscellaneous freight were handled. During the first twenty-six days of control by M.R.S. troops the tonnage handled on the B. & A. was increased 46 per cent.

On passenger trains operated by the M.R.S., beginning in March 1944 and ending in September 1945, the M.R.S. handled a total of 5,559 passenger trains, which averaged 310 trains per month, 10 trains per day.

There were three directors and managers of the M.R.S. in India. Brigadier General Appleton served from 25 December 1943 to 27 April 1944 when he was transferred for service in England and France. He was succeeded by Colonel Stanley H. Bray from 28 April 1944 to 17 May 1944. Colonel (later Brigadier General) Paul F. Yount had been transferred from Iran and succeeded to command of M.R.S. in India 18 May 1944 until 25 October 1945.

Orders were received for the M.R.S. troops to return the operation of the railroad to its owner and then leave India for return to the United States. The turnover covering the period from 1 September to 15 October 1945 was done smoothly and easily. The last unit departed from India for the United States and inactivation 27 October 1945.

12

Operations in the Philippine Islands, New Caledonia, Australia, and Japan

1942-1945

The Philippine Islands were under Spanish rule from their discovery by Magellan in 1521 until Spain ceded the islands to the United States in the treaty following defeat in the Spanish-American War in 1898. Aguinaldo led a revolution in the Philippine Islands against the Spanish which he continued against the Americans. It was not put down until 1901. The administration of the islands by the United States started as a territory with a Governor General and staff administering the affairs. The first governor was William Howard Taft, appointed in 1901 by President Theodore Roosevelt.

In 1907 a Philippine Assembly was authorized which assisted the Governor General in the administration of the affairs of the islands. The Jones Act of 1916 gave them an elective legislature composed of both a Senate and a House of Representatives. In 1934 the Congress of the United States provided for complete independence to become effective at the end of a ten-year period. The Philippines were to have a constitution similar to that of the United States. They elected their first president, the grand old man of the Philippines, Manuel Quezon.

In providing for their security, the Philippine government had authorized two armed forces—the Philippine Scouts and the Philippine Constabulary, which were originally officered by American Army officers on detached

Brigadier General Paul W. Johnston, Military Railway Service.

service. President Quezon, desiring to perfect that defense force, secured the services of General Douglas MacArthur as military adviser to the Commonwealth Government of the Philippines in 1935. He was well along in the establishment of the standing military forces of the Commonwealth when within four hours after the Japanese sneak attack on Pearl Harbor Japanese bombers attacked Manila with a raid which occurred at noon on 7 December 1941.

On 22 December 1941 the Japanese landed in many places in the Philippines. The United States and Philippine troops were thrown back by superior forces and took their final stand in Corregidor. This fortress fell on 5 May 1942 with the surrender of the United States forces under General Wainwright. General MacArthur had been ordered by the President of the United States to Australia on 17 March 1942. He took up command there, and told the Filipinos he would return and liberate them from the Japanese.

Plans with respect to rail transportation in the Pacific had their inception in the appointment in the grade of Colonel (later Brigadier General) of Mr. Paul W. Johnston, Assistant Vice President of the Erie Railroad. He was permitted to choose certain assistants who were likewise commissioned and departed with him for Australia in March 1942. The men who accompanied Colonel Johnston were L. S. Kurfess, Chief Shop Inspector, H. M. Shepard, Chief Draftsman, G. B. DeGroat, Road Foreman of Engines, A. J. Sanok, Trainmaster (all men from the Erie Railroad), and O. C. Gruenberg, Superintendent of Motive Power, New York, Susquehanna and Western Railroad Company. They arrived in Australia at about the same time that General MacArthur reached there from the Philippines.

Australia had a rather complicated railroad system of many and varied gauges. Colonel Johnston's original orders were to inspect and report back to the United States the amount of railroad facilities required as to additions and with particular reference to equipment and supplies. The success in the Pacific occasioned by the defeat of the Japanese at Midway and the Coral Islands changed the situation and instead of Australia being a battleground, it became a base for logistical supply to the Army and Navy fighting back to the Philippines.

M.R.S. troops, therefore, were never sent to Australia, and neither Colonel Johnston nor his men had any responsibility in the direct operation of the railroads. He and his staff, and others who were assigned to him, coordinated logistical activities and manufacture of supplies for General MacArthur's armies generally under the Lend-Lease or Mutual Aid plan as between the Australian and United States Governments.

When Colonel Johnston reached Australia he found that in that large island continent there were approximately 30,000 miles of railroad running almost entirely around the coast line with the greatest percentage of the mileage on the south side, extending from Perth on the west to Melbourne and Sydney on the east. There was only one rail line up into the central plain area which extended northward 720 miles from the south to Alice Springs.

The railroads were of five gauges, from 2 feet to 5′3″, the greatest amount being 3′ 6″ for 13,000 miles. The gauge with the next largest amount of mileage was 4′ 8½″ for 7,300 miles and there was only 30 miles of 2′ gauge. The weight of rail was from 41 to 110 pounds; the maximum grade was 2.5 per cent and the maximum curvature was 4° 20″.

There were 750 miles of electrified railroad. There was a total of 3,608 steam locomotives between the 4-6-2 and the 4-8-4 types; there were 88,330 freight cars and 8,748 passenger cars of all types.

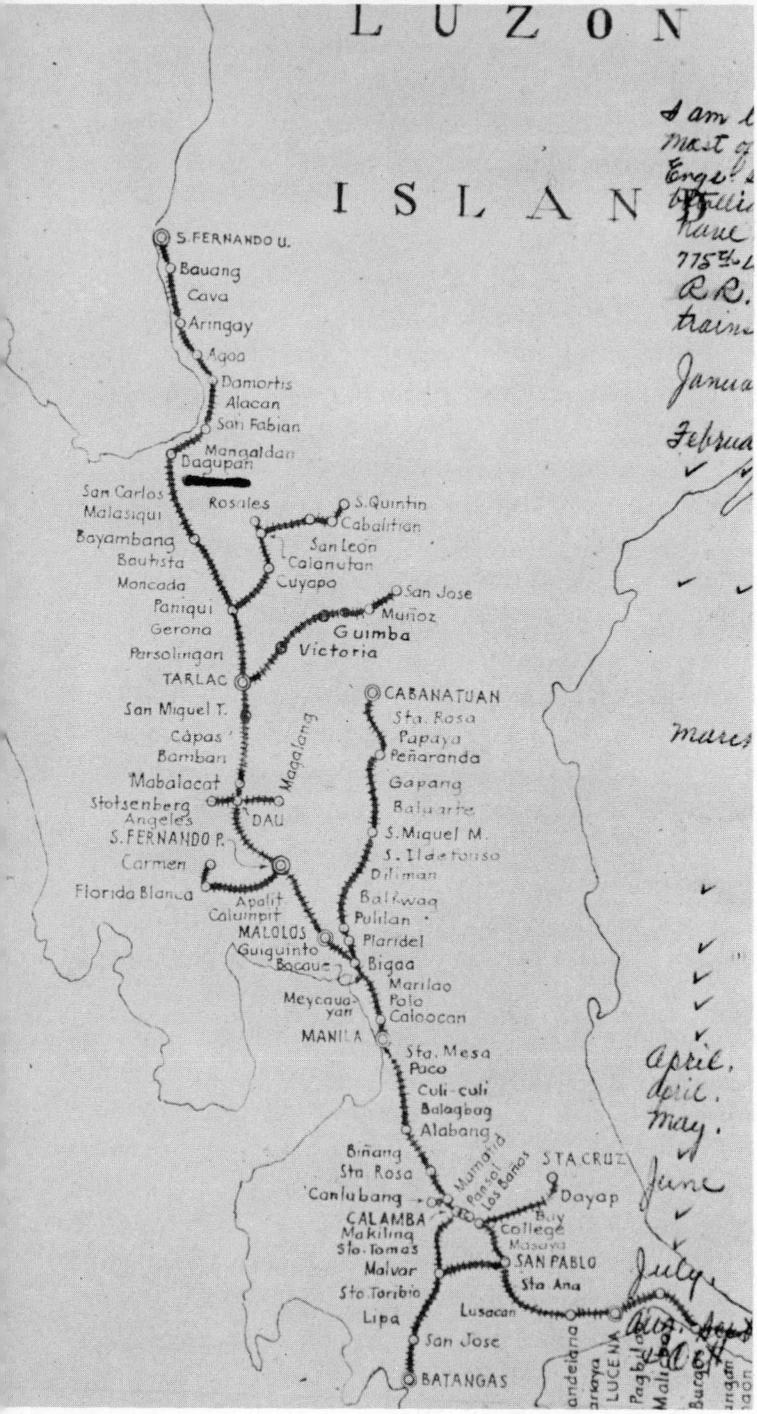

Railroad on Luzon, P.I.

The largest commodity handled was coal and coke, followed by grain and grain products, then minerals and livestock. The volume of business handled in the fiscal year 1937-1938 was 42 million tons of freight and 386 million passengers.

Colonel Johnston and his men remained in Australia and other M.R.S. staff officers joined them. Finally, the original party of Colonel Johnston and his Erie railroad men were returned to the United States in August of 1945 and other M.R.S. personnel in Australia were sent to the Philippine Islands and Japan.

The Americans' first landings on the Philippine Islands were in the Lingayen Gulf area, the closest railroad being at Dagupan. An augmented R.G.D., the 775 R.G.D., was organized to be sent to Luzon. The first M.R.S. troops to arrive were those of the 790 Railway Operating Company (not affiliated) commanded by Captain R. V. Lea, on 11 January 1945. This company had seen service in New Caledonia from July 1943 until that time. They immediately started to rehabilitate so they could operate the railroad south toward Manila. The railroad was in horrible shape because of neglected maintenance and bombs and Japanese destruction and thievery.

The 5202 Engineers began the rehabilitation of bridges while the mechanical men of the 790 R.O.C. assisted by all began the repair of locomotives and cars found in that general vicinity.

The Manila Railway Company's total mileage on the island of Luzon was 712. The portion used by the American forces was only a total of 234 miles. It was designated by the American forces as the Luzon Military Railway. The trunk line of the Manila Railroad Company was north and south from Manila, north to San Fernando (La Unión), a distance of 165 miles, and south to Calamba, a distance of 35 miles. It was all 42-inch gauge and was mostly of 60 to 80 pound rail. Since the equipment was light, that made sufficient strength of rail to make it possible to align and service it when rehabilitated to make a pretty good railroad.

There was no coal available to M.R.S. troops and engines were fired from driftwood, pulpwood, and coconut hulls. The 790 R.O.C. was successful in getting the railroad together and they ran their first train from Dagupan to Bayambang on 19 January 1945, a distance of 30 miles. They continued southward and reached Capas, 70 miles, on 24 January.

Jeep switcher, Philippine Islands.

Railroad formerly used for sugar plantation and refinery at San José, Mindoro Island, P.I., during the war was utilized to transport rations and supplies from beach to town.

On 10 February 1945 the Headquarters, 775 R.G.D. (not affiliated), commanded by Lieutenant Colonel H. G. Balch, arrived from the United States. It took over direction of the rehabilitation and operation of the Luzon Military Railway, including responsibility for security of the freight. Headquarters were established at Manila on 23 February 1945. Rehabilitation progressed satisfactorily and the first train was run into Manila from the north on 15 March 1945.

The 737 R.O.B. (New York Central), Major Charles Buchanan commanding, and the 749 R.O.B. (The New York, New Haven and Hartford Railroad Company), Lieutenant Colonel Harry F. Donnelly commanding, arrived from the United States 1 April 1945, and realignment of units of the M.R.S. resulted.

The 790 R.O.C. was given the operation of the San José branch line. The 737 R.O.B. took over the railroad from San Fernando (Pampanga) north to San Fernando (La Unión), a distance of 127 miles. The 749 R.O.B. was assigned the territory from San Fernando (Pampanga) south through Manila and on to Calamba, a total distance of 70 miles. It also operated a bus service from Calamba to Batangas.

Three Railway Workshops Mobile arrived 25 March 1945: the 131 R.W.M., commanded by First Lieutenant Bert L. Brown, was assigned to Caloocan; the 132 R.W.M., commanded by First Lieutenant H. L. Anderson, was assigned to San Fernando (Pampanga); and the 133 R.W.M., commanded by First Lieutenant F. E. Seiller, was assigned to San Fernando (La Unión).

The 753 R.S.B. (Big Four), commanded by Lieutenant Colonel C. O. Butler, arrived from Italy on 20 September 1945 and was placed in the Caloocan shops. On arrival the 753 R.S.B. absorbed the 5250 Provisional R.S.B., which had been formed on 3 July 1945.

From lessons learned in the Mediterranean and European Theaters there was sent to the Philippine Islands from experienced stores men available the 793 Base Depot Company. It arrived there 1 April 1945 and took over the question of requisitions, supplies, and storage of all railroad material.

The M.R.S. in the Philippines reached its peak in October 1945, when it had 126 officers, 3,074 enlisted men, and employed and used 6,010

Major General George C. Stewart, Chief of Transportation NATOUSA, Asst. Chief of Transportation, ETOUSA, Chief of Transportation, Philippine Islands.

civilians. The Chief of Transportation in the Philippines was Brigadier General George C. Stewart who had served as Chief of Transportation in North Africa, Italy, and southern France, and Assistant Chief of Transportation in ETOUSA. The Deputy Chief of Transportation was Colonel R. B. Lincoln. The Director and General Manager of M.R.S. was Colonel F. E. Russell, and Lieutenant Colonel J. F. O'Connell commanded the 775 R.G.D. as General Superintendent after Lieutenant Colonel Balch had been assigned to the Third T.M.R.S.

There were M.R.S. troops that took up temporary residence in the Philippines. One of these was the Third T.M.R.S., which arrived in August and used the Philippines as a springboard before going on to Japan. This was likewise true of the 770 R.O.B. which had arrived in August off the White Pass and Yukon Route, Alaska. It went on to the Japan-Korea Theater in October 1945.

Railway supplies started coming in on 13 February 1945 with the arrival of the first ship bringing much needed locomotives, cars, track material, and shop machines. The ultimate number of American-built locomotives and cars to be used by the M.R.S. in the Philippines totaled 53 locomotives and 990 cars.

The Luzon Military Railway issued a timecard which covered the operation of trains north and south of Manila. While the railroad carried much normal freight, its main object was to handle military freight. Between San Fernando (La Unión) and Manila there were two passenger trains daily in each direction and four mixed trains. On the Manila-Caloocan shuttle service, 23 trains were operated daily in each direction, while the Manila-Paco shuttle service operated five trains daily in each direction. On the San José branch two mixed trains were operated daily.

On the southern division between Manila and Calamba one train was operated daily.

Business on the Luzon Military Railway grew steadily; they handled a total of 865,695 net tons from 1 March 1945 to 31 December 1945. For the period from 1 June 1945 to 31 December 1945 they operated a total of 7,410 trains and moved 48,321 cars. Their biggest month of operation was July 1945 when they handled 1,131 trains containing 10,839 cars in which were loaded 152,628 net tons.

At the same time, passenger business was heavy both for natives and for military on leave. Its total from 1 April 1945 through 31 December 1945, not including July 1945, was 1,595,353.

Native Filipino civilian employees began to return to work on the railroads immediately and they enjoyed working for the United States Army, for full pay was certain and on time.

The final blows in the war with Japan occurred on 6 August 1945, when the atom bomb was dropped on Hiroshima, and on 8 August 1945, when the second atom bomb was dropped on Nagasaki. VJ-Day was 14 August 1945, when the Japanese accepted the Allied peace terms; hostilities officially ceased 2 September 1945.

The Board of Directors of the Manila Railway Company were notified that the Army would return the railroad to civilian control, and the date was announced as 1 January 1946.

On 15 August the 737 R.O.B., the 790 R.O.C., the 793 B.D.C. and the 131 R.W.M. were relieved of all duty in the Philippine Islands, and departed for Japan and Korea.

American 2-8-2 locomotive in the Philippine Islands.

Railroad engines in the yard at San Fernando Pampanga on Luzon, P.I.

The 775 R.G.D. was materially reduced in size after the turnback of the railroad to civilian operation and was ultimately inactivated on 31 May 1946. The 749 R.O. B. departed for Korea in February 1946; the 753 R.S.B. was inactivated 1 April 1946; and the 132 and 133 R.W.M. were inactivated 25 January 1946.

The war in the Pacific was mainly a naval and air war, particularly from a transportation standpoint. Japan was an island empire of many islands, totaling 147,611 square miles, and centered on the three main islands of Honshu, Hokkaido, and Kyushu, the main one, of course, being Honshu.

Japan's first railroad was started in 1870, and was built of standard-gauge track from Yokohama to Shinbashi, a distance of fifteen miles. In 1889 the Tokaido main line was completed between Tokyo and Kobe. By 1942 Japan had approximately 20,000 miles of railroads and they were very modern. The profile and alignment of the railroads were, however, very unusual because of the mountains, rivers, and islands. There were 2,630 tunnels, the longest of which was 31,831 feet, and there were 39,026 bridges, the longest of which was 4,080 feet.

Because of the very mountainous country, the engineers had to resort

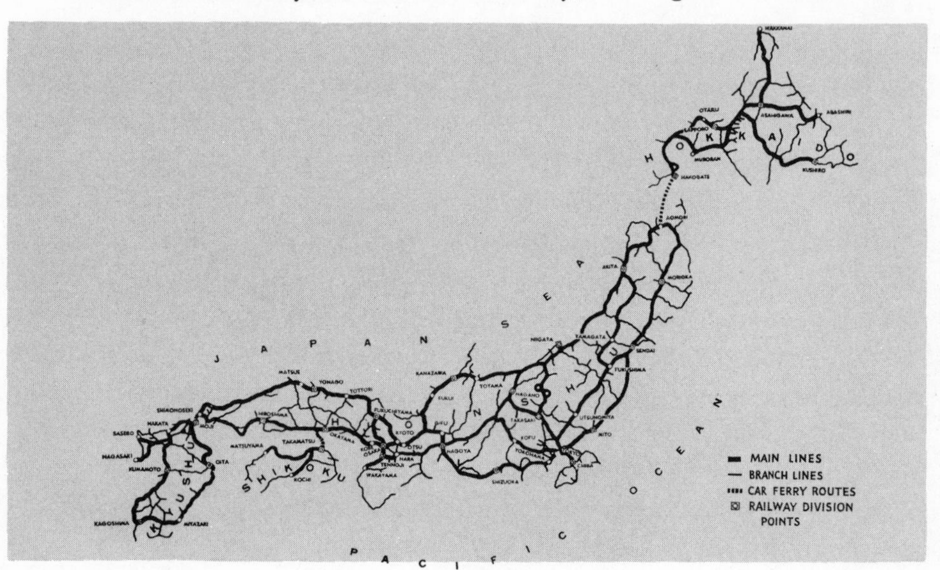

Railroads of Japan.

to switchbacks in order to secure altitude quickly. A total of twenty-three switchbacks was built. The unusual operation through switchbacks is to put a locomotive with tender at each end of the train, and one engine hauls the train to the switchback, and then when the direction is reversed, what was the rear locomotive takes over as the lead locomotive and so on up the mountain through the switchbacks.

Another unique stretch of railroad was that between Marugame and Nagasaki, which is a distance of approximately five miles. The grade for most of this distance is 6.67 per cent. Within this distance there are 24 tunnels aggregating 14,660 feet, putting over 50 per cent of this section underground. This is electrically operated. Traction is not by wheels, but by cog form of traction operating on a cog rack in the center of the track, such as the cog railroad up Pike's Peak in Colorado. Normal trains on the railroad consist of nine cars. It requires three electric locomotives to handle the train up and down because braking downgrade is as important as traction upgrade.

The particular portion of the Japanese National Railways that the M.R.S. took over and operated was the line from Sapporo on Hokkaido Island in the north, across the train ferry between Hakodate on Hokkaido to Aomori on Honshu. These car ferries were not like the ones that Americans are accustomed to, but are in reality bow and stern ships. Whole passenger trains, without their engines, are shoved aboard coupled and pulled off at the other end of the run. The same is true of freight trains. While making the five-hour trip, passengers leave the railroad cars and travel in lounges on the upper deck and eat in the dining room of the ship.

Proceeding south on Honshu Island, the M.R.S. operated on the east coast thereof through Yokohama and Tokyo to Shimonoseki on the southernmost tip of Honshu, and then by an underwater tunnel to Moji on Kyushu Island, a distance of 2.2 miles. Actually, there are two tunnels, single track each, the number-one tunnel having been started in 1936 and completed in 1942. Number-two tunnel was started in 1940 and completed in 1944. In Number-one tunnel 5,160 feet are under water, and 4,265 feet of Number-two tunnel are under water. The ordinary tunneling method of cement grouting was applied to the sections of the Shimonoseki side and the shield method was applied to the Moji side.

On the island of Kyushu, the railroad continues from Moji to Sapporo.

American occupation forces landed on Honshu Island on 28 August 1945 and took over the occupation of Japan. M.R.S. forces were then established and utilized in the supply of occcupying forces.

Headquarters, Third T.M.R.S. arrived in Japan 25 October 1945. It was inactivated on 25 January 1950 to form the 8010 T.M.R.S., was reactivated on 25 August 1950 from the 8059 T.M.R.S., which was formed in Japan in July 1950 for duty in Korea. Brigadier General F. S. Besson, Jr., was the General Manager on arrival in Japan, and it was subsequently commanded by Colonel L. W. Anderson, Colonel H. E. Owens, and then during service in Korea was commanded by Colonel W. S. Carr.

Three detachments of the 737 R.O.B. (whose headquarters were in Korea) were sent from there to Japan to assist temporarily in the supervision of operations there. One detachment each was placed at Yokohama, Osaka, and Sasebo.

The 8010 T.M.R.S., since 26 January 1950 called the 8010 Transportation Traffic Regulating Group, is on duty at the present time in Japan.

The 793 Base Depot Company, which was relieved in the Philippine Islands 15 August 1945, arrived in Japan on 26 October 1945, where it took up usual stores duties peculiar to a unit of its type and remained on duty in Japan until 25 September 1949, when it was inactivated.

The 8059 T.M.R.S. was formed in Japan on 1 July 1950 for duty in Korea. Its first Commanding Officer was Lieutenant Colonel Smith, and next Major Victor E. Estrem. It left Japan on 8 July 1950 and arrived at Pusan, Korea, 9 July 1950. The 8059 T.M.R.S. was subsequently commanded by Lieutenant Colonel J. R. Truden. It was inactivated and Headquarters, Third T.M.R.S., was formed in its stead 26 August 1950 in Korea. Colonel W. S. Carr became Director and General Manager.

The principle of the M.R.S. in the control and handling of the Japanese railroads was Phase III type of operation. This means the entire direction and control was by Headquarters, M.R.S., with men placed on each train and directing the operations, all carried out by the native Japanese.

In Japan, the M.R.S. exercised full operational control of railroads and rail facilities as was required for the support of the occupation forces. Headquarters were set up in the N.Y.K. building in Tokyo and the manner in which they carried out their work may be described as coordinating the requirements for the occupation troops with that of the normal civilian traffic so as to interfere in the least possible way with civilian requirements. It was not so much a job of operating a railroad as it was of traffic control and the distribution of cars and trains to serve Army and civilian requirements.

The Army required regularly scheduled passenger train service between certain points and these trains were given Yankee names. Possibly the most prominent were the *Yankee Limited* between Yokohama and Sapporo, Hokkaido, the *Dixie Limited* and *Allied Limited* between Tokyo and Sasebo. Each of these trains had first-class equipment, including sleeping cars and diners. Ten sets of equipment were required to operate these three trains.

As finally established, the Japanese railway under the M.R.S. was operated in four divisions. 1. The Tokyo Division which included the operations in the greater Tokyo-Yokohama area, and extended from Yokohama westward to Niigata. 2. The Sendai Division with headquarters at Sendai extended over the northern portion of Honshu Island and the entire island of Hokkaido. 3. Osaka Division with headquarters at Osaka was responsible for central and south central Honshu Island and the island of Shikoku. 4. Fukuoka Division, with headquarters at Hakada, Kyushu, comprised the area of southern Honshu and the island of Kyushu.

As indicated previously the railroads are government owned and operated. Prior to the war, in honor of the Emperor, trains were numbered starting at Tokyo. All trains leaving Tokyo were odd numbered and all trains arriving at Tokyo from any direction were even numbered. In addition all even-numbered trains were called "Up" trains and all odd-numbered trains were called "Down" trains. Approximately 1,370 scheduled passenger trains arrived and departed from Tokyo Central Station daily; 1,270 went in and out of Yokohama Central Station.

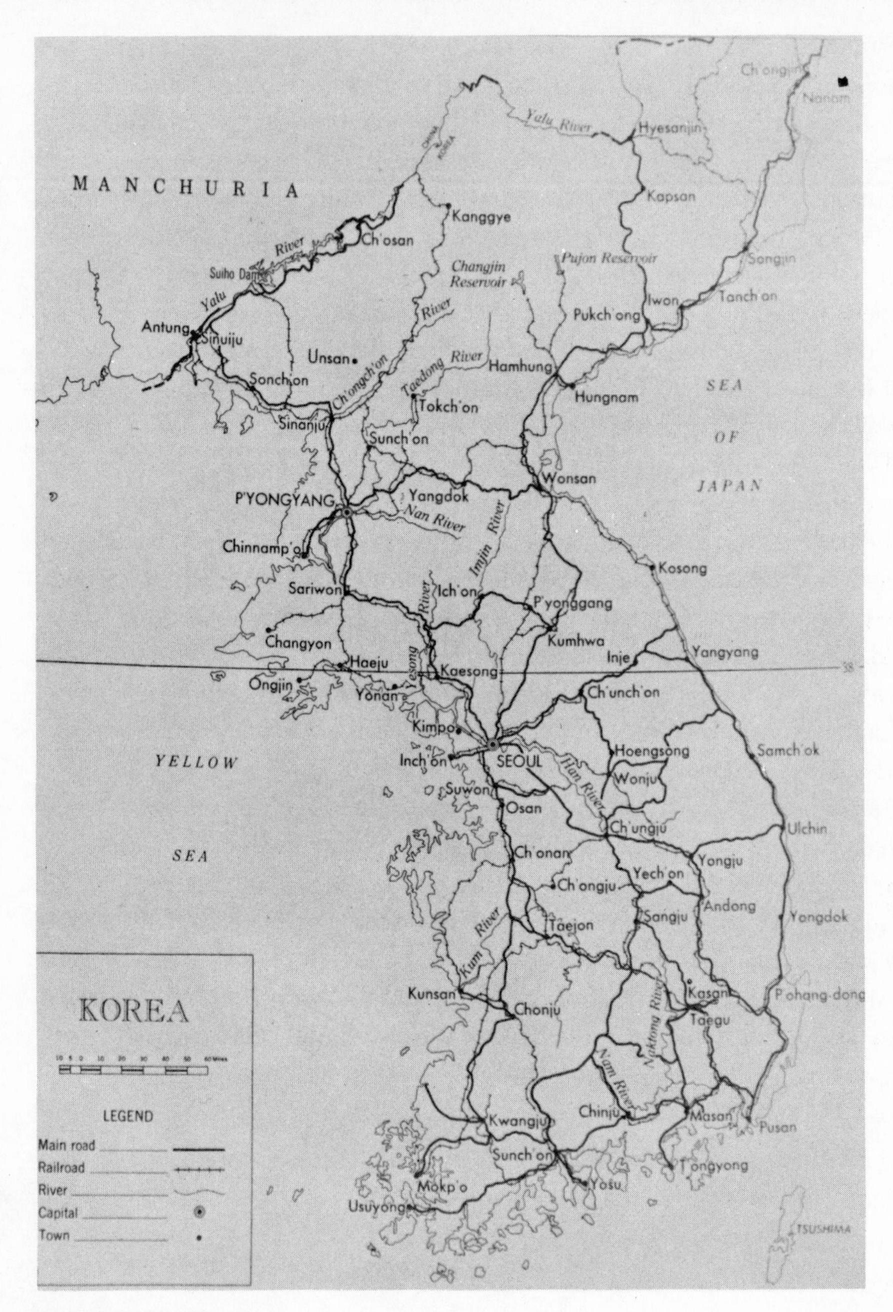

Korean railroads.

13

Operations in Korea

1945-1953

KOREA, AS WE CALL IT and know it now, was originally called Chosen, and was dominated by and under direction of China for a thousand years prior to 1894. Japan began its ambitious expansion, and finally went to war with China in 1894. In 1895 there was a treaty which considered Korea as an independent nation.

This continued with constant trouble between Russia and Japan, and was mainly responsible for the Russo-Japanese War in 1904. By a treaty which was signed at Portsmouth, New Hampshire, in 1905, Japan was given many concessions, among them a dominant directive authority in Korea. This the Japanese expanded until they actually annexed Korea in 1910.

Japan continued to rule Korea until the end of World War II in 1945, when, by the surrender terms signed in Tokyo Bay, Korea was separated from Japan and divided at the 38° parallel, that area south of the parallel going to United States control and that part north, bordering on Manchuria, to Russian control.

Difficulties began almost immediately between the Russians and the Americans in connection with their respective activities in Korea. When the Soviet-United States Commission talks broke down, the United Nations stepped in and proclaimed a free election for all of Korea in 1948 under its supervision. In 1950 the Allied Nations and the North Koreans under Russian Communist direction engaged again in war.

Demolition of Yongsan yard.

The M.R.S. operations in Korea were divided into two separate periods, the first as logistical supporters of the short-lived Army of Occupation following the close of World War II, and the second in logistical support of the United Nations as they engaged the Russian-dominated Communistic armies of North Korea in 1950.

The savage guerrilla type of warfare which ensued, as well as the tremendous numerical advantage of the enemy, caused the resources of the M.R.S. to be used many times in Korea in moving large combat units from one place on the front line to another. This use in tactical maneuvers stopped the fast-moving enemy troops and assisted materially in plugging breakthroughs in the Allied lines. One notable example of this was when, in one twenty-four-hour period, the railway picked up the entire 25th United States Division and attached units at Waegwan and transported them 100 miles to the vicinity of Masan, where they went into position and blocked the enemy.

Korea is a country with rice paddies in the lowlands interlaced by narrow roads, where if a truck or tank goes off the road, it sinks almost out of sight. Railroads bridge the marshes and tunnel through the mountains.

In 1945 the railroads of all Korea, developed mainly by the Japanese, consisted of 4,000 miles, 100 per cent steam operated. South of the 38°

parallel there were 1,700 miles of railroad. Generally speaking, the railroads were laid out for strategy in military purposes and between most major terminals there were alternate lines.

The first railroad to be constructed in Korea was a private railroad built and financed by Americans which ran from Seoul to Inchon. It was completed in 1896. Railroads were later developed under Japanese direction, and lines were opened as follows: from Sinuiju on the Manchurian border to Seoul in 1906; from Seoul to Pusan in 1908; a branch line to Mokpo in 1914; and a line from Seoul to Wonsan, and eventual extension to Manchuria, opened in 1928. The government took control of most of the Korean railways in 1924.

The railroads were built with standard 4′ 8½″ gauge track while a few miles were of narrow gauge, 30 inches. The standard-gauge railroad was government owned and the narrow-gauge was privately owned.

There is an interesting story as to why the standard gauge of 4′ 8½″ is used almost universally. Tests and research through the years caused the

Yongsan Station Yard—near Seoul Railroad Office.

adoption of the 4′ 8½″ gauge, the wheel spread of the Roman chariot, as being the best spread between wheels in connection with the stability of the carriage on curves and elevations.

The rails on main lines averaged 90 pounds. Ties were of a miscellaneous assortment of hardwoods. Ballast was crushed rock and river sand. There was a total of 239 tunnels and 1,724 bridges on Korean railroads.

The Korean Railway had two back shops for the over-all repair of standard-gauge locomotives and cars, the largest of which was at Seoul and the other located at Pusan. Privately owned railroads for narrow-gauge equipment had shops at Inchon and Yongdungpo. The standard-gauge repair shops were in good condition and were modern, with all the necessary heavy machinery and overhead traveling cranes. During the fiscal year of 1946-1947 these two shops gave over-all repairs to 232 locomotives, 341 passenger cars, and 1,467 freight cars. At full capacity, which was not reached, the Seoul shops could employ 5,000, but during this period there were only 3,000 at work; the Pusan shops could employ 3,000; however, only 1,800 were at work. Output of these shops was 65 per cent by the Seoul shops and 35 per cent by the Pusan shops. In addition to main repairs at the shops, many parts were manufactured and distributed to roundhouses along the line of railroad. Many more repair parts and stock had to be secured from Japan.

When the M.R.S. moved into Korea in September of 1945, the condition of the locomotives and rolling stock was from good to bad. Over-all there was a total of 474 locomotives, almost wholly of Japanese design and manufacture, of which 65 per cent were beyond repair. This left some 166 serviceable and repairable locomotives in South Korea. This was not enough, so the M.R.S. immediately requisitioned American locomotives now no longer needed in Europe. The first of these arrived 19 March 1947. Eventually 101 American locomotives were thus brought onto the Korean railroads. By September 1948 the M.R.S. troops had a total of 656 locomotives in operation including the original standard and narrow-gauge Korean locomotives, 101 of the 2-8-0 American locomotives, and 15 locomotives from Japan. There was almost every type of wheel arrangement from the 2-2-0 to the 2-10-0.

Passenger equipment totaled about 500 cars and they were predominately influenced by Japanese specifications. There were second- and third-class cars, all coaches, and second-class cars of parlor or sleepers, baggage and combination cars. It is interesting to note that 80 per cent of the Korean train mileage is passenger and only 20 per cent freight.

In order to improve morale and stimulate interest among the Korean officials and employees two trains were placed in service on 20 May 1946 between Pusan and Seoul, covering that 280 miles in nine and one-half hours. One was called the *Liberator* and the other the *West Coast Section* of the *Liberator*. The equipment used was 50 roller-bearing passenger coaches and they were painted orange with a broad black stripe.

Freight equipment was divided almost equally between boxcars and gondolas and flatcars with a small number of cattle and refrigerator cars. They were of an average 33-ton capacity and had four-wheel bogie trucks. An interesting fact is that both freight and passenger equipment had automatic couplers instead of the European styled link and pin.

The manpower running the Korean railroads totaled 55,000 employees of which one-third were Japanese who occupied all the management positions and the two-thirds rank and file were native Korean. After the defeat of Japan and the occupation by the Americans in South Korea, this presented a real problem, because the Koreans immediately manifested an unwillingness to take Japanese direction. The Japanese, on the other hand, refused to continue responsibility. It was on the basis of this hiatus of desire or unwillingness to work that the first phase of M.R.S. management was established.

Lieutenant Colonel A. J. Cornelson, Transportation Officer of the United States Armed Forces occupying Korea, realized that the operation of the railroads by the M.R.S. was the only solution to the rail problem in Korea. He requisitioned sufficient M.R.S. troops to manage and operate required mileage of the Korean railroads.

Four officers headed by Lieutenant Colonel S. H. Pulliam, and including Majors H. H. Cosgray, W. H. Hay, and Harry P. French, arrived 28 September 1945, took up headquarters at Seoul, and began the survey of requirements for handling the business of the Korean railroads. Colonel Pulliam had to return to the United States and Lieutenant Colonel J. M. McLellan arrived on 7 December 1945 and took over management of the M.R.S.

The 790 R.O.C. and the 131 R.W.M. were the first units to arrive. They came from the Philippine Islands and landed on 28 September 1945. They immediately took up headquarters and duties at Seoul. The 30 Transportation Traffic Regulating Group was formed on 30 October and established traffic-control centers through the southern part of the country on the Korean railroads. The 737 R.O.B. arrived from the Philippine Islands 10 November 1945 and was set up to operate the Seoul region, the Taejon terminals, and had supervision of lines in the southwest.

The 770 R.O.B. arrived from the Philippine Islands on 24 November and was assigned as operating territory the Pusan region and main line up to Taejon. Headquarters were at Pusan.

The 749 R.O.B. did not arrive until 2 March 1946. It really was not used as it was inactivated on arrival.

On 30 July 1947 the 30 T.T.R.G. was reorganized as the 500 T.R.G.D. and Lieutenant Colonel J. M. McLellan was named General Superintendent. By that date the 131 R.W.M., the 737 and 770 T.R.O.B. had been inactivated, so that by 1 August 1947 the only M.R.S. troops in Korea were the 500 T.R.G.D. and the 790 R.O.B. which had been increased on 18 June 1946 from a company to a battalion. The 790 R.O.B. departed Korea 16 December 1948 for Japan, where it was inactivated 25 January 1949. The 500 T.R.G.D. was inactivated in Korea the same date.

Train service on the Korean railroads was non-existent until 15 September 1945 when two trains were operated from Seoul to Pusan. Occupation troops were moving in, and supplies for their maintenance and relief supplies for civilians began to arrive. By the middle of October the 40th Infantry Division arrived and headquartered at Pusan. The 6th Infantry Division arrived and took station in southwest Korea.

It was absolutely necessary to clear the ports and transport these supplies to where needed. As indicated, Japanese supervision refused to work and Korean employees left their jobs. Finally, train operation was built up by Herculean efforts until by November 1947 the handling was an average of twelve to fourteen freight trains daily between Pusan, Taejon, and Seoul in addition to the passenger trains.

Ultimately Korean employees began to return to work. One of the most extraordinary conditions found in Korea by the M.R.S. men was that the

2-8-2 locomotive used in Korea.

Switching, Korean fashion.

Engineer was the boss of all he surveyed. He designated how many cars his engine would take out of terminal and haul, and he left and arrived according to time of his own schedule. Conductors had nothing to say about the operation of the trains. American standards soon established what the locomotive could haul and ultimately secured satisfactory tonnage per train mile.

Building from the ground up, Major Alter A. Hill, Third Army Headquarters, loaned to the department of Transportation, started with the roundhouse at Yongsan and soon had it operating on American standards. Other roundhouses followed in line, all due to the basic principles laid down and supervised by Major Hill.

During this whole period sabotage of the most barbarous nature was constantly interfering with and disrupting normal operations. The motive power was not yet in the best shape and these saboteurs would break water glasses and gauges, damage or steal injectors and air pumps; they poured sand and metal filings in journal boxes and other moving parts.

Nature added its fury to sabotage, inexperienced personnel, and deferred maintenance. In June 1946 there was one of the most disastrous floods in the history of the country. There were more than 300 washouts including five bridges, the largest of which were at Waegwan and Pyongtaek. The bridge at Waegwan took the most time to restore; it consisted of twelve spans each 156 feet, of which seven were over water. Repairs on it started in April 1946 and were completed in January 1948. The bridge was opened for railroad use 22 February 1948. During the reconstruction period, traffic was rerouted. Increased truck and air delivery augmented the handling of supplies by rail.

From a dead railroad it was made operative and equipment repaired. Business picked up unbelievably. For the fiscal year 1947-1948 nearly 65 million passengers were handled, an increase of approximately 12 per cent. Also during the early period after the liberation there were about one million Japanese nationals who were transported over the lines to ports of embarkation for return to the homeland. At the same time nearly two and one-half million Korean nationals returned home and were transported by rail from ports of debarkation to their homes throughout Korea.

With the liberation, business and industry resumed. A miscellaneous assortment of all kinds of freight began to be moved by rail. At first it was lumber and then all commodities moved freely. During the first six months there was handled on the railroad more than one million tons. Tonnage grew, and during the following year three and one-half million tons moved. For the year ending in March 1948 five million tons moved. Freight trains were scheduled and those schedules maintained. There was established regular eighteen-hour freight train service between Pusan and Seoul, a distance of 280 miles.

The Japanese had fixed extremely low wages, freight, and passenger rates on the Korean railroads in order to move manufactured goods from Japan into Korea and raw materials from Korea to Japan at low cost to themselves. Upon the liberation, conditions immediately changed, and the economic structure had to be stabilized. A series of increases in freight and passenger rates and wages to employees was immediately inaugurated. The first rate increase was in March 1946, when freight rates were increased 300 per cent and passenger rates increased 100 per cent. This was followed by another increase in May 1946 of 150 per cent in freight and 125 per cent in passenger rates.

On 1 December 1946 passenger rates were again increased 100 per cent, and in January 1947, 150 per cent. Further increases occurred in August 1947, when both freight and passenger rates increased 50 per cent. In February 1948 passenger fares increased 33½ per cent and freight rates increased another 300 per cent. Wages and salaries followed the same trend.

The final step in the restoration of the South Korean railroads was taken on 10 August 1948 when by executive order the last private railroad was taken into the Korean National Railroads, leaving out only electrically operated streetcar and suburban service lines. Continuing from 1948 to 1950, rail transportation was coordinated by R.T.O.'s under the logistical command in Korea.

The second phase of M.R.S. operations in Korea came with the invasion of South Korea by the Russian Communist-directed North Koreans on 25 June 1950. The United Nations Security Council acted promptly. On 27 June it recommended that the members of the United Nations furnish sufficient forces to repel and drive out the North Koreans. Eleven days later,

Colonel W. S. Carr, General Manager, Third Transportation Military Railway Service.

by request of the Security Council, President Truman appointed General of the Army Douglas MacArthur as Commander in Chief, United Nations Command.

The 8059 T.M.R.S. arrived in Korea on 9 July 1950, commanded by Major Victor E. Estrem. It took over the direction of the R.T.O. On 26 August 1950 that unit was inactivated and its personnel transferred to Headquarters, Third T.M.R.S., which reported to the Commanding General of the Eighth Army in Korea.

Colonel W. S. Carr, General Superintendent of the 708 R.G.D. in the European Theater, was again called to active duty 23 July 1950 and ordered to command in Korea. He was flown there with an advance echelon to be assigned to Headquarters, Third T.M.R.S.

By General Order No. 88, Headquarters, Eighth United States Army in Korea, dated 30 September 1950, he was placed on duty as Director General of Transportation, M.R.S., in Korea, with headquarters at Pusan.

On 26 August 1950 the 714 R.O.B., commanded by Major H. W. Martens and the 765 R.S.B., commanded by Major James K. Hanks, arrived for duty with the Third T.M.R.S. in Korea. These two units had become a part of the regular army on 9 March 1949.

None of the units was up to strength. The total number of officers and men in the headquarters and its assigned units on 30 August was only 229. This was increased during the month of September, so that as of 1 October 1950 there were 427. The most serious difficulty was the fact that, contrary to the conditions existing in Europe in World War II, only 20 per cent of this M.R.S. assignment were experienced railroad men.

Headquarters, Third T.M.R.S., was first set up at Pusan. The mileage under its direction on 1 September was 272. On 1 October this mileage had been increased by the taking over of responsibilities for the railroad including the station limits of Chinju in the southwest and Waegwan in the north, giving the M.R.S. a total of 359 miles of railroad. Headquarters, Third T.M.R.S., moved to Taegu and opened there 25 September 1950.

Equipment available was 153 locomotives, all classifications, 344 passenger cars, and 3,655 freight cars, all types. Arrangements were made to transfer equipment in from the United States and from Japan.

Operation was directive, or, as it was called in the European Theater, Phase III. Virtually all of the train and engine crews, switchmen, stationmen, and shop and enginehouse men were native Korean employees of the Korean National Railroad.

Business was good. During the month of September 1,540 trains were dispatched handling 265,553 tons. During October the strength of the M.R.S. increased to 379 officers and men. Mileage likewise increased to 1,074. For the first time in Korea, however, the M.R.S. was handicapped by the action of the retreating enemy who demolished bridges, tunnels, roadbed, and rolling stock. During October 988 trains were dispatched, hauling 205,074 tons of military supplies. Casualties were reasonably heavy and as a result the 66 hospital cars in Korea by that time were in constant use.

On 11 October 1950 headquarters of Third T.M.R.S. were closed at Taegu, moved forward by rail, and a mobile headquarters set up at Yongdongpo. Then on 18 October headquarters were established at Yongsan (Seoul) in the large K.N.R. building there.

With the expansion of the railroad, it became necessary to turn over more and more actual work to the native employees of the Korean railroads. On 13 November the back shops at Yongdungpo were turned over to the Koreans. During November, with 233 operable locomotives, M.R.S. handled 294,594 tons of military freight.

Great reliance was placed upon the experienced railroad men of the M.R.S. Among those who had served throughout the European Theater and who utilized their capacity and experience gained in World War II were Lieutenant Colonels J. R. Truden, C. O. Butler, and F. H. Drake; Majors L. A. Hartley and J. G. Woodall; Captains W. L. Grimes, M. E. Hale, R. B. Melton, and R. L. Steinke.

The M.R.S. in Korea lacked in their Table of Organization the services of a Chaplain. This was corrected on 8 November 1950 when Chaplain (Major) Lester J. Houghteling was assigned to the Third T.M.R.S

The 712 R.O.B. (Central Railroad of New Jersey), commanded by Major Arthur C. Palmer, arrived in Korea 23 December 1950. During the month of December one million Chinese Communist forces began a very definite offensive southward. For the first time the American Army and with it, of course, the M.R.S., retreated southward. This enemy offensive had been anticipated, although not on the scale in which it was launched.

Our plans had been formulated and fixed covering the retreat if and when necessary, specifying when and how strategic railroad property would be destroyed to check and hinder the advance of the enemy. The fulfillment of these plans was especially well coordinated as between the tactical units of the Army and the M.R.S. and were thoroughly understood by the management of the K.N.R.

The southern thrust of the enemy had become such that on 10 December it was deemed advisable to destroy the yards at Sinmak. As the advance continued, additional facilities on the double-track railroad on the west coast line were destroyed. This was at Susack and in the Hamhung-Hungnam Sector. On 26 December the Director General gave orders to destroy all railroad facilities north of Uijongbu.

By 14 December the situation around Seoul had become so critical that the Headquarters, Third T.M.R.S., started moving back to establish head-

South Han River bridge at Tanyang.

Bridge demolition, Korea.

quarters at their old location in Taegu, which was fully accomplished shortly after the first of the year.

The farthest south the enemy advanced was on a line east and west across the peninsula south of Suwon and Wonju, which cut the two railroads out of Taejon and Taegu. This was as of 1 February 1951.

On the offensive which the United Nations began with the American troops on the left flank, the situation improved to the extent that by 1 March they had recaptured the port of Inchon and were on the south bank of the Han River across from Seoul. On the east coast the line was just north of Samchok. By 1 April they had pushed north of the 38° parallel just south of Haeju and had in their possession the town of Yangyang on the east coast. There the line remained except for some fluctuations in the east sector until the cessation of hostilities on 27 July 1953.

One additional M.R.S. battalion, the 724 R.O.B. (Pennsylvania Railroad), commanded by Major Albert M. Schofield, arrived in Korea on 25 June 1951.

In the drive back the M.R.S. made slow progress because of the terrific destruction of railroad facilities both by themselves and by the now retreating enemy. As an illustration, the yards at Kaesong had been completely destroyed by American air force bombardments. Not a track remained intact in those extensive yards. The same was true at Wonju and Suwon.

One of the most unusual rehabilitation procedures was the manner of repair to certain bridges. There was no piling, timber, or steel available, and so Korean labor filled sandbags and built up a dump across the stream bed. It was the dry season, with no water in the river. The highest bridge thus built on these sandbags was 65 feet high. It held up remarkably well under severe traffic. Steel and piling replaced them before the rainy season.

The retreating North Koreans added further destruction specializing on blowing tunnels, many of which were through mountains of free-running sand. Another expedient that was necessary is illustrated by the action taken to cross the river at Pyongyang. The bridge was demolished and there wasn't material or time to construct one, so a pontoon bridge was fabricated. Goods were moved to the south bank by train, then lifted over the pontoon bridge, reloaded on cars, and forwarded. To make this possible 20 locomotives and

Anyang Highway River bridge.

Han River bridge.

Waegwan Railroad bridge being repaired.

approximately 500 freight cars were found on the railroad just north of the river.

Sabotage was terrific. Roving bands of guerrillas added materially to the danger and difficulties of rail transportation. While M.R.S. men are soldiers, they are not really expected to engage in combat, but in Korea on several occasions they had to, and gave an excellent account of themselves. On one occasion a unit of the M.R.S. was attacked by 1,000 guerrillas. The fighting was furious but they were finally driven off, leaving 40 enemy dead and two prisoners, while the M.R.S. losses were one dead. In all there were more than fifty actual battle engagements between M.R.S. units and the enemy.

To protect lading on all trains forwarded in danger areas, gondolas filled with sandbags and manned by combat troops with automatic weapons were placed on the front and rear of each train.

During June and July 1951 the fighting had become stationary. The South Koreans were taking over more and more of the operation of their railroads. Colonel Carr returned home on 6 March 1951. On 24 August 1951 the 714 R.O.B. was returned to the United States. The 765 R.S.B. was inactivated in Korea on 1 December 1954 and the 712 R.O.B. was inactivated in Korea on 20 January 1955. Still remaining in Korea, giving general management direction, is the Headquarters, Third T.M.R.S. and the 724 R.O.B.

14

Summations and Conclusions

IN THE PRECEDING CHAPTERS there has been given a recital of the use of railroads by the American Army in five wars. World War II, of course, was bigger than all of the rest combined, for 16,535,000 Americans went forth to protect our way of life.

In the War Between the States, 2,192,000 Americans participated on the Northern side. The M.R.S. forces in the War Between the States were 24,964.

In World War I, 4,744,000 men participated. There were organized and sent to France 51 M.R.S. units aggregating 69,000 men. In addition, M.R.S. troops were either organized or in the process of organization in the United States, numbering 14,000. This totals 83,000 men of the M.R.S. organized in World War I.

Out of the 16,535,000 who participated in World War II, 43,500 were soldier-railroaders. The World War II armies required many times greater logistical support per man than armies in all other wars. The greater percentage of these 43,500 American railroad men utilized in World War II were primarily experienced railroad men who had learned the job of railroading the hard way and therefore were capable, by virtue of their experience, to produce the unbelievable freight handling records recorded herein.

Every unit of the M.R.S. received many citations from Supreme Headquarters of the various theaters for the logistical support which they furnished. Individual members of the M.R.S. were awarded medals for their valor and individual accomplishments. Unfortunately all units did not keep a record of individual decorations, but for those units that served in the

Mediterranean and European Theaters, there is recorded as awarded the following:

Distinguished Service Medal	1
Legion of Merit	50
Silver Star	3
Soldier's Medal	68
Bronze Star Medal	184
Purple Heart	301
Commendation Medal	1
War Cross of Italy	1
Order of the Crown of Italy	8
Croix de Guerre with palm (French)	18
Croix de Guerre with Gold Star (French)	19
Croix de Guerre with Silver Star (French)	4
Croix de Guerre with Brown Star (French)	1
Legion of Honor (French)	2
Médaille de la Réconnaissance (French)	1
Commander, Order of the British Empire	1
Officer, Order of the British Empire	1
Commander, Order of the Crown of Belgium	1

Railroad men gained much stature and experience in the period 1942-1945 in the M.R.S. When they entered service, there were only two officers in the whole organization who were general officers of a railroad. Today, there are proudly recognized six railroad presidents. Alphabetically, they are:

John M. Budd, President of the Great Northern Railway
William N. Deramus, III, President of the Chicago Great Western Railway
Paul W. Johnston, President of the Erie Railroad
Fred W. Okie, President of the Bessemer and Lake Erie Railroad Company and the Union Railroad Company (Pittsburgh)
W. Thomas Rice, President of the Richmond, Fredericksburg and Potomac Railroad Company
Arthur E. Stoddard, President, Union Pacific System.

The mileage of these railroads totals 22,294 miles.

"All work and no play makes Jack a dull boy" is an old but true saying. The various units of the M.R.S. created baseball teams, even football teams, and engaged in many activities of a recreational and entertainment nature.

Possibly the most outstanding achievement of these soldier-railroaders was the formation of a male chorus from the men in the Headquarters, First M.R.S. Their success was so definite that it is believed a brief recital of their formation and subsequent performances is justified.

After mobilization on 15 May 1942 at Fort Snelling, Minnesota, one of the final actions in training was a five-mile hike. In training were not only Headquarters, First M.R.S., but the headquarters of the 701, 702, and 703 R.G.D., a total of some five or six hundred men. As they were marching along, Major F. E. Cheshire, the training officer, got the men to singing in order to get their minds off their fatigue. He noticed there were some very excellent voices.

At parade that night he indicated what he had heard and told them that if they desired to form a chorus or glee club he would provide a leader. They desired this club, and the first leader was Mr. Merle Larson, W.P.A. director at Fort Snelling. Shortly afterward a new director was secured, a Mr. Walter Mallory. The chorus accompanist was Mr. D. Morris Jeffrey, whose son, Robert, was in the Headquarters Company. The first business manager was Technician Fourth Grade Donald R. McFadden of the 702 R.G.D. Upon his being transferred, Master Sergeant Roy J. E. Olson was appointed business manager and continued thereafter. Private First Class J. B. Myhers was soloist.

Rehearsals were held constantly, the voices were superb, and the chorus soon gained an enviable reputation. Their first real public appearance was a broadcast over station WMIN, St. Paul-Minneapolis on 9 July 1942. They soon became regular participants in the U.S.O. programs in St. Paul.

In September Mr. Ralph Mather, President of the St. Paul Civic Opera, indicated to the Manager that the opera company was going to produce *Desert Song* and that they desired to utilize Private First Class Myhers in the lead, if they could be assured that Myhers would be there through mid-February 1943. This, of course, was impossible, but a promise was made that Myhers would be the last soldier of the headquarters to leave Fort Snelling.

With that assurance, Myhers was chosen and rehearsals started. The balance of the chorus was used as the male chorus of the opera. They gave outstanding performances on 4, 5 and 6 February 1943.

"The Red Shadow,"
Pfc. Myhers.

Headquarters, M.R.S., was ordered to the North African Theater and departed for there on 29 April 1943. When the chorus went overseas they could not, of course, take the civilian director and accompanist along. Private First Class Myhers was elected director and Technician Fifth Grade Herbert Wigley became the accompanist.

It wasn't long after their arrival in North Africa on 11 May 1943 that they reestablished their chorus and performances for the benefit of themselves and the command in North Africa. The members of the chorus then were: Master Sergeants Harold J. Buring and Roy J. E. Olson; Technical Sergeant Jack W. D. Mann, Jr.; Staff Sergeant William P. Carey; Technician Third Grade Clarence A. Berman; Technicians Fourth Grade George D. Anders, Howard G. Bielefeldt, Clarence W. Bunde, George T. Dinsdale, Gerald T. Gardell, Rodney E. Johnson, Walter C. Marlow, George O. Nygaard, Maurice Peacock, Jr., Elroy M. Pierson, Larry E. Schreiber, Wendell K. Strandberg; Technicians Fifth Grade Henry P. Binney, John W. Ewald, Paul C. Ivory, Homer C. Johansen, Nathaniel E. Kernell, James G. Maloy, Don A. Mears, Mason O. Myers, Irvin C. Meyett, Albert M. Pett, Thomas E. Wicker and Herbert J. Wigley; Privates First Class George S.

Aumer, Robert W. Finney, Charles S. Haum, John B. Myhers, Robert C. Rehberg, Raymond C. Stromquist, and Paul Warren Wallgren; Privates Douglas L. Hanson, Donald N. Hacking, Joseph H. Margl, Alfred L. Nelson, and Edmond F. Velat.

The chorus was invited by the Senior Chaplain of the theater, Colonel Parker, to participate in weekly broadcasts of the "Church of the Air" program over Radio Algiers; then they appeared on a series of broadcasts called "Soldiers Chapel of the Air" and in a series of programs called "Franco Allied Music Hall." On 30 May 1943, at El Alia National Cemetery just outside of Algiers, the chorus participated in the Memorial Day program attended by General Eisenhower.

The headquarters moved to Naples, Italy, and opened there on 12 November 1943. Immediately the chorus began concerts throughout the Naples and Rome area. Director Myhers in his off-duty time started studying voice under Caruso's old teacher who did the same thing for Myhers that he had done for Caruso; that was to change him from a baritone to a tenor.

Director Myhers and a few other members of the chorus were transferred to Headquarters, 774 R.G.D., and remained in Italy when Headquar-

Military Railway Service Chorus on their regular broadcast, Algiers, 1943.

Memorial Day, National Cemetery, Algiers, 1943.

ters, First M.R.S., went to Lyon, France. This separation of the director and certain members of the chorus unfortunately caused the permanent dismemberment of the chorus. Myhers continued his musical study until he was returned to the States for discharge.

The M.R.S. Chorus not only added to the relief from tension of the M.R.S. but because of their radio performances they entertained members of the whole combat command and exercised a very excellent public relationship with the soldiers and civilians of the Allied nations.

The American likes to know what's going on, and the American soldier-railroader had that instinct developed to the "nth" degree. One of the pieces of necessary equipment furnished the Engineering Department of the Headquarters, First M.R.S., was a map reproduction plant. Beginning with Volume I, No. 1, published 7 October 1943, there was produced on it a four-to-eight-page weekly newspaper called most appropriately *The Yankee Boomer*. It was dedicated to the personnel of the M.R.S. and came out every

Thursday. In its life to 27 September 1945 it published two volumes of 52 numbers each.

The staff consisted of Captains R. K. Bard and N. T. Kenny, Technician Third Grade J. D. McGrory, Technicians Fourth Grade R. C. Doelle and G. D. Anderson, Technicians Fifth Grade C. S. Haum and N. E. Kernell, and Privates First Class R. K. Waldron and J. L. Sheehan. Captains Bard and Kenny remained with *The Yankee Boomer* only in its infancy. Technician Fifth Grade N. E. Kernell and Private First Class Waldron were responsible for its publication throughout the years.

The Yankee Boomer was published in North Africa, Italy, and France. When the Headquarters moved from North Africa to Naples the map reproduction plant was dismantled. During that time Volume I, Nos. 11-18, were mimeographed. Later, when the Headquarters moved from Rome to Lyon, France, Volume I, No. 41, was mimeographed.

It first appeared in color with Volume I, No. 29, of 20 April 1944, when it carried on the front of the sheet in three colors the Fifth Army Plaque which had recently been awarded by General Clark to the Allied Forces Military Railway Service. Color was not used again until its final issue, when its cover was in four colors. That issue was a résumé of the outstanding events carried in previous issues. The editorial on the front page was entitled: "Good-Bye and 30."

The newspaper was extensively illustrated with pictures and intimate stories of individual heroisms and promotions of individuals. Activities of units were fully given. Eight of its issues were entirely pictorial reviews of activities. It still stands as one of the outstanding publications of any unit of the war.

America has the finest railroads in the world. The ingenuity of their officers and employees is unsurpassed. They are patriotic true Americans and may be counted upon to respond to a call to duty in any further difficulties that require their military service. There is no surer way to success than to get a man who knows how to do a job, give him the responsibility and authority, and then support him. This is the secret of the success of the M.R.S. in World War II.

References and Authorities Used

Aciéries de Longwy, 1880–1917, Braun & Cie, Mulhouse

Alaska Defense Command, Headquarters
  Excerpts from
    Bulletins
    General Orders
    Official Correspondence
    Special Orders

Alaskan Department, Headquarters
  Excerpts from
    Bulletins
    General Orders
    Official Correspondence
    Special Orders

Allied Forces Headquarters (AFHQ)
  Excerpts from
    Bulletins
    General Orders
    Official Correspondence
    Special Orders

American Armies and Battlefields in Europe, American Battle Monuments Commission, 1938

Army, Department of
  Publications:
    Army Almanac, 1950
    European Theater of Operations, The Supreme Command, 1954
    History of the Persian Gulf Command, Office of Chief of Military History
    Korea, 1950, Office of Chief of Military History, 1952
    Korea, 1951–1953, Office of Chief of Military History, August, 1954
    Organization and Role of the Army Service Forces, 1954
    Persian Corridor and Aid to Russia, 1952
    Pictorial Record: The War Against Germany and Italy: Mediterranean and Adjacent Areas, 1951
    Rail Operation in the Philippines
    Transportation Corps: Responsibilities, Organization and Operation, 1951
    United States Army in the Korean Conflict, Chief of Military History
    War Against Germany: Europe and Adjacent Areas, 1951

World Atlas, Rand McNally & Company, 1942 edition

The Battle Is the Pay Off, Ralph Ingersoll, 1943

Beschreibung und Betriebsanweisung der 1 E-Henschel-Kondenslokomotive, Henschel & Sohn, Kassel, 1943

Britain's Homage to 28,000 American Dead, the London *Times,* 1952

Chaplains of the Methodist Church in World War II, Methodist Commission on Chaplains, 1948

CONAD Compendium, 1945

CONAD History, September, 1945

Congratulatory Messages Received at the Conclusion of the Tunisian Campaign by the Commander in Chief Allied Forces, May, 1943

Crusade in Europe, Dwight D. Eisenhower, Doubleday & Co., Inc., 1948

Department of Transportation Since Liberation, South Korean Interim Government, 15 August, 1948

Eighth British Army, Headquarters
  Excerpts from
    Bulletins
    Official Correspondence

Eighth United States Army, Headquarters
  Excerpts from
    Bulletins
    General Orders
    Official Correspondence
    Special Orders

Engineers, Chief of (United States Government)
  Excerpts from
    Bulletins
    Official Correspondence

European Theater of Operations United States Army (ETOUSA), Headquarters
  Excerpts from
    Bulletins
    General Orders
    Official Correspondence
    Special Orders
Federal Records Center
  Adjutant General's Section
  Department Records Branch
  Directory Section
  Transportation Corps Historical Research Office
Fifteenth Army Group Headquarters
  Excerpts from
    Bulletins
    General Orders
    Official Correspondence
    Special Orders
Fifth United States Army Headquarters
  Excerpts from
    Bulletins
    General Orders
    Official Correspondence
    Special Orders
Final Report on the Vesuvius Emergency Operation, Allied Control Commission, March, 1944
Foreign Inland Transportation, Major Raymond L. Steinke, American University Press, 1954
French Railroads and the War, Colonel LeHenaff and Captain Bornecque, 1922
G. I. Railroader, Chaplain (Captain) R. E. Musser, February, 1945
Historical Report, Chief Engineer, A.E.F., World War I.
Historical Report, 714 Railway Operating Battalion
History of World War II, Universal Book and Bible House, 1945
Information Please 1955 Almanac, St. Paul Pioneer Press Edition, 1955
Iran-Iraq Service Command, Headquarters
  Excerpts from
    Bulletins
    General Orders
    Official Correspondence
    Special Orders
Korea, I. & E. Section, Far East Command
Les Locomotives à Vapeur de la SNCF, J. Fournereau, 1947
L'Oeuvre des Services de la SNCF et des Enterprises Françaises, SNCF
Mediterranean Theater of Operations, United States Army (MTOUSA) Headquarters
  Excerpts from
    Bulletins
    General Orders
    Official Correspondence
    Special Orders
Men of the Erie, Edward Hungerford, 1946
Military Personnel Records Center, St. Louis, Missouri
Military Railway Service
  General Headquarters
  Headquarters, First Military Railway Service
  Headquarters, Second Military Railway Service
  Headquarters, Third Military Railway Service
  Headquarters, Railway Grand Divisions: 701, 702, 703, 704, 705, 706, 707, 708, 709, 710, 774, 775, Paris Provisional
  Railway Operating Battalions: 711, 712, 713, 714, 715, 716, 717, 718, 719, 720, 721, 722, 723, 724, 725, 726, 727, 728, 729, 730, 732, 733, 734, 735, 737, 740, 741, 743, 744, 745, 746, 748, 749, 750, 752, 759, 770, 790, 791
  Railway Shop Battalions: 753, 754, 755, 756, 757, 758, 760, 762, 763, 764, 765, 766
  Railway Transportation Company: 761
  Base Depot Companies: 783, 788, 793
    Bulletins
    Official Correspondence
    General Orders
    Histories, Official
    Histories, Published:
      Claiborne & Polk Military Railway (711 R.O.B.), 1942
      Company A, 713 Railway Op. Bn., 1946
      Company B, 722nd Rwy Op. Bn., 1946
      Extra 704 West, 1945
      Highlights of History of the 709th Railway Grand Division, May, 1945
      History of the 706th Railway Grand Division, June, 1945
      History of the 718th Railway Operating Battalion, Transportation Corps, 1945
      History of the 756 Ry Shop Bn, September, 1945
      Mileposts (774 R.G.D.), 1945
      Photographs of Damaged Bridges (706 R.G.D.), 1945
      Pictorial History Headquarters Second Military Railway Service in the E.T.O., 1945
      Report of the Engineering Section, 706th Railway Grand Division, 1945
      714th Railway Operating Battalion, 1946
      759th Railway Operating Battalion World War II, 1949
      760 Ry Shop Bn. Diesel, 1945
      765 Railway Shop Battalion,
      The Saga of the 708, 1947
      The Santa Fe Battalion in World War II (713 R.O.B.), 1946

The Soldier-Railroaders' Story of the 716th Railway Operating Battalion, 1945
The 727th Railway Operating Battalion in World War II, 1948
Memoranda
Publications:
Area Railway Maps, October, 1942
Equipment Data Book, French Locomotives
Equipment Data Book, German Locomotives
Equipment Data Book, Italian Locomotives, Freight Cars and Misc. Rolling Stock
Guide to Rail Operation, Japan
Operating, Signal and Interlocking Rules, German State Railways, June, 1945
Railways of Australia, July, 1942
Railways of Belgium, Netherlands and Northern France, January, 1943
Railways of the British Isles, August, 1942
Railways of Egypt and Libia, November, 1942
Railways of Italy, Greece and Yugoslavia, August, 1943
Railways of Iraq and Iran, October, 1942
Railways of Portugal, Spain and Southern France, January, 1943
Railways of Tunisia, Algeria and Morocco, October, 1942
Report on Railway Construction and Repair North African Campaign, August, 1943
Standard Plans Roadway Track and Structures, October, 1942
Theater Railway Maps, 1942–1944
U.S.A. Equipment Data Book, Locomotives, Freight Cars and Misc. Rolling Stock
Records:
Guest Book, Headquarters, 1943–1945
Yankee Boomer, Volume I, No. 1, October 7, 1943, to Volume II, No. 52, September 27, 1945
Log of Train 400, Italy, France, Belgium, and Germany, December 29, 1943, to October 30, 1945
Military Review, Command and General Staff College, Vol. XXVIII, No. 2, May, 1948, and Vol. XXVIII, No. 3, June, 1948
National Defense Act, The Pay Readjustment Act, Army Pay Tables, Seventy-Ninth Congress, January, 1945
Navy Department: *The United States Naval Railway Batteries in France,* 1942
Nineteen Days from the Apennines to the Alps, Fifth Army, 1945
North African Theater of Operations, United States Army (NATOUSA) Headquarters
Excerpts from
Bulletins
General Orders
Official Correspondence
Special Orders
Northwest Service Command, Headquarters
Excerpts from
Bulletins
General Orders
Official Correspondence
Special Orders
Persian Gulf Command, Headquarters
Excerpts from
Bulletins
General Orders
Official Correspondence
Special Orders
Persian Gulf Service Command, Headquarters
Excerpts from
Bulletins
General Orders
Official Correspondence
Special Orders
Pietrarsa, Officina Locomotive Ferroviaria, 1940
Photographs, Official
Belgian Government
French Government
German Government
Italian Government
Military Railway Service
Official Photographers: T/4 D. S. Lidikay, Headquarters, M.R.S.; T/5 M. S. Krinke, 713 R.O.B.
Netherlands Government
United States Signal Corps.
Railroads at War, S. Kip Farrington, Jr., Coward-McCann, 1944
Railroads in Defense and War, Association of American Railroads, 1953
Railway Reconstruction Italy, Royal Engineers, British, 1946
Railways of 30 Nations, P. H. Middleton, Prentice-Hall, Inc., 1937
Roster, Headquarters, CONAD, 1945
Sixth Army Group Headquarters (United States)
Excerpts from
Bulletins
General Orders
Official Correspondence
Special Orders
Southern Line of Communications, Headquarters (SOLOC)
Excerpts from
Bulletins
General Orders
Official Correspondence
Special Orders

Publications:
From the Sahara to the Rhine, February, 1945
American Rails in Eight Countries
Southwest Pacific Area, Headquarters
Excerpts from
Bulletins
General Orders
Official Correspondence
Special Orders
Supreme Headquarters, Allied Expeditionary Force, SHAEF
Excerpts from
Bulletins
General Orders
Official Correspondence
Special Orders
Theater Service Forces, European Theater (TSFET) Headquarters
Excerpts from
Bulletins
General Orders
Official Correspondence
Special Orders
Transport for War, Edward Hungerford, 1943
Transportation, Chief of
Annual Report, 1919
Excerpts from
Bulletins
Official Correspondence
Historical Research Office
Publications:
Pictorial Handbook of Military Transportation, 1 August, 1945
U. S. Army Transportation and the Conquest of North Africa, January, 1945
U. S. Army Transportation and the Conquest of Sicily, March, 1945
U. S. Army Transportation and the Italian Campaign, September, 1945
U. S. Army Transportation in the European Theater of Operations, June, 1946
Technical Liaison Office
Transporting the A.E.F. in Western Europe, 1917–1919, by Wilgus, printed by Columbia University Press, New York, 1931
Twelfth Army Group, Headquarters (United States)
Excerpts from
Bulletins
General Orders
Official Correspondence
Special Orders
United States Army Forces, China-Burma-India, Headquarters
Excerpts from
Bulletins
General Orders
Official Correspondence
Special Orders
United States Army Forces in the Far East, Headquarters (USAFFE)
Excerpts from
Bulletins
General Orders
Official Correspondence
Special Orders
United States Army Forces in the Pacific, Headquarters (AFPAC)
Excerpts from
Bulletins
General Orders
Official Correspondence
Special Orders
United States Army Forces, Middle Pacific, Headquarters
Excerpts from
Bulletins
General Orders
Official Correspondence
Special Orders
United States Forces, European Theater, Headquarters (USFET)
Excerpts from
Bulletins
General Orders
Official Correspondence
Special Orders
Publication: *American Enterprise in Europe*, 1945
United States Forces, India-Burma Theater, Headquarters
Excerpts from
Bulletins
General Orders
Official Correspondence
Special Orders
U. S. Official Pictures of the World War, Pictorial Bureau, Washington, D. C., 1920
Victory Rode the Rails, J. Edgar Turner, Bobbs-Merrill Company, 1953
War Department
Adjutant General's Office
General Officers' Section
Awards and Decorations Section
Organization and Directory Section
General Orders, Excerpts from
Official Correspondence, Excerpts from
Publications:
Field Manual 55–60, Transportation Corps, Military Railroads and the Military Railway Service, 27 March, 1944
Field Manual 55–55, Transportation Corps, Railway Operating Battalion, 4 February, 1944
Field Manual 55–60, Transportation Corps, Railway Shop Battalion, January, 1944

REFERENCES AND AUTHORITIES USED

Historical Report of the Chief Engineer, Including all Operations of the Engineer Department, American Expeditionary Forces, 1917–1918, War Department Document No. 907, Office of the Adjutant General, 8 July, 1919

Maintenance of Way Manual, Military Railway Service, September, 1942

Manual Transportation Rules, Military Railway Service, 1942

Military Engineering, Volume VIII—Transportation, 1952

Operating Manual, Military Railway Service, 1941

Report of the Chief of Transportation Army Service Forces, World War II, 30 November, 1945

The Engineer Field Manual, Volume I, Engineer Troops, 1929

Report on Military Railway Service in War Between the States by Brigadier General D. C. McCallum to the Secretary of War

Records, World War I, February 1, 1917, to January 1, 1926, Excerpts from

Special Orders, Excerpts from

Tables of Organization, 1918 to 1954

World War II, a Concise History, Washington Infantry Journal Press, 1946

INDEX

Index

Aachen, Germany, 175, 178, 179
Abainville, France, 16
Adams, Lieut. Col. H. H., 10
Adriatic Sea, 106, 158
Affiliation Plan, adoption by Association of American Railroads, 24
AFHQ: *See* Allied Force Headquarters
Africa, North: *See* North Africa
Agrigento, Sicily, 100
Agropoli, Italy, 128
Aguinaldo, Emilio, 284
Ahwaz, Iran, 257, 261, 262, 264, 265, 266, 268
Aix-en-Provence to Grenoble line, 198
Akhaura, India, 269
Alamosa, Col., 41
Alaska: M.R.S. in, 41-55, 291
Alaska Boundary Survey Commission, 52
Alaska Defense Command, 53
Alaska Mineral Resources, Division of Geological Survey, 50
Alaska Railroad, 50-55
Alaska Railroad Commission, members of, 50
Alaska Railroad General Office, 54
Alaskan Engineering Commission, 52
Albach, Germany, 240
Alcan Highway, 42, 46, 50
Alessandria, Italy, 107
Alexander, Field Marshal Sir Harold R. L. G., 142
Alexander, Maj. R. F., 75, 229
Alexandria, La., 32, 33
Algeria, 57, 61
Algiers, Algeria, 29, 57, 61, 62, 64, 67-69, 71, 78, 83, 85, 88, 94, 109, 134, 320; British landing at, 57; AFHQ set up, 62
Algiers Base Area, 81
Alice Springs, Australia, 286
Allied Air Forces, 245
Allied Conference, Cairo, 259
Allied Control Commission, 134
Allied Force Headquarters (AFHQ), 69, 71, 109, 110, 128, 133, 147, 157; negotiations on railroads, 58-60; AFHQ set up in Algiers, 62; staff, 62-64; Field Memoranda on Italian Railways, 111-112; Movement Control Section, 134; staff conferences, 134
Allied Force Military Railway Service, Fifth Army Plaque presented to, 148, 322
Allied Joint Chiefs of Staff, 142
Allied Limited (train), 297
Allied navies, 99
Alps, the, 200
American Bailey type bridging: *See* Bridging, American Bailey type
American Expeditionary Force, Chief Engineer, 15
American Locomotive Company, 136
American Military Cemetery, Bensheim, Germany, 228
American Military Government, G-4 Section, 244
American Red Cross, 140, 226; Clubmobile Division, 140
Amingaon, India, 275
Amsterdam, Netherlands, 176
Ancona, Italy, 107, 158, 161
Anders, T/4 George D., 319
Anderson, Capt. Chris H., 165
Anderson, T/4 George D., 60, 322
Anderson, Lieut. H. L., 290
Anderson, Col. L. W., 296
Andilly, France, 218
Andimeshk, Iran, 261, 262, 264, 265
Andreoli, T/4 Bernard, 69
Angel, T/5 Leonard R., 189
Antwerp, Belgium, 175, 178, 179, 182, 186, 238; Port of, 188, 240
Aomori, Japan, 295
Apennine Mountains, 107
Applebaum, T/5 George, 216
Appleton, Brig. Gen. J. A., 172, 271, 272; director, 283
Arabs, 212, 264
Arak, Iran, 257, 262
Ardoin, M., Director, Chemins de Fer du Maroc, 71, 75
Arezzo, Italy, 158, 161
Argentan, France, 179, 187
Armistice, Italian, 1943, 105
Armistice, World War I, 1918, 14
Army Groups: Sixth Army Group, 174, 194, 195, 200, 201, 216, 218, 219, 224, 225, Headquarters, 141-142, G-4 Section, 244; Twelfth Army Group, 170, 174, 175, 184, 188, 190, 194, 195, 219, 236, G-4 Section, 244; Fifteenth Army Group, com-

manding officers, Headquarters, 112, Lieutenant General Mark W. Clark succeeds to command, 142, Italian railroad lines used by, 158, under British direction, 160; Twenty-first Army Group, 144, 169, 173, 174, 175, 178, 219, 236, Army of Occupation, in Cuba, 8; in Germany, 254; in Korea, 300
Army Service Forces, 39, 41
Arnall, 2nd Lieut. A. W., 143
Arnheim, Holland, 219
Assam, India, 48, 269, 270, 271
Association of American Railroads: adoption of Affiliation Plan, 24; M.R.S. units sponsored by, 25-27, 185
Atchison, Topeka and Santa Fe Railway Company, 25, 26, 27, 185, 272
Athus, Belgium, 187
Atlanta, Georgia, 12
Atlantic Coast Line Railroad Company, 25, 28, 135
Atterbury, Brig. Gen. W. W., 10
Augsburg, Germany, 237, 238, 240, 248, 254, 255
Aumer, Pfc. George S., 319-320
Ausland, Maj. John E., 46, 48
Australia, 29, 259, 285, 286; M.R.S. troops not sent to, 286; M.R.S. staff officers in, 288
Austria, 176, 237
Auxonne Bridge, Lyon, France, 201
Avellino, Italy, 128, 145
Aversa, Italy, 109, 118, 126, 127, 129, 154
Avignon, France, 205, 215
Awards, military, 148, 192, 264, 268, 317
Axis, the, 61, 62
Aye, Lieut. Walter, 261
Azan, General: Commander, French Headquarters at Avignon, 215

"B & B" Platoon (713 R.O.B., M.R.S.), 128
Back, Lieut. Nicholas V., 239
Bad Sulza, Germany, 221
Bagnoli, Italy, 127
Balch, Lieut. Col. H. G., 290, 291
Baldwin Locomotive Company, 15, 94, 136, 147
Baltic Sea, 237
Baltimore, Md., 2
Baltimore and Ohio Railroad Company, 25, 166, 178, 182
Bandar Shah, Iran, 256, 257, 258, 265
Bandar Shapour, Iran, 256, 257, 261, 262, 264
Bangor and Aroostook Railroad Company, 135
Barbout, M., Director, Chemins de Fer de Tunisie, 71, 89
Bard, Capt. R. K., 322
Bari, Italy, 105, 107, 108, 109, 110, 111, 147
Bari Compartimento, 147
Barnes, Lieut. Col. E. F., 134
Barnett, Lieutenant, 240
Barnwell, Major, 68
Barrett, Lieut. Col. Edward T., 165
Barry, John, 36
Bartholomew, T/5 Hugh, 96
Base Depot Companies, M.R.S., 23, 27, 254
783 Base Depot Company, 216
788 Base Depot Company, 144, 154, 196
793 Base Depot Company, 290, 292, 296
2682 Base Depot Company, 144
Basilica of San Lorenzo, 103
Basra, Iraq, 261
Basse Yutz Shops, 226
Bastogne, Belgium, 189
Bastogne Bulge, 188
Batangas, P. I., 290
Bates, Lieut. Col. H. U., 167, 200, 229
Bathurst, Gambia, 69
Batignolles Yard, 183, 187
Battipaglia, Italy, 128, 132, 144, 145
Battle of the Bulge, 182, 188, 189, 231
Bauer, Herr, 239, 247
Baughn, Lt. Col. H. C., 48, 49, 185
Bay British Steel Trestling: *See* Trestling, Bay British Steel
Bayambang, P. I., 288
Bayeux, France, 180
Beach, 2nd Lieut. D. C., 143
Bean, Capt. Ralph E., 228
Beard, Capt. James G., 81, 215
Beatty, Tom, 140
Beauvais, France, 187
Bebra, Germany, 221, 252, 254
Beggs, Maj. Stanley R., 60, 143, 220
Beki River, India, 278
Belfort-Mulhouse priority line, 216
Belgium, 29, 66, 179, 182, 251-253; M.R.S. operations in, 186-191
Bell, Lieut. Col. J. E., 67, 72
Benedict, George A., 41
Benevento, Italy, 107, 144
Bengal, India, 270
Bengal and Assam Railway, 269, 270, 271, 273, 275, 276, 278, 280, 281, 282, 283
Beni Mancour, Algeria, 77, 88
Bensheim, Germany, 228
Bergess, General: French member, Inter-Allied Railway Commission, 172
Berlin, Germany, 176, 232, 237, 247; occupation of, 244-245
Berman, T/3 Clarence A., 319
Besançon, France, 201, 207
Bessemer and Lake Erie Railroad Company, 317
Besson, Col. Frank S., Jr., 296
Bhulkdoba River, India, 278
Bicocca, Italy, 100
Bielefeldt, T/4 Howard G., 319
Bietigheim, Germany, 240
Big Cut Bridge, 32
Big Four: *See* 753 Railway Shop Battalion
Bingen, Germany, 221
Bingham, Col. S. H., 175, 247
Binney, T/5 Henry P., 319
Bischheim, Germany, 237
Bizerte, Tunisia, 72, 82, 89
Black, Maj. Gen. William M., 9
Bleialf, Germany, 227-228

INDEX

Blizard, Lieutenant, 230
Blum-Byrnes agreements, 224
Bogpani, India, 280
Boice, Sgt. Woodrow, 126
BOLERO (Operation of planning and building up troops and supplies in England), 165
Boles, Capt. J. M., 100
Bologna, Italy, 107, 157, 158, 161
Bombay, India, 275
Bône, Algeria, 78, 88
Bône-La Calle line, 78, 81, 88
Bonn, Germany, 238
Bordeaux, France, 12, 195
Bosporus, the, 267
Boston, Mass., 12, 252
Boston and Albany Railroad, 27, 178
Boston and Maine Railroad, 26, 27, 135, 178, 186
Boston *Globe* (newspaper), 36
Botta, Maj. Francesco: commander 13th Railway Battalion (Italian), 116
Bou Arada, North Africa, 76, 81
Bougie, Algeria, 88
Bourg-Railhead, France, 200
Boxer Rebellion: foreword
Bradley, Pfc. Harvey D., 126
Bradley, Gen. Omar N., 170, 219
Brahmaputra River, 269, 275, 280, 281, 282
Branch, Lieut. Col. George, 271, 278
Bray, Col. Stanley H., 271, 273, 283
"Breathing bridges," 175
Bremen, Germany, 240, 245, 252, 254; Port of, 254
Bremerhaven, Germany, 240, 252, 254; Port of, 254
Brennan, Sergeant Patrick, 228
Brennan, Lieut. Col. T. J., 185
Brest, France, 12, 179, 186, 195
Brenner Pass, 107, 158, 161
Bridge and Building Platoon, No. 711, M.R.S., 32, 33
Bridging, American Bailey type, 103, 131-132
Bridging, Roth Waagner, 127, 128-129, 130-131, 160, 205
Bridging, U.C.R.B., 207
Brindisi, Italy, 105, 107, 108, 109, 110
Brisbine, Col. Dawes G., 50
Bristol-Savoy Hotel, Lyon, France, 196
Bristow, Capt. Lyle, 69
British, the, 57, 59-60, 62, 64, 244, 253, 254, 257, 259, 265, 268, 271, 272, 273
British Army, 60, 61, 62, 179, 272; First British Army, 61, 62, 76, 81, 82, 88; First British Army Command, 61; Second British Army, 170, 176, 232; Eighth British Army, 77, 81, 82, 85, 99, 105-107, 109, 112, 142, 144, 148, 157, 160, 163, 176
British Columbia, 43
British Columbia Yukon Railway Company, 43
British Transportation Service (BTS), 87, 173; Headquarters office, 60, 62; units in, 62; Director of, 64, 71, 144, 157, 160, 169; units in North African Theatre, 67-68, 77-78; in Sicily and Italy, 100, 109, 144, 157; units in Italy, 157; in Iran, 257; in India, 272-273
British Transportation Service units: Line Maintenance Section, No. 42, 68; Mechanical Equipment Company, 157; 187 Mechanical Equipment Company, 68; Mechanical Equipment Sections, No. 45 and No. 46, 68; Railway Bridging Company, No. 167, 75 Railway Bridging Sections, 100, 157; 1 Railway Bridging Section, 68; 2 Railway Bridging Section, 68; Railway Construction Companies, 100, 157, 273; 150 Railway Construction Company, 68; 160 Railway Construction Company, 68; 161 Railway Construction Company, 68, 150; Railway Construction Company of South African Engineer Corps, 157; Railway Construction Group, 100; First Railway Construction Group, 72; South African Construction Group, 157; Railway Construction and Maintenance Group, 157; Headquarters, 157; First Railway Construction and Maintenance Group, 67; Railway Operating Companies, 62, 100, 157, 273; 154 Railway Operating Company, 67, 78, 88; 189 Railway Operating Company, 67, 78, 88; 192 Railway Operating Company, 128; Railway Operating Group, 62; First Railway Operating Group, 67, 72, 78, 88, 100; Railway Survey Company, 157; 29 Railway Survey Company, 68; Railway Telegraph Companies, 157; 3 Railway Telegraph Company, 68; South African Railway Telegraph Company, 157; Railway Telegraph Companies, 157; 3 Railway Telegraph Company, 68; South African Railway Telegraph Company, 157; Railway Workshop Companies, 62, 100, 157; 163 Railway Workshop Company, 67, 78, 88; Railway Workshops Mobile, 62; 2 Railway Workshop Mobile, 67, 78, 88; 5 Railway Workshop Mobile, 67, 78, 88; Section Railway Survey Company, 100; Separate Mechanical Equipment Company, 100; South African Tunnelling Group, 157; Stores Company, No. 155, 67; Tele-Op Section, No. 76, 68
British War Office, 61, 62
Brooks, Alfred H.: Vice-Chairman Alaska Railroad Commission, 50
Brown, Lieut. Bert L., 290
Bruce, Lieut. Col. Aubrey M., 262, 268
Brünn, Austria, 237
Brussels, Belgium, 221, 226, 227, 237, 238, 252
Bruyères-St. Dié-Saales priority line, 216
Bryant, 2nd Lieut. R. H., 143
Buchanan, Maj. Charles, 290
Bucyrus, Ohio, 31
Budd, Lieut. Col. John M., 69, 160, 221, 317
Büderich, Germany, 232
Buford, C. H., 28
Buick (Detroit), 259
Bulgaria, 29
Bunde, T/4 Clarence W., 319
Buring, M/Sgt. Harold J., 319
Burke, Lieut. W. E., 67
Burma, 270-273
Burma Roads, 271
Burpee, Brig. Gen. Clarence L., 64, 66, 72, 81, 107,

108, 110, 111, 118, 128, 134, 142, 166, 170, 171, 177, 183
Bush, Capt. Allan A., 68
Busigny, France, 187
Butler, Lieut. Col. C. O., 100, 102, 290, 310
Butler, Col. Frederick B., 78, 79

Caen, France, 178, 179, 180, 187
Cairo, Egypt, 259
Calabria, Italy, 114, 163
Calais, France, 217, 252
Calamba, P. I., 288, 290, 292
Calcasieu River, 32
Calcutta, India, 269, 270, 275, 276, 278, 279
California, 12, 135, 140
Caloocan, P. I., 290
Caltanissetta, Sicily, 99, 101
Cambrai, France, 187
Cameron, Simon, 2
Campbell, Col. A. W., 84, 134, 153, 160, 220, 221
Campi Flegrei, Italy, 138, 154
Campo Leone, Italy, 154
Campobello, Sicily, 100
Camps: Claiborne, 32, 33, 34, 47, 53, 54, 55, 137; Plauche, 37; Polk, 32, 33; Shelby, 31, 165; Thomas A. Scott, 36; William G. Reid, 31
Canada, 43, 45
Canadian Army, 179; Canadian First Army, 170, 176
Canadian National Railways, 50
Canadian Pacific Railway, 136
Cancello, Italy, 145, 154
Capas, P. I., 288
Capra, Staff Sergeant Alfred L., 69
Capua, Italy, 128, 129
"Caravan" for Eisenhower, 89
Carcross, Yukon, 48
Carentan, France, 178, 180, 187
Carey, S/Sgt. William P., 319
Carmel, Cal., 140
Carpi, Captain Tommaso, commander, 21st Railway Company (Italian), 116
Carr, Col. W. S., 166, 296, 308, 315
Carroll, Miss Madeleine, 226
Carteret, France, 187
Caruso, Enrico, 320
Casablanca, Morocco, 57, 61, 64, 66, 67, 68, 69, 83, 108
Casablanca Conference, 68
Caserta, Italy, 107, 118, 126, 127, 128, 144, 150, 151
Caserta Yard, 144
Caspian Sea, 256
Cassino, Italy, 148, 149, 151
Castiglione, Italy, 144
Catania, Sicily, 100, 103
Caucasian Railways, 258
Cava, Italy, 144
Cearfoss, 1st Sgt. William J., 275, 276
Cefalu, Sicily, 103
Celo, Capt. Antonio, commander 20th Railway Company (Italian), 116
Cemeteries: American Military Cemetery, Bensheim, Germany, 228; El Alia National Cemetery, Algiers, Algeria, 320
Central of Georgia Railway Company, 26, 185
Central Railroad Company of New Jersey, 25, 166, 178, 310
Central Vermont Railway, Inc., 27, 178
Centrale Yard Freight House, Palermo, Italy, 102
Cervaro, Italy, 154
Châlons-sur-Marne, France, 217
Chandler, Pvt. Clarence, 191
Chaplains: in M.R.S., 75; in Third T.M.R.S., 310
Charleroi, France, 187, 188, 238
Charleroi Yard, 188
Charleston, S. C., 137
Chartres, France, 179
Châteaudun, France, 179
Chatelineau-Chatelet, Belgium, 191
Chattanooga, Tenn., 8
Chemins de Fer Algériens (C.F.A.), 61, 67, 75, 77, 83, 85, 88, 90
Chemins de Fer du Maroc (C.F.M.), 61, 71, 75, 83, 88
Chemins de Fer de Tunisie (C.F.T.), 61, 71, 75, 83, 89, 90
"Cheminote," 85, 200, 226
Cherbourg, France, 175, 178, 179, 180, 186, 187, 188, 193, 195, 248, 252; Port of, 179, 192
Cherbourg Peninsula, 171, 178
Chesapeake and Ohio Railway Company 26, 178
Cheshire, Col. F. E., 185, 318
Cheval Blanc-Pertuis line, 198
Chevrolet (Detroit), 259
Chicago, Ill., 10, 12
Chicago, Burlington and Quincy Railroad, 10, 26, 135, 272
Chicago Great Western Railway Company, 9, 10, 26, 136, 317
Chicago, Milwaukee and Gary Railway, 10-11
Chicago, Milwaukee, St. Paul and Pacific Railroad, 26, 27, 136, 167, 178, 185
Chicago and North Western Railway Company, 25, 135, 167, 178
Chicago, Rock Island and Pacific Railroad Company, 26, 136, 271
Chicago, St. Paul, Minneapolis and Omaha Railway, 25, 33, 53, 136
Chief Dispatcher, M.R.S., 18, 135
China, 270, 271, 273, 299
Chinju, Korea, 309
Chiusi, Italy, 158
Chorus, M.R.S., 318-321
Chosen: *See* Korea
Christmas parties, 214-216, 226
"Church of the Air," 320
Churchill, Sir Winston, 61, 259
Churchill tanks, 164
Ciampino, Italy, 154
Cittagong, India, 269
City Security Guard, 192
Civil War: *See* War Between the States

INDEX

Civitavecchia, Italy, 154, 159
Civitavecchia Marino, Italy, 154
Claiborne and Polk Military Railway (C.&P.), 33-36, 53, 55, 109
Clark, General Mark W., 57-58, 85, 105, 109, 142, 143; presents Fifth Army Plaque to M.R.S., 147-148, 322; 148-149, 153
Clay, Lieut. Gen. Lucius Du B., 241
Cleveland, Cincinnati, Chicago and St. Louis Railway, 25, 26, 178
Close Brothers, 45
Clovis, N. M., 31, 46
Clutz, Lieut. Col. J. J., 256, 261, 267, 268
Cobble, Lieut. W. E., 143
Codola, Italy, 128, 154
Cole, Lieut. C. E. J., 67
Cole, Lieut. Col. Oscar E., 256, 268
Collins, Gen. J. Lawton, 143
Colmar, France, 219
Cologne, Germany, 232, 233
Colorado and Southern Railway Company, 47
Commercy, France, 186
Communications Zone, European Theatre of Operations, United States Army, 194-195, 220, 253
Communists, 209, 300, 307, 310
Compagne Internationale des Wagons-Lits, 213
Compiègne, France, 186, 187, 238
COMZONE, ETOUSA: *See* Communications Zone, European Theatre of Operations, United States Army
Confederate States of America, 5
Conflans, France, 186
Conlisk, Lieut. Col. Clarence V., 272
Connerat, Lieut. B., 79
Connolly, Maj. Gen. Donald H., 259
Constantine, Algeria, 67, 71, 77, 78, 81, 83, 88, 89, 90, 108
Constantine-Casablanca railroad schedule, 83
Cook, Lieut. Col. F. G., 185
Copenhagen, Denmark, 259
Coral Islands, 286
Cornelson, Lieut. Col. A. J., 303
Corregidor, P. I., 285
Cosenza, Italy, 144
Cosgray, Maj. H. H., 303
Couch, Johnson, 34
Coudraux, Col. Henri, Director French M.R.S., 212
Coulommiers, France, 187
Coutances, France, 187
Covert, Lieut. Col. George W., 183
Covin, Col. L. E., 108, 142
Cox, Leonard M., 50
Crane, Lieut. Col. Robert J., 68, 72, 220
Creil, France, 187, 226
Crerar, General, heads Canadian First Army, 170
Crill, Col. O. D., 185
Crosland, Col. B. H., 29, 34, 69, 72, 73, 90, 107, 128, 134, 207
Crouser, Capt. Claude S., 66
"Crummies," 85
Crusade in Europe, by General Eisenhower: tribute to M.R.S. (quotation), 96-97; directive to SHAEF (quotation), 170
Crymes, Lieut. Col. T. P., 84, 144, 147
Cuba: foreword, 8
Curtis, Capt. Leslie D., 262
Curtiss, Capt. Herbert M., 267
Cushman, Sgt. Joseph, 191
Czechoslovakia, 237, 259

D-Day, 166, 167, 175, 177, 178; date fixed, 170
Dagupan, P. I., 288
Dahlin, T/5 Paul H., 126
Dardenelles, the, 267
Darjeeling, India, 269
Darlan, Admiral, 57-58
Dassel, Germany, 176
Daugherty, Lieut. Col. John J., 67, 89, 145
Davidson, Brig. Gen. Garrison H., 207
Davis, Jefferson, 5
Davis, Lieut. S. P., 215
Davis, Brig. Gen. T. J., 70
Davis, Lieut. Col. Wynn, 109
Dawes, Lieut. Col. Charles G., Vice-President of U. S., Ambassador to Great Britain, 11
Dawes, Capt. Henry, 262
Deakyne, 2nd Lieut. J. B., 143
Decker, Col. Benjamin H., 68, 200, 211
Decorations, military: *See* Awards, military
De Gaulle, General, 89
De Groat, G. B., 286
deLambert, 2nd Lieut. G. M., 143
Delaney, Lieut. Raymond F., 192
Delaware and Hudson Railroad, 27, 178
Delaware, Lackawanna and Western Railroad Company, 27, 136, 167, 185
Dempsey, General: commands British Second Army, 170
Denain, France, 187
Denmark, 29, 176, 259
Dennis, Lieutenant Colonel, 134
Denver and Rio Grande Western Railroad Company, 26, 41, 46, 136
Denver and Salt Lake Railroad, 136
Deramus, William, Sr., 34
Deramus, William, III, 317
Desert Song, 318
Dessau, Germany, 237
Detroit, Mich., 12, 259
Devers, Gen. Jacob L., 112, 141, 151, 160, 194, 201-205, 212, 216, 219
Diamond, Maj. Oscar R., 69
Diamond, Col. Oscar A., 229
Dibrugarh, India, 276
Dieppe, France, 175
Diesel autorail car, 182
Diesel Electric Locomotive Repair Company, M.R.S., 23
Diesel electric road switchers, 211, 265
Diesel locomotives, 137, 138, 163, 168, 169, 191, 211, 226, 234, 240

Diesel power, 20, 23, 114, 122, 132, 137, 138, 151, 153, 183, 186, 214, 217, 260, 264, 265, 280
Dijon, France, 175, 178, 194, 200, 201, 205, 218, 225
Dijon-Railhead, 200
Dillon, Brig. Gen. J. V., 85
Dinozé, France, 207
Dinsdale, T/4 George T., 319
Director General, M.R.S.: command organized, 21; Allied staff in North Africa, 71; Reconstruction Division office established, 111-112; closes M.R.S. Headquarters in North Africa, 133; opens M.R.S. Headquarters in Naples, 133; relieved of railroad responsibility in North Africa, 157; southern French railroads under control of, 196-198; letter from General Devers, 201-205; Paris Headquarters, 237; in Korea, 310
Director of Military Transports (French), 58
Director of Military Training, M.R.S., 53
Dixie Limited (train), 297
Djedeida, Tunisia, 81
Dodge (Detroit), 259
Doelle, T/4 R. C., 322
Dohazari, India, 269
Dol, France, 185
Domgermain, France, 192
Donovan, Maj. Gen. Richard, 33
Donnelley, Lieut. Col. Harry F., 290
DoRoud, Iran, 261, 262
Dorpmüller, Dr. Julius H., 246, 247, 248
Doud, Lieut. Col. F. R., 166, 178
Dougherty, Col. C. F., 34, 71-72
Doughty, Engineer Emmet P., 275
Downing, Pfc. Glenn E., 228
Draguignan, France, 200
Drake, Lieut. Col. F. H., 310
Drake, T/4 Terry E., 68
Dresden, Germany, 176, 237
Dreux, France, 179, 187
Ducluzeau, M., Director C.F.A., 71
Duisburg, Germany, 232, 233, 234, 239
Dunmire, T/4 Bill, 234
Durance River, France, 205, 217; Valley of, 200
Dusina, T/4 Oswald B., 95
Düsseldorf, Germany, 232, 233
Dutch Navy, 99
Dutto, Col. Umberto: commander, "Raggrupamento Ferrovieri," 116
Duvivier, Algeria, 88
Dwyer, Pfc. Anthony P., 95
Dykes, Lieut. Gardner E., 33

Earle, Admiral Ralph, 14
East Yard Limit Board, Oujda, Morocco, 88
Edes, William C., 52
Egypt, 29, 57, 77, 107, 138
Eisenach, Germany, 221
Eisenhower, Gen. Dwight D.: Commander in Chief, AFHQ, 62, 70, 89; "caravan" for, 89; *Crusade in Europe* quoted, 96-97; announces surrender of Italy, 105; General of the Army, 141; Allied Commander in Europe, 141; Commanding General of NATOUSA, 141; leaves for England, 141; commands SHAEF divisions in field, 169; directive to SHAEF, 170; sets up Inter-Allied Railway Commission, 172-173; on German railroads, 246, 247; attends Memorial Day program, 320
El Alia National Cemetery, Algiers, 320
Elbe River, 176, 236, 237
Electro-Motive Corporation, 136
Ellsworth, Kansas, 140
Emmanuel, Lieut. Col. Karl F., 271
Enfidaville, Tunisia, 81, 90
England, Major, 68
England, 29, 62, 66, 166, 169, 177, 259; M.R.S. in, 27, 165, 167-168
English Channel, 141, 142, 144, 175, 178
English Railroad Rules, 165
Enna, Sicily, 101
Epinal-Blainville-Luneville-Sarrebourg-Strasbourg line, 212
Epinal-St. Dié-Strasbourg line, 212
Equipment Department, Second M.R.S., 193
Erfurt, Germany, 221
Erie Railroad, 2, 27, 186, 285, 286, 288, 317
Ernée, France, 180
Erquelinnes, French-Belgian border, 187
Essen, Germany, 259
Esslingen, Germany, 238
Estrem, Maj. Victor E., 296, 308
Etheridge, Lieutenant, 230
Etna, Mount, Sicily, 199
ETOUSA: *See* European Theatre of Operations, United States Army
European Theatre of Operations, 106, 99-255, 317
European Theatre of Operations, United States Army (ETOUSA), 194-195, 229, 254, 308, 309, 310; Office of Chief of Transportation, 167-168, 171; M.R.S. participation in, 271; Fiscal Director, 214; Headquarters, 219, 224; G-4 Section, 244
Evans, Maj. Gen. V., 270
Ewald, T/5 John W., 319

Fairbanks, Alaska, 50, 52
Falck-Kreuznach Division, 244
Falson, Sgt. George C., 64-66
Farrell, Col. Thomas, 271
Fascist, surrender in Italy, 161, 164
Faulkner, Pvt. John J., 228
Fedala, Morocco, 64
Felton, Samuel M., Jr., 9
Felton, Samuel M., Sr., 2
Fey, Chaplain Lieut. Col., 229
Fez, Morocco, 83
Fidecadori, Capt. Mario: commander 2nd Railway Company (Italian), 116
Fields, S/Sgt. Estil H., 228
Fifth Army Plaque and Clasp, 148, 322
Finney, Pfc. Robert W., 320
"First In-First Out," 87, 254
Fiscal Section, M.R.S., North Africa, 60
Fiumetorto, Italy, 100
Flannagan, 2nd Lieut. Richard J., 64, 143

Flensburg, Denmark, 247
Flers, France, 179, 180
Florence, Italy, 107, 158
Foggia, Italy, 106, 107, 109, 110, 144, 158
Foglia River, Italy, 157
Folligny, France, 184, 185, 187
Fondouk, Tunisia, 76, 77
Ford (Detroit), 259
Formia, Italy, 144
Forts: Belvoir, 29; Eustis, 55, 252; Francis E. Warren, 37; Leonard Wood, 37; Sam Houston, 37; Slocum, 37; Snelling, 29, 47, 317; Sumter, 2; Totten, 12
Fort Wayne, Indiana, 36
Fougères, France, 179, 180, 185
Foulks, Lieut. Col. Ernest E., 126
Fourth of July, celebrated in Rome, 151
Fox, T/5 Richard H., 228
France: foreword, 10, 12, 14, 15, 17, 29, 48, 58, 65, 66, 107, 114, 167-218, 219-255, 259, 316-322; Southern, 27, 29; invasion plans for, 159-160; M.R.S. in, 194-218; Northern, 29; M.R.S. in, 167-193; Director of Military Transports, 58, 71; railroads of, 58, 173; Government of, 60; Provisional Government, 172, 223; invasion of (operation OVERLORD), 165; western, invasion of, 177; Premier of, 213; Ministry of Public Works and Transports, 224; War Office, 224
"Franco Allied Music Hall," 320
Frankfurt, Germany, 221, 237, 247, 248, 252, 253, 254
Franks, Engineer George, 90
Fransi, Signor, Director Italian State Railways, 110, 147
Freeman, Lieut. Col. C. J., 167, 178
Fréjus, France, 200
French, Maj. Harry P., 303
French Army, 57, 60, 62, 76, 82, 114, 179, 216, 223; First French Army, 176, 194, 212, 217
French Military Railway Service, 212; 57 French M.R.S. Company, 75
French National Railways, 179
French Ordnance, 228
French-Singhalese troops, 80
Frye, 2nd Lieut. R. D., 143
Fuith, T/Sgt. Julius, 68
Fulda, Germany, 221
Fuller, Capt. James N., 90
Fürth, Germany, 237, 238, 252
Fuknoka Division (railway), 297

Gabes-Graiba, Tunisia, 90
Gafsa, Tunisia, 76, 77, 78, 79
Gage, Rex F. O'Dowd, Brigadier, 71, 77, 112, 114, 160; Director of British Transportation, AFHQ, 64; named Deputy to Director General, M.R.S., 133; commands British Transportation troops, 21st Army Group, 144; Chief of British Transportation, 169
Gale, Sir Humphrey, Chief Administrative Officer, AFHQ, 62, 69, 109
Gardanne, France, 200
Gardell, T/4 Gerald T., 319
Garibaldi Station, Naples, 151
Garigliano River, Italy, 129
Garino, Sgt. Anthony L., 228, 234
Gauhati, India, 275
Gela-Licata-Empedocle Area, Italy, 105
Gelnhausen, Germany, 221
Gembloux, Belgium, 187, 188
Genoa, Italy, 107, 157, 158, 161
Georgetown, British Guiana, 69
Geribini, Sicily, 103
German State Railways, 246 (*See also:* Reichs Eisenbahn)
German-Netherlands border, 219
Germans, 61, 73, 79, 81, 228, 231, 232; offensive in North Africa, 78, 79; in Sicily and Italy, 99, 101, 105, 106, 118-138; surrender in Italy, 161, 164; in Northern France and Belgium, 182, 190, 193; in Southern France, 205, 211
Germany, 29, 66, 187, 227, 228, 232, 257, 259, 270; Italy declares war on, 116; declares war on U. S., 165; Armed Forces ordered destroyed, 170; unconditional surrender of, 216-217, 236, 237, 240, 254; M.R.S. in, 219-255; occupation of, 244-245; Iran declares war on, 266
Gerstungen, Germany, 221
Ghardimeau, North Africa, 78, 88
Giessen, Germany, 192
Gildea, Lieut. Col. James H., 261, 267, 268
Gillan, Maj. Gen. A. C., 33
Gilland, Brig. Gen. Morris W., 194
Gillespie, Lieut. S. S., 143
Glacier (White Pass & Yukon Route), 49
Glendenning, Major, 68
Gongaware, Lieutenant, 191
"Good-Bye and 30" (editorial), 322
"Gooseberry" (anchorage), 175
Gotha, Germany, 221
Gothic Line, 157
Gott, Lieut. Julius R., 96
Gouldin, Maj. Robert A., 232
Goursat, M., Director General, S.N.C.F., 213
Graham, 2nd Lieut. J. R., 143
Granville, France, 179, 187
Gray, Major General Carl R., Jr. (referred to as the author): transferred from Corps Area Command 326 Engineers (Combat), 101 Division, to Arm and Service assignment, office, Chief of Engineers, 20; assigned as Manager, M.R.S., Engineering Headquarters, Railway, 20; Supreme Commander, M.R.S., 31
Great Britain, 62
Great Northern Railway, 25, 26, 84, 135, 136, 185, 218, 317
Greece, 29
Greek Navy, 99
Green, Lieut. Joseph P., 239
Greiner, Lieut Col. W. W., 166, 177
Grenoble, France, 200, 201
Grenoble-Bourg line, 200

Gresham, Lieut. Col. Doyle, 185
Gricignano, Italy, 127
Griffin, Lieut. L. B., 143
Grimes, Capt. W. L., 310
Gross, Gen. Charles P., 23, 68, 69, 142
Gruenberg, O. C., 286
Guelma, Algeria, 78, 88
Guilfoyle, Col. J. E., 84, 144
Gulf, Mobile and Ohio Railroad, 26, 185

Haag, Sgt. Jim, 244
Hacking, Pvt. Donald N., 320
Hadjeb-El Aioun, Tunisia, 75
Haeju, Korea, 312
Hainault, Belgium, 169
Hakadu, Japan, 297
Hakodate, Japan, 295
Hale, Capt. M. E., 310
Haltern-Herne, Germany, 252
Hamburg, Germany, 176
Hamhung-Hungnam Sector, Korea, 310
Hamilton, Sir George, 45
Hamm, Germany, 237, 239; Passenger Station of, 239
Hammond, Lieut. Col. Lionel E., 262
Han River, Korea, 312
Hanau, Germany, 221, 231, 237
Hanks, Maj. James K., 309
Hanley, Maj. E. C., 229
Hanover, Germany, 237, 239, 240, 254
Hanover Division, 240
Hanson, Pvt. Douglas L., 320
Harding, Col. Chester K., 142
Harding, President Warren G., 52
Harriman, W. A., 259, 260
Harrisburg, Pa., 2
Harrison, General, 271
Harrison, George M., 28
Hartley, Maj. L. A., 310
Hartzel, Capt. R. W., 135
Hartzog, Major, 134
Hastedt, Lieut. Col. W., 53
Hastings, Lieut. D. C., 182
Hatley, Capt. Lloyd E., 149
Hattiesburg, Mississippi, 31
Haum, Pfc. Charles S., 320, 322
Haupt, Brig. Gen. Herman, 3, 5
Havana Harbor, 8
Hay, Maj. W. H., 303
Hayes, Capt. George P., 185, 227
Hayes, Capt. James T., 34, 68, 220
Headquarters and Service Company, M.R.S., 18, 79, 100
Hedlam, Maj. Gen. John, 14
Heflin, Capt. R. M., 182
Heilbronn, Germany, 237, 238
Henchir Saoutir, North Africa, 79
Henschel plants (Germany), 248
Henschel and Sons, 251
Hentz, Maj. Albert G., 69
Herford, Germany, 240
Heron, Capt. James H., 69
Hersfeld, Germany, 221
Hess, Fireman Ed, 90
Hickey, Lieutenant, 230
Hill, Maj. Alter A., 306
Hillyer-Deutsches-Edwards Logging Road, 32, 33
Himalaya Mountains, 272
Hiroshima, Japan, atom bombing of, 292
Hirson, France, 221
Hise, Col. C. E., 39, 53
Hitler, Adolf, 246, 257, 266, 270
Hobbs, Lieut. Col. E. K., 200
Hoblitzell, Lieut. W. T., 85
Hodge, Gen. John R., 170
Hoge, Gen. William M., 41
Hokkaido, Japan, 294, 295, 297
Holland (*See also* Netherlands, the), 176, 187, 241, 253; Navy, 99
Holman, Lieut. Col. J. R., 11
Holmes, Lieut. James R., 228
Homberg, Germany, D.P. camp at, 248
Honshu Island, Japan, 294, 295, 296, 297
Hooper, 2nd Lieut. James S., 262
Hoosac Tunnel, Massachusetts, 3
Horschel, Germany, 221
Horton, Lieut. M. L., 100
Hosack, Col. Frank R., 72, 220, 254
Hospital Train Maintenance Crews, M.R.S., 23, 27
Hospital Train Maintenance Detachments, M.R.S., 254; 117 H.T.M.D., M.R.S., 253; 119 H.T.M.D., M.R.S., 253; 120 H.T.M.D., M.R.S., 253; 140 H.T.M.D., M.R.S., 253; 141 H.T.M.D., M.R.S., 253
Hospital Train Maintenance Sections, M.R.S., 23
Hospital trains: for United States Army, 139, 140, 214; for French, 214
Hotchkiss, Lieut. Col. W. J., 185
Hotel Bristol-Savoy, Lyon, France, 196
Hotel Cavour, Naples, Italy, 144
Houghteling, Chaplain (Maj.) Lester J., 310
Hovis, Lieut. Claude W., 266
Howard, Lieut. L. W., 143
Howard, Lieut. Col. N. L., 10
Howie, Lieut. Franklin S., 79, 100, 143
Hubble, 1st Sgt. Paul J., 215
Hughes, Maj. Gen. E. B., 69, 70, 71, 85
Hulen, Colonel, 233
Hume, Maj. Gen. E. E., 151
Hunt, Lieut. Col. A. L., 267
Huron, Lieut. Col. Herbert S., 53
Huston, 1st Sgt. Floyd L., 215

Illingworth, Lieut. Col. V. R., 67, 72
Illinois Central Railroad, 25, 26, 84, 136, 185
Inchon, Korea, 301, 302
India: M.R.S. in, 27, 269-283; Viceroy of, 272; caste system, 276
India-Burma Theatre, 270-283
Indian and Burmese Rail Transportation units (Br.): Railway Bridging Companies, Railway Construction Companies, Railway Construction

and Maintenance Group Headquarters, Railway Control Groups, Railway Maintenance Companies, Railway Operating Companies, Railway Operating Group Headquarters, Railway Survey Companies, Railway Telegraph Maintenance Section, Railway Workshops Companies, Railway Workshops Groups Headquarters, Railway Yard Operating Companies, 273
Indian Transportation Troops, 271, 273
Ingersoll, Colin M., 50
Inglis, Sir Robert, General Manager, London and North Eastern Railway, 272
Innsbruck, Austria, 176
Inter-Allied Railway Commission, 172, 173
International Power Congress, 247
Interstate Commerce Commission, 46
Iran, 29, 36, 220, 269, 271, 283; M.R.S. in, 23, 256-268; Queen Mother of, 265; declares war on Germany, 266
Iranian State Railway (I.S.R.), 256, 257, 258, 260, 261
Iran-Iraq Service Command, 259
Irak, 29, 259
Ireland, Maj. C. A., 67
"Irish" bridges, 279
Isoletta, Italy, 150, 151
Italian Army: "Raggrupamento Ferrovieri," organization of, 116
Italian Engineer Construction troops, 116, 128, 129
Italian Railway Engineers: 9 Company, 161; 23 Company, 161
Italian State Railroads (I.S.R.), 107-164
Italy, 27, 29, 48, 61, 66, 85, 87, 92, 169, 171, 173, 176, 195, 198, 200, 207, 212, 225, 251, 259, 266, 273, 290, 322; M.R.S. in, 99-164; Allied invasion, 105; surrender of, 105, 116, 161; declares war on Germany, 116; declares war on United States, 165
Ivory, T/5 Paul C., 319

Jackson, Sgt. James J., 228
Jamison, Col. L. G., 177, 182-183, 234
Japan, 164, 259, 291, 292, 297; attacks Pearl Harbor, 25, 29, 285; surrender of, 164, 292; M.R.S. in, 296-297; Emperor of, 297; war with China, 299; in Korea, 299-309
Japan-Korea Theatre, 291
Japanese, 270, 271, 272, 281, 285, 286
Japanese National Railways, 295
Jaules, Sgt. Yves, 216
Jeffers, William J., 260
Jeffrey, D. Morris, 318
Jeffrey, Robert, 318
Jensen, Maj. Ralph D., 166
Jepp, Miss Mary, 140
Jerrow, Capt. Thomas A., 69
Johansen, T/5 Homer C., 319
Johnson, Lieut. Col. John P., 261
Johnson, Gen. H. H., 150, 151, 153
Johnson, Lieut. H. W., 143
Johnson, Lieut. Col. R. E., 186
Johnson, T/4 Rodney E., 319
Johnson, M/Sgt. Virgil M., 69
Johnston, Brig. Gen. Paul W., 285, 286, 288, 317
Jones, Governor Sam Houston (Louisiana), 34
Jones, Sgt. William B., 90
Jones Act, 1916, 284
Julfa, Iran, 258

Kaesong, Korea, 312
Kairouan, Tunisia, 76
Kaiserlauten, Germany, 219
Kamakhaya, India, 275
Kansas City Railway Company, 32
Kansas City Southern Railway Company, 32, 33, 34, 136
Kansas City Terminal, 10
Karlsbad, Germany, 237
Karlsruhe, Germany, 182, 234, 238, 254
Karoune River, Iran, 257
Kassel, Germany, 238, 239, 248
Kasserine, North Africa, 90
Kasserine Pass, North Africa, 76, 78, 81
Keating, Capt. Stephen J., 68
Kebibia, Tunisia, 82
Keiser, Brig. Gen. Laurence B., 148
Kelly, 2nd Lieut. M. D., 143
Kelly, Ralph, President Baldwin Locomotive Company, 147
Kelly, Brig. W. T.: member Inter-Allied Railway Commission, 172
Kempster, Lieut. Col. Oliver W., 223
Kenny, Capt. N. T., 322
Kernell, T/5 Nathaniel E., 319, 322
Kernkamp, Capt. M. F., 85
"Khalassis" (Indian caste), 276
Khatikar, India, 269, 270, 275
Khorramshahr, Iran, 256-257, 261, 262, 264, 265
King, T/4 Hugh M., 228
Kingman, Brig. Gen. John J., 19, 20
Kirn, Germany, 221
Klondike Gold Rush, 42
Knapp, Col. Ralph E., 262
Knight, Col. W. G., 34
K.N.R. Building, Seoul, Korea, 309
Kobe, Japan, 294
Korea, 292, 293, 296, 299-315; M.R.S. in, 300-315; railroads of, 301-303; North Korea, 299, 301, 307, 312; South Korea, 302, 303, 314; invasion of South Korea, 307
Korean National Railroads (K.N.R.), 307, 309
Kossuth, Capt. Frank J., 93, 140
Krefeld, Germany (Rhine River City), 228
Kreuger, Lieut. Gen. W. E., 33
Kroubs, Algeria, 77, 88
Krupp of Essen, 259
Kruse, Capt. Charles A., 245
Kurfess, L. S., 286
Kyushu Island, Japan, 294-297

La Calle, North Africa, 76, 78, 88
Lacamp, La., 33
La Chappelle, France, 180

INDEX

Lagonegro, Italy, 145
Lake, Maj. W. J., 67
Laksam, India, 269
Lalmanirhat, India, 275
Lamberton Projection Formula, 29
Lamezia, Italy, 144
Landen, Belgium, 187, 190
Lane, M/Sgt. Robert E., 190
Langres, France, 218
Laon, France, 184, 186, 187
La Pallice, France, 12
Largs Bay (transport, British), 136
Larkin, Maj. Gen. T. B., 194, 195
Larson, Merle, W.P.A. director, 318
La Spezia, Italy, 157
Latham, 2nd Lieut. H. E., 143
Laurent, 2nd Lieut. R. J., 143
Lawrence, 2nd Lieut., 143
LCT (car ferries), 175, 186
Lea, Capt. R. V., 288
Ledo, India, 269, 270, 271, 276
Ledo Road, 272
Lee, Lieut. Gen. John C. H., 171, 195
Lee, Gen. Robert E., 5
Leer, Capt. E. J., 85
Leese, Lieut. Col. J. F. M., Assistant Director Tn-1, 72
Leese, Lieut. Gen. Sir Oliver W. H., commands British Eighth Army, 142
Leghorn, Italy, 157
Le Havre, France, 12, 187, 252
Lehigh Valley Railroad Company, 26, 27, 136, 185-186
Leipzig, Germany, 221
Le Mans, France, 12, 179, 180, 181
Lend-Lease Act, 83, 214, 224, 260, 268, 276, 286
Le Nesueray, M., President General of French Railways, 183
Lévi, M., Chief Engineer, S.N.C.F., 213
Lewis, 2nd Lieut. Francis J., 262
Lewis, Lieut. Col. L. H., 186
Liberator (train), 303; West Coast Section of, 303
Libya, 29, 77, 138
Licata, Sicily, 99, 100, 101, 102, 105
Liége, Belgium, 182, 187, 226, 227, 230, 238
Lincoln, President Abraham, 9, 36; seizes railroads, 2
Lincoln, Col. R. B., 291
Linehan, Lieutenant, 230
Ling, Engineer J. O., 79
Lingayen Gulf, P. I., 288
Linningston, Lieut. H. E., 143
Linthwaite, Capt. G. F., 85
Linz, Austria, 176
Liri River, Italy, 150; Valley, 106
Lisieux, France, 180, 187
Lison, France, 180, 187
Livron Bridge, Lyon, France, 201
Locomotive No. 1864, M.R.S., report on, 94-96
Locomotives, Diesel, 137, 138, 163. 168, 169, 211, 226, 234
Locomotives, oil-burning, 225, 231
Locomotives, steam, 163, 169, 211, 225, 251, 265
London, England, 45, 61; European strategy planned at, 106, 141
London and North Eastern Railway, 272
Loneker, Sgt. Edward E., 189
Long Island Railroad, 96
"Long Toms" (artillery), 245
Longuyon, France, 253
Louisville and Nashville Railroad Company, 26, 167, 185
Louvain, Belgium, 238
Love, Lieut. Col. C. D., 167, 185
LST (car ferries), 175, 186
Lucas, Lieut. F. D., 135
Ludwigshaven, Germany, 234, 237
Lumding, India, 275, 276, 280
Lure-Belfort priority line, 216
Luscaleet, 2nd Lieut. W., 143
Luxembourg, 175, 186, 187, 227, 251, 253
Luxembourg City, 227, 253
Luzon, P. I., 288
Luzon Military Railway, 288, 290, 292
Lyon, France, 196, 198, 200, 201, 215, 218, 223, 226, 228, 321, 322; Terminal, 200
Lyon-Chagny-Grenoble line, 200

Maastricht, Netherlands, 238
McAdoo, William G., Director General, U. S. Railroad Administration, 16
MacArthur, General Douglas, 285, 286, 308
McCafferty, T/5 Keith, 95
McCallum, Brig. Gen. D. C., Military Director and Superintendent of Railroads in United States, 2, 4, 5, 8
McCarty, 2nd Lieut. L. C., 143
McCoach, Brig. Gen. David, Jr., 33
McConnell, 2nd Lieut. C. H., 143
McFadden, T/4 Donald R., 318
McFadden, Col. E. F., 34, 83, 216, 220
McGee, Capt. R. D., 126, 143
McGrory, T/3 J. D., 322
McLellan, Lieut. Col. J. M., 135, 303, 304
McMeans, T/4 William J., 126
McNarney, Maj. Gen. Joseph T., 142
McRee, Lieut. Col. C. A., 185
Madisonville, Texas, 96
Magdeburg, Germany, 236, 245
Magellan, Ferdinand, 284
Maguire, Capt. George T., 192
Maiatico, Maj. Alberico, commander 3rd Railway Battalion (Italian), 116
Maine, State of, 135
Maine, sinking of, 8
Mainz, Germany, 232, 233, 234, 252
Maison-Carrée, Algeria, 88
Maknassy, North Africa, 77
Mallory, Walter, 318
Maloy, T/5 James G., 319
Malta, 65
Manager of Light Railways, M.R.S., 15

Manchuria, 299, 301
Manila, P. I., 252, 288, 290, 292; Japanese attack on, 285
Manila-Caloocan Shuttle Service, 292
Manila-Paco Shuttle Service, 292
Manila Railway Company, 288, 292
Manipur, India, 280
Mann, T/Sgt. Jack W. D., Jr., 228, 229, 230, 319
Mann, 2nd Lieut. R. B., 143
Mannheim, Germany, 252, 254
Margl, Pvt. Joseph H., 320
Margonia, Sicily, 101
Mariana, India, 276, 281
Marin, T/4 Paul, 96
"Mark Clark Special" (train), 109
Marlow, T/4 Walter C., 319
Marrakech, Morocco, 69
Mars (Marsowicz), Pfc., 267
Marsala, Sicily, 99
Marseille, France, 12, 159, 160, 185, 194, 195, 196, 198, 200, 201, 205, 211, 214, 216, 217, 218, 226, 229, 230, 237, 252; Port of, 200, 201
Marseille Terminal, 198
Marseille-La Barque line, 198
Marseille-Valence line, 198
Marson, Lieut. Col. L. B., 72
Martens, A. H., 45
Martens, Maj. H. W., 309
Martin, Capt. William M., 261
Martinetti, Capt. Arduino, commander 8th Railway Company (Italian), 116
Marugame, Japan, 295
Maruscak, Pvt. Michael A., 267
Maryland, State of, 8
Masan, Korea, 300
Mason, Master Sergeant, 230
Mast, General (French Army), 57
Mather, Ralph, 318
Matheson, Col. John D., 109
Mattson, Lieut Col. 266, 267, 268
Mauney, Capt. H. C., 215
Maxfield, Lieut. Col. H. H., 11
Mayenne, France, 179, 180, 181, 182, 184, 185
Mayer, René, Chairman of Board, Compagnie Internationale des Wagons-Lits, 216
Mears, T/5 Don A., 319
Mears, Lieut. Frederick, 52
"Meatball Express," 192
Meaux, France, 186
Mediterranean, the, 57, 76, 82, 251
Mediterranean Theatre of Operations, United States Army, 141, 164, 195, 317; changed from NATOUSA, 142, 194
Melbourne, Australia, 286
Melbourne Military Railway, 165
Melton, Capt. R. B., 310
Memorial Day, in 1945, 268; in 1943, 320
Meridian, Miss., 31
Mers-el-Kebir, North Africa, 67
Merzig, Germany, 221
Messina, Sicily, 99, 100
Messina, Strait of, 100, 105
Metaponto, Italy, 132, 145
Metlaoui, North Africa, 79, 80
Metz, France, 175, 178, 237
Metz-Thionville area, 234
Mexican War: foreword
Meyett, T/5 Irvin C., 319
Mézidon, France, 180
Miami, Fla., 69
Mianeh, Iran, 257, 258
Michaud, Capt. Philip W., 261
Michigan Central Railroad, 11
Middle East, 107, 137, 138, 157, 163, 256-268, 269-283
Midway Islands, 286
Milan, Italy, 107, 157, 161
Mileposts 15-17, 20.9 Alaska, 48, 49
Military Police Battalions, M.R.S., 27, 85, 87, 223
382 Military Police Battalion, 223
383 Military Police Battalion, 223
385 Military Police Battalion, 223
388 Military Police Battalion, 223
390 Military Police Battalion, 223
392 Military Police Battalion, 223
400 Military Police Battalion, 223
794 Military Police Battalion, 85, 136, 196, 211, 215, 223; Company "B," 136; 794 M.P.B. (Rome), 154
Military Police Companies, 27, 85
181 Military Police Company, 85
182 Military Police Company, 223
185 Military Police Company, 85
186 Military Police Company, 85
187 Military Police Company, 85
189 Military Police Company, 223
193 Military Police Company, 85
Military Railways of Italy, Col. Clarence L. Burpee named Director, 134; Col. A. W. Campbell named Director, 160
Military Railway of North Africa, Col. A. W. Campbell assigned as Director, 134
Military Railway Service (M.R.S.): first organization of in U. S. Army, 2; in War Between the States, 2-8; in World War I, 10-16; first railroad operation by, 12; reorganization of (1919-1942), 17-23; units at start of World War II, 25-27; organizational setup, 27; activation of units, 37-39; first overseas assignments, World War II, 41-56; First M.R.S. Headquarters assigned to North Africa, 68-69; integration in Allied staff of Director General, North Africa, 71; Headquarters, M.R.S. established in Italy, 133; railroads represented in, 135-136; Second M.R.S. established, 142; training of units in England, 167-168; additional units assigned to Second M.R.S., 185-186; General Headquarters, M.R.S., established, 193, 219; staff assignments to General Headquarters, M.R.S., 220; boundaries between First and Second M.R.S. established, 221; office of General Manager, Headquarters, M.R.S., bombed, 228; troop assignments in First and Second M.R.S. at time of

Germany's surrender; boundaries between First and Second M.R.S. changed, 251-252; disposal of units in ETOUSA after war, 254-255; Third M.R.S. Headquarters formed, 256; staff in Iran, 261-262; staff reorganization, Third Headquarters, M.R.S., 267; directors and managers in India, 283; M.R.S. staff in Philippines, 290-291; Third T.M.R.S., 291, 296; 8010 T.M.R.S. formed, 296; 8059 T.M.R.S. formed, 296; 500 T.R.G.D. formed in Korea, 304; Third T.M.R.S. in Korea, 308, 309, 310, 314; statistics on M.R.S., 316
Miller, Lieut. Glenn E., 261
Miller, Major, 68
Mills, 2nd Lieut. Lyman R., 126, 143
Miloston, T/5 Raymond F., 60
Milwaukee, Wis., 19
Minneapolis, Minn., 318
Minneapolis and St. Louis Railway Company, 136
Minneapolis, St. Paul and Sault Ste. Marie Railroad Company, 136
Minturno, Italy, 154
Miramas, France, 198
Mississippi, State of, 8, 165
Missouri-Kansas-Texas Railroad Company, 26, 186
Missouri Pacific Railroad, 26, 33, 84, 95, 96, 136
Mitsui and Mitsubishi (Tokyo), 259
Mittman, Herr, 182
Moe, Lieut. Col. J. W., 167, 178, 248
Moji, Japan, 295, 296
Mokpo, Korea, 301
Molsheim, France, 216
Moncrieff, Captain, 68
Mons, France, 188
Montebourg, France, 180
Montepescali, Italy, 158
Montevarchi, Italy, 158
Montgomery, Field Marshal Sir Bernard L., 77, 99; accompanies General Eisenhower to England, 142; commands Twenty-first Army Group, 169-170
Montmelion, France, 200
"Moonbeam" (elephant), 280
Moran, Lieut. Thomas C., 192
Morocco, 29, 61, 65
Morris, Lieut. J. H., 143
Morris, Lieut. Col. W. C., 185
Morrow, Maj. Jay J., Chairman, Alaska Railroad Commission, 50
Morton, Pvt. George, 234
Morton-on-Lug, England, 169
Moselle Valley, 228
Moslems, 89, 268
Moss, Maj. Roy P., 79, 102
Motta, Sicily, 100
Mountbatten, Lord Louis, Supreme Commander in Chief, Southeast Asia Command, 270
"Movement Control" Board, 279
MTOUSA: *See* Mediterranean Theatre of Operations, United States Army
"Mulberry" (anchorage), 175
Mulhouse, France, 176, 219, 224
Muller, Col. W. J., 102, 188
München-Gladbach, Germany, 237
Munich, Germany, 248, 254
Münster, Germany, 232
Murphy, Captain, 134
Murphy, Robert, American Consul at Algiers, 57
Mussolini, Premier Benito, 103, 266
Myers, T/5 Mason O., 319
Myhers, Pfc. John B., 318, 319, 320, 321
"Mystery" (Indian caste), 276

Nagasaki, Japan, 295; atom bombing of, 292
Namur, Belgium, 179, 187, 188, 236, 238
Nancy, France, 186, 218, 227, 237
Napier, Maj. Gen. C. S., Chief, British MOV and Tn Branch, G-4 Division, 174
Naples, Italy, 104, 105, 106, 107, 108, 109, 110, 111, 118, 122, 127, 129, 138, 320, 322; reconstruction work of R.O.B., M.R.S., 116; Headquarters, M.R.S. in, 133, 134
Naples, Bay of, 136
Naples, Compartimento, 111
Naples, Port of, 109, 114, 163
Naples Terminal, 144, 154
Nashville, Tenn., 8
Natal, Brazil, 69
National Defense Act of 1916, 24; provisions of, 9
Natour, North Africa, 81
NATOUSA: *See* North African Theatre of Occupation, United States Army
Navy Special black fuel oil, 217
Nazis, 246, 247
Nelson, Pvt. Alfred L., 320
Netherlands, the (*See also* Holland), 29, 251, 252; Navy, 99
Netherton, 2nd Lieut. T. C., 143
Nettuno, Italy, 154
Neu Offingen, Germany, 240
Neu Ulm, Germany, 240
Neuringen, Germany, 240
Neustadt, Germany, 237, 238, 248
Nevers, France, 12, 218
Nevers (France) Cut-Off, 12
New Caledonia, M.R.S. in, 27, 288
New Delhi, India, 273, 278
New Orleans, La., 31, 39, 142
New Orleans Unit Training Center (Camp Plauche), 37
New York Central Railroad, 25, 26, 31, 84, 136, 271, 290
New York, N. Y., 50, 96
New York, Chicago and St. Louis Railroad Company, 136
New York, New Haven and Hartford Railroad Company, 26, 136, 166, 178, 240, 290
New York, Ontario and Western Railway, 136
New York, Susquehanna and Western Railroad Company, 286
Niiagata, Japan, 297
Nocera, Italy, 154
Nocera Inferiore, Italy, 133, 145
Nordhausen, Germany, 245

INDEX

Norfolk and Western Railway, 26, 136, 167, 178
Normandy Beach, France, 175
Norris, Lieut. J. M., 100
North Africa, 101, 114, 173, 223, 269; M.R.S. operations in, 27, 29, 48, 49, 57-98, 107, 108, 115, 142, 143, 144, 154, 157, 160, 163, 169, 171, 211, 212, 213, 225, 261, 266, 273, 319, 322; General Mark Clark lands, 57; Sir Winston Churchill quoted on, 61; Allied plan of attack, 61-64; armed resistance ends, 84; M.R.S. Headquarters closed, 133
North African Theatre of Operations, United States Army (NATOUSA), 69-70; General Eisenhower Commanding General of, 141; Lieutenant General Jacob L. Devers becomes Commanding General, 141; Lieutenant General Joseph T. McNarney named Commanding General, 142; redesignated MTOUSA, 142, 194; plans invasion of southern France, 159
North Carolina, State of, 8
North Pacific Theatre of Operations, 53
North Sea, 176, 251
Northeim, Germany, 245
Northern Pacific Railway, 136, 256
Northwest Service Command, 46, 49
Norway, 29
Notgrass, Lieut. Col. Charles D., 67
Nürnberg, Germany, 237, 238, 239, 248, 254
Nygaard, T/4 George O., 60, 319
N.Y.K. Building, Tokyo, 296

Oakland, Calif., 95
O'Brien, Pvt. H. J., 231
O'Connell, Lieut. Col. J. F., 291
Oder River, 237
Odum, Sgt. Bill, 234
Officers Reserve Corps, 9
Ogg, Lieut. Col. Alva C., 272
Ohlson, Otto F., General Manager Alaska Railroad, 52
Okie, Col. Fred W., 67, 79, 80, 81, 100, 101, 102, 221, 317
"Old Crime and Punishment" (C. & P. Railway), 35
Oliphant, Lieut. Col. Fred L., 223
Olson, M/Sgt. Roy J. E., 318, 319
Omaha Beach, France, 171; landing on, 175, 182
Oran, Algeria, 61, 66, 67, 82, 83, 84, 85, 88, 89, 93; British land at 57; Port of, 83, 93, 94, 108, 149
Order of the Crown of Italy, 148, 317
Order of the Fatherland, First Class (Russian), 268
Order of the Fatherland, Second Class (Russian), 268
Order of the Red Star (Russian), 268
Oregon-Washington Railroad and Navigation Company, 11
Orgon, France, 205
Orléans, France, 179
Orléansville, Algeria, 61, 85, 88
Orte, Italy, 158, 161
Osaka, Japan, 296, 297; Division, 297
Osawatomie, Kansas, 96
Otley, Pfc. Herbert, 267
Ottawa, Canada, 45
Otz, Germany, 221
Oudh and Tirhut Railway, 275
Oued Keberit, North Africa, 77, 81, 88
Oujda, Morocco, 83, 88
Ouled Rhamoun, North Africa, 67, 77, 78, 88, 93
OVERLORD (invasion of France operation), 165, 166
Oviatt, Capt. E. F., 143
Owen, Lieut. Col. Frederick H., 85, 87, 196, 220, 223
Owens, Col. H. E., 296

Pachino, Sicily, 99
Pacific and Arctic Railway and Navigation Company, 43
Pacific Theatre of War Operations, 164, 226, 254, 271, 284-298
Pahlevi, Reza Shah, 256
Palermo, Sicily, 99, 100, 101, 102, 105, 127
Palestine, 138
Palmer, Maj. Arthur C., 310
Palmisano, T/4 Frank, 181
Pandu, India, 275, 281
Pannel, Maj. L. C., 60
Pantin Yard, Paris, 186
Paola, Italy, 144
Parbatipur, India, 269, 275
Paris, France, 12, 179, 180, 182, 183, 184, 186, 187, 188, 195, 219, 221, 223, 226, 227, 238, 247, 252, 253, 254, 259; capture of, 177, 179
"Paris-Frankfurt Express," 253-254
Paris-Orléans Railway, 12
Paris Railway Grand Division (Provisional), 252, 253
Parker, Pvt. Alexander, 125
Parker, Senior Chaplain, Colonel, 320
Parkes, Col. E. L., DD, Tn, 72, 90, 144; commands Reconstruction Division, M.R.S., 112; named Deputy to Director General, M.R.S., 133-134
Parsons, Lieut. Col. William B., 10
Pasing, Germany, 240
Patch, Lieut. Gen. A. M., Jr., 194
Patterson, Capt. C., 143
Patterson, Capt. Thomas R., 69
Pattison and Bufola shops, I.S.R., Naples, 145
Patton, General George S., Jr., 85, 99; commends 727 R.O.B., M.R.S., 104-105, 170, 180; on work train over Rhine, 233
Payner, Cpl. Lloyd N., 228
Peacock, T/4 Maurice, Jr., 319
Pearl Harbor, 28; Japanese attack on, 25, 285
Peeler, Capt. J. G., M.C., 103
Pelley, John J., 28
Pendleton, Col. H. M., 34
Pennsylvania, State of, 8, 12
Pennsylvania Railroad, 2, 3, 10, 11, 25, 26, 27, 29, 31, 36, 37, 95, 136, 167, 172, 177, 185, 200, 256, 271, 312
Père Marquette Railroad, 136

Perkins, Lieut. Col. Albert T., 10
Perl, Germany, 228
Pershing, Gen. John J., expedition against Villa, 9, 10; Armies of in World War I, 16
Persian Gulf, 256
Persian Gulf Command, 259, 265, 266-267, 268
Persian Gulf Service Command, 259
Perth, Australia, 286
Pesaro, Italy, 157
Pescara, Italy, 144, 149, 158
Petits Fils de François de Vandel et Cie., les (Paris), 259
Pett, T/5 Albert M., 319
Philadelphia, Pa., 12
Philadelphia, Wilmington and Baltimore Railroad, 2
Philipe, Brigadier A. T., Director of MOV and Tn, AFHQ staff, 62
Philippeville, Algeria, 77, 88, 90
Philippine Assembly, 284
Philippine Constabulary, 284
Philippine Insurrection, 8, 9
Philippine Islands, 284-292; Japanese land in, 285; M.R.S. in, 288-292, 304
Philippine Scouts, 284
Phillips, Capt. Herbert R., 83, 144
Piacenza, Italy, 107, 161
Piazzy, Pfc. James, 275, 276
Pierson, T/4 Elroy M., 319
Pike's Peak, Colorado, 295
Pilcher, Lieut. Col. Harvey, 271
Pilsen, Czechoslovakia, 176
Pisa, Italy, 157, 158
Pisa-Florence line, I.S.R., 158
Pittsburgh, Pa., 12
Plechinger, Germany, 240
Plunkett, Admiral C. P., 515
Po River, Italy, 161
POL, 191
Pola, Italy, 157
Poland, 259
Polish, the, 268
Pont du Fahs, North Africa, 81, 82
Pontabault, France, 179, 184
Pontorson, France, 185
Port-de Bouc-Avignon via Miramas line, 198
Portsmouth, England, 171
Portsmouth, N. H., 299
Portugal, 29
Potenza, Italy, 108, 114, 128, 132, 144, 145, 154
Pottle, Colonel, DD, Tn, made Commanding Officer, First District, Railways of Italy, 111
Powell, Pvt. Herbert J., 264
Prague, Czechoslovakia, 259
Price, Capt. C. G., Jr., 192
Price, Lieut. Col. E. M., 84, 154
Prince Umberto Square, No. 35, Naples, 108
Protoille, North Africa, 82
Pruitt, Lieut. Col. W. C., 186
Pueblo, Col., 41
Puerto Rican Army, 65th Infantry Regiment, 2nd Battalion, 196
Pulliam, Lieut. Col. S. H., 178, 303
Pullman Company, the, 136, 143
Purcell, Lieut. Col. James, 167, 186
Pusan, Korea, 296, 301, 302, 303, 304, 307, 308, 309
Pyongtaek, Korea, 306
Pyongyang, Korea, 312

Quenard, Col. E., Director of Military Transports, French, 58, 71, 72, 90, 114
Quezon, Manuel, President of the Philippines, 284, 285
Quiévrain, French-Belgian border, 187
Quist, 2nd Lieut. C. E., 143
Qum, the Holy City, Iran, 268

Rabat, Morocco, 71, 83
Radio Algiers, 320
"Raggrupamento Ferrovieri" (Italian Army construction engineers), 116
Ragusa, Sicily, 99
Rail Transportation Offices, Sicily, 100, 105
Railroads, American, military operation up to 1954 (summary), foreword; employee representation in World War II, foreword; M.R.S. created, 2; seizure by President Wilson, 16; organization of, 20-21, 85; Affiliation Plan adopted, 24; M.R.S. representation in, 25-27, 135-136; (see also under names of individual railroads)
Railroads, Australian, 286
Railroads, British: (*See* Railroads of United Kingdom, also British Transportation Service)
Railroads, French, 58-60, 75, 173, 179-180, 196-218; (see also under S.N.C.F.)
Railroads, German, 182, 246-251; (see also under Reichs Eisenbahn)
Railroads, Iranian, 256-268
Railroads, Italian, 99-164
Railroads, Japanese, 294-297
Railroads, Korean, 300-314
Railroads, North African, 58-61, 67, 71-72, 75, 77-78, 83, 85, 88-90
Railroads, Polish, 246
Railroads, Sicilian, 103, 128; (see also under Railroads, Italian)
Railroads of United Kingdom, 167, 168, 180, 190
"Rails, The," 215
Railway Age (magazine), 147
Railway Battalion, Corps of Engineers, M.R.S., 18
Railway Company of an Engineering Battalion, M.R.S., 18
Railway Detachment 9646-A, M.R.S., 46
Railway Grand Divisions, M.R.S., 27, 28, 61, 62, 160, 186, 207, 214, 237, 261, 271; formation of, 21; Headquarters, 72, 160, 166, 177, 254; Stores Department, 216
701 R.G.D., 25, 37, 69, 107, 149, 154, 160, 161, 318; Engineering Section, 161; Headquarters, 84, 88, 144, 164, 318, 320
702 R. G. D., 25, 36, 37, 220, 256, 261; Headquar-

ters, 256, 261-262, 318
703 R. G. D., 25, 28, 29, 37, 64, 66, 72, 77, 81, 88, 100, 104, 107, 111, 134, 143, 144, 145, 154, 160, 196, 201, 207, 221, 226, 237, 261, 318; Headquarters, 29, 77, 81, 108, 195, 227, 318
704 R. G. D., 25, 37, 85, 88, 107, 200, 218, 225, 227, 234, 237, 238; Headquarters, 68, 69, 84, 85, 153, 154, 160, 227, 271, 318
705 R. G. D., 25, 37, 273, 275
706 R. G. D., 25, 37, 143, 179, 181, 182, 183, 186, 188, 226, 227, 228, 237, 252; Headquarters, 177; Company "C," 226
707 R. G. D., 25, 37, 180, 187, 227, 237, 252; Headquarters, 166, 177, 179, 227
708 R. G. D., 25, 37, 188, 193, 227, 237, 239, 252, 308; Headquarters, 166, 178, 179, 227
709 R. G. D., 25, 37, 185, 187, 188, 190, 192, 238, 252; Headquarters, 227, 254
710 R. G. D., 25, 37, 185, 187, 227, 238, 252, 254; Headquarters, 227
774 R. G. D., 27, 160
775 R. G. D., 288, 290, 294; Headquarters, 290, 291
Railway Labor Executives Association, 28
Railway Operating Battalions, M.R.S., 17, 18, 20, 27, 28, 61, 62, 72, 73, 160, 165, 178, 186, 190, 214, 254; "A" Companies, 17, 18, 73, 207; "B" Companies, 17, 18; "C" Companies, 17, 18, 87; "D" Companies, 20; Headquarters, 18, 19, 216, 254; Headquarters and Service Companies, 18, 19
711 R. O. B., 25, 29, 32, 33, 37, 109, 256, 261, 262, 264, 265, 267, 268; Company "C," 264
712 R. O. B., 25, 37, 75, 166, 178, 181, 183, 187, 226, 231, 237, 253, 310, 315; Company "A," 181; Company "B," 181; Company "C," 189
713 R. O. B., 25, 29, 31, 37, 46, 67, 77, 88, 90, 104, 107, 122, 125, 126, 128, 154, 160, 165, 196, 205, 207, 237; Company "A," 128, 129, 154, 195; "B & B" Platoon, 128
714 R. O. B., 25, 37, 39, 53, 54, 55, 309, 315; Company "A," 53
715 R. O. B., 25, 37, 84, 88, 90, 107, 144, 147, 153, 154, 160, 161, 164; Company "A," 116, 129
716 R. O. B., 25, 37, 185, 231, 237, 252, 255
717 R. O. B., 25, 37, 167; Company "A," 239; Detachment "A," 185, 227; Detachment "B," 227; Detachment "C," 227
718 R. O. B., 25, 37, 178, 184, 187, 188, 189, 227, 234, 237; Company "C," 191
719 R. O. B., 25, 37, 84, 88, 90, 107, 144, 145, 154, 160, 161, 164; Company "A," 90, 116, 129, 144, 154, 161
720 R. O. B., 25, 37, 167, 178, 180, 187, 233, 237, 252
721 R. O. B., 25, 38, 271, 275; Headquarters, 275
722 R. O. B., 25, 38, 185, 187, 188, 237, 240, 245, 252
723 R. O. B., 25, 38, 185, 187, 237, 252
724 R. O. B., 26, 38, 185, 186, 187, 226, 238, 244, 253, 310, 315
725 R. O. B., 26, 38, 271; Headquarters, 275
726 R. O. B., 26, 38, 271, 275
727 R. O. B., 26, 29, 31, 38, 46, 67, 75, 77, 78, 81, 88, 100, 101, 102, 103, 104, 105, 144, 154, 157, 160, 165, 195, 198, 205, 215, 221, 234, 237; Company "A," 79, 100-102, 104, 127-129, 144, 195, 215, 216; Company "B," 100, 104; Company "C," 79, 100, 104; Headquarters Company, 127, Headquarters and Headquarters Company, 104
728 R. O. B., 26, 38, 167, 185, 237, 238; Company "B," 238
729 R. O. B., 26, 38, 166, 178, 179, 187, 188, 233, 234, 237, 240, 245, 252
730 R. O. B., 26, 29, 36, 37, 38, 165, 256, 262, 266, 267, 268; Company "A," 266; Company "C," 268
731 R. O. B., 26, 38
732 R. O. B., 26, 38, 185, 187, 188, 189, 225, 228, 233, 237, 244; Headquarters, 254
733 R. O. B., 26, 38, 185, 187, 192, 239, 248, 253
734 R. O. B., 26, 38, 186, 238, 241, 252, 255
735 R. O. B., 26, 38, 185, 187, 190, 237, 239, 241, 252, 255; Bridge and Building Platoon, 239; Company "C," 190; Second Track Platoon, 239
737 R. O. B., 26, 38, 290, 292, 296, 304
738 R. O. B., 26, 38
739 R. O. B., 26, 38
740 R. O. B., 26, 38, 178, 180, 238, 252, 253; Company "A," 181; Headquarters, 226; Maintenance & Equipment Company, 181
741 R. O. B., 26, 38, 185, 187, 228, 237, 241, 252, 255; Company "A," 231; Company "C," 228
742 R. O. B., 26, 38
743 R. O. B., 26, 38, 185, 187, 188, 238, 240
744 R. O. B., 26, 38, 185, 187, 188, 191, 238, 252
745 R. O. B., 26, 38, 48, 272, 276
746 R. O. B., 26, 38, 192, 238, 252, 255; Company "B," 192; Company "D" (Diesel), 186
747 R. O. B., 26, 38
748 R. O. B., 26, 38, 272, 276, 280
749 R. O. B., 26, 38, 290, 294, 304
750 R. O. B., 26, 38, 185, 200, 216, 237, 252, 255
751 R. O. B., 26, 38
752 R. O. B., 26, 38, 186, 236, 238, 252, 255
759 R. O. B. (Missouri Pacific), 26, 38, 84, 88, 90, 107, 154, 160, 198, 231, 237; Company "A," 90, 116, 144, 154, 196, 207
770 R. O. B., 27, 38, 47, 48, 49, 50, 291, 304
790 R. O. B., 38
791 R. O. B., 38, 256 (First Provisional Operating Battalion), 262, 267, 268
Railway Operating Company, No. 790, 27, 288, 290, 292, 304
Railway Operating Detachment, No. 770, 46
Railway Security Department, Provisional, Headquarters, Second M.R.S., 223
Railway Shop Battalions, M.R.S., 22, 23, 27, 28, 61, 62, 72, 160, 165, 168, 178, 186, 254; "A," "B," and "C" Companies, 23; Headquarters Companies, 216, 254; Headquarters and Service Company, 23
753 R. S. B., 26, 29, 31, 39, 67, 77, 88, 89, 93, 104, 107, 145, 146, 148, 154, 164, 290, 293; "A" Company, 93, 104; "B" Company, 104; "C" Company,

67, 89, 104, 140
754 R. S. B., 26, 37, 39, 252
755 R. S. B., 26, 39, 167, 178, 179, 187, 238, 242
756 R. S. B., 27, 39, 167, 200, 218, 226, 228, 229, 230, 237, 309
757 R. S. B., 27, 39, 167, 178, 179, 181, 187, 238, 248, 250, 252
758 R. S. B., 27, 39, 272, 276; "B" Company, 276
760 R. S. B., 39
762 R. S. B., 39, 252
763 R. S. B., 27, 39, 167, 185, 238
764 R. S. B., 27, 39, 178, 179, 181, 187, 230, 238
765 R. S. B., 27, 39, 186, 226, 237, 315; Headquarters, 254
766 R. S. B., 27, 39 (M.R.S.), 200, 237, 255
Railway Shop Battalions Diesel, M.R.S., 23, 27
760 R. S. B. Diesel, 107, 136, 137-138, 154, 160, 164
762 R. S. B. Diesel (Alco), 256, 262, 268
Railway Shop Battalion Provisional, No. 5250, 290
Railway Shop Battalions Steam, M.R.S., 27, 256, 262
754 R. S. B. Steam, 267, 268
Railway Supervisory Group, No. 7107, 164
Railway Supervisory Group, No. 6603, 164
Railway Transportation Companies, M.R.S., 27, 254
761 R. T. C., 39, 66, 88, 107, 149, 154, 160, 165, 200, 237
Railway Workshops Mobile, M.R.S., 23, 27, 254, 290
131 R. W. M., 290, 292, 304
132 R. W. M., 290, 294
133 R. W. M., 290, 294
Raimondo, Maj. Gen. Giovanni di, Director of Military Railways, I. S. R., 109, 112, 114, 116, 153
Ramillies Yard, 190
Rapino, Maj. Salvatore, commander 1st Railway Battalion (Italian), 116
Ratter, Lieut. Col. J., Assistant Director, Tn-2, 107
Reading Company, 166, 178
Red River and Gulf Railroad, 32
Reconstruction Division, M.R.S., 111-112
Redeyef, North Africa, 80
Regensburg, Germany, 254
Reggio-Calabria Compartimenti, 111
Reggio de Calabria, Italy, 100, 105, 107, 109, 145; line, 147
Rehberg, Pfc. Robert C., 320
Reichs Eisenbahn, 228, 239, 240, 246
Reims, France, 186, 187
Reims Deployment Area, 252
Remagen, Germany, 232
Rennes, France, 179, 184, 185
Resurrection Bay, Alaska, 52
Revere, Italy, 161
Revolutionary War, American, foreword
Reybold, Maj. Gen. Eugene, 33, 41
Reynolds, Maj. D. C. L., 67
Rhine River, 161, 174, 175, 176, 178, 190, 213, 219, 231, 232, 233, 234, 239
Rhine River City (Krefeld), Germany, 228
Rhône River, 201, 205; Bridge, 201; Route, 212; Valley, 12, 194, 195, 201
Riach, Staff Sergeant, 230
Rice, Maj. W. Thomas, 267, 317
Richards, Capt. Frederick T., 69
Richmond, Fredericksburg and Potomac Railroad Company, 136, 317
Rickenbacker, Capt. Eddie, 265
Ricketts, T/5 Alfred C., 126
Ridgway, Gen. Matthew B., Eighty-second Airborne Division, 33; member, Class of 1917, West Point, 143
Rigby, Capt. Jourdan, 262
Riggs, Thomas, Jr., 52
Ringberg, Lieutenant Colonel, 178
Ritter, Capt. J. H., 143
Riviera, French, 218
Robertson, Lieut. Gen. Sir Brian H., British Second District, 110
Röderau, Germany, 221
Rogers, C. J., 44
Rogers, Maj. William C., 256
Rome, Italy, 103, 107, 129, 150, 151, 153, 154, 158, 159, 161, 163, 196, 320, 322; Fifth Army captures, 149, 150; Fourth of July celebration, 151; receives coal from Secretary of War, 151
Rome Railroad Terminal, 151, 153, 154
Rommel, Field Marshal Erwin, 77
Roosevelt, President Theodore, 284
Roscofsky, Colonel, 245
Ross, Brig. Gen. Lewis T., 28, 31
Ross, Maj. Gen. F. T., 171
Roth Waagner, bridging: *See* Bridging, Roth Waagner
Rouen, France, 252
R. T. O., 307, 308
"Rubber Czar," 260
Rüdesheim, Germany, 221
Ruhr, the, 219, 233, 234, 241
Ruhr Valley, 245
Rundstedt, Field Marshal Karl von, 188
Russell, Col. F. E., 291
Russia, 248, 257, 259, 260, 267, 299, 300
Russians, the, 237, 244, 245, 257, 258, 264, 265, 267-268, 270, 271
Russo-Japanese War, 299
Ryan, Col. Norman A., 165

Saales, France, 216
Saar Region, 219
Saar River, 239
Saar Salient, 236
Saarbrücken, Germany, 237
Sagstetter, Mr., 41
St. Barbe de Tletat, North Africa, 83
St. Dié, France, 216
Saint-Lazare Station, Paris, 183, 253-254
Saint-Lô, France, 175, 178, 179, 180, 187
St. Louis, Mo., 12, 95
St. Louis-San Francisco Railway Company, 26, 136, 185, 200
St. Marie, France, 216
St. Maximin, France, 200

Saint Nazaire, 12, 15, 195
St. Paul, Minn., 29, 34, 39, 41, 68, 69, 165, 231, 318
St. Paul Civic Opera, 318
St. Raphael, France, 194, 200
St. Raphael-Toulon line, 198
St. Tropez, France, 194
Sakkhoa Ghat, India, 269
Salerno, Italy, 105, 106, 108, 114, 127, 128, 144
Salida, Col., 41
Samchok, Korea, 312
San Fernando (La Unión), P. I., 288, 290, 292
San Fernando (Pampanga), P. I., 290
San Francisco, Cal., 12
San Giovanni Barra, Italy, 128, 145
San José, P. I., 290
San Juan Hill, Cuba, 8
San Lorenzo Railway Yards, 103
San Stefano, Sicily, 101
Sanderson, Lieut. Col. C. S., 72, 108
Sanok, A. J., 286
Sant' Eufemia, Italy, 144
Sant' Eufemia Marina, Italy, 145
Santa Claus, 214
Santa Elena (transport), 83
Santa Fe Railway, 29, 31, 67
Santiago, Cuba, 8
Sapporo, Japan, 295, 296, 297
Sardinia, Island of, Col. Chester K. Harding appointed Allied Military Governor, 142
Sarrebourg, France, 200
Sarrebourg-Berthelnung-Sarralbe priority line, 216
Sasebo, Japan, 296, 297
Saturday Evening Post, 36
Savage, Maj. Merle F., 228
Sbeitla, Tunisia, 76, 90
Sbeitla-Sousse line, 75
Scannell, Capt. Carl O., 261
"Scarifier," 118-119, 150, 153
Scarnecchia, Capt. Paolo, commander 7th Railway Company (Italian), 116
Schaefer, Pfc. Victor F., 126
Scheuble, Maj. Carl C., 68
Schofield, Maj. Albert M., 312
Schopper, Lieut. Col. W. P., 192
Schreiber, T/4 Larry E., 319
Schulchtern, Germany, 221
Schulz, Brig. Gen. J. W. N., 33
Schulze, Lieut. W. A., 85
Schuyler, Lieut. Commander Garret L., 15
Scordia, Sicily, 100
Scotland, 165
Scott, Capt. J. W., 126
Scott, Thomas A., 2
Seaboard Air Line Railroad Company, 25, 185, 240
Seattle, Wash., 12, 42
Security Section, M.R.S., 87
Seddon, James A., 5
Seiller, Lieut. F. E., 290
Seine, Bay of, 171
Sélestat, France, 216
Sendai Division, Japan, 297
Sened, North Africa, 79
Seoul, Korea, 301, 302, 303, 304, 307, 310, 312
"Sergeant Tomer's Reclamation Department," 125-126
Sétif, Algeria, 67, 88
Seward, Alaska, 52
Sézanne, France, 187
Sfax-Gafsa Railroad, Tunisia, 61, 67, 78
SHAEF: *See* Supreme Headquarters, Allied Expeditionary Force
Shah Reza Pahlevi, 256
Shannon, 2nd Lieut. J. W., 143
Shappell, Col. M. M., 253, 267
Sharood, Capt. R. A., 143
Shea, Lieut. Col. J. D., 185
Sheehan, Pfc. J. L., 322
Shepard, H. M., 286
Shepherd, Cpl. Clyde P., 228
Sherman tanks, 164
Shields, Lieut. L. G., 126
Shikoku, Japan, 297
Shinbashi, Japan, 294
Shimonoseki, Japan, 295
Sibari, Italy, 132
Siboney, Cuba, 8
Sicignano, Italy, 145
Sicily, 48, 61, 85, 87, 92, 127, 142
Sicily and Italy, M.R.S. operations in, 99-164
Sidi-bel-Abbès, Algeria, 67
Sidi Bou Baker, North Africa, 79
Sidi-Mabrouk, Algeria, 67, 88, 89, 93
Siegfried Defenses, 190
Siegfried Line, 175
Signal Engineer, M.R.S., 18
Siliguri, India, 269
Simpson, Captain, 68
Sinclair, Maj. J., 67
Singapore, 272
Sinmack, Korea, 310
Sinuiju, Korea, 301
Sisteron, France, 200
Sisteron-Grenoble Route, 212
Skagway, Alaska, 42, 43, 46, 48
Skoda of Prague, 259
Slick, T/5 Harry, 268
Smith, Captain, 60
Smith, Maj. Gen. W. B., 70
Smith, Lieut. Col. Worthington C., 178, 256, 267, 268, 296
S. N. C. B. Telephone Networks, 236
S. N. C. F., 211, 213, 215, 221, 223, 224, 226, 228; officers of, 213, 236; Nord (North) Region, 253; Est (East) Region, 253; Ouest (West) Region, 253; Sud Est (Southeast) Region, 211, 218, 224
S. N. C. F. Actors Guild, 215
S. N. C. F. Stores, 182
Snipes, Cpl. Flody C., 245
Soissons, France, 186, 187, 192
"Soldiers Chapel of the Air," 320
Soldier's Medal award, 192, 264, 317

SOLOC: *See* Southern Line of Communications
Somervell, General B. B., in Alaska, 41, 43; in AFHQ, Algiers, 68; commands M.R.S. troops in India, 272
Sommesous, France, 186
Sottevast, France, 180, 187
Souk Arbe, Tunisia, 76
Souk-Ahras, Algeria, 72, 77, 81, 88
Sousse, North Africa, 81, 88, 90
South America, 46
South Atlantic, 69
Southeast Asia Command, 270
Southern Army (War Between the States), 5
Southern Line of Communications (SOLOC), 194, 214, 216
Southern Pacific Company, 25, 26, 52, 95, 96, 135, 136, 185, 256, 271
Southern Railway Company, 25, 26, 31, 67, 166, 177
Soviet frontier, 258
Soviet-United States Commission, 299
Soviet Transport Department, 268
Spain, 29, 284
Spanish-American War, foreword, 8, 284
Sparanise, Italy, 154
Sparks, Lieut. Harvey H., 190
Spellman, Most Reverend Francis J., Archbishop of New York, Military Vicar of the United States Armed Forces, 265
Spezzano, Italy, 132
Spring Creek Bridge, 32
Stalingrad, Russia, 245
Standard Steel Car Company, 15
Stanton, Edwin M., Secretary of War, 2
Station Agency Detachment, M.R.S., 23
Steeves, Capt. Carl E., 262
Steinke, Capt. R. L., 310
Stendal, Germany, 244
Sterling, Lieut. J. R., 79, 81, 100
Steubenville, Ohio, 95
Stevens, Lieut. Col. M. G., 167, 178
Stewart, Brig. Gen. George C., 291
Stilwell, Lieut. Gen. J. W., 270, 272
Stilwell Road, 271
Stimson, Lieutenant, 230
Stockard, Lieut. Col. J. J., 185, 200, 216
Stoddard, Col. Arthur E., 220, 229, 256, 261, 262, 267, 317
Stone, Sgt. N. L., 102
Storch-Nielsen (Copenhagen), 259
Strader, Chaplain Val B., 216
Strandberg, T/4 Wendell K., 319
Strasbourg, France, 176, 211, 214, 217, 218, 228, 237
Strieff, Lieut. C. J., 143
Stromquist, Pfc. Raymond C., 320
Stump, Fireman J. L., 79
Sturtevant, Lieut. Col. Carleton W., 11
Stuttgart, Germany, 248
Sugarman, Capt. W., 85
Sulton, Lieut. Gen. D. I., 270
Superintendent of Transportation, M.R.S., 135
Superintendents, M.R.S., 75; Division, 18, 31; General, 31, 75, 77; Railway, 22; Shop, 31, 75
Supreme Headquarters, Allied Expeditionary Force, 179, 254; General Eisenhower commands, 169; status of M.R.S., 169; directive from General Eisenhower, 170; sets up Inter-Allied Railway Commission, 172; G-4 Section, 244; discontinuance of, 241
Surdon, France, 179
Surles, Lieut. Harry J., 68
Susack, Korea, 310
Suwon, Korea, 310, 312
Swan, Sgt. C., 102
Sweden, 29, 259
Switzerland, 175, 176, 217, 219, 251, 259
Sydney, Australia, 286
Sykora, 1st Sgt., 215
Syracuse, Sicily, 99
Syria, 138

Tabarka, Tunisia, 76
Tabriz, Iran, 258
Taegu, Korea, 309, 310, 312
Taejon, Korea, 304, 312
Taft, William Howard, President of the United States, 50; Governor of Philippine Islands, 284
Tanana River, 52
Tangier Fez (railroad), 61
Tanuma, Iran, 262
Taranto, Italy, 107, 108, 110, 114
Tardieu, Capt. André, 14
Tassigny, General of the Army, Jean de Lattre de, 194
Tate, T/4 Benjamin, 191
Tate, Colonel, 106; G-4 of Fifth Army, 110
Taylor, Maj. George, 267
Tébessa, Algeria, 67, 76, 77, 78, 79, 80, 81, 88
Tebourba, Tunisia, 82
Teets, Capt. Arthur G., 69
Teheran, Iran, 256, 257, 258, 261, 262
Tempelhof Airport, 244
Tergnier, France, 187
Terni, Italy, 158
Terry, Maj. Gen. T. A., 270
Tessier, M., 57
Texas and New Orleans Railroad Company, 25, 26, 84, 186
Texas and Pacific Railway Company, 26, 272
Thelepte, North Africa, 81
Thionville, France, 226, 228, 237
Thomas, Maj. Herbert, 165
Thompson, Cpl. William S., 216
Thomson, J. Edgar, 2
Thorne, Capt. James R., 245
Thornton, Lieut. Col. L. E., 185
Tiber River, 105
Tiburtina and Rome Terminal Yards, 154
Tinsukia, India, 269, 276
T. M. R. S.: *See* Transportation Military Railway Service, M.R.S.
Tokaido, Japan, 294

Tokyo, Japan, 259, 294, 295, 297; Bay, 299; Division, 297; Central Station, 297
Tokyo-Yokohama area, 297
Tomer, Sgt. Fred A., 125-126
Toomey, Capt. Justin G., 68
"Toot Sweet Special," 193
Topa, Lieut. Filippo, commander 31st Railway Company (Italian), 116
TORCH (Allied invasion of North Africa), 57
Torrenza, Italy, 132
Toul, France, 186, 187
Tours, France, 12
Townsend, F. D., 4
Train Movement Section, Hanover Division, 240
Trans-Iranian Railroad, 257, 258
Transportation Corps Composite Company, No. 61, M.R.S., 27, 276
Transportation Military Railway Service, M.R.S., 21
Transportation Railway Command, M.R.S., 21
Transportation Railway Grand Division, M.R.S.: *See* T. R. G. D.
Transportation Railway Group, M.R.S., 21
Transportation Railway Operating Battalion. M.R.S.: *See* T. R. O. B.
Transportation Traffic Regulating Groups, M.R.S.:
30 T. T. R. G., 304
8010 T. T. R. G., 296
Treasure, Major, 68
T. R. G. D., No. 500, M.R.S., 304
Trestling, Bay British Steel, 129
Trieste, 176
Triggs, Lieut. Col. R. E., 186
T. R. O. B., M.R.S.:
737 T. R. O. B., 304
770, T. R. O. B., 304
Troxler, 2nd Lieut. T. E., 143
Truax, T/Sgt. Sidney W., 68
Truden, Lieut. Col. J. R., 296, 310
Truesdell, Maj. S. R., 143
Truman, President Harry S., 308
Truscott, Lieut. Gen. Lucian K., 142
T. T. R. G.: *See* Transportation Traffic Regulating Groups
Tully, Colonel James K., 143, 220
Tunis, 29, 61, 62, 71, 72, 82, 89
Tunisia, 61, 62, 67, 72, 73, 76, 78, 81, 88, 99, 100
Turin, Italy, 107, 157, 161

Uijongbu, Korea, 310
Ulm, Germany, 240, 254
Umberto, His Royal Highness, Prince of Piedmont, Lieutenant General of the Realm, visits Headquarters, M.R.S., 148
Union Pacific Railroad, 25, 26, 36, 135, 185, 220, 256, 260, 317
Union Railroad Company, Pittsburgh, 317
United Kingdom, 167, 168, 180, 190
United Nations, 299, 300, 307, 310; Command, 308; Security Council, 307, 308
United States, 82, 165, 247, 259, 260
United States, Armed Forces of, 9, 57, 58, 244
United States, Army of, foreword, 1, 2, 9, 12, 57, 60, 139-140, 270;
Adjutant General's Department, 9;
Airborne Division, Eighty-second, 33;
Armies:
First Army, 170, 176, 177, 186, 219, 226, 232, 253;
Third Army, 170, 176, 186, 188, 189, 219, 225, 226, 228, 232, 236, 253; G-4, 188;
Fifth Army, 85, 105, 106, 112, 142, 144, 148, 149, 157, 160, 163, 176, 322; G-4, 106;
Seventh Army, 85, 99, 101-105, 176, 189, 194, 207, 212, 217, 219, 236, 253; G-4, 102;
Eighth Army, 308;
Ninth Army, 176, 219, 233, 245, 253;
Fifteenth Army, 176-177, 253.
Armored Divisions, First, 76;
Corps (except Engineers):
Air Corps, 9;
Corps of Chaplains, 75;
Eighth Corps Area, 33;
Medical Corps, 140;
II U. S. Corps, 67, 75, 76, 78, 82; Quartermaster (II Corps), 79;
Signal Corps, 9, 207, 228, 236;
Transportation Corps, 23, 111; 3483 Quartermaster Truck Company (Trans. Corps), 161; 3491 Quartermaster Truck Company (Trans. Corps), 161; 3901 Quartermaster Truck Company (Trans. Corps), 233; 4260 Quartermaster Truck Company (Trans. Corps), 233; Transportation Corps, Diesel, 234;
Depots, 167
Divisions:
Third Division, 100;
Twenty-fifth Division, 300;
Engineers, 73, 231-233;
Chief of Engineers, 9;
Corps of Engineers, 9, 10, 12, 18, 23, 29, 31, 52;
Engineer Battalions, 18;
91 Engineer Battalion, 32;
93 Engineer Battalion, 32;
98 Engineer Battalion, 32;
Engineer Combat Groups:
40 Engineer Combat Group, 207;
326 Engineer Combat Group, 20;
540 Engineer Combat Group, 207;
1175 Engineer Combat Group, 207;
Engineer Construction Battalions:
371 Engineer Construction Battalion, 233;
Engineer D. T. Companies:
433 E. D. T. Company, 233;
1533 E. D. T. Company, 233;
Engineer General Service Battalions, 225;
Engineer General Service Regiments, 225;
94 Engineer General Service Regiment, 207;
341 Engineer General Service Regiment (First Battalion), 233;
343 Engineer General Service Regiment, 207;
344 Engineer General Service Regiment, 207;

345 Engineer General Service Regiment (Company "A"), 109;
347 Engineer General Service Regiment, 233;
355 Engineer General Service Regiment, 233;
368 Engineer General Service Regiment, 233;
1051 Engineer General Service Regiment, 205;
1317 Engineer General Service Regiment, 233;
Engineer General Service Units:
175 (First Battalion) Engineer General Service Unit, 161;
Engineer Heavy Equipment Company:
482 Engineer Heavy Equipment Company, 233;
Engineer P. C. & R. Group:
1056 Engineer P. C. & R. Group, 233;
Engineer Regiments: Third, 10; Eleventh, 10, 12; Twelfth, 10, 12; Thirteenth, 10, 12; Fourteenth, 11, 12; Fifteenth, 11, 12; Sixteenth, 11, 12; Seventeenth, 11, 12; Eighteenth, 11, 12; Nineteenth, 11, 12; Twentieth (Company "C"), 103;
Engineer Reserve Officers, 17;
5202 Engineers, 288;
Enlisted Reserve Corps, 9;
Field Artillery, 225;
General Staff, G-4, 91;
Infantry Divisions, 214:
First, 76; Sixth, 304; Ninth, 76; Eighteenth (First Division), 64; Thirty-fourth, 76; Fortieth, 304; Seventieth, 214;
National Guard, 9;
Officers Reserve Corps, 9;
Organized Reserve, 9, 28;
Regular Army, 9, 10, 55;
Signal Construction Battalion, No. 26, 33;
Signal Service Companies:
980 Signal Service Company, 233; 3112 Signal Service Company, 233
United States Army Forces in China-Burma-India Theatre, 270
United States Congress, 3, 50, 284
U. S. Engine 1776, 85
United States Forces in India Burma Theatre, 270
United States Intelligence Service, 246
United States Military Iranian Mission, 259
United States Military Railway, 252
United States Navy, 5, 14-15, 286; 469 Amphibious Truck Company, Sea-Bees, 233
United States, President of, 2, 3, 16, 50, 259, 260, 285
United States Railroad Administration, 16, 45, 50
United States Secretary of War, 2, 4, 5, 151-153
United States Service Forces installations, 271
United States Theatre Service Forces, European Theatre Headquarters, 224
United States War Department, 4, 23, 25, 27, 28, 31, 46, 69, 93, 261, 276
Unterturckheim, Germany, 240
Upshaw, Pfc. Ralph, 234
USAFCBI: *See* United States Army Forces in China-Burma-India Theatre
USFIB: *See* United States Forces in India Burma Theatre
USO programs, 318
Utah Beach, France, 171, 175, 184

Valence-Lyon line, 200
Valence-Morains line, 198
Valenciennes, France, 187
Valenton Yard, Paris, 186, 187
Valognes, France, 180
V-E Day, 176, 236, 240, 251
Velat, Pvt. Edmond F., 320
Venice, Italy, 107
Verdun, France, 186, 226
Verona, Italy, 107, 158, 161
Versailles, France, 179; Palace of, 247
Versailles-Matelots Yard, 187
Vesoul, France, 201
Vesoul-Lure-Belfort-Mulhouse line, 212
Vesuvius, Mount, 132-133
Victor Emmanuel World War I Memorial, 151
"Victory Bridge," 234
Vienna, Austria, 237
Villa, Pancho, 9
Villa Literno, 118, 154
Vire, France, 179, 187
Virginia, State of, 8
V-J Day, 252, 292
Volturno River, Italy, 128; Bridge, 150
Vopatek, Lieut. J. A., 60

Wabash Railroad Company, 26, 271
Waegwan, Korea, 300, 306, 309
Waghorn, Brigadier, 144; Director (Br.) M.R.S. in Italy, 160
Wagner, Col. Otto, 33
Wainwright, Gen. Jonathan, 285
Waldron, Pfc. R. K., 322
Walker, Lieut. Col. A. R., 137, 138
Wallgren, Pfc. Paul Warren, 320
War of 1812, foreword
War Between the States, foreword, 1-8; M.R.S. in, 2-8, 14, 316
Warburg, Germany, 237, 238, 252
Ward, 2nd Lieut. L. E., 143
Warren, Lieut. Col. C. T., 267
Wars, American, numbers participating in, foreword
Wartchow, Capt. John R., 90
Washington, D. C., 4, 41, 69, 142, 261, 272
Weatherill, T/4 George C., 4
Webb, Lieut. Col. George H., 11
Weimar, Germany, 221
Welch, Lieut. Col. George M., 33, 256, 261
Wesel, Germany, 161, 174, 227, 232, 233, 234, 237; Bridge, 174; Yard, 233
Weser River, 234; Bridge, 234
(West Point) Class of 1917, 143
West Virginia, State of, 43
West Yard Limit Board, at Sétif, Algeria, 88; at Orléansville, Algeria, 88
Western Maryland Railway, 136

Wheeler, Brig. Gen. Raymond W., 259
Wheeler, Lieut. Gen. W. A., 270
White, Maj. Cecil A., 69
White, Capt. H. H., 90
White Horse, Yukon Territory, 41, 42, 43, 44
White Pass and Yukon Company, Ltd., 44
White Pass and Yukon Route, 27, 41-50, 291
Whittier, Alaska, 52
Wicker, T/5 Thomas E., 319
Wiesbaden, Germany, 221
Wigley, T/5 Herbert J., 319
Wilder, Lieut. T. E., Jr., 140
Williams, Lieut. Col. Robert F., 84, 145
Wilson, T/4 S., 183
Wilson, General Sir Henry Maitland, assumes command, AFHQ, Mediterranean Theatre, 141; with Allied Joint Chiefs of Staff, 142
Wilson, Col. W. P., 47, 48, 160, 272
Wilson, President Woodrow, 16, 52
Wismar, Germany, 237
Winfree, Lieut. W. J., 143
Wittekind, Capt. H. N., 100
WMIN (broadcast station), St. Paul-Minneapolis, Minn., 318
Wonnenberg, Maj. Raymond H., 262
Wonju, Korea, 310, 312
Wonsan, Korea, 301
Woodall, Maj. J. G., 310
World War I, 5, 45, 46, 65, 143, 181, 195, 265, 316; M.R.S. in, 10-16, 316
World War II, foreword, 164, 299, 300, 309, 310, 316, 322; M.R.S. in, 27, 41-298
"Worst Railroad on Earth" (C. & P. Railway), 35
W. P. A., 318
Wright, Lieut. Col. R. A., 178, 234
Würzburg, Germany, 231, 237, 254
Wurzen, Germany, 221

Xertigny, France, 207

Yangyang, Korea, 312
Yankee Boomer, The (newspaper), 321-322
"Yankee Dipper" (railroad car), 140, 141
Yankee Limited (train), 297
Yokohama, Japan, 294, 295, 296, 297; Central Station, 297
Yongdungpo, Korea, 302, 309, 310
Yongsan, Korea, 306, 309
Young, Col. C. D., 31
Yount, Col. Paul F., 256, 261, 267, 283
Yugoslavia, 29, 237
Yukon Territory, 41, 42, 43, 44
"Yum Dum" (Bathurst, Gambia), 69

Zagreb, Yugoslavia, 237
Zelmer, Sgt. Lee, 183
Zimmerman, Capt. V. O., 143, 190